How to
Master Skills for the

Second Edition

TOEFL® iBT
READING · Intermediate

DARAKWON

How to
Master Skills for the
Second Edition

TOEFL® iBT

READING Intermediate

Publisher Kyudo Chung
Editor Sangik Cho
Authors Timothy Hall, Arthur H. Milch, Denise McCormack, E2K
Proofreaders Michael A. Putlack, Will Link
Designers Minji Kim, Kyuok Jeong

First Published in February 2007 By Darakwon, Inc.
Second edition first published in November 2024 by Darakwon, Inc.
Darakwon Bldg., 211, Munbal-ro, Paju-si, Gyeonggi-do 10881
Republic of Korea
Tel: 02-736-2031 (Ext. 250)
Fax: 02-732-2037

ISBN 978-89-277-8089-2 14740
       978-89-277-8084-7 14740 (set)

www.darakwon.co.kr

Photo Credits
Shutterstock.com

Components Main Book / Answer Key / Free MP3 Downloads
7 6 5 4 3 2 1   24 25 26 27 28

Table of
Contents

INTRODUCTION

1 Information on the TOEFL® iBT

A The Format of the TOEFL® iBT

Section	Number of Questions or Tasks	Timing	Score

Reading	**20 Questions**
	
	• 2 reading passages
	  – with 10 questions per passage
	  – approximately 700 words long each
		35 Minutes	30 Points

Listening	**28 Questions**
	
	• 2 conversations
	  – 5 questions per conversation
	  – 3 minutes each
	
	• 3 lectures
	  – 6 questions per lecture
	  – 3-5 minutes each
		36 Minutes	30 Points

Speaking	**4 Tasks**
	
	• 1 independent speaking task
	  – 1 personal choice/opinion/experience
	  – preparation: 15 sec. / response: 45 sec.
	
	• 2 integrated speaking tasks: Read-Listen-Speak
	  – 1 campus situation topic
	    reading: 75-100 words (45 sec.)
	    conversation: 150-180 words (60-80 sec.)
	  – 1 academic course topic
	    reading: 75-100 words (50 sec.)
	    lecture: 150-220 words (60-120 sec.)
	  – preparation: 30 sec. / response: 60 sec.
	
	• 1 integrated speaking task: Listen-Speak
	  – 1 academic course topic
	    lecture: 230-280 words (90-120 sec.)
	  – preparation: 20 sec. / response: 60 sec.
		17 Minutes	30 Points

Writing	**2 Tasks**
	
	• 1 integrated writing task: Read-Listen-Write
	  – reading: 230-300 words (3 min.)
	  – lecture: 230-300 words (2 min.)
	  – a summary of 150-225 words (20 min.)
	
	• 1 academic discussion task
	  – a minimum 100-word essay (10 min.)
		30 Minutes	30 Points

B What Is New about the TOEFL® iBT?

- The TOEFL® iBT is delivered through the Internet in secure test centers around the world at the same time.
- It tests all four language skills and is taken in the order of Reading, Listening, Speaking, and Writing.
- The test is about 2 hours long, and all of the four test sections will be completed in one day.
- Note taking is allowed throughout the entire test, including the Reading section. At the end of the test, all notes are collected and destroyed at the test center.
- In the Listening section, one lecture may be spoken with a British or Australian accent.
- There are integrated tasks requiring test takers to combine more than one language skill in the Speaking and Writing sections.
- In the Speaking section, test takers wear headphones and speak into a microphone when they respond. The responses are recorded and transmitted to ETS's Online Scoring Network.
- In the Writing section, test takers must type their responses. Handwriting is not possible.
- Test scores will be reported online. Test takers can see their scores online 4-8 business days after the test and can also receive a copy of their score report by mail.

2 Information on the Reading Section

The Reading section of the TOEFL® iBT measures test takers' ability to understand university-level academic texts. This section has 2 passages, and the length of each passage is about 700 words. Some passages may have underlined words or phrases in blue. Test takers can click on them to see a definition or explanation. Test takers have to answer 10 questions per passage. 35 minutes are given to complete this section, including the time spent reading the passages and answering the questions.

A Types of Reading Passages

- Exposition: Material that provides an explanation of a topic
- Argumentation: Material that presents a point of view about a topic and provides evidence to support it
- Historical narrative: An account of a past event or of a person's life, narrated or written by someone else

B Types of Reading Questions

- Basic Comprehension Questions
  - Vocabulary Question (1-3 questions per passage): This type of question asks you to identify the meanings of words and phrases in the reading passage.
  - Reference Question (0-1 questions per passage): This type of question asks you to identify the referential relationship between the words in the passage.
  - Factual Information Question (1-3 questions per passage): This type of question asks you to identify specific information that is explicitly stated in the passage.

- Negative Factual Information Question (0-2 questions per passage): This type of question asks you to check what information is NOT mentioned in the passage.
- Sentence Simplification Question (0-1 question per passage): This type of question asks you to choose the sentence that best paraphrases the essential information in the highlighted sentence.

- Inference Questions
  - Inference Question (0-2 questions per passage): This type of question asks you to identify an idea that is not explicitly stated in the passage.
  - Rhetorical Purpose Question (1-2 questions per passage): This type of question asks you why the author uses particular words, phrases, or sentences.
  - Insert Text Question (1 question per passage): This type of question provides an example sentence and asks you to decide where the best place for that sentence would be in the passage.

- Reading to Learn Questions
  - Prose Summary Questions (0-1 question per passage): This type of question asks you to complete a summary chart with major ideas from the passage. It is worth up to 2 points, and partial credit is given. This type of question does not occur with a Fill in a Table question in one passage.
  - Fill in a Table Question (0-1 question per passage): This type of question asks you to identify and organize the major ideas of the passage into table categories. It is worth up to 3 points for tables with 5 correct answers and 4 points for tables with 7 correct answers. Partial credit is given. This type of question does not occur with a Prose Summary question in one passage.

C Question Formats

- There are three question formats in the Reading section: Four-choice questions with a single answer in traditional multiple-choice format, four-choice questions with a single answer that ask test takers to insert a sentence where it fits best in a passage, and Reading to Learn questions with more than four choices and more than one answer

HOW TO USE THIS BOOK

How to Master Skills for the TOEFL® iBT Reading Intermediate is designed to be used either as a textbook for a TOEFL® iBT reading preparation course or as a tool for individual learners who are preparing for the TOEFL® test on their own. With a total of ten units, this book is organized to prepare you for the test with a comprehensive understanding of the test and a thorough analysis of every question type. Each unit consists of six parts and provides a step-by-step program that provides question-solving strategies and the development of test-taking abilities. At the back of the book are two actual tests of the Reading section of the TOEFL® iBT.

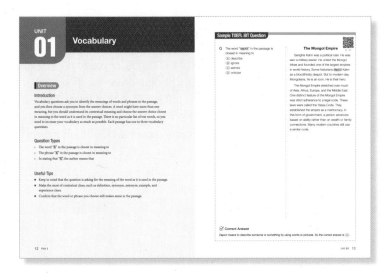

❶ Overview

This part is designed to prepare you for the type of question the unit covers. You will be given a full description of the question type and its application in the passage. You will also be given some useful tips as well as an illustrated introduction and sample.

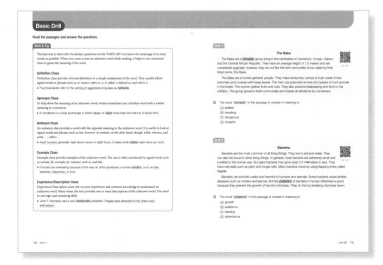

❷ Basic Drill

The purpose of this section is to ensure that you understand the new types of questions that were described in the overview. You will be given a chance to confirm your understanding in brief texts before starting on the practice exercises. You will read some simple passages and answer questions of a particular type. This part will help you learn how to deal with each type of question on the Reading section of the TOEFL® iBT.

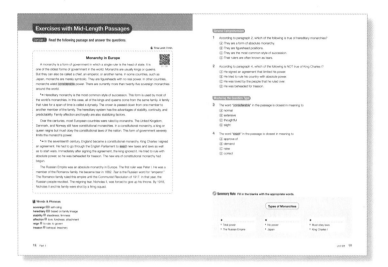

❸ Exercises with Mid-Length Passages

This section allows you to practice reading TOEFL® passages. Six mid-length passages are provided, and a time limit is given for reading each passage. You first read the passage within a time limit and then solve general comprehension questions and the questions of the type that is mainly dealt with in the unit. A glossary of important words is listed in each passage to help increase your understanding. In addition, summary notes are provided to help you grasp the overall organization of each passage and understand important points.

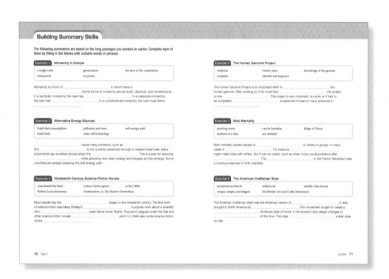

❹ Building Summary Skills

The purpose of this part is for you to understand the previous mid-length passages thoroughly by completing the summaries of them. This will also help you enhance your paraphrasing skills, which are strongly recommended to those who are preparing for the TOEFL® iBT.

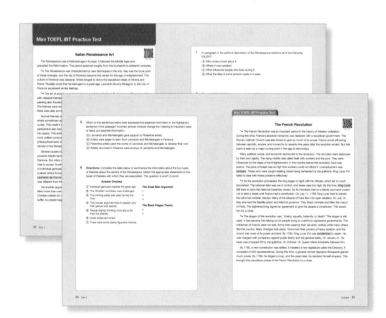

❺ Mini TOEFL iBT Practice Test

This part gives you a chance to experience an actual TOEFL® iBT test in a shortened form. You will be given two passages with 6 questions each. The topics are similar to those on the actual TOEFL® test, as are the questions.

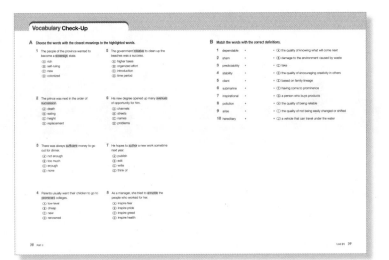

❻ Vocabulary Check-Up

This part offers you a chance to review some of the words you need to remember after finishing each unit. Vocabulary words for each unit are also provided at the back of the book to help you prepare for each unit.

❼ Actual Test

This part offers two full practice tests that are modeled on the Reading section of the TOEFL® iBT. This will familiarize you with the actual test format of the TOEFL® iBT.

PART I

Basic Comprehension

In this part, the reading comprehension questions include vocabulary, reference, factual information, negative factual information, and sentence simplification. The learning objectives of these reading comprehension questions are to identify individual words, referential relations between words in the passage, factual information, and essential sentences.

Vocabulary

Overview

Introduction

Vocabulary questions ask you to identify the meanings of words and phrases in the passage, and you then choose a synonym from the answer choices. A word might have more than one meaning, but you should understand its contextual meaning and choose the answer choice closest in meaning to the word as it is used in the passage. There is no particular list of test words, so you need to increase your vocabulary as much as possible. Each passage has one to three vocabulary questions.

Question Types

▶ The word "X" in the passage is closest in meaning to

▶ The phrase "X" in the passage is closest in meaning to

▶ In stating that "X", the author means that

Useful Tips

■ Keep in mind that the question is asking for the meaning of the word as it is used in the passage.

■ Make the most of contextual clues, such as definition, synonym, antonym, example, and experience clues.

■ Confirm that the word or phrase you choose still makes sense in the passage.

01-01

Q The word "depict" in the passage is closest in meaning to

- Ⓐ describe
- Ⓑ ignore
- Ⓒ admire
- Ⓓ criticize

The Mongol Empire

Genghis Kahn was a political ruler. He was also a military leader. He united the Mongol tribes and founded one of the largest empires in world history. Some historians depict Kahn as a bloodthirsty despot. But to modern-day Mongolians, he is an icon. He is their hero.

The Mongol Empire stretched over much of Asia, Africa, Europe, and the Middle East. One distinct feature of the Mongol Empire was strict adherence to a legal code. These laws were called the Yassa Code. They established the empire as a meritocracy. In this form of government, a person advances based on ability rather than on wealth or family connections. Many modern countries still use a similar code.

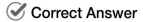 **Correct Answer**

Depict means to describe someone or something by using words or pictures. So the correct answer is Ⓐ.

Basic Drill

Read the passages and answer the questions.

Skill & Tip

The best way to deal with Vocabulary questions on the TOEFL iBT is to know the meanings of as many words as possible. When you come across an unknown word while reading, it helps to use contextual clues to guess the meaning of the word.

Definition Clues

Definition clues provide a formal definition or a simple restatement of the word. They usually follow signal words or phrases such as *or, means, refers to, is, is called, is defined as*, and *which is*.

- Psychoanalysts *refer to* the venting of aggressive impulses as catharsis.

Synonym Clues

To help show the meaning of an unknown word, writers sometimes use a familiar word with a similar meaning or a synonym.

- A condenser is a heat exchanger in which steam *or* vapor loses heat and returns to liquid form.

Antonym Clues

An antonym clue provides a word with the opposite meaning to the unknown word. It is useful to look at signal words and phrases such as *but, however, in contrast, on the other hand, though, while, whereas*, and *some . . .; others . . .*

- Adult humans generally need about seven or eight hours of sleep *while* infants need twice as much.

Example Clues

Example clues provide examples of the unknown word. The clue is often introduced by signal words such as *include, for example, for instance, such as*, and *like*.

- Portraits are interesting because of the way an artist expresses a human emotion, *such as* fear, sadness, happiness, or love.

Experience/Description Clues

Experience/Description clues rely on your experience and common knowledge to understand an unknown word. Many times, the text provides one or more descriptions of the unknown word. You need to use logic and reasoning skills.

- John F. Kennedy was a very charismatic president. People were attracted to his charm and enthusiasm.

Drill 1

The Baka

01-02

The Baka are a nomadic group living in the rainforests of Cameroon, Congo, Gabon, and the Central African Republic. They have an average height of 1.5 meters and are considered pygmies; however, they do not like this term and prefer to be called by their tribal name, the Baka.

The Baka are a hunter-gatherer people. They make temporary camps of huts made of tree branches and covered with large leaves. The men use poisoned arrows and spears to hunt animals in the forest. The women gather fruits and nuts. They also practice beekeeping and tend to the children. The group governs itself communally and makes all decisions by consensus.

Q   The word "nomadic" in the passage is closest in meaning to
   Ⓐ settled
   Ⓑ traveling
   Ⓒ dangerous
   Ⓓ cheerful

Drill 2

Bacteria

01-03

Bacteria are the most common of all living things. They live in soil and water. They can also be found in other living things. In general, most bacteria are extremely small and invisible to the human eye. But giant bacteria may grow past 0.5 millimeters in size. They have cell walls such as plant and fungal cells. Many bacteria move by using flapping limbs called flagella.

Bacteria can be both useful and harmful to humans and animals. Some bacteria cause terrible diseases such as cholera and leprosy. But the presence of bacteria in human intestines is good because they prevent the growth of harmful microbes. They do this by breaking microbes down.

Q   The word "presence" in the passage is closest in meaning to
   Ⓐ growth
   Ⓑ existence
   Ⓒ bearing
   Ⓓ attendance

Drought

01-04

A drought is an abnormally long spell of dry weather. It is a time when there is not enough water to support farming, urban, or environmental needs. It usually refers to an extended period of below-normal rainfall. But it can be caused by anything that reduces the amount of water circulation.

Humans cannot control the weather, so the causes that lead to drought cannot be stopped. The most common causes are a lack of water and hot temperatures. Many scientists believe that recent droughts have happened because of global warming. They claim that if we can reduce the damage done to the ozone layer, there will be fewer droughts.

Q The word "spell" in the passage is closest in meaning to

Ⓐ charm

Ⓑ zone

Ⓒ signal

Ⓓ period

Metaphors

01-05

A metaphor is a part of language that is a direct comparison between two unrelated things. The metaphor describes a first subject as being equal to the second subject in some way. There are many types of metaphors, such as mixed, active, and dead. A mixed metaphor combines two commonly used metaphors to create a nonsensical image. An example of this is, "He stepped up to the plate and grabbed the bull by the horns." An active metaphor is not part of daily language, such as, "You are my sun." A dead metaphor is used to describe a metaphorical cliché, such as "to break the ice."

Q The word "cliché" in the passage is closest in meaning to

Ⓐ indirect expression

Ⓑ novel expression

Ⓒ overused expression

Ⓓ old-fashioned expression

Queen Elizabeth I

01- 06

Queen Elizabeth I ruled England and Ireland. She sat on the throne from 1558 to 1603. She was also considered the queen of France, but she had no power there. She was the fifth and final monarch of the Tudor Dynasty. Elizabeth was called the Virgin Queen because she never married.

The time of Elizabeth's reign is called the Elizabethan Era. Many great accomplishments took place under her reign. Shakespeare wrote his plays, and Sir Francis Drake circled the globe. The English colonized North America. Shortly after her death, the American colony of Virginia was established. It was named in honor of the Virgin Queen.

Q In stating that Sir Francis Drake "circled the globe", the author means that he

ⒶＡ drew a map
ⒷＢ measured a model globe
ⒸＣ traveled around the world
ⒹＤ ran in a circle

The Paramecium

01- 07

A paramecium is an organism which is also known as a slipper because it has the shape of a slipper. Paramecia represent a group of single-celled organisms called the ciliate group. The reason is that their bodies are covered with cilia, which are thin tail-like limbs. Their constant motion allows the paramecium to move. The cell has a deep oral groove. This is a kind of mouth that is also filled with cilia. The mouth is used to expel water. Paramecia are commonly found in freshwater areas, especially in scum. They are attracted by acidic conditions.

Q The word "expel" in the passage is closest in meaning to

ⒶＡ push out
ⒷＢ pull in
ⒸＣ take in
ⒹＤ throw away

Exercise 1 Read the following passage and answer the questions.

🕐 Time Limit: 3 min.

Monarchy in Europe

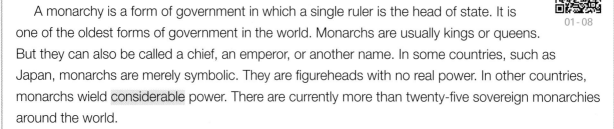

01-08

A monarchy is a form of government in which a single ruler is the head of state. It is one of the oldest forms of government in the world. Monarchs are usually kings or queens. But they can also be called a chief, an emperor, or another name. In some countries, such as Japan, monarchs are merely symbolic. They are figureheads with no real power. In other countries, monarchs wield considerable power. There are currently more than twenty-five sovereign monarchies around the world.

2 ➡ Hereditary monarchy is the most common style of succession. This form is used by most of the world's monarchies. In this case, all of the kings and queens come from the same family. A family that rules for a span of time is called a dynasty. The crown is passed down from one member to another member of the family. The hereditary system has the advantages of stability, continuity, and predictability. Family affection and loyalty are also stabilizing factors.

Over the centuries, most European countries were ruled by monarchs. The United Kingdom, Denmark, and Norway still have constitutional monarchies. In a constitutional monarchy, a king or queen reigns but must obey the constitutional laws of the nation. This form of government severely limits the monarch's power.

4 ➡ In the seventeenth century, England became a constitutional monarchy. King Charles I signed an agreement. He had to go through the English Parliament to exact new taxes and laws as well as to start wars. Immediately after signing the agreement, the king ignored it. He tried to rule with absolute power, so he was beheaded for treason. The new era of constitutional monarchy had begun.

The Russian Empire was an absolute monarchy in Europe. The first ruler was Peter I. He was a member of the Romanov family. He became tsar in 1682. *Tsar* is the Russian word for "emperor." The Romanov family ruled this empire until the Communist Revolution of 1917. In that year, the Russian people revolted. The reigning tsar, Nicholas II, was forced to give up his throne. By 1918, Nicholas II and his family were shot by a firing squad.

📖 **Words & Phrases**

sovereign (adj) self-ruling
hereditary (adj) based on family lineage
stability (n) steadiness; firmness
affection (n) love; fondness; attachment
reign (v) to rule; to govern
treason (n) betrayal; treachery

1   According to paragraph 2, which of the following is true of hereditary monarchies?

    (A) They are a form of absolute monarchy.

    (B) They are figurehead positions.

    (C) They are the most common style of succession.

    (D) Their rulers are often known as tsars.

2   According to paragraph 4, which of the following is NOT true of King Charles I?

    (A) He signed an agreement that limited his power.

    (B) He tried to rule his country with absolute power.

    (C) He was loved by the people that he ruled over.

    (D) He was beheaded for treason.

Mastering the Question Type

3   The word "considerable" in the passage is closest in meaning to

    (A) normal

    (B) extensive

    (C) thoughtful

    (D) slight

4   The word "exact" in the passage is closest in meaning to

    (A) approve of

    (B) demand

    (C) raise

    (D) correct

Summary Note Fill in the blanks with the appropriate words.

Types of Monarchies

❶ _____	❷ _____	❸ _____
• Total power	• No power	• Must obey laws
• The Russian Empire	• Japan	• King Charles I

Alternative Energy Sources

01 - 09

Fossil fuels are the cause of many problems. They create terrible pollution, which leads to global warming. Many wars are fought to control oil and gas fields. Fossil fuels are also nonrenewable resources, so they will be exhausted someday. Societies around the world suffer when fuel shortages occur.

Some people believe that solar power can completely replace fossil fuels. Solar power is clean, safe, and inexpensive. However, the idea of replacing fossil fuels with solar power alone is totally unrealistic. Current solar cell technology is not advanced enough. Solar cells are not dependable. They are useless in cloudy and rainy weather as well as at night. They also take up too much space. Finally, they fail to produce sufficient amounts of power.

³➡ The soft-energy path is a good alternative to fossil-fuel reliance. The soft-energy path is an energy conservation plan. It is an alternative to the hard-energy path. Hard energy is defined as harmful and nonrenewable. Fossil fuels and nuclear power are considered hard energy. On the other hand, soft energy is defined as renewable and environmentally safe energy. Solar and wind power are examples of soft energy. Biofuel and geothermal energy are also two types of it.

There are many proponents of the soft-energy path. They believe the solution lies in new energy production methods. The first step is to practice careful conservation in the use of hard-energy technologies. Then, many new soft-energy sources will be phased into use as soft-energy technology improves.

Some critics claim this will damage all energy production. They feel fossil fuels are important. They want to control as much oil production as possible. They think fossil-fuel consumption is good for industry.

⁶➡ Countries such as Canada and Sweden are taking the soft-energy path. Canada is currently lessening its reliance on gasoline. In the next few years, all gasoline sold in Canada will contain a percentage of biofuel. Sweden has committed to decrease its reliance on oil by forty percent. Its government says the country can do this within a few years.

📖 Words & Phrases

nonrenewable `adj` not able to be replaced after use
dependable `adj` reliable; trustworthy
conservation `n` the protection of the natural environment
proponent `n` a supporter; an advocate
consumption `n` the act of using energy, food, or materials

1 According to paragraph 3, which of the following is true of the soft-energy path?

 Ⓐ It is an energy-conservation plan.

 Ⓑ It refers to harmful and nonrenewable fuel.

 Ⓒ It is useless in cloudy and rainy weather.

 Ⓓ It includes biofuel and geothermal energy.

2 In paragraph 6, all of the following questions are answered EXCEPT:

 Ⓐ Which countries have adopted the soft-energy path?

 Ⓑ What will all gasoline in Canada include in a few years?

 Ⓒ How much has Sweden reduced its consumption of oil by recently?

 Ⓓ What does the Swedish government believe it can do soon?

Mastering the Question Type

3 The word "exhausted" in the passage is closest in meaning to

 Ⓐ wasted

 Ⓑ used up

 Ⓒ worn out

 Ⓓ burned

4 In stating that many soft-energy sources will "be phased into use", the author means that they will

 Ⓐ be an alternative to the hard-energy path

 Ⓑ be used gradually over time

 Ⓒ be adopted by Sweden and Canada

 Ⓓ damage all energy production

Summary Note Fill in the blanks with the appropriate words.

Ways to Meet Energy Needs	

❶ _____
(oil, coal, nuclear power)
• Good
  – meets current needs
• Bad
  – nonrenewable, making pollution, and
    causing wars
	❷ _____
	(biofuel, solar, wind, hydro, geothermal)
	• Good
	  – clean, inexpensive, and safe
	• Bad
	  – can't meet current needs

🕐 Time Limit: 2 min. 40 sec.

Nineteenth-Century Science-Fiction Novels

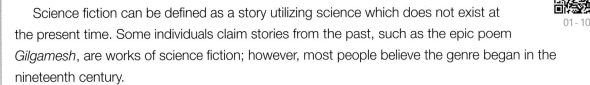

01-10

Science fiction can be defined as a story utilizing science which does not exist at the present time. Some individuals claim stories from the past, such as the epic poem *Gilgamesh*, are works of science fiction; however, most people believe the genre began in the nineteenth century.

2 ➡ The first widely accepted work of science fiction was written by Mary Shelley in 1818 and was her novel *Frankenstein: or, The Modern Prometheus*. It featured a scientist who used electricity to reanimate the dead and then dealt with the consequences of the man's actions. Her book was extremely popular and has remained in print ever since it first came out.

3 ➡ Many of the stories written by Jules Verne, another notable figure of the 1880s, employed elements of science fiction. Arguably the best known of these novels is *Twenty Thousand Leagues under the Sea*, which describes the story of Captain Nemo and his advanced submarine, the *Nautilus*, on its adventures underneath the world's oceans. One of Verne's first works of science fiction was entitled *Paris in the Twentieth Century*. It covers how Verne believed Paris would look in future times. He also authored the novels *From the Earth to the Moon* and *Five Weeks in a Balloon*.

A popular science-fiction novel from this period is *The Strange Case of Dr. Jekyll and Mr. Hyde*, which was written by Robert Louis Stevenson. In it, Dr. Jekyll creates a potion which transforms him into Mr. Hyde, his alter ego. H.G. Wells published several works of science fiction. He wrote *The Time Machine*, which tells the story of how one man travels far back into the Earth's past as well as into its distant future. *The War of the Worlds* is about how aliens from Mars attack the Earth. Wells also wrote *The Invisible Man*, a story about a man who cannot be seen by others.

These works all led to the increasing popularity of science fiction. In the 1900s, it would become one of the most popular of all genres in literature.

📖 Words & Phrases

epic poem ⓝ a long poem that often features heroes, gods, and monsters
genre ⓝ a type; a kind
reanimate ⓥ to bring back to life
consequence ⓝ a result of an action
submarine ⓝ a vehicle that can travel under the water
author ⓥ to write something such as a book or article
alter ego ⓝ a different version of oneself

1 In paragraph 2, the author's description of *Frankenstein: or, The Modern Prometheus* mentions all of the following EXCEPT:

    Ⓐ The year in which it was published

    Ⓑ The subject matter of the work

    Ⓒ The name of the author of the book

    Ⓓ The number of copies the book has sold

2 According to paragraph 3, the Jules Verne book that focused on the future is

    Ⓐ *Five Weeks in a Balloon*

    Ⓑ *Paris in the Twentieth Century*

    Ⓒ *From the Earth to the Moon*

    Ⓓ *Twenty Thousand Leagues under the Sea*

3 The word "elements" in the passage is closest in meaning to

    Ⓐ aspects

    Ⓑ definitions

    Ⓒ memories

    Ⓓ considerations

4 The word "transforms" in the passage is closest in meaning to

    Ⓐ destroys

    Ⓑ removes

    Ⓒ alters

    Ⓓ features

Summary Note Fill in the blanks with the appropriate words.

Science-Fiction Novelists

❶	❷	❸	❹
• Wrote *Frankenstein: or, The Modern Prometheus* • About the results of a scientist who reanimates the dead	• Wrote *Twenty Thousand Leagues under the Sea* • Wrote several other works of science fiction	• Wrote *The Strange Case of Dr. Jekyll and Mr. Hyde* • About Dr. Jekyll and his alter ego	• Wrote *The Time Machine* about a man's trips to the past and the future • Wrote *The War of the Worlds* about an alien invasion

Time Limit: 2 min. 40 sec.

The Human Genome Project

01 - 11

The Human Genome Project (HGP) was a very important effort in science. It was an attempt to map and sequence the human genome. There are three billion codes in the human genome. All of these had been identified. But they still needed to be sequenced. The project also hoped to identify all the genes present in the human body.

2 ➡ The international HGP was launched in 1986 by Charles DeLisi. A 1987 report stated, "The ultimate goal of this initiative is to understand the human genome. Knowledge of the human genome is necessary to the continuing progress of medicine and other health sciences, as human anatomy has been for the present state of medicine." This three-billion-dollar project was formally founded in 1990. It was expected to take fifteen years to complete. The international consortium included geneticists from around the world.

3 ➡ After years of work, the claim was made that the genome map had been completed in 2003. However, at that point, the HGP had complete mapping around ninety-two percent of the human genome. As a result, work on the project continued. Thanks to improvements in mapping and sequencing technologies, progress on the remaining eight percent was steadily made. Nevertheless, the central region of each chromosome contains highly repetitive DNA sequences. It was very difficult for the existing technology to put them in order. Finally, in 2022, the work was completed, and the human genome was entirely mapped.

4 ➡ This clear map of the human genome provided by HGP will give doctors very much important information. It will allow them to make medical advances. This knowledge will, for example, lead to significant advances in the early diagnosis of breast cancer. It will also improve doctors' ability to deal with liver and Alzheimer's disease. Analysis of the genome promises to open new avenues in the study of human evolution. The sequence of human DNA is stored on the Internet. It is housed in a database called Genebank. This data is available for anyone to view.

📖 Words & Phrases

identify ⓥ to become thoroughly familiar with
launch ⓥ to start; to begin
progress ⓝ development; advance
anatomy ⓝ the parts of the human body
initiative ⓝ an organized effort
consortium ⓝ a group of organizations that have agreed to cooperate with one another

1 Select the TWO answer choices from paragraphs 2 and 3 that identify the work done on the Human Genome Project. *To receive credit, you must select TWO answers.*

ⓐ The majority of the work was finished in 2003.

ⓑ It was supposed to take twenty years to complete.

ⓒ By 2022, around eight percent of the human genome had not been mapped.

ⓓ Its goal was to improve knowledge of the human genome.

2 In paragraph 4, the author's description of the HGP mentions all of the following EXCEPT:

ⓐ Who can access the information it learned

ⓑ How the knowledge it provides will help doctors

ⓒ Where the information it discovered can be found

ⓓ How many sick people it has already benefitted

3 In stating that the codes in the human genome still need to "be sequenced", the author means that the codes still have to

ⓐ be taken apart

ⓑ be put in order

ⓒ be discovered

ⓓ be processed

4 In stating that analysis of the genome promises to "open new avenues" in the study of human evolution, the author means that it will

ⓐ build new roads

ⓑ create new possibilities

ⓒ save people

ⓓ try new methods

Summary Note Fill in the blanks with the appropriate words.

The Human Genome Project

- What: a scientific effort to map and sequence ❶ _____
- Why: to advance medicine and other health sciences
- When: formally founded in ❷ _____
- Current state: human genome completely mapped in 2022
- Future benefits
  – early diagnosis of breast cancer possible
  – improved treatment of ❸ _____
  – progress in the study of human evolution

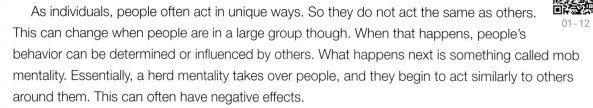

🕐 Time Limit: 2 min. 50 sec.

Mob Mentality

01-12

As individuals, people often act in unique ways. So they do not act the same as others. This can change when people are in a large group though. When that happens, people's behavior can be determined or influenced by others. What happens next is something called mob mentality. Essentially, a herd mentality takes over people, and they begin to act similarly to others around them. This can often have negative effects.

[2] → Mob mentality can be seen in many facets of life. For instance, schoolchildren in classrooms may start making noise if other students are loud. Likewise, office workers in meetings sometimes display mob mentality. Some individuals may not agree with a point being made. However, when they see the others in the group agreeing with it, they refuse to speak up but instead go along with the crowd. Fans at sporting events may begin cheering after large numbers of other individuals begin a chant or a cheer. These are all relatively harmless examples of mob mentality.

Unfortunately, there are many instances where mob mentality leads to violence and other problems. In the United States, after a sports team wins a championship, fans of the winning team often gather in large groups. They can then rapidly turn to violence. Building windows may be broken, cars may be smashed, and bonfires may be started on city streets. In some instances, there have been shootings once mob mentality takes over.

[4] → In the past, one of the most notorious instances of mob mentality happened during the French Revolution in the late 1700s. In the middle of the revolution, the Reign of Terror took place from 1793 to 1794. During it, tens of thousands of people were executed by mobs. They were beheaded in most cases either for being aristocrats or for lacking revolutionary spirit. During the Reign of Terror, members of the working class often banded together and accused various people. These individuals, in turn, were given sham trials and often speedily executed. This happened until the mob wore itself out and stopped the mass killings.

📖 **Words & Phrases**

mob (n) a large group of people
mentality (n) a way of thinking
facet (n) an aspect
relatively (adv) basically; fairly
bonfire (n) a large fire
execute (v) to kill, often by order of the government
sham (adj) fake

1 According to paragraph 2, which of the following is NOT true of mob mentality?

    Ⓐ It can affect people at workplaces.

    Ⓑ Its results may be harmless.

    Ⓒ It can have deadly consequences.

    Ⓓ It can take place in many places.

2 In paragraph 4, the author's description of the Reign of Terror mentions which of the following?

    Ⓐ The exact number of people killed during it

    Ⓑ The reason that it finally stopped

    Ⓒ The month in 1793 when it began

    Ⓓ The name of the person who led it

Mastering the Question Type

3 The word "smashed" in the passage is closest in meaning to

    Ⓐ stolen

    Ⓑ destroyed

    Ⓒ removed

    Ⓓ traded

4 The word "notorious" in the passage is closest in meaning to

    Ⓐ violent

    Ⓑ spectacular

    Ⓒ infamous

    Ⓓ discussed

Summary Note Fill in the blanks with the appropriate words.

Mob Mentality

Harmless Examples

- Schoolchildren making noise when other students do that
- Office workers agreeing with others despite not feeling that way
- ❶ _____ cheering together with others

Harmful Examples

- Fans of winning sports teams gathering and turning violent
- ❷ _____ during the French Revolution
  - tens of thousands were executed by mobs
  - killed people for not having ❸ _____

🕐 Time Limit: 2 min. 50 sec.

01 - 13

The American Craftsman Style

The American Craftsman style is a type of design. It was popular from 1900 to the 1930s. It changed the style of building in the United States.

The craftsman style originated in Europe. The British Arts and Crafts style arose in the 1860s. The unique designs of this movement tried to ennoble the common person. Handmade items were preferred because they were considered better than items that were mass-produced. But this British style was still Victorian and only served the wealthiest clients.

[3] ➡ In 1897, a group of Boston architects brought these handcrafted styles to the United States. They planned a show of craft objects, which turned out to be a huge success. They realized the potential and established the Society of Arts and Crafts on June 28, 1897. Its slogan was "to develop and encourage higher standards in the handicrafts." The American style began as the Victorian Era was ending. It emphasized handmade work, and originality and simplicity were highly valued. Local materials and the quality of the handicrafts were very important. These traits were meant to dignify the modest homes of the middle class.

[4] ➡ These simple designs used glass and wood that were produced locally. They were also very elegant. The metalwork was a reaction to Victorian opulence. The increase of mass-produced housing items was rejected. The American Craftsman used clean lines while relying on sturdy structures. Natural materials were always used in these houses if possible. This style introduced many changes to the average American home. New designs were made for families without servants. This was a trait of the new middle class. The kitchen went from being a hidden room to a prominent one. Another development was the breakfast nook. This new area provided the family with a place to gather any time of day.

In addition, inspirational to the Craftsman style were the Shaker and Mission designs. The American Craftsman style led to the Art Deco movement of the 1930s.

📖 Words & Phrases

originally `adv` at first; in the beginning
arise `v` to happen
unique `adj` one of a kind
potential `n` possibility
sturdy `adj` durable; well-built
inspirational `adj` motivating; encouraging creativity
nook `n` a small, quiet place set back from the rest of a room

1 According to paragraph 3, the American Craftsman style became popular in the United States because

Ⓐ the style was original yet complicated

Ⓑ it imitated works done in Victorian England

Ⓒ a handicrafts show was a major success

Ⓓ it served the needs of wealthy individuals

2 According to paragraph 4, which of the following is NOT true of the American Craftsman style?

Ⓐ The breakfast nook provided the family with a place to gather.

Ⓑ The kitchen became a more prominent room.

Ⓒ It did not make any changes to the middle-class American home.

Ⓓ Houses were designed for a new middle class with no servants.

3 The word "ennoble" in the passage is closest in meaning to

Ⓐ enlighten

Ⓑ satisfy

Ⓒ surprise

Ⓓ dignify

4 The word "opulence" in the passage is closest in meaning to

Ⓐ richness

Ⓑ greed

Ⓒ ugliness

Ⓓ distaste

✎ **Summary Note** Fill in the blanks with the appropriate words.

> ### The American Craftsman Style
>
> **Didn't use or create**
> - ❶ _____
> - Rooms for servants
> - Victorian opulence
> - Hidden kitchens
>
> **Developed new designs and methods of**
> - Homes for ❷ _____
> - Handcrafted items
> - ❸ _____
> - Sturdy structures
> - Prominent kitchens
> - Breakfast nooks

Building Summary Skills

The following summaries are based on the long passages you worked on earlier. Complete each of them by filling in the blanks with suitable words or phrases.

Exercise 1 Monarchy in Europe

a single ruler	government	the laws of the constitution
total power	no power	

Monarchy is a form of _____ in which there is _____. Some forms of monarchy are symbolic, absolute, and constitutional. In a symbolic monarchy, the ruler has _____. In an absolute monarchy, the ruler has _____. In a constitutional monarchy, the ruler must follow _____.

Exercise 2 Alternative Energy Sources

fossil-fuel consumption	pollution and wars	soft-energy path
fossil fuels	solar-cell technology	

_____ cause many problems, such as _____. But _____ is not currently advanced enough to replace fossil fuels. Many proponents say societies should adopt the _____. This is a plan for reducing _____ while adopting new clean-energy technologies as they emerge. Some countries are already adopting the soft-energy path.

Exercise 3 Nineteenth-Century Science-Fiction Novels

reanimated the dead	science-fiction genre	in the 1800s
Robert Louis Stevenson	*Frankenstein: or, The Modern Prometheus*	

Most people say the _____ began in the nineteenth century. The first work of science fiction was Mary Shelley's _____, a popular work about a scientist who _____. Jules Verne wrote *Twenty Thousand Leagues under the Sea* and other science-fiction novels. _____ and H.G. Wells also wrote science-fiction works _____.

Exercise 4 — The Human Genome Project

| medicine | twenty years | knowledge of the genome |
| complete | identify and sequence | |

The Human Genome Project is an important effort to _____ the human genome. After working on it for more than _____, the project is now _____. This project is very important, so work on it had to be completed. _____ is expected to lead to many advances in _____.

Exercise 5 — Mob Mentality

| sporting events | can be harmless | Reign of Terror |
| students in a class | act similarly | |

Mob mentality causes people to _____ to others in groups. In many cases, it _____. For instance, _____ might make noise with others. But it can be violent, such as when mobs cause problems after _____. The _____ in the French Revolution was a notorious example of mob mentality.

Exercise 6 — The American Craftsman Style

| prominent architects | influenced | middle-class homes |
| unique, simple, and elegant | the British Arts and Crafts Movement | |

The American Craftsman style was the American version of _____. It was brought to North America by _____. This movement sought to create a _____ American style of home. It introduced many design changes to _____ of the time. This style _____ a later style as well.

Italian Renaissance Art

01-14

The Renaissance was a historical age in Europe. It followed the Middle Ages and preceded the Reformation. This period spanned roughly from the fourteenth to sixteenth centuries.

2 ➡ The Renaissance was characterized by new techniques in the arts. Italy was the focal point of these changes, and the city of Florence became the center for this age of enlightenment. The culture in Florence was classical. Artists longed to revive the republican ideals of Athens and Rome. Rucellai wrote that he belonged to a great age. Leonardo Bruni's *Panegyric to the City of Florence* expressed similar feelings.

3 ➡ The art of sculpture made great progress during this time. Sculptors used Roman models with classical themes. Nude statues with expressions of human dignity abounded. The art of painting also flourished. Huge leaps forward were made by artists like Giotto and Fra Angelico. The themes were mainly religious because the church was the main client of these artists. But there were also some plainly figurative themes.

Normal themes were often treated via mythological or religious representation. For instance, artists sometimes used the biblical characters of Adam and Eve to represent male and female nudes. This made it morally acceptable. A fig leaf was often used to hide the genitals. The use of perspective also became prominent. This was the first time the painting was treated as a window into space. This added to the realistic presentation of architecture. It moved painters to use more unified compositions. The printing press was used during this time, too. Many humanistic philosophical texts by Plato and Aristotle were published and read. This led to the intellectual climate of the Renaissance.

Several causes for the rise of the Renaissance have been offered. One theory is that the powerful Medici family brought this age about. This family patronized many of the artists of Florence. But critics argue that the Renaissance began in the early 1400s before the Medici family rose to power. Another theory is called the Great Man Argument. It claims that the existence of individual geniuses sparked this great age. Great artists such as Donatello and Brunelleschi pushed others forward. The artists of Florence stood on the shoulders of the great artists Leonardo da Vinci and Michelangelo. But this circular argument fails to explain why their genius was different from the genius of any other age.

Yet another argument is the Black Plague Theory. In the fourteenth century, the Black Plague killed more than one-third of Europe's population. It killed kings and priests as well as the poor. Christian beliefs did not protect anyone from this scourge. It caused the Christian world view to suffer, so people began to think more about life than the afterlife.

1 In paragraph 2, the author's description of the Renaissance mentions all of the following EXCEPT:

Ⓐ Who wrote a book about it

Ⓑ Where it was centered

Ⓒ What influenced people who lived during it

Ⓓ What the titles of some artwork made in it were

2 The word "abounded" in the passage is closest in meaning to

Ⓐ revealed

Ⓑ thrived

Ⓒ loomed

Ⓓ approved

3 In paragraph 3, the author uses "Giotto and Fra Angelico" as examples of

Ⓐ writers who praised the ideals of the Renaissance

Ⓑ sculptors who revived classical themes

Ⓒ individuals who purchased Renaissance paintings

Ⓓ artists who made progress in the art of painting

4 The word "prominent" in the passage is closest in meaning to

Ⓐ popular

Ⓑ recommended

Ⓒ apparent

Ⓓ studied

5 Which of the sentences below best expresses the essential information in the highlighted sentence in the passage? *Incorrect* answer choices change the meaning in important ways or leave out essential information.

(A) Leonardo and Michelangelo gave support to Florentine artists.

(B) Artists were eager to learn from Leonardo and Michelangelo in Florence.

(C) Florentine artists used the works of Leonardo and Michelangelo to develop their own.

(D) Artists who lived in Florence were envious of Leonardo and Michelangelo.

6 **Directions:** Complete the table below to summarize the information about the two types of theories about the advent of the Renaissance. Match the appropriate statements to the types of theories with which they are associated. *This question is worth 3 points.*

Answer Choices

1. Individual geniuses inspired the great age.
2. The Christian worldview was challenged.
3. The printing press was used during this time.
4. This circular argument fails to explain why their genius was special.
5. People started thinking more about life than the afterlife.
6. Great artists led others.
7. There were some plainly figurative themes.

The Great Man Argument

-
-
-

The Black Plague Theory

-
-

The French Revolution

01-15

1 ➡ The French Revolution was an important period in the history of Western civilization. During this time, France's absolute monarchy was replaced with a republican government. The Roman Catholic Church was also forced to give up much of its power. France would still swing between republic, empire, and monarchy for seventy-five years after the revolution ended. But this event is seen as a major turning point in the age of democracy.

Many political, social, and economic factors led to the revolution. The old rulers were destroyed by their own rigidity. The rising middle class allied itself with workers and the poor. They were influenced by the ideas of the Enlightenment. In the months before the revolution, food was scarce. The price of bread was so high that workers could not afford it. Unemployment was rampant. Those who were caught stealing risked being beheaded by the guillotine. King Louis XVI failed to deal with these problems effectively.

3 ➡ As the revolution proceeded, the king began to fight with his officials, which led to much bloodshed. The national debt was out of control, and taxes were too high. By this time, King Louis XVI tried to have the National Assembly closed. So its members met on a tennis court and vowed not to take a break until France had a constitution. On July 11, 1789, King Louis tried to banish the reformist minister, Necker. Many of the citizens of Paris flew into open rebellion. On July 14, they stormed the Bastille prison and killed its governor. They freed criminals and killed the mayor of Paris. The frightened king signed an agreement to give the people a constitution. This saved him for a while.

4 ➡ The slogan of the revolution was, "Liberty, equality, fraternity, or death!" This slogan is still used. It has become the rallying cry for people trying to overthrow oppressive governments. The noblemen of France were not safe. Some tried wearing their servants' clothes while many others fled the country. Many changes took place. Towns lost their powers of heavy taxation, and the church lost most of its power and land. By 1793, King Louis XVI was condemned to death. He was charged with conspiracy against public liberty and the general safety. On January 21, his head was chopped off by the guillotine. On October 16, Queen Marie Antoinette followed him.

By 1795, a new constitution was ratified. It installed a new legislature called the Directory. It consisted of 500 representatives. During this time, a general named Napoleon Bonaparte gained much power. By 1799, he staged a coup, and five years later, he declared himself emperor. This brought the republican phase of the French Revolution to a close.

7 According to paragraph 1, which of the following is NOT true of the French Revolution?

Ⓐ It was a significant event in Western history.

Ⓑ Absolute monarchs controlled France before it.

Ⓒ The French people formed a new government after it.

Ⓓ The Roman Catholic Church welcomed it.

8 The word "rampant" in the passage is closest in meaning to

Ⓐ serious

Ⓑ widespread

Ⓒ uncommon

Ⓓ increasing

9 The author discusses "King Louis XVI" in paragraph 3 in order to

Ⓐ argue that he should have acted differently

Ⓑ claim he tried to stop the violence of the French Revolution

Ⓒ describe his role in the French Revolution

Ⓓ compare his actions with those of Necker

10 The word "condemned" in the passage is closest in meaning to

Ⓐ accused

Ⓑ sentenced

Ⓒ tortured

Ⓓ claimed

11 In paragraph 4, which of the following can be inferred about the guillotine?

Ⓐ It was a chair for royalty to sit upon.

Ⓑ It was highly regarded by the king of France.

Ⓒ It was a device used to enact death sentences.

Ⓓ It was used to chop off the hands of criminals.

12 According to paragraph 4, some noblemen fled France because

Ⓐ they were in great danger

Ⓑ they did not like living a lower-class lifestyle

Ⓒ the Roman Catholic Church had too much power

Ⓓ King Louis XVI was sentenced to death

Vocabulary Check-Up

A **Choose the words with the closest meanings to the highlighted words.**

1 The people of the province wanted to become a sovereign state.

- Ⓐ rich
- Ⓑ self-ruling
- Ⓒ new
- Ⓓ colonized

2 The prince was next in the order of succession.

- Ⓐ death
- Ⓑ eating
- Ⓒ height
- Ⓓ replacement

3 There was always sufficient money to go out for dinner.

- Ⓐ not enough
- Ⓑ too much
- Ⓒ enough
- Ⓓ none

4 Parents usually want their children to go to prominent colleges.

- Ⓐ low-level
- Ⓑ cheap
- Ⓒ new
- Ⓓ renowned

5 The government initiative to clean up the beaches was a success.

- Ⓐ higher taxes
- Ⓑ organized effort
- Ⓒ introduction
- Ⓓ time period

6 His new degree opened up many avenues of opportunity for him.

- Ⓐ channels
- Ⓑ streets
- Ⓒ names
- Ⓓ problems

7 He hopes to author a new work sometime next year.

- Ⓐ publish
- Ⓑ edit
- Ⓒ write
- Ⓓ think of

8 As a manager, she tried to ennoble the people who worked for her.

- Ⓐ inspire fear
- Ⓑ inspire pride
- Ⓒ inspire greed
- Ⓓ inspire health

B **Match the words with the correct definitions.**

1   dependable   •   • Ⓐ the quality of knowing what will come next

2   sham   •   • Ⓑ damage to the environment caused by waste

3   predictability   •   • Ⓒ fake

4   stability   •   • Ⓓ the quality of encouraging creativity in others

5   client   •   • Ⓔ based on family lineage

6   submarine   •   • Ⓕ having come to prominence

7   inspirational   •   • Ⓖ a person who buys products

8   pollution   •   • Ⓗ the quality of being reliable

9   arise   •   • Ⓘ the quality of not being easily changed or shifted

10 hereditary   •   • Ⓙ a vehicle that can travel under the water

Overview

Introduction

Reference questions ask you to understand the relationship between a pronoun and the word which the pronoun refers to. Usually, personal pronouns *such as he, she, it, they,* and *them* are tested on the TOEFL iBT. Sometimes other reference words such as *which, this, one, the former,* and *the latter* are also asked.

Question Types

▷ The word "X" in the passage refers to

▷ The phrase "X" in the passage refers to

Useful Tips

■ The referent (the word to which a pronoun refers) usually appears before the pronoun in the same sentence or shows up in an earlier sentence. Sometimes, however, the referent might be found after the pronoun.

■ Substitute your answer for the highlighted word or words in the passage.

■ Make sure that your answer is the same number (singular or plural), gender (male or female), and case (first, second, or third person) as the highlighted pronoun.

02-01

Q The word "they" in the passage refers to

- Ⓐ giant floods
- Ⓑ the effects
- Ⓒ these storms
- Ⓓ humans

Hurricanes

The scientific name for a hurricane is a tropical cyclone. It is fueled by the heat that is released when moist air rises and condenses. Hurricanes rotate counterclockwise in the Northern Hemisphere and clockwise in the Southern Hemisphere.

Hurricanes can produce extremely strong winds, tornadoes, heavy rains, and huge waves called storm surges. The heavy rains and huge waves create giant floods. Though the effects of these storms on humans can be catastrophic, they are also known to relieve drought conditions.

Hurricanes also carry heat away from the tropics. This is an important part of global circulation and is the way balance is maintained in the Earth's troposphere.

✅ Correct Answer

The highlighted word *they* is a part of the sentence which explains the effects of hurricanes on human beings. So the pronoun *they* refers to the phrase *these storms*, which is mentioned earlier in the same sentence. The correct answer is Ⓒ.

Basic Drill

Read the passages and answer the questions.

In order to deal with Reference questions, you need to understand the relationships between pronouns and the words which they refer to. There are four kinds of referential relationships which are asked on the TOEFL iBT.

Personal Pronouns

Personal pronouns refer back to someone or something previously mentioned in the passage. Sometimes they can refer forward to what is mentioned later in the passage. On the TOEFL iBT, third-person pronouns such as *it, they,* and *them* are frequently asked.

- Capuchins crack walnuts by repeatedly pounding them with stones.
- When it was first introduced in Europe, coffee was sold in pharmacies as a medicinal remedy.

Demonstratives

Demonstratives are pronouns or adjectives pointing out which item is being referred to. In English, they include *this, that, these,* and *those*. Sometimes *the former* and *the latter* are also asked on the TOEFL iBT.

- Although the initial cost of a timber house is less than that of one made of brick or concrete, the long-term expense is greater.
- An organization designed to accomplish some task is called a utilitarian organization. Businesses are one example of this.

Relative Pronouns

Relative pronouns such as *which, that, who, whose,* and *whom* introduce a clause that modifies the noun or noun phrase right before them. Sometimes *which* can refer to the entire previous clause.

- Penicillin kills a wide variety of bacteria, many of which cause disease in humans.
- In the early 1850s, many daguerreotypists, most of whom were in the business to make money, not art, were practicing in the United States.

Indefinite Pronouns

Indefinite pronouns refer to an unknown or undetermined person, place, or thing. Indefinite pronouns include words with *some, any, every,* or *no* (e.g. *someone, anyone, everyone,* and *no one*) and *one, another, some, others, each,* and *none*.

- Diffusion is the process of introducing cultural elements from one society into another.
- By looking at examples of atoms, one discovers that each contains an equal number of electrons and protons in the nucleus.
- Lactose, a sugar present in milk, is one of the simple sugars used in food preparations for infants.

The Formation of Fog

02-02

Fog is a cloud in contact with the ground. It only differs from other clouds in that it touches the Earth's surface. Most types of fog form when the relative humidity reaches 100% at ground level. Fog can form suddenly and can dissipate just as rapidly, depending on what side of the dew point the temperature is on. Evaporation fog and precipitation fog are two kinds. The former is caused by water changing into gas very quickly while the other is caused by the release of water.

The foggiest place on the Earth is the Grand Banks of Newfoundland, Canada. Frequent fog in this area is caused by the meeting of the cold Labrador Current from the north and the much warmer Gulf Stream from the south.

Q   The phrase "the other" in the passage refers to

    Ⓐ evaporation fog

    Ⓑ precipitation fog

    Ⓒ water changing into gas

    Ⓓ the release of water

The Dragonfly

02-03

The dragonfly is an insect with large multifaceted eyes that allow 360 degrees of vision. It has two pairs of strong, transparent wings in addition to a stretched-out body.

Dragonflies usually consume mosquitoes, flies, and other small insects. Many humans like them because they feed on these pests. Dragonflies live near lakes, ponds, streams, and wetlands, and their larvae, called nymphs, are aquatic.

The life cycle of a dragonfly, going from the egg to the death of the adult, can last anywhere from six months to six or seven years. Most of this life cycle is spent in the larval state, during which time the nymph uses its gills to breathe and eats tadpoles or fish.

Q   The word "them" in the passage refers to

    Ⓐ dragonflies

    Ⓑ mosquitoes

    Ⓒ flies

    Ⓓ other insects

Drill 3

Ecology

02-04

Ecology is the study of living things in their habitats. It studies why they live in certain areas and how many of a species can survive in those places. It also looks at species' interactions with other living things.

The environment of a living thing includes various physical factors. Some such factors are sunlight and climate. Geology is another factor. The other living things that share a habitat make up yet another factor.

Ecology is a broad science. One branch is behavior ecology, which looks at the way a single living thing adapts to its habitat. Population ecology studies a single species. There are many more branches of this science.

Q The phrase "this science" in the passage refers to

Ⓐ geology

Ⓑ ecology

Ⓒ behavior ecology

Ⓓ population ecology

Drill 4

Hypothesis

02-05

A hypothesis is a suggested explanation of an event that is not already understood by science. It suggests a possible connection between two or more phenomena in a reasoned way. Scientists base hypotheses on their observations or on theories.

The scientific method requires that one can test a hypothesis. Many members of the scientific community demand that a hypothesis be falsifiable. This means that it can possibly be proven false.

A famous example posits a man who goes to a new country and sees only white sheep. He forms a hypothesis that all the sheep in the country are white. But if one black sheep is observed, the hypothesis would be proven false.

Q The word "it" in the passage refers to

Ⓐ the scientific method

Ⓑ one

Ⓒ the scientific community

Ⓓ a hypothesis

Newton's Laws of Motion

02-06

Newton's Laws of Motion are three physical laws. To understand the first law, imagine an apple resting on a table. If a force, such as a hand, pushes the apple, it will gain inertia and begin moving.

For the second law, imagine a hand pushing the same apple softly, therefore causing it to move just a little. If the hand hits it with increased force, the force will make it hit a wall in the direction and with the momentum with which it was hit.

An example of Newton's third law is the reaction occurring after the apple hits the wall. Every action requires an equal and opposite reaction, which, in this case, could be a dent in the wall or the apple exploding into bits.

Q The word "it" in the passage refers to

Ⓐ a hand

Ⓑ the same apple

Ⓒ increased force

Ⓓ the momentum

Biological Kingdoms

02-07

In 1735, Carolus Linnaeus published a book about kingdoms. In his book, he distinguished two kingdoms of living things: the animal kingdom and the vegetable kingdom. Everything on the Earth fell into one category or the other. He later created a third kingdom for minerals.

Years later, bacteria were discovered. Biologists realized that they did not fit into any of the three kingdoms. Another kingdom was named for them. This was called the Monera kingdom.

As science progressed and learned more about living things, new kingdoms were needed. In 1969, Robert Whittaker recognized a fifth kingdom. This kingdom was named for fungi. By 1980, yet another kingdom was named. It was named to distinguish various microscopic organisms.

Q The word "them" in the passage refers to

Ⓐ minerals

Ⓑ bacteria

Ⓒ biologists

Ⓓ the three kingdoms

Exercises with Mid-Length Passages

Exercise 1 Read the following passage and answer the questions.

⏱ Time Limit: 3 min.

El Nino and La Nina

02-08

1 ➡ El Nino and La Nina are phenomena that take place between the ocean and the atmosphere on a global scale. During them, there are major temperature changes in the surface waters of the tropical Pacific Ocean. El Nino indicates a rise of 0.5 degrees Celsius or more. La Nina indicates a drop of around the same degree. These changes must be sustained for a period longer than five months to be called El Nino or La Nina.

Many of the countries affected by these climatic changes are developing nations in South America and Africa. Their economies are largely dependent on the farming and fishing sectors. These industries are a major source of food supply, employment, and foreign exchange. So new methods for predicting these changes in the climate can have a great socioeconomic impact for these countries.

3 ➡ El Nino and La Nina episodes usually occur irregularly. In recent times, they have happened every two to seven years. They usually last for one or two years. The effects of El Nino are very wide ranging. Many places experience weather that is the reverse of their normal climate. Some areas even experience terrible flooding due to heavy rainfall. There are also many forest fires because of extreme droughts. On the other hand, the effects of La Nina begin to develop worldwide. During a La Nina, trade winds can become very strong, and an abnormal accumulation of colder-than-normal water can occur in the Central and Eastern Pacific regions.

In the normal Pacific pattern of ocean atmosphere system, equatorial winds gather, and then warm water pools toward the west. Cold water upswells along the South American coast. This brings fish up the coast, where they support the local fishing industry because they follow the cool, nutrient-rich water. When El Nino takes effect, the warm water flows toward the South American coast. The absence of cold upswelling increases warming. This sends the fish population swimming out to sea instead of being along the coast. These conditions severely damage the local fishing industries.

The causes of El Nino and La Nina are still undiscovered. But many scientists are dedicating their careers to understanding these global weather phenomena better.

📖 **Words & Phrases**

phenomenon Ⓝ a natural occurrence that requires scientific explanation
impact Ⓝ a strong effect
drought Ⓝ a period of abnormally dry weather
upswell Ⓥ to rush up toward the surface

1 According to paragraph 1, which of the following is NOT true of El Nino and La Nina?

Ⓐ They result in the water temperature changing.

Ⓑ They can affect places around the world.

Ⓒ They originate in the Pacific Ocean.

Ⓓ They usually last fewer than five months.

2 The author's description of El Nino in paragraph 3 mentions which of the following?

Ⓐ The speed it makes trade winds blow

Ⓑ Some countries it has no effect on

Ⓒ The frequency that it tends to occur

Ⓓ The places where it causes flooding

Mastering the Question Type

3 The word "Their" in the passage refers to

Ⓐ The countries

Ⓑ These climatic changes

Ⓒ Developing nations

Ⓓ South America and Africa

4 The word "This" in the passage refers to

Ⓐ El Nino

Ⓑ The warm water

Ⓒ The South American coast

Ⓓ Warming

Summary Note Fill in the blanks with the appropriate words.

El Nino vs. La Nina

❶ _____

- Temperature rise of 0.5°C or more for a period longer than 5 months
- Heavy rainfall ➡ flooding
- Drought ➡ forest fires

❷ _____

- Temperature drop of 0.5°C or more for a period longer than 5 months
- Strong trade winds
  - accumulation of cold water
  - change in fish migration patterns
  - damage to fishing industry

🕐 Time Limit: 2 min. 50 sec.

The Decline of Biodiversity

02-09

Biodiversity is the range of living things in an area. During the last 100 years, scientists have seen a great decline in biodiversity. This means a great loss for humans as stewards of the planet Earth.

Some studies show that one in eight plant species is threatened with extinction. It is estimated that 140,000 species of plants are lost each year. This is due to the use of unsustainable ecological practices. Many of these lost plants could have been very useful in creating new drugs to combat disease.

3 ➡ Most of the extinctions in the last thousand years are due to humans. The main cause is the chopping down of tropical rainforests. These habitats are being turned into pastures, farmlands, and orchards. Most of this destruction is done to create pastures for beef cattle. It is also done to clear places for farmers to raise crops and to grow fruit trees for human consumption.

4 ➡ The introduction of exotic species is another threat. When exotic species are introduced to a habitat, they try to establish a self-sustaining population. Then, they threaten the local species. These foreign species may be predators or parasites. Or they may simply be aggressive. They deprive local species of nutrients. Because the local species have not had a chance to evolve, they often lack defenses and cannot compete against these exotic species.

The rich diversity across the world exists only because of barriers. The main barriers are seas and oceans. These barriers could never be crossed by natural means. But since humans invented ships and airplanes, it is now possible for species to meet. There is no time for them to adapt, but humans continue to combine species from different regions. The world's ecosystems will soon be dominated by very few aggressive super-species.

In order to reverse these problems, people need to minimize their consumption. They need to consume less beef and other products that cause damage to the natural environment. Governments also need to impose strict rules against destroying natural land and introducing exotic species.

📖 Words & Phrases

decline ⓝ a decrease
unsustainable adj unable to be maintained for a period of time
chop down ⓥ to cut down
aggressive adj threatening or dangerous toward others
exotic adj foreign; strange

1 According to paragraph 3, which of the following is true of most extinctions in the last thousand years?

Ⓐ They have been caused by biodiversity.

Ⓑ They have been caused by humans.

Ⓒ They may have been caused by predators or parasites.

Ⓓ They have been caused by combining species from different regions.

2 In paragraph 4, all of the following questions are answered EXCEPT:

Ⓐ Why do many native species lack defenses against foreign invaders?

Ⓑ How do foreign invaders harm native species?

Ⓒ What do invasive species do when they are introduced to a new habit?

Ⓓ What are the most common types of invasive species nowadays?

3 The word "This" in the passage refers to

Ⓐ Biodiversity

Ⓑ The range of living things

Ⓒ A great decline in biodiversity

Ⓓ A great loss for humans

4 The word "Many" in the passage refers to

Ⓐ Some studies

Ⓑ Plant species

Ⓒ These lost plants

Ⓓ New drugs

✏ **Summary Note** Fill in the blanks with the appropriate words.

Threats to Biodiversity

Chopping down of ❶ _____ to create pastures and farmland

Introduction of ❷ _____ predators (super species)

Effects

Increased rate of extinction of plant life

Increased extinction of indigenous animal life that is unable to adapt or compete

❸ _____ of biodiversity

Tidal Power Plants

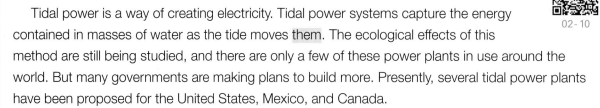

02-10

Tidal power is a way of creating electricity. Tidal power systems capture the energy contained in masses of water as the tide moves them. The ecological effects of this method are still being studied, and there are only a few of these power plants in use around the world. But many governments are making plans to build more. Presently, several tidal power plants have been proposed for the United States, Mexico, and Canada.

2➡ The Rance Tidal Power Plant was the world's first electrical generating station powered by tidal energy. It is located on the Rance River in Bretagne, France. The construction of this plant necessitated the draining of the surrounding area. Two dams were built over two years. Construction of the actual plant began on July 20, 1963. At that time, the Rance was entirely blocked by the two dams. The plant was completed in 1966. On December 4, 1967, it was connected to the French national power grid. The plant cost about 524 million euros to build. It currently produces three percent of the power consumed by Bretagne. The project had very high costs, but those costs have been recovered. The power from this plant is cheaper than using nuclear power.

The plant's barrage has caused progressive silting of the Rance ecosystem. Sand eels and plaice have disappeared. But sea bass and cuttlefish have returned to the river. Tides still flow in the estuary. The operators of the plant are still trying to minimize the biological impact.

4➡ The first tidal power plant in North America was the Annapolis Royal Generating Station. It was located in Annapolis Royal in Canada. It was originally constructed in 1984 to look at alternative methods for generating electricity but was decommissioned in 2019. However, it also caused changes in the local environment. The water and the air temperature in the area changed. Moreover, the siltation patterns of the river shifted, and the riverbanks on both sides of the dam increased in size.

📖 Words & Phrases

contain Ⓥ to hold something within another thing
necessitate Ⓥ to create a need
barrage Ⓝ repeated hits on something
estuary Ⓝ a place where fresh water and salt water mix
minimize Ⓥ to shrink; to make smaller
generate Ⓥ to produce; to create

1 According to paragraph 2, which of the following is true of the Rance Tidal Power Plant?

Ⓐ It is located in North America.

Ⓑ It was constructed in the 1960s.

Ⓒ It provides the majority of electricity in Bretagne.

Ⓓ It is considered to be a waste of money.

2 According to paragraph 4, the author's description of the Annapolis Royal Generating Station mentions all of the following EXCEPT:

Ⓐ The year that it was built

Ⓑ Some of the changes it has caused

Ⓒ The cities it supplies with electricity

Ⓓ The place where it is located

Mastering the Question Type

3 The word "them" in the passage refers to

Ⓐ tidal power systems

Ⓑ masses of water

Ⓒ the ecological effects of this method

Ⓓ these power plants

4 The word "it" in the passage refers to

Ⓐ North America

Ⓑ the Annapolis Royal Generating Station

Ⓒ electricity

Ⓓ the local environment

✏ **Summary Note** Fill in the blanks with the appropriate words.

```
                            ( Tidal Power Plants )

• Create ❶ _____
• Cheaper/safer/cleaner than ❷ _____
• ❸ _____
   ➡ the world's first power plant
• The first tidal power plant in North America
   ➡ Annapolis Royal Generating Station in Annapolis, Royal, Canada
```

🕒 Time Limit: 3 min.

The Komodo Dragon

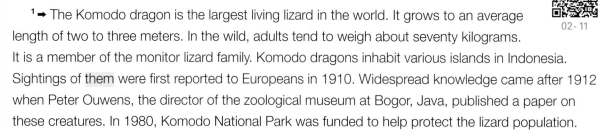

02-11

¹➡ The Komodo dragon is the largest living lizard in the world. It grows to an average length of two to three meters. In the wild, adults tend to weigh about seventy kilograms. It is a member of the monitor lizard family. Komodo dragons inhabit various islands in Indonesia. Sightings of them were first reported to Europeans in 1910. Widespread knowledge came after 1912 when Peter Ouwens, the director of the zoological museum at Bogor, Java, published a paper on these creatures. In 1980, Komodo National Park was funded to help protect the lizard population.

Komodo dragons are carnivorous. Although they enjoy the flesh of dead animals, they hunt live prey. They begin with a stealthy approach and then launch into a short, sudden charge. During this time, they can run briefly at speeds of up to twenty kilometers per hour.

³➡ The Komodo dragon is not considered venomous, but its teeth are home to more than fifty strains of bacteria. If the initial bite does not kill its prey, deadly infections will kill the creature within a week. Then, the Komodo dragon finds its victim by following the smell, whereupon it feeds on the dead flesh. The dragon also has large claws that it uses when it is young. It uses these to climb trees to escape from the jaws of older dragons. But when it becomes older, the claws are used mainly as weapons.

The Komodo dragon has a wide range of prey, including wild pigs, goats, deer, and water buffaloes. In the wild, it has also been observed eating smaller dragons. Occasionally, it devours humans and human corpses. More than a dozen human deaths have been attributed to dragon bites in the last 100 years.

The Komodo dragon is a vulnerable species as there are approximately 6,000 of them living today. Mating occurs between May and August with eggs laid in September. The female lays eggs in the ground or in tree hollows, providing them with some protection. Clutches usually contain an average of twenty eggs. Once born, the animals take about five years to mature, and they live for around thirty years.

📖 Words & Phrases

inhabit Ⓥ to live somewhere
carnivorous [adj] meat-eating
prey [n] a living thing that is hunted and killed by other animals
stealthy [adj] secretive
charge [n] an attack

1 According to paragraph 1, which of the following is true of Komodo dragons?

Ⓐ Some of them are more than three meters long.

Ⓑ Europeans learned about them centuries ago.

Ⓒ They mostly live on islands in Indonesia.

Ⓓ They have an average lifespan of seventy years.

2 According to paragraph 3, which of the following is NOT true of the Komodo dragon?

Ⓐ It has large claws that help it when it hunts.

Ⓑ It uses venom to kill animals it attacks.

Ⓒ It can kill some prey by biting it.

Ⓓ Bacteria in its body can kill other animals.

3 The word "them" in the passage refers to

Ⓐ Komodo dragons

Ⓑ various islands

Ⓒ Europeans

Ⓓ Komodo National Park

4 The word "these" in the passage refers to

Ⓐ large claws

Ⓑ trees

Ⓒ the jaws of older dragons

Ⓓ weapons

✎ **Summary Note** Fill in the blanks with the appropriate words.

The Komodo Dragon

- ❶ _____ in the world: 2 to 3 meters long
- A member of the monitor lizard family
- Inhabits ❷ _____
- First sighted by Europeans in 1910
- Teeth hold more than 50 strains of bacteria
- Eats wild pigs, goats, deer, water buffaloes, and humans
- ❸ _____ Komodo dragons currently living

🕐 Time Limit: 2 min. 40 sec.

Nanotechnology

02-12

1 ➡ Nanotechnology is a relatively new field of applied science. It is an effort to create very tiny machines on a nano scale. A nano is a unit of measurement which stands for ten to the negative power of nine. It is used to describe very small things. One example of nanotechnology in modern use is the making of polymers. These are based on molecular structure. Another is the design of computer chip layouts. These are based on surface science.

At the nano-size level, the properties of many materials change. For example, copper changes from opaque to clear. Solid gold becomes liquid at room temperature. Insulators like silicon become conductors. All of these activities open up many potential risks. Due to their altered states, nano particles become more mobile. They are also more likely to react with other things. There are four ways for nano particles to enter the human body. They can be inhaled, swallowed, absorbed through the skin, or injected. Once these particles are in the body, they are highly mobile.

In fact, the way these particles react inside living things is still not fully understood. But scientists guess that these tiny objects could easily overload defensive cells. This would weaken a body's defenses against diseases. Humans could easily lose control of particles this size. This would lead to mass epidemics that would cause widespread disease and death.

4 ➡ Another concern about nanotechnology regards the environmental risks. One report details the possible disaster of the Earth being covered in a gray sticky substance. This terrible event is attributed to the unrestrained self-replication of microscopic robots. These robots are called nanobots and are able to control themselves. Therefore, scientists need to collect much more data before they are allowed to create and release nanobots. They should be highly regulated by laws that only allow licensed scientists to do safe experiments.

📖 Words & Phrases

apply Ⓥ to use something
regulate Ⓥ to control something by using laws
opaque adj unable to be seen through
inhale Ⓥ to breathe in
epidemic Ⓝ a wave of sickness that sweeps over a group of people

1 According to paragraph 1, which of the following is NOT true of nanotechnology?

Ⓐ Its name describes things that are very small.

Ⓑ It describes the effort to make machines on a tiny scale.

Ⓒ Its name describes the measurement of ten to the negative power of nine.

Ⓓ It is a fairly old field of theoretical science.

2 According to paragraph 4, some people are concerned about nanotechnology because

Ⓐ it could cause problems on a global scale

Ⓑ nanobots might try to kill humans

Ⓒ there are not enough laws restricting it

Ⓓ very little is understood about it today

3 The word "These" in the passage refers to

Ⓐ Ten to the negative power of nine

Ⓑ Very small things

Ⓒ Polymers

Ⓓ Computer chip layouts

4 The word "They" in the passage refers to

Ⓐ Scientists

Ⓑ Much more data

Ⓒ Nanobots

Ⓓ Laws

Summary Note Fill in the blanks with the appropriate words.

Computer chip layout

❶ .... Polymers

Nanotechnology

The properties of materials change

❷ .... Humans could lose control of self-replicating nanobots

Nano particles can enter the human body

🕐 Time Limit: 2 min. 30 sec.

The Dust Bowl

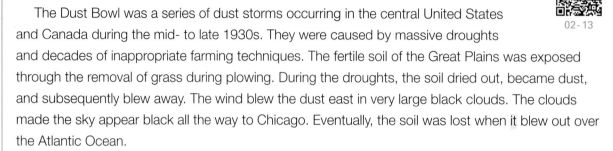
02-13

The Dust Bowl was a series of dust storms occurring in the central United States and Canada during the mid- to late 1930s. They were caused by massive droughts and decades of inappropriate farming techniques. The fertile soil of the Great Plains was exposed through the removal of grass during plowing. During the droughts, the soil dried out, became dust, and subsequently blew away. The wind blew the dust east in very large black clouds. The clouds made the sky appear black all the way to Chicago. Eventually, the soil was lost when it blew out over the Atlantic Ocean.

2 ➡ The Dust Bowl began in 1934 and lasted until 1939. On November 11, 1933, a very strong dust storm stripped topsoil from parched South Dakota farmlands. It was just one of a series of terrible dust storms that year. Then, on May 11, 1934, a strong two-day storm removed massive amounts of Great Plains topsoil in one of the worst storms of the Dust Bowl. Once again, the dust clouds blew all the way to Chicago, where the filth fell like snow. April 14, 1935, is known as Black Sunday. That was when one of the worst "black blizzards" occurred during the Dust Bowl. It caused extensive damage and turned the day to night. Witnesses reported that they could not see five feet in front of them at certain points.

3 ➡ Topsoil across millions of acres was blown away because the indigenous sod had been broken for wheat farming. Vast herds of buffalo were no longer fertilizing the rest of the indigenous grasses. This ecological disaster caused an exodus from Texas, Arkansas, Oklahoma, and the surrounding Great Plains. Over 500,000 Americans became homeless. Many of these homeless people migrated west looking for work. These people were referred to as Okies even when they were not from Oklahoma.

📖 **Words & Phrases**

inappropriate adj unsuitable; improper
plow v to break through the top layer of soil and to mix it before planting
soil n dirt; dust; earth
blizzard n a terrible snowstorm with strong winds
extensive adj broad; far-reaching; large-scale
indigenous adj born or coming from a certain place

1   According to paragraph 2, which of the following is true of the Dust Bowl?
    Ⓐ It lasted for several years in the 1930s.
    Ⓑ Tidal waves caused the dust storms during it.
    Ⓒ The worst dust storm occurred on April 1, 1930.
    Ⓓ Most storms during it lasted for weeks.

2   According to paragraph 3, which of the following is NOT true of the Dust Bowl?
    Ⓐ Buffalo no longer fertilized large amounts of grass during it.
    Ⓑ Topsoil was lost during it due to the actions of wheat farmers.
    Ⓒ Some of the topsoil lost during it was recovered by farmers.
    Ⓓ Many desperate farmers left their lands in Texas, Arkansas, and Oklahoma.

3   The word "it" in the passage refers to
    Ⓐ the sky
    Ⓑ Chicago
    Ⓒ the soil
    Ⓓ the Atlantic Ocean

4   The phrase "that year" in the passage refers to
    Ⓐ 1934
    Ⓑ 1939
    Ⓒ 1933
    Ⓓ 1935

Summary Note Fill in the blanks with the appropriate words.

Important Dates of the Dust Bowl of the 1930s

❶ _____
- A very strong dust storm stripped topsoil from South Dakota farmlands

❷ _____
- A strong two-day storm removed massive amounts of Great Plains topsoil

❸ _____
- Black Sunday ➡ one of the worst "black blizzards" occurred

Results: By 1939, more than 500,000 Americans were homeless

Building Summary Skills

The following summaries are based on the long passages you worked on earlier. Complete each of them by filling in the blanks with suitable words or phrases.

Exercise 1   El Nino and La Nina

South America and Africa	temperature changes	irregularly
migratory patterns	drought, flooding, and forest fires	

El Nino and La Nina cause major _____ that affect a large portion of the world's climate. The economies of many nations in _____ are strongly affected by these changes in the climate. El Nino and La Nina occur _____ and can cause some damaging effects such as _____. These changes also affect the _____ of fish, which affects the fishing industry. Scientists do not fully understand El Nino and La Nina yet, but they are studying them very closely.

Exercise 2   The Decline of Biodiversity

living things	foreign species	biodiversity
rainforests	unsustainable environmental practices	

_____, which describes the range of _____, has been declining rapidly over the past century. Many species of plants are becoming extinct because of _____. Humans are the biggest cause of these environmental problems mainly because they chop down so many parts of _____. Another threat to biodiversity is the introduction of _____, which overtake local species. Humans need to take strong steps to stop the decline of biodiversity.

Exercise 3   Tidal Power Plants

local ecosystem	moving water	time and money
Annapolis Royal	generating electricity	

Tidal power plants are a method of _____ through the power of _____ and are gaining popularity around the world. The Rance Tidal Power Plant in France was the first power plant in the world to use this method. The construction of the Rance Tidal Power Plant took a lot of _____, but it has generated enough power to cover its costs. Tidal power plants do affect the _____, and scientists are still studying how. The first tidal power plant in North America was in _____ in Canada.

Exercise 4 The Komodo Dragon

their own species	infects their prey	largest lizards
population	some islands in Indonesia	

Komodo dragons are the _____ in the world today. They
live on _____. They eat meat, which they kill by a bite that
_____ and kills it over a period of days. Komodo dragons eat a wide range of
other animals, including _____. Today, the _____
of Komodo dragons is not very large.

Exercise 5 Nanotechnology

human bodies	microscopic machines	nanotechnology
unpredictable	self-replicating nanobots	

_____ is the risky science of building _____.
This technology could be very useful, but it is _____ since the properties of
many materials change at the microscopic level. Some scientists worry that machines this small could
easily enter _____ and cause effects that nobody can predict. Another
concern is that _____ could damage the environment on a very large and
unexpected scale. Experiments with nanotechnology should be done in a very cautious fashion as
regulated by the government.

Exercise 6 The Dust Bowl

blown away	a series of terrible storms	natural disaster
dusty, infertile ground	the United States and Canada	

The Dust Bowl was _____ in the 1930s that damaged the farming industries
in _____. Farming was damaged because the fertile layer of topsoil was
_____ by powerful winds, leaving only _____.
Some of these storms were so bad that the sky turned black, and no one could see the sun. Many
farmers were made homeless by this _____ and were forced to travel west
to look for work.

Meteorology

02-14

¹→ Meteorology is the study of the Earth's atmosphere. It focuses on weather processes and forecasting and explaining weather events. These events are bound by the factors that exist in the atmosphere, such as temperature, air pressure, and water vapor. These factors interact to create climate patterns. The term *meteorology* was coined by Aristotle in 350 B.C. He was the first person to observe and record the process by which water evaporates. He noticed how the hot sun turned it into mist and then the cool air returned it to the Earth on the following day.

In 1607, Galileo made the first tool to measure temperature. A few years later, his assistant made the first barometer. By 1648, Pascal saw that air pressure falls with height. He also guessed that there is a vacuum above the atmosphere. In 1667, Robert Hooke built a tool to measure the speed of wind. Later, Edmund Haley mapped the trade winds for sailors. He also deduced that changes in the atmosphere are driven by solar heat. By the twentieth century, science began to understand many important weather events. Perhaps the most important concept was how the rotation of the Earth affects the flow of air. This large-scale force was named the Coriolis Effect.

³→ In 1904, a Norwegian scientist said that it was possible to predict the weather by means of calculations based on natural laws. This led to the field of modern weather forecasting. By the 1950s, forecasters began using computers. These early machines helped them do experiments. The first forecasts were produced by using models of low and high temperatures. After about a decade, the first weather satellite was launched. This event led to the age of global weather information. Satellites became important tools for studying everything from forest fires to El Nino. They gave scientists a large-scale view of the planet.

These days, climate models are used to compare weather data from past years. The historical data is cross-referenced with current conditions. This gives scientists data to study long-term climate shifts. Effects such as global warming are now better understood. Currently, powerful new supercomputers are being used. With them, it is possible to create working models of the atmosphere.

Many human methods of weather forecasting are also employed. These methods rely on the skill and judgment of the forecasters who used them. Many of the methods allow an accuracy rate of more than fifty percent. In this age of weather forecasting, many people depend on information about the weather. It increases the successful production of food. It also saves lives when natural disasters strike. Mankind's ability to predict the weather has reached new levels of unprecedented accuracy.

1   According to paragraph 1, which of the following is true of meteorology?
    Ⓐ It explains the science of outer space bodies such as meteors.
    Ⓑ It explains biological phenomena.
    Ⓒ It explains events that occur related to the weather.
    Ⓓ It explains the science of things that fall to the Earth such as rain and snow.

2   According to paragraph 1, which of the following is NOT true of Aristotle?
    Ⓐ He was the first person to use the term *meteorology*.
    Ⓑ He was the first person to examine the evaporation process.
    Ⓒ He could predict the weather up to a week in advance.
    Ⓓ He saw how the hot sun turned water into mist.

3   The word "deduced" in the passage is closest in meaning to
    Ⓐ reduced
    Ⓑ inferred
    Ⓒ told
    Ⓓ eliminated

4   In paragraph 3, why does the author mention "a Norwegian scientist"?
    Ⓐ To explain why the purposes of weather forecasting changed
    Ⓑ To show how modern methods of weather forecasting began
    Ⓒ To describe when scientific concepts began to be used in weather forecasting
    Ⓓ To claim that weather forecasting should be based on natural laws

5 According to paragraph 3, what can be inferred about satellites and weather forecasting?

    Ⓐ Global weather information was not available before the launch of satellites.

    Ⓑ Satellites enabled scientists to identify the causes of El Nino.

    Ⓒ Satellites are responsible for influencing weather patterns.

    Ⓓ Human methods of weather forecasting have become useless because of satellites.

6 The word "them" in the passage refers to

    Ⓐ data

    Ⓑ long-term climate shifts

    Ⓒ effects such as global warming

    Ⓓ powerful new supercomputers

Chipmunks

02-15

A Siberian chipmunk eating a cone

The Earth is covered with millions of species of animals, and each is responsible for filling an important niche in the delicate ecosystem of the planet. The chipmunk, although small in size, is vital to the health of its habitat. Chipmunks are small rodents that inhabit the forests of North America and Asia. There are twenty-five species of chipmunks. Many of them are marked by their reddish-brown fur with white and black stripes that cover the length of their bodies.

2 ➡ Unlike many of its rodent relatives, the chipmunk has two breeding seasons a year. The first spans from February to April, and the second runs from June to August. The average number of offspring for a chipmunk is four, but there can be litters as small as one and as big as nine. Mothers keep their young hidden underground in their homes for up to six weeks until they are old enough to fend for themselves. Some of their natural predators include cats, dogs, eagles, hawks, foxes, coyotes, and wolves. In the wild, a chipmunk's lifespan is typically only a year, but some have been known to live for up to five years.

3 ➡ Although mating season is an exception, chipmunks spend most of their time alone building their homes, looking for food, and hiding from predators. They are often found climbing in trees to look for food. Chipmunks are traditionally hoarders. They spend spring and summer stocking their burrows with nuts, seeds, insects, berries, and other foods in order to hibernate during the long winter without starving. Other sources of food include fungi, bird's eggs, grain, and worms.

4 ➡ One of the most remarkable features of chipmunks is their cheeks. Chipmunks have special pouches on both sides of their head that can be stretched and filled with food. Once completely filled, each cheek can become as large as the chipmunk's head. This ability allows chipmunks to carry a large amount of food to and from their burrows with ease.

Chipmunks, like other small rodents, are known as spreaders. They are responsible for the spreading of seeds, fungi, and other types of vegetation. For instance, sometimes seeds that chipmunks take to their burrows get left behind or dropped along the way. These begin to grow, in turn providing more food and shelter for other animals in the habitat. Whether they are spreading seeds or becoming the prey of other animals, chipmunks are an important part of their habitats. They are very much a part of the ever-evolving cycle present in nature.

7 The phrase "fend for" in the passage is closest in meaning to

Ⓐ take care of

Ⓑ move

Ⓒ feed

Ⓓ look for

8 According to paragraph 2, which of the following is NOT true of chipmunks?

Ⓐ They breed during two seasons every year.

Ⓑ Their average number of offspring is six.

Ⓒ Chipmunk mothers hide their young underground.

Ⓓ Chipmunks have various kinds of natural predators.

9 The word "hoarders" in the passage is closest in meaning to

Ⓐ searchers

Ⓑ eaters

Ⓒ hunters

Ⓓ collectors

10 According to paragraph 3, which of the following can be inferred about chipmunks?

Ⓐ Many of them live together in burrows.

Ⓑ They are not normal social animals.

Ⓒ They tend to eat one or two types of food.

Ⓓ They put on weight during the winter months.

11 In paragraph 4, why does the author mention chipmunks' "cheeks"?

Ⓐ To show that chipmunks use them to defend themselves

Ⓑ To explain that they help chipmunks carry and store food

Ⓒ To prove that they are extremely large

Ⓓ To describe chipmunks' ability to eat a lot of food

12 The word "These" in the passage refers to

Ⓐ Other types of vegetation

Ⓑ Seeds

Ⓒ Chipmunks

Ⓓ Their burrows

Vocabulary Check-Up

A Choose the words with the closest meanings to the highlighted words.

1 The sign indicates the correct direction to the store.
- (A) looks
- (B) shows
- (C) says
- (D) needs

2 The impact of the tsunami on the coast was terrible.
- (A) time
- (B) cost
- (C) effect
- (D) use

3 The decline of the African elephant can be linked to poaching.
- (A) decrease
- (B) change
- (C) growth
- (D) limitation

4 Because of his hard work, he was able to recover his losses from the accident.
- (A) find
- (B) sell
- (C) take back
- (D) escape

5 This dinosaur was known to be carnivorous.
- (A) vegetative
- (B) nocturnal
- (C) tardy
- (D) flesh eating

6 His approach was so stealthy that no one noticed him coming.
- (A) fast
- (B) secretive
- (C) expected
- (D) noisy

7 He is applying everything he learned in photography class at his new job.
- (A) using
- (B) needing
- (C) saying
- (D) wanting

8 If you look at the watch, you can tell it is exotic.
- (A) sharp
- (B) normal
- (C) original
- (D) unusual

B **Match the words with the correct definitions.**

1 upswell   •   • (A) to cut down

2 soil   •   • (B) to break through the top layer of soil and to mix it before planting

3 phenomenon   •   • (C) a wave of sickness that sweeps over a group of people

4 plow   •   • (D) the forceful movement of water rushing up toward the surface

5 chop down   •   • (E) a natural occurrence that requires a scientific explanation

6 epidemic   •   • (F) to control something by using laws

7 barrage   •   • (G) a living thing that is hunted and killed by other animals

8 regulate   •   • (H) to create a need

9 necessitate   •   • (I) a nutrient-rich layer of dirt for planting

10 prey   •   • (J) repeated hits on something

Factual Information

Overview

Introduction

Factual Information questions ask you to identify facts, details, or other information that is explicitly mentioned in the passage. The information is often found in just one or two paragraphs of the passage. So you can find the correct answer without even reading the whole passage. You just need to find the right spot in the passage that has the information about which the question asks. This is one of the most frequent question types on the TOEFL iBT.

Question Types

▷ According to the passage, which of the following is true of X?

▷ According to paragraph X, who [when/ where/ what/ how/ why] Y?

▷ The author's description of X mentions which of the following?

▷ According to the paragraph, X occurred because . . .

▷ Select the TWO answer choices from paragraph 1 that identify X. *To receive credit, you must select TWO answers.*

Useful Tips

■ Read the questions first to know what exactly is being asked.

■ Scan the passage to find out where the relevant information is in the passage.

■ Remove the choices that are not relevant to the passage.

■ Do not choose an answer just because it is mentioned in the passage.

03-01

Q According to the passage, what are ballet dancers famous for?

Ⓐ Their dancing, miming, acting, and music

Ⓑ Their clothes and shoes

Ⓒ Their elegant movements

Ⓓ Their balancing skills

Ballet

Ballet is an art form that makes use of dancing, miming, acting, and music. It can be performed alone or with an opera. Ballet dancers are famous for their gracefulness. They are also known for amazing feats of physical strength. Many ballet techniques resemble positions and footwork used in fencing. Both ballet and fencing have similar requirements of balance and movement. Both of these forms also developed during the same historical period. Ballet became popular in the royal courts of Italy and France during the Renaissance. For the past four hundred years, this dance form has been refined, most notably by Russian dance companies that travel and perform. Today, ballet is one of the best-preserved dances in the world.

✔ Correct Answer

The question asks what ballet dancers are known for doing. The third sentence of the passage reads that they are famous for their gracefulness. So the correct answer is Ⓒ because "elegant movements" is a similar expression for "gracefulness."

Basic Drill

Read the passages and answer the questions.

Skill & Tip

The key to success in Factual Information questions is the ability to scan for correct information in the passage. You need to practice reading the questions first and then spotting the relevant information in the passage quickly. You do not have to read every part of the passage.

Drill 1

Opinions

03-02

An opinion is a thought or idea held about something important to the holder. It is not a fact so cannot be proven correct or incorrect. But in the case of the United States Supreme Court, the word "opinion" has a different meaning. For the court, an opinion is a decision that establishes the way a law will be followed in the future. The court gave an opinion in the 1971 case of *Roe vs. Wade* that was in favor of abortion being legal. This made it possible for pregnant women in the United States to have abortions. This is an example of an opinion that has caused controversy. This controversy has continued for many years after it was issued.

Q According to the passage, what does a court's opinion establish?

Ⓐ Thoughts or ideas about a particular event
Ⓑ Controversy over important issues
Ⓒ Future interpretations of the law
Ⓓ Facts about legal matters

Drill 2

Quilting

03-03

Quilts were traditionally used to cover beds as warm top blankets. But these days, many quilts are treated as works of art and hang on walls to be displayed. In colonial times, many women spent time weaving and making clothing. But wealthy women were able to spend their time making fine quilts. These women formed groups called quilting bees. Quilts are often sewn to commemorate important events such as weddings or births. Quilters sew important dates or names into a quilt by using a needlepoint technique. They also incorporate pieces of a person's clothing or important flags in quilts to create historical documents.

Q According to the passage, why do people often sew quilts?

Ⓐ To remind other individuals of historic events
Ⓑ To make flags that people can enjoy and use to represent them
Ⓒ To make lots of money for use by the federal government in wars
Ⓓ To have them displayed in cultural exhibits

The History of Medicine

03-04

In 1960, the earliest proof of medicine was found buried with a prehistoric man. With him were eight kinds of plants. All of these are still used for their healing benefits today. In cultures around the world, medicine has developed differently. In traditional Chinese medicine, doctors heal by changing the flow of energy through the body. In India, doctors heal by trying to restore harmony between the mind, the body, and the soul. Western medicine first developed in Europe. Doctors focus mainly on diet and hygiene as a way to restore health. Now, as technology grows and the world becomes smaller, doctors are using the best parts of medicine from all over the world.

Q According to the passage, what do doctors do with medicine from all over the world?

Ⓐ They bury it with prehistoric men in order to create historical records.

Ⓑ They develop it in European clinics.

Ⓒ They use it to heal the minds, the bodies, and the souls of wounded people.

Ⓓ They combine it and use the most effective parts.

Print Journalism

03-05

Print journalism can be split into several categories. They are newspapers, news magazines, and general interest magazines. There are also trade and hobby magazines. Finally, there are newsletters, private publications, online news pages, and blogs.

Newspaper journalists use the inverted pyramid style. This style is used for straight or hard news reports rather than for features. Written hard news reports are expected to be spare in the use of words and to list all of the important information first. The story can be cut from the bottom when there is not enough space for it. Feature stories are written in a looser style.

Q According to the passage, what is a characteristic of written hard news reports?

Ⓐ They are long and wordy.

Ⓑ They do not use many words.

Ⓒ They deal with as few facts as possible.

Ⓓ They are printed in magazines.

Exercise 1 Read the following passage and answer the questions.

🕐 Time Limit: 2 min. 30 sec.

Optical Fibers

03-06

Optical fibers are thin and transparent fibers made of glass or plastic. They are used to send light signals that can carry information or light. Optical fibers are commonly used in communication systems.

2 ➡ The study of optical fibers and their uses is called fiber optics. Optical fibers transmit light because of a scientific principle called total internal reflection. According to the principle, light continues to bounce through an optical fiber when the outer layer of the fiber is thicker than in the center.

The history of fiber optics began in England during the Victorian Era. At that time, scientists used the total internal reflection principle to light streams of water in public fountains. In the middle of the twentieth century, fiber optics was used by doctors. A tool called the gastroscope was created. It allowed doctors to see into a patient's stomach and intestines. By 1977, telephone companies began to use fiber optic cables. The companies used them to send telephone signals very long distances.

4 ➡ In the past, copper cables were used to send electric signals. But optical fibers have become more popular because they offer several advantages over copper cables. Optical fibers can send signals very long distances with low loss. They are also much lighter than copper. Just seven kilograms of optical fibers can replace twenty tons of copper cable. This is very useful for aircraft. The only disadvantages of optical fibers are found in short distances. In small amounts, optical fibers can be more expensive than copper cables. They are also harder to splice, and they cannot send power along with a signal.

In this age of computers, there is an increased need for bandwidth. Optical fibers can send huge amounts of data over long distances. The science of fiber optics is more useful than ever.

📖 Words & Phrases

transparent (adj) clear and easy to see through
internal (adj) inside
bounce (v) to rebound off of something
intestine (n) the tubes in a human body that process food and carry waste out of the body
splice (v) to connect two cables

1 The word "transmit" in the passage is closest in meaning to

Ⓐ send

Ⓑ control

Ⓒ trap

Ⓓ save

2 The word "them" in the passage refers to

Ⓐ telephone companies

Ⓑ fiber optic cables

Ⓒ telephone signals

Ⓓ very long distances

Mastering the Question Type

3 In paragraph 2, the author's description of total internal reflection mentions which of the following?

Ⓐ The explosion of light

Ⓑ A vacuum of light

Ⓒ The continuous bouncing of light

Ⓓ The absence of light

4 According to paragraph 4, copper cables were used in the past to

Ⓐ make optical fibers

Ⓑ send light through streams of water

Ⓒ see into patients' stomachs

Ⓓ send electric signals

✎ **Summary Note** Fill in the blanks with the appropriate words.

Optical Fibers vs. Copper Cables

Advantages of Optical Fibers
- Send signals ❶ _____ with low loss
- ❷ _____
- Increased bandwidth

Advantages of Copper Cables
- ❸ _____ for short distances
- Easier to splice
- Send electrical power with signals

⏱ Time Limit: 2 min. 30 sec.

The American Revolution

03-07

¹ ➡ The American Revolution ended British rule over its colonies in North America. The result was the formation of the United States after the war ended. The American Revolution began with a shift in ideology. The Americans were unhappy with the British monarchy. Founding Fathers such as Thomas Jefferson and Samuel Adams led the new way of thinking. People from all classes wanted to have a voice in the government. Corruption was seen as the greatest evil. Civic virtue was seen as the greatest good. Family status no longer decided a person's place in society.

The unrest that led to the Revolutionary War can be linked to three events. First, in 1765, the British Parliament passed the Stamp Act. This tax on all paper goods was passed to pay for more British troops in America. The colonists complained because they were already being taxed to pay for troops to put them down. This led to more protests and disobedience. The Stamp Act was repealed.

The second wave began in 1767. Parliament passed the Townshend Acts. These acts taxed goods such as glass, paint, and paper. Colonists organized boycotts of these products. More British troops arrived in Boston, and violence broke out. British soldiers fired their guns into an angry mob and killed five colonists. This was called the Boston Massacre.

⁴ ➡ The third event leading to the revolution took place in 1773. Although the British government repealed the Townshend Acts, it left behind one tax on tea. A group of angry Bostonians boarded a British ship. They dumped all of its tea into the harbor. This event was called the Boston Tea Party.

The British government and the American colonists could not repair their relationship. By 1775, fighting broke out in Lexington. In 1776, the American Declaration of Independence was passed. By 1781, the fighting ended, and the British withdrew from America.

📖 **Words & Phrases**

ideology Ⓝ a way of thinking
corruption Ⓝ dishonesty
unrest Ⓝ dissatisfaction; a protest
repeal Ⓥ to cancel a law
board Ⓥ to get on; to embark
boycott Ⓝ an organized effort by a group of people not to buy something as a means of complaining
massacre Ⓝ a slaughter, often of a large number of people

1 In stating that people from all classes wanted to "have a voice" in the government, the author means that they wanted to

Ⓐ speak out in favor of the government

Ⓑ overturn the government

Ⓒ participate in the government

Ⓓ be united in their opinions about the government

2 The word "them" in the passage refers to

Ⓐ paper goods

Ⓑ the colonists

Ⓒ troops

Ⓓ more protests

3 According to paragraph 1, which of the following is true of the American Revolution?

Ⓐ It helped the British gain more land.

Ⓑ It freed America from British rule.

Ⓒ It was a minor war.

Ⓓ It was triggered by the British government's corruption.

4 According to paragraph 4, why did the American colonists have the Boston Tea Party?

Ⓐ They were angry about a British tax on tea.

Ⓑ They did not want the Townshend Acts.

Ⓒ They wanted to fight the British.

Ⓓ They wanted to go back to Britain.

Summary Note Fill in the blanks with the appropriate words.

Events Leading to the American Revolution

1765
- Stamp Act
- Colonists complained, protested, and disobeyed
- Stamp Act repealed

1767
- Townshend Acts
- Colonists organized boycott
- ❶ _____

1773
- Tax on tea remained
- ❷ _____

1776
- ❸ _____
  published

1775
- Fighting broke out

🕐 Time Limit: 2 min. 50 sec.

American Newspapers in the Nineteenth Century

03-08

¹ ➡ In 1844, the telegraph became widely used. Thanks to it, newspapers could get reports from far away. A wire service called the Associated Press (AP) was started to gather news. With fresh daily news reports, local newspapers began all around the country. But New York City was the center of the newspaper industry.

Newspapers around the nation entered an age of growth. This lasted until the Civil War broke out in 1861. During this time, newspapers improved. Methods of printing and delivery were perfected, and writing and reporting became clearer and fresher. Editors such as Samuel Bowles and Horace Greeley made editorials popular again. At that time, editorials had fallen into disfavor. Most people felt they were just tools for the propaganda of political parties. Through his editorials, Greeley became a leading voice against slavery.

In 1851, Henry J. Raymond began the *New York Times*. This paper greatly improved upon the other newspapers. People thought that Greeley's *New York Tribune* was too political. On the opposite end, James G. Bennett's *New York Herald* was only concerned with looking nice and selling more copies. But the *New York Times* had both journalistic integrity and visual appeal. It reached a new height of excellence. The *New York Times* became the most respected newspaper in the country.

⁴ ➡ By 1895, two men ruled media empires. Both Joseph Pulitzer and William Randolph Hearst owned newspapers in cities around the country. In New York, Pulitzer's *New York World* and Hearst's *New York Journal* battled to win readers. They were both accused of focusing on crime stories and deaths. People felt they were exaggerating headlines. They only wanted to attract the curiosity of readers. This practice was termed "yellow journalism." It was called "yellow" for two reasons. One reason was that both papers published a cartoon about the same popular character named the Yellow Kid. The other reason is that yellow was the color used to describe anything cowardly and dishonest. Many people think this problem still exists in journalism today.

📖 Words & Phrases

editorial ⓝ a written opinion published in a newspaper
disfavor ⓝ dislike; disapproval
propaganda ⓝ material that promotes the views of one group
integrity ⓝ honesty; uprightness

1 The word "they" in the passage refers to

Ⓐ newspapers

Ⓑ methods of printing and delivery

Ⓒ Samuel Bowles and Horace Greeley

Ⓓ editorials

2 The word "integrity" in the passage is closest in meaning to

Ⓐ authority

Ⓑ preciseness

Ⓒ morality

Ⓓ swiftness

Mastering the Question Type

3 According to paragraph 1, newspapers were able to get reports from far away because

Ⓐ they had long-distance reporters

Ⓑ the telegraph was used to send information

Ⓒ New York City started a wire service

Ⓓ lots of local newspapers began throughout the country

4 According to paragraph 4, why was the practice of exaggerating headlines to win readers called "yellow journalism"?

Ⓐ The color yellow described actions thought to be cowardly.

Ⓑ Yellow was the color that stood for both the *New York World* and the *New York Journal*.

Ⓒ People liked a cartoon character called the Yellow Kid.

Ⓓ The newspapers were printed on yellow paper.

✎ **Summary Note** Fill in the blanks with the appropriate words.

American Newspapers in the Nineteenth Century

1844
- Advent of
  ❶ _____
- Wire service called AP started
- New York City
  – the center of the newspaper industry

1851
- ❷ _____
  – journalistic integrity and visual appeal
- *New York Tribune*
  – too political
- *New York Herald*
  – too commercial

1895
- ❸ _____
  – competition between Joseph Pulitzer's *New York World* and William Randolph Hearst's *New York Journal*

Read the following passage and answer the questions.

Time Limit: 2 min. 50 sec.

03-09

The Statue of Liberty and the Liberty Bell

In the United States, two monuments symbolize the ideal of freedom that the country holds dear. The Statue of Liberty and the Liberty Bell represent freedom in different ways. The Statue of Liberty brings about feelings of hope for freedom to immigrants who enter the USA. The Liberty Bell commemorates the struggle for freedom that marks America's past.

2 ➡ In the past, the Statue of Liberty was the first thing people saw when their boats approached America. The statue stands over forty-five meters tall. It was given as a gift to the United States by France in 1885. The date was chosen to mark the centennial of the establishment of the United States.

The sculpture is made of copper. The internal structure was designed by Gustave Eiffel, who also designed the famous tower bearing his name in Paris. The statue is located on Liberty Island in New York Harbor. In her right hand, Lady Liberty holds a torch. It is meant to light the way of freedom across the land. In her left hand, she holds a tablet with the date 1776 inscribed on it. This is to commemorate the year America declared its independence from Great Britain. It is possible to go inside the statue. Many people enjoy climbing the stairs to enter its head and torch.

4 ➡ The Liberty Bell is located in Philadelphia, Pennsylvania, and is most famous for being rung on July 8, 1776. It was rung to summon citizens for the first public reading of the Declaration of Independence. It was also rung in 1774 to announce the opening of the First Continental Congress. Inside the bell is cast an inscription from the Bible's Leviticus 25:10. This passage states, "Proclaim liberty throughout all the land unto all the inhabitants thereof." The Liberty Bell was originally cast in 1752. It got its famous crack in 1753 the first time it was rung.

In 1965, the FBI uncovered a plot by terrorists to destroy the Statue of Liberty and the Liberty Bell. But these attacks on the symbols of freedom were quickly stopped.

📖 Words & Phrases

monument n an object meant to symbolize an important event or concept
immigrant n a person who moves from one country to another
commemorate v to celebrate
struggle n a fight; a conflict
centennial n a 100-year birthday
sculpture n a structure that represents an image of something

1   The word "commemorates" in the passage is closest in meaning to
    Ⓐ celebrates
    Ⓑ commences
    Ⓒ destroys
    Ⓓ claims

2   The word "its" in the passage refers to
    Ⓐ America
    Ⓑ Great Britain
    Ⓒ the statue
    Ⓓ head

Mastering the Question Type

3   According to paragraph 2, France gave the Statue of Liberty to the United States to
    Ⓐ pay off a debt
    Ⓑ improve the friendship between both countries
    Ⓒ make New York Harbor look nicer
    Ⓓ celebrate the hundred-year birthday of the United States

4   According to paragraph 4, when is the Liberty Bell the most famous for being rung?
    Ⓐ On July 4, 1776
    Ⓑ On July 8, 1776
    Ⓒ On December 25, 1776
    Ⓓ On January 1, 1776

🖉 **Summary Note** Fill in the blanks with the appropriate words.

Symbols of American Freedom

❶ ....
- A gift from France
- Stands forty-five meters tall
- Designed by Gustave Eiffel
- Lady Liberty holds the freedom torch and a tablet marked with 1776

❷ ....
- Located in Philadelphia, Pennsylvania
- Famously rung on July 8, 1776
- Inside the bell is cast an inscription from Bible's Leviticus 25:10
- Cracked the first time it was rung in 1753

🕐 Time Limit: 2 min. 50 sec.

Acid Rain

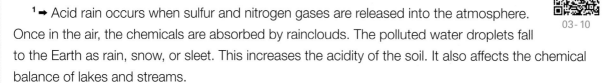

03-10

¹➡ Acid rain occurs when sulfur and nitrogen gases are released into the atmosphere. Once in the air, the chemicals are absorbed by rainclouds. The polluted water droplets fall to the Earth as rain, snow, or sleet. This increases the acidity of the soil. It also affects the chemical balance of lakes and streams.

²➡ The United States Environmental Protection Agency says that acid rain is a serious problem which affects large parts of the United States and Canada. It damages rivers, streams, lakes, and forests. The best way to show the increase in acid rain is to check glacial ice. Scientists can see the drastic increase of acid levels. These changes have been occurring since the Industrial Revolution.

This industrial acid rain is also a large problem in China, Eastern Europe, and Russia. Areas downwind from these places, such as Korea and Japan, suffer the negative effects. Acid rain was first reported in Manchester, England. This was an important city during the British Industrial Revolution. But the acid rain problem was not studied closely until the late 1960s. A Canadian scientist named Harold Harvey was the first to research a "dead" lake. In the 1990s, the *New York Times* published reports about acid rain effects. This brought the problem into public awareness.

Acid rain can be caused by natural occurrences such as the eruption of a volcano. But the main causes of acid rain are from fossil fuel combustion and industry. Factories, motor vehicles, and electricity generation are the leading causes of this problem. Acid rain kills many forms of animal life, such as birds, fish, and insects. It also damages buildings. It is even suspected to have negative health effects on humans. In addition, acid rain damages soil. This makes it difficult for farmers to grow food.

Scientists are searching for ways to reverse the effects of acid rain. There are some international treaties that hope to reduce this global problem. One such treaty is the Convention on Long Range Transboundary Air Pollution, which is intended to protect human environments from air pollution.

📖 **Words & Phrases**

absorb Ⓥ to soak up; to take in
droplet Ⓝ the form in which water collects when in motion
sleet Ⓝ icy rain
glacial adj related to ice or glaciers
awareness Ⓝ alertness; consciousness
eruption Ⓝ an explosion; an ejection

1   The word "drastic" in the passage is closest in meaning to
    Ⓐ slight
    Ⓑ endless
    Ⓒ moderate
    Ⓓ radical

2   The word "This" in the passage refers to
    Ⓐ Korea
    Ⓑ Japan
    Ⓒ Acid rain
    Ⓓ Manchester, England

Mastering the Question Type

3   According to paragraph 1, acid rain occurs
    Ⓐ when the sun is too hot and burns the atmosphere
    Ⓑ when sulfur and nitrogen gases escape into the air
    Ⓒ when airplanes pollute the atmosphere
    Ⓓ when greenhouses release gas into the atmosphere

4   According to paragraph 2, what is the best way to show the increase in acid rain?
    Ⓐ Checking the floor of the ocean
    Ⓑ Checking many small animals
    Ⓒ Checking the ice on glaciers
    Ⓓ Checking with many scientists

Summary Note Fill in the blanks with the appropriate words.

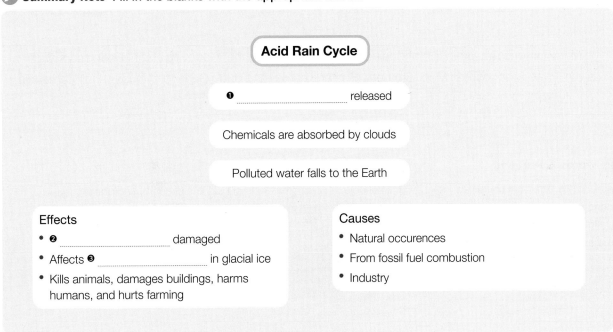

Acid Rain Cycle

❶ _____ released

Chemicals are absorbed by clouds

Polluted water falls to the Earth

Effects
* ❷ _____ damaged
* Affects ❸ _____ in glacial ice
* Kills animals, damages buildings, harms humans, and hurts farming

Causes
* Natural occurences
* From fossil fuel combustion
* Industry

Vaudeville

03-11

Before the age of radio, movies, and television, many people enjoyed variety theater. In America this entertainment theater was called vaudeville. The term *vaudeville* comes from the French *voix de ville*, which means "voice of the city." For just five cents, people could be entertained. Popular acts included music, comics, magic, animal acts, acrobatics, and even lectures.

2 ➡ A routine vaudeville show usually began with a silly act featuring acrobats or trick bicyclists. This allowed audience members to arrive late and to find their seats. The show peaked in the middle with the headliner, the act that was usually the best of the show. The show would conclude with a chaser act, which was considered good enough to feature but dull enough to make the audience members leave the theater.

Between the years 1880 and 1920, vaudeville enjoyed great popularity. The economy was growing in the United States, so people had enough money to spend on entertainment. Many theaters tried very hard to appear polite and family oriented to attract middle-class customers. Performers were not allowed to use bad language. They could not even say the word "hell." But the performers often disobeyed the rules, and this delighted the audiences.

Successful theater owners insisted their theaters appear rich and majestic. The curtains and the seats were covered with the finest red velvet while the beautiful woodwork was gilded with gold trim. They made the theaters look like palaces. Still, they featured silly acts such as juggling dogs. By the 1890s, vaudeville peaked. It became equal to churches and public schools in popularity. It was a great place for people to gather.

5 ➡ There was no exact end to vaudeville. But in 1910, movie theaters opened. They offered entertaining films at lower prices. They steadily shrank vaudeville's audience. Ironically, movies were first shown in vaudeville theaters. By the 1930s, the Great Depression hit the country, and vaudeville disappeared.

Many famous American film and television stars began on the vaudeville stage. Performers such as the Three Stooges, the Marx Brothers, Buster Keaton, and Judy Garland all began their careers in vaudeville.

📖 **Words & Phrases**

acrobatics Ⓝ a form of entertainment in which people perform great feats of balance, strength, and bravery
conclude Ⓥ to finish
delight Ⓥ to please immensely
majestic adj appearing royal; grand

1 The word "peaked" in the passage is closest in meaning to

Ⓐ thrived

Ⓑ climaxed

Ⓒ began

Ⓓ disappeared

2 The word "they" in the passage refers to

Ⓐ successful theater owners

Ⓑ the curtains and the seats

Ⓒ the theaters

Ⓓ palaces

3 According to paragraph 2, why did a vaudeville show usually start with a silly act?

Ⓐ Because the audience needed time to be seated in the theater

Ⓑ Because the audience preferred to begin with silly acts

Ⓒ Because silly acts got the audience ready for serious ones

Ⓓ Because that was the only type of act the theater owner could find

4 According to paragraph 5, what led to the disappearance of vaudeville? *To receive credit, you must select TWO answers.*

Ⓐ The invention of radio and television

Ⓑ The Great Depression

Ⓒ Politicians and religious figures

Ⓓ Movie theaters

🖉 **Summary Note** Fill in the blanks with the appropriate words.

The History of Vaudeville

1880
- Vaudeville begins in U.S.
- Consists of opener, headliner, and
  ❶ _____

1890s
- The most popular entertainment

1910
- Appearance of
  ❷ _____
- Decrease in Vaudeville audiences

1930s
- ❸ _____
- Vaudeville disappears

Building Summary Skills

The following summaries are based on the long passages you worked on earlier. Complete each of them by filling in the blanks with suitable words or phrases.

Exercise 1   Optical Fiber

in England	copper cables	glass or plastic
medical equipment	light and information	

Optical fibers are made of _____ and are very useful for sending _____. The study of fiber optics has shown that light can be bounced continuously down an optical fiber. The concept behind optical fibers was discovered _____ and later adapted for _____. Optical fibers have many advantages over _____. In this age of information, optical fibers are very useful.

Exercise 2   The American Revolution

Thomas Jefferson	the Boston Tea Party	British rule
the United States	the Revolutionary War	

The American Revolution was the war that ended _____ over some of its colonies in North America and established _____ as a country. The revolution began with a shift in ideology that was led by great men such as _____ and Samuel Adams. Three main events led up to _____. These events were the Stamp Act of 1765, the Townshend Acts of 1767, and _____ in 1773. By 1781, the fighting ended, and the British withdrew from the American colonies.

Exercise 3   American Newspapers in the Nineteenth Century

New York Times	Joseph Pulitzer	the newspaper industry
the telegraph	the writing and visual presentation	

In the middle of the 1800s, the wide use of _____ enabled newspapers to get reports from far away. This led to a new age of growth in _____. During this time, everything from _____ to the delivery of newspapers improved. New York was the most competitive place, and the _____ emerged as the most respected newspaper in the country. Meanwhile, two newspaper owners, William Randolph Hearst and _____, battled to win readers, giving rise to the unethical practice of yellow journalism.

Exercise 4 — The Statue of Liberty and the Liberty Bell

Philadelphia, Pennsylvania	America's ideal of freedom	Gustave Eiffel
the Declaration of Independence	the 100-year birthday	

Two monuments are the best symbols of _____: the Statue of Liberty and the Liberty Bell. The Statue of Liberty was given to the United States by France as a gift in 1885 to mark _____ of the United States. It was designed by _____ and stands about forty-five meters tall in New York Harbor. The Liberty Bell is located in _____, and was most famously rung on July 8, 1776, to announce the first public reading of _____. It has a crack which was made when it was rung for the first time.

Exercise 5 — Acid Rain

sulfur and nitrogen gases	the health of humans	acid rain
industrialized countries	poisoning bodies of water	

_____ is a pollution problem caused by the release of _____ into the air. This problem has been observed in many _____. Acid rain causes many problems such as _____, killing animals, damaging soil, and harming _____. Scientists are searching for ways to reduce this problem.

Exercise 6 — Vaudeville

a variety of acts	the Great Depression	inexpensive live entertainment
a headliner	the late 1800s and the early 1900s	

Vaudeville was a form of _____ that was very popular in the United States in _____. Vaudeville entertained the audience with _____, including trained animals, acrobats, magic, comedy, musical performances, and lecturers. A typical vaudeville show began with an opener, peaked with _____, and closed with a chaser. At the height of its popularity, vaudeville theaters were among the most popular places for people to gather. By the early 1900s, movie theaters and _____ caused vaudeville to disappear.

President Andrew Jackson

03-12

1 ➡ Andrew Jackson was the seventh president of the United States and the first governor of Florida. Jackson was known to be a very tough soldier, so his nickname was "Old Hickory" after the hard wood.

2 ➡ At age thirteen, Jackson joined the army to fight against the British in the Revolutionary War. He and his brother were captured. He was cut in the face and the hand by a British soldier because he refused to clean the soldier's boots, leading him always to despise the British. After being released, Jackson's brother died, and then Jackson returned home and found his mother and the rest of his family dead.

3 ➡ In the Battle of New Orleans in 1815, Jackson led 6,000 soldiers against 12,000 British soldiers yet still emerged victorious. The British army lost 2,000 soldiers while only eight of Jackson's men died. In 1817, Jackson led his men against the Spanish and the Seminole Indians in Florida, and he crushed the Seminoles. Then, he forced the Spanish to cede power in Florida to the United States, whereupon he was made the first American governor of Florida.

4 ➡ Andrew Jackson ran for president in the election of 1824. Many people, like Thomas Jefferson, thought he was too lawless to be president. Jackson lost the election to John Quincy Adams. By the election of 1828, Jackson was able to come back. He defeated Adams and became president. The most controversial part of Jackson's presidency was his treatment of American Indians. In 1830, his Indian Removal Act became a law. At that time, 45,000 Cherokee Indians were forced to give up their land and move west. Thousands died on a march called "the trail of tears." One historian called this period "one of the unhappiest chapters in American history." On January 30, 1835, Richard Lawrence tried to assassinate President Jackson. The mentally ill man approached Jackson and fired two pistols at him. The bullets missed Jackson, and the president then attacked Lawrence with his cane.

Andrew Jackson married his wife Rachel after she divorced her first husband. Afterward, many people attacked her honor, so Jackson fought 103 duels to defend his wife's honor. Despite fighting so many duels, Jackson only killed one man, named Charles Dickenson. He insulted Jackson's wife, so they had a duel. Dickenson shot first, and his bullet hit Andrew Jackson in his ribs. Then, Jackson shot and killed Dickenson. Jackson had many wounds from his numerous duels, and they hurt him for the rest of his life. He often coughed up blood. He died of tuberculosis and heart failure at the age of seventy-eight.

1 According to paragraph 1, the meaning of Andrew Jackson's nickname was

(A) sharp steel

(B) hard wood

(C) strong wind

(D) tough leather

2 According to paragraph 2, which of the following is NOT true of Andrew Jackson?

(A) He joined the army in his late teens.

(B) He and his brother were captured by the British.

(C) He was wounded by a British soldier.

(D) He returned home to find his family was all dead.

3 Which of the following can be inferred from paragraph 3 about Andrew Jackson?

(A) He liked to swim in Florida.

(B) He did not like Seminole culture.

(C) He was a strong military leader.

(D) He wanted to be president of the United States.

4 The word "assassinate" in the passage is closest in meaning to

(A) help

(B) kill

(C) elect

(D) hurt

5 In paragraph 4, the author discusses Andrew Jackson's treatment of the Native Americans in order to

Ⓐ show the negative side of Andrew Jackson's presidency

Ⓑ show that Andrew Jackson was a ruthless leader

Ⓒ show that Andrew Jackson helped his country

Ⓓ show how patriotic Andrew Jackson was

6 The word "they" in the passage refers to

Ⓐ his ribs

Ⓑ many wounds

Ⓒ his numerous duels

Ⓓ tuberculosis and heart failure

Aristotle and the Development of Science in Ancient Greece

03-13

1 ➡ Western science comes from ancient Greece, and Aristotle was a great thinker from this era. Although he was not the first scientist or philosopher, he was the most influential. He was a student of Plato and the teacher of Alexander the Great.

2 ➡ From the ages of eighteen to thirty-seven, Aristotle was a student. He attended Plato's school, called the Academy. Then, he traveled for a few years and studied biology on various islands. Later, King Philip of Macedon called for Aristotle because he wanted Aristotle to teach his son Alexander, who was then thirteen. Years later, Alexander left Aristotle and went on to conquer parts of Asia. Aristotle returned to Athens and opened an academy called the Lyceum, where he trained scientists.

3 ➡ Aristotle wrote books on many subjects. His works covered every topic. He was aware of everything from science to art. None of his books has survived in their entirety; however, Aristotle's studies became the foundation of Western philosophy and science. Aristotle valued knowledge gained from the five senses. He used his senses and dialectic to seek truth. Dialectic originated with Plato, but Aristotle refined it. Aristotle's dialectic relied on logic. It was a way of answering a question with another question. The answers could then be used to find truth. These methods are called inductive and deductive logic.

4 ➡ Based on Aristotle's logic, the scientific method was formed. The scientific method is a process used by scientists. First, they make a hypothesis, and then, they test it with an experiment. The scientific method is the most important method in modern Western science. Aristotle did not do many experiments himself, but his system of logic led others to discover many things. Sir Isaac Newton and Galileo used the scientific method. Their discoveries are an example of Aristotle's influence. Aristotle also created the idea of categories. He studied every branch of science possible and then separated them into different groups. He was familiar with every subject from zoology to geology. His written works make up a huge body of Greek knowledge.

Aristotle has many critics as well. Some scholars think he did not have respect for women while others believe his work is too confusing. He often seems not to obey his own logical rules. And in the Middle Ages, his work, which was treated as infallible, was used to oppress people. But Aristotle's work has been referenced for thousands of years. His studies are one of the pillars that hold up modern society.

7   According to paragraphs 1 and 2, which of the following is NOT true of Aristotle?

    Ⓐ He became the leader of ancient Greece.

    Ⓑ He was a student of Plato.

    Ⓒ He spent time on islands studying biology.

    Ⓓ He opened an academy called the Lyceum.

8   According to paragraph 2, Aristotle was hired by King Philip of Macedon to

    Ⓐ teach at the Academy with Plato

    Ⓑ write books focusing on biology

    Ⓒ set up a school for teaching scientists

    Ⓓ provide instruction for Philip's son

9   The word "It" in the passage refers to

    Ⓐ Knowledge

    Ⓑ Truth

    Ⓒ Aristotle's dialectic

    Ⓓ Logic

10   Which of the following can be inferred from paragraph 3 about Aristotle?

    Ⓐ He did not like to think about science.

    Ⓑ He was very interested in drama.

    Ⓒ He was primarily a poet.

    Ⓓ He was of very high intelligence.

11 According to paragraph 4, why does the author mention "Aristotle's logic"?

    Ⓐ To show how smart he was

    Ⓑ To prove that he was the greatest thinker of all time

    Ⓒ To show his influence on the formation of the scientific method

    Ⓓ To prove that Plato was a greater thinker than Aristotle

12 The word "infallible" in the passage is closest in meaning to

    Ⓐ correct

    Ⓑ valuable

    Ⓒ logical

    Ⓓ doubtful

Vocabulary Check-Up

A Choose the words with the closest meanings to the highlighted words.

1 The computer was experiencing an internal problem.

- (A) international
- (B) inner
- (C) outside
- (D) lasting forever

2 His job was to splice electrical wires inside houses.

- (A) destroy
- (B) remove
- (C) connect
- (D) buy

3 The group had an ideology that many other people found offensive.

- (A) vehicle
- (B) smell
- (C) haircut
- (D) way of thinking

4 The citizens protested until the unfair law was repealed.

- (A) canceled
- (B) noticed
- (C) joined
- (D) doubled

5 The actress fell into disfavor when she changed her style.

- (A) fame
- (B) unpopularity
- (C) wealth
- (D) debt

6 The park was unveiled to commemorate the veterans of World War I.

- (A) remember
- (B) scold
- (C) thank
- (D) show

7 The worker's struggle to receive fair pay was finally successful.

- (A) long question
- (B) long time
- (C) long fight
- (D) long speech

8 Their new house looks very majestic with its huge columns and beautiful entryway.

- (A) splendid
- (B) enormous
- (C) expensive
- (D) attractive

B Match the words with the correct definitions.

1 propaganda •

2 unrest •

3 corruption •

4 integrity •

5 glacial •

6 massacre •

7 eruption •

8 monument •

9 intestine •

10 droplet •

• Ⓐ the quality of coming from a large ice mass

• Ⓑ an internal explosion that causes outward movement

• Ⓒ the tubes in a human body that process food and carry waste out of the body

• Ⓓ an event in which three or more innocent people are killed

• Ⓔ material that promotes the views of one group

• Ⓕ the form in which water collects when in motion

• Ⓖ an object meant to symbolize an important event or concept

• Ⓗ dishonesty in a publicly held office

• Ⓘ dissatisfaction; protest

• Ⓙ the quality of being honest and upright

Overview

Introduction

Negative Factual Information questions ask you to find wrong information that is not mentioned in the passage. You should decide which of the answer choices is not discussed in the passage or does not agree with one or more statements in the passage. Like Factual Information questions, scanning is the key skill for this question type. However, you need to scan more of the passage to make sure that your answer is correct.

Question Types

▶ The author's description of X mentions all of the following EXCEPT:

▶ Which of the following is NOT mentioned in the passage?

▶ All of the following questions are answered EXCEPT:

Useful Tips

■ Make use of the key words in the question and the answer choices to spot relevant information in the passage.

■ Do not forget that the necessary information may be spread out over one or two paragraphs.

■ Make sure that your answer is NOT mentioned in the passage and does not contradict the passage.

Q According to paragraphs 2 and 3, which of the following is NOT true of ladybugs?

(A) They are helpful for gardening.

(B) They are hunted by aphids and fruit flies.

(C) They are insectivores.

(D) They can be purchased at garden supply shops.

Ladybugs

04-01

Many people do not like insects and may scream or attempt to squash bugs upon seeing them. One exception is the ladybug as people frequently regard this colorful little beetle as a friend.

2 ➡ The ladybug is an especially useful friend to gardeners. Many garden supply shops sell these beetles, which gardeners buy and put in their gardens. The reason is that ladybugs consume harmful insects.

3 ➡ Once in a garden, ladybugs hunt and devour all sorts of pests. Aphids and fruit flies become meals for these insectivores. These pests would otherwise threaten the plants in the garden. Some gardeners even install special rows of grass called beetle-bunkers to give ladybugs places to thrive.

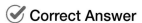 **Correct Answer**

Check and make sure which choice is not true according to the passage. Ladybugs hunt aphids and fruit flies. They are not hunted by those insects. So the correct answer is (B).

Read the questions and the answer choices first. Then, scan for the information you need to answer the questions. Try to eliminate obviously wrong answer choices.

Skill & Tip

Scanning is the key skill to deal with Negative Factual Information questions. But unlike Factual Information questions, you should scan more of the passage because relevant information may be spread out over more than one part of the passage. You need to decide which of the answer choices is not true or not mentioned in the passage.

Drill 1

04-02

Caterpillars

A caterpillar is the larval form of a butterfly or moth. It has a long, segmented body which is soft. This allows it to grow quickly, like a balloon, as it consumes great amounts of food. Caterpillars are eating machines as they prepare to enter the pupa stage.

Like all insects, caterpillars do not breathe through their mouths but instead pull in air through tubes along the sides of their bodies. Their eyesight is very poor, so they use antennae to locate food. Caterpillars have various defenses to protect themselves from birds and other animals. Their bodies are capable of utilizing camouflage, so some caterpillars resemble snakes or leaves. Some caterpillars also eat poison leaves and become toxic.

Q Which of the following is NOT true of the caterpillar?

    (A) It locates food with feelers and eats a lot.   (B) It protects itself in various ways.

    (C) It is the larval form of all insects.   (D) It breathes through the sides of its body.

Drill 2

04-03

The Refrigerator

One invention that changed the daily lives of humans is the refrigerator. Prior to its invention, people had to spend very much time gathering fresh food every day. The only way to keep food cold was to have a large block of ice delivered to the home, which was costly and inconvenient.

The first home refrigerators came onto the market in 1911. At that time, a refrigerator cost almost twice as much as a new car. Early models took up so much space in homes that sometimes two rooms were needed. By 1927, General Electric introduced the Monitor-Top refrigerator. This was the first model to be widely used and is still functional today.

Q The author's description of the refrigerator mentions all of the following EXCEPT:

    (A) The prices of the first refrigerators   (B) The convenience of refrigerators

    (C) The sizes of early refrigerators   (D) The popularization of refrigerators

Kinds of Wind

04-04

Wind is the movement of air over the Earth's surface and is caused by the uneven heating of the atmosphere. The two major influences on wind are the heating between the equator and the poles and the Earth's rotation.

One way to classify different kinds of wind is by the forces that cause it. Prevailing winds, such as the trade winds, the westerlies, and the jet streams, are caused by global circulation. Synoptic winds are caused by warm and cold fronts clashing while mesoscale winds are produced by thunderstorms. Microscale winds are very short bursts that happen suddenly. Winds are some of the most common yet powerful forces shaping people's lives and the planet every day.

Q Which of the following is NOT true of wind?

Ⓐ The clash of cold fronts causes synoptic winds.

Ⓑ Very short, sudden bursts of wind are called microscale winds.

Ⓒ The trade winds are caused by global rotation.

Ⓓ Thunderstorms produce mesoscale winds.

Hummingbirds

04-05

Hummingbirds are known for their ability to hover in mid-air by rapidly flapping their wings, which they can do fifteen to eighty times per second. This action enables it to maintain its position while drinking from flower blossoms. The hummingbird received its name from the humming sound made by its wings flapping.

The bee hummingbird, weighing 1.8 grams, is the smallest bird in the world while the rufous hummingbird is more typical, weighing three grams. The giant hummingbird weighs as much as twenty-four grams. Hummingbirds have the highest metabolism of any animal other than insects. Their hearts can beat as many as 1,260 times per minute. To sustain this rapid rate, they must consume more than their own body weight in food each day.

Q All of the following questions are answered EXCEPT:

Ⓐ How often can a hummingbird's heart beat each minute?

Ⓑ How does the metabolism of the hummingbird relate to that of insects?

Ⓒ What kinds of foods do hummingbirds usually eat?

Ⓓ What is the smallest bird in the world?

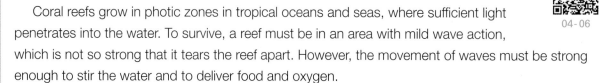

Exercises with Mid-Length Passages

Exercise 1 **Read the following passage and answer the questions.**

⏱ Time Limit: 2 min. 50 sec.

Coral Reefs

04-06

Coral reefs grow in photic zones in tropical oceans and seas, where sufficient light penetrates into the water. To survive, a reef must be in an area with mild wave action, which is not so strong that it tears the reef apart. However, the movement of waves must be strong enough to stir the water and to deliver food and oxygen.

2 ➡ Coral reefs are made of millions of skeletons from small animals called polyps. After polyps die, waves and fish break down their skeletons. Then, the fragments settle into the reef, causing it to grow. Algae feed on the skeletons and convert the material to limestone, which is deposited over the reef and subsequently forms a protective crust. These algae grow best in clear, shallow water.

Most of the world's reefs are located in the tropical waters of the Pacific and Indian oceans. There are few reefs on the western coasts of North and South America and Africa. This is due to the strong, cold coastal currents in these areas. Coral reefs support a vast array of biodiversity. They create habitats for many species of fish and plant life to thrive. Without reefs, many of these species would face extinction.

Currently, there are several threats to the world's reefs. Some pollutants that run off from factories and farms kill coral reef life. The water quality in these areas often becomes poisonous, killing coral reefs and the creatures that live in and around them.

5 ➡ Another threat to coral reefs is overfishing and destructive fishing by humans. Many fishermen who trap exotic fish for pet shops use cyanide gas to stun fish. This process decreases the lifespan of the captured fish and poisons reefs. Dynamite fishing is another method that damages reef ecosystems. It kills coral, which is the habitat for a healthy reef. Many conservation groups are actively trying to protect coral reefs around the world.

📖 **Words & Phrases**

photic adj penetrated by light, especially that of the sun
stir v to mix; to shake
fragment n a small piece
shallow adj not deep
current n a force of waves that do not break the surface of a body of water
habitat n a place where one or more species of living organisms thrives

1 The word "convert" in the passage is closest in meaning to

Ⓐ destroy

Ⓑ change

Ⓒ condense

Ⓓ eliminate

2 The word "them" in the passage refers to

Ⓐ factories and farms

Ⓑ these areas

Ⓒ coral reefs

Ⓓ the creatures

3 In paragraph 2, the author's description of coral reefs mentions all of the following EXCEPT:

Ⓐ Where algae grow best

Ⓑ The role of algae in forming them

Ⓒ How they are formed

Ⓓ What polyps look like

4 According to paragraph 5, which of the following is NOT true of coral reefs?

Ⓐ Many fishermen catch exotic fish for profit by using helium gas.

Ⓑ Coral reefs can be damaged by overfishing.

Ⓒ A lot of conservation groups work hard to protect coral reefs.

Ⓓ The process of cyanide fishing poisons coral reefs.

Summary Note Fill in the blanks with the appropriate words.

(**Coral Reefs**)

Conditions for growth

- ❶ _____ in the tropical Pacific and Indian oceans
- ❷ _____ to deliver food and oxygen
- Algae to build coral reefs

❸ _____

- Pollution from factories and farming
- Overfishing and destructive fishing with dynamite or cyanide gas

Read the following passage and answer the questions.

Mass Production and the Ford Model-T

04-07

The manufacturing of large amounts of items on an assembly line is called mass production. The advent of the production line changed the way people worked and lived in the twentieth century. This method became popular when Henry Ford's Ford Motor Company began manufacturing the Model-T car in 1908.

2 ➡ Henry Ford was the inventor of the car and the president of the company. He was always searching for more efficient methods of production. In 1913, he introduced moving assembly lines to his production plants. By 1914, the Ford assembly line was so efficient that it only took ninety-three minutes to produce one Model-T. They came off the assembly line every three minutes. Ford produced more cars than all of its competitors combined.

In addition, Ford's assembly line introduced a new level of worker safety. This method of having workers stay in assigned positions led to fewer accidents. Ford also shocked the nation with an unprecedented pay scale of five dollars a day. This effort on the part of Ford to attract talented workers more than doubled the minimum wage.

In 1908, the price of a Model-T was 825 dollars, and it fell every year afterward. By 1916, the price of the Model-T had dropped to 360 dollars. There were more Model-T's than any other car on the road. The only color available in this model was black. The reason was that black paint was cheaper and dried faster, so it kept production costs down. Henry Ford was once heard to have joked, "Any customer can have a car painted any color he wants so long as it is black."

5 ➡ By the 1920s, 15 million Model-T's had been produced. This was a record that was not broken for thirty years. Many people learned to drive in a Model-T and had very fond memories of the car. The Model-T revolution changed the way people around the world worked and traveled. Today, assembly lines employ people in every industrial nation. People also use cars in their everyday lives.

📖 Words & Phrases

assembly Ⓝ the act of putting something together
manufacture Ⓥ to make; to produce
efficient 〔adj〕 productive; competent
competitor Ⓝ a rival
unprecedented 〔adj〕 not having happened before; unusual
have fond memories of 〔phr〕 to remember something with affection and pleasure

1 The word "advent" in the passage is closest in meaning to

Ⓐ improvement

Ⓑ increase

Ⓒ appearance

Ⓓ efficiency

2 The word "it" in passage refers to

Ⓐ any customer

Ⓑ a car

Ⓒ any color

Ⓓ black

3 According to paragraph 2, which of the following is NOT true of Henry Ford?

Ⓐ He taught workers to build a Model-T in only three minutes.

Ⓑ He was the president of the Ford Motor Company.

Ⓒ He tried to find new and better ways to produce cars cheaply.

Ⓓ He brought automated assembly lines into the Ford production plants in 1913.

4 In paragraph 5, the author's description of the Model-T revolution mentions all of the following EXCEPT:

Ⓐ The difficulty of manufacturing the Model-T

Ⓑ The changes the Model-T produced in society

Ⓒ The importance of the Model-T to many people

Ⓓ The number of Model-T's produced in a single year

✎ Summary Note Fill in the blanks with the appropriate words.

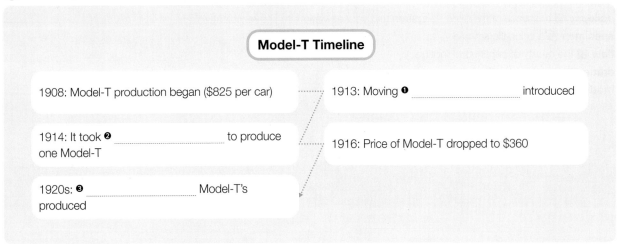

Model-T Timeline

1908: Model-T production began ($825 per car) ⟶ 1913: Moving ❶ _____ introduced

1914: It took ❷ _____ to produce one Model-T

1916: Price of Model-T dropped to $360

1920s: ❸ _____ Model-T's produced

⏱ Time Limit: 2 min. 30 sec.

Pioneers in Neurology

04-08

[1]➡ The history of neurology dates back to ancient Egypt. Scrolls depict disorders of the brain. The Egyptians had a basic understanding of the nervous system and even performed simple brain surgery. In ancient Greece, the famous physician Hippocrates was convinced epilepsy had a physical cause. Before him, it was considered a punishment by the gods. Another Greek physician, Galen, looked at the nervous system in specimens. He cut a certain nerve in the brain of an ape. Then, he noticed the ape lost its voice.

In 1664, Thomas Willis published *Anatomy of the Brain*. In it he described the circle of Willis, which enables the flow of blood through the brain. He was also the first to use the word *neurology*. In the 1700s, Bailie and Cruveilhier published the first illustrations of the brain, which helped doctors and scientists. They began to understand diseases such as brain damage in strokes.

[3]➡ In 1837, J.E. Purkinje was the first to look at neurons when he saw them through a microscope. This led to an understanding that progressed past crude drawings. The famous philosopher Rene Descartes thought about the brain. He had a theory about behavior. He believed every activity of an animal was a necessary reaction to an external stimulus. Some doctors conducted experiments on patients. They were able to understand more about the nervous system. A new understanding of neurological behavior was reached by Ivan Pavlov, a Russian physiologist. He trained his dogs to salivate at the ring of a bell. This established that a simple reflex could be modified by higher brain functions.

By 1878, William McEwen removed a brain tumor from a patient. The patient lived for many years afterward. When he performed his surgeries, he used tools such as the tendon hammer. X-rays and the CT scan were not far behind. These developments led to the field of neurology that helps people today.

📖 **Words & Phrases**

depict Ⓥ to describe; to show
epilepsy Ⓝ a disease of the nervous system that causes victims to shake violently
specimen Ⓝ a scientific sample
flow Ⓝ the quality of continuous motion
crude adj simple; not advanced
modify Ⓥ to change

1 The word "crude" in the passage is closest in meaning to

Ⓐ detailed

Ⓑ rough

Ⓒ natural

Ⓓ original

2 The word "They" in the passage refers to

Ⓐ Crude drawings

Ⓑ Some doctors

Ⓒ Experiments

Ⓓ Patients

3 In paragraph 1, the author's description of the ancient Egyptians mentions all of the following EXCEPT:

Ⓐ How they studied and learned about the brain

Ⓑ Their level of knowledge of the nervous system

Ⓒ Where they wrote information about the brain

Ⓓ A type of surgery they conducted

4 In paragraph 3, all of the following questions are answered EXCEPT:

Ⓐ Who conducted experiments with dogs?

Ⓑ How did J.E. Purkinje contribute to science?

Ⓒ What did Rene Descartes believe?

Ⓓ What kinds of experiments did scientists conduct on patients?

✎ Summary Note Fill in the blanks with the appropriate words.

Development of Neurology Timeline

Ancient Egypt: scrolls depicted brain disorders; simple brain surgery performed

❶ _____ : epilepsy has physical cause; physician experimented on ape's brain

1664: Thomas Willis published
❷ _____

1700s: Bailie and Cruveilhier published first illustrations of the brain

1837: J. E. Purkinje examined neurons through a microscope

1878: William McEwen removed
❸ _____ from a patient

After 1878: the tendon hammer, X-rays, and the CT scan developed

🕐 Time Limit: 2 min. 40 sec.

The Effects of Desert Weather

1 ➡ A desert is a type of landscape that receives little precipitation. Deserts are normally defined as areas that receive annual precipitation of fewer than 250 millimeters. Nevertheless, some places such as Tucson, Arizona, receive more but are still called deserts because they have a high rate of evaporation.

2 ➡ Many environmentalists argue that desert regions are increasing through a process called desertification. This happens when useful soil is blown away by the wind. Then, the temperature rises, and a region that was once fertile becomes desert. This can be due to global warming as well as overdevelopment, both of which are major threats to humanity.

True deserts have very sparse vegetation. These deserts exist in the most arid regions of the Earth. In these places, rainfall is rare and infrequent. Deserts have a reputation for supporting little life, yet this is not true. Deserts have many animals that hide during daylight. Approximately one-fifth of the Earth's land surface is covered by deserts.

4 ➡ Desert landscapes are often composed of sand and rocky surfaces. Sand dunes and stony surfaces called regs are often found in deserts. Cold deserts have similar features but receive snow instead of rain. Antarctica is the largest cold desert while the largest hot desert is the Sahara. Most deserts have an extreme temperature range. The temperature can be very low at night because the air is so dry that it holds little heat. The desert cools as soon as the sun sets. Cloudless skies also increase the release of heat at night.

Sand covers only about twenty percent of the Earth's deserts. There are six forms of deserts. One of the forms is a mountain or a basin desert. Hamada deserts are comprised of plateau landforms, regs consist of rock pavements, and ergs are formed by sand seas. Intermontane basins occur at high elevations while badlands are arid regions comprised of clay-rich soil.

📙 Words & Phrases

precipitation (n) rain, snow, sleet, or hail
evaporation (n) the process by which water is turned into gas by heat
fertile (adj) productive; fecund; rich
reputation (n) fame; renown
arid (adj) very dry; lacking moisture

1 The word "precipitation" in the passage is closest in meaning to

Ⓐ heat

Ⓑ desertification

Ⓒ moisture

Ⓓ sand

2 The word "it" in the passage refers to

Ⓐ the temperature

Ⓑ night

Ⓒ the air

Ⓓ little heat

3 According to paragraphs 1 and 2, which of the following is NOT true of deserts?

Ⓐ Their numbers are increasing nowadays.

Ⓑ Their evaporation rates are low.

Ⓒ They get small amounts of rain or snow.

Ⓓ They may be created by overdevelopment.

4 In paragraph 4, the author's description of deserts mentions all of the following EXCEPT:

Ⓐ The reason deserts have extreme temperature ranges

Ⓑ The name of the world's largest cold desert

Ⓒ The location of the Sahara Desert

Ⓓ The composition of many desert landscapes

✎ **Summary Note** Fill in the blanks with the appropriate words.

Little precipitation (fewer than ❶ _____)

Increasing through ❷ _____

Deserts

Have sparse vegetation, but many animals

Composed of sand and ❸ _____

6 forms of deserts

Read the following passage and answer the questions.

🕐 Time Limit: 2 min. 30 sec.

The Migration of the Monarch Butterfly

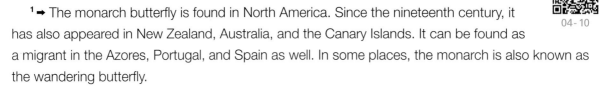
04-10

1 ➡ The monarch butterfly is found in North America. Since the nineteenth century, it has also appeared in New Zealand, Australia, and the Canary Islands. It can be found as a migrant in the Azores, Portugal, and Spain as well. In some places, the monarch is also known as the wandering butterfly.

2 ➡ Monarchs are known for flying long distances annually. They fly southward in large numbers from August through October. Then, in spring, they migrate northward. During their migrations, females deposit eggs for the next generation. North American monarchs are separated into two populations. One group lives east of the Rocky Mountains and spends its winters in Michoacan, Mexico. The group that lives in the west spends winter in central California, mainly in Pacific Grove and Santa Cruz.

The length of the monarch's migration is longer than a single butterfly's lifespan. Butterflies born in early summer live fewer than two months. The final generation of the summer lives about seven months. During this time, the butterflies fly to their winter home. This generation does not reproduce until it leaves the winter location in the spring.

Scientists still do not understand how the species can return to the same winter location over a gap in generations. This is the subject of much research. It is assumed that knowledge of the flight patterns is inherited. Studies suggest that they are based on a combination of circadian rhythm and the position of the sun in the sky. A new study suggests that monarchs have special ultraviolet photoreceptors that give them a sense of direction.

5 ➡ A few monarchs appear in Great Britain in years with favorable conditions. Some also live on the island of Hawaii. These butterflies do not migrate. They live for six to eight weeks if the gardens they dwell in have enough nectar-producing flowers to support them.

📖 **Words & Phrases**

generation ⓝ a group of the same species born around the same time
reproduce ⓥ to have babies
inherit ⓥ to receive certain traits from one's parents
circadian rhythm ⓝ biological behavior based on day and night cycles
nectar ⓝ the sweet, nutritious fluid within the blossom of a flower

1 The word "migrate" in the passage is closest in meaning to

    Ⓐ travel seasonally

    Ⓑ escape from danger

    Ⓒ search for food

    Ⓓ prepare for winter

2 The word "they" in the passage refers to

    Ⓐ the species

    Ⓑ generations

    Ⓒ the flight patterns

    Ⓓ studies

3 The author's description of the monarch butterfly in paragraphs 1 and 2 mentions all of the following EXCEPT:

    Ⓐ The places where it lives

    Ⓑ Its migration route

    Ⓒ Its nickname

    Ⓓ The time and direction of its migration

4 According to paragraph 5, which of the following is NOT true of monarch butterflies?

    Ⓐ Hawaiian butterflies do not migrate.

    Ⓑ Some appear in Great Britain every year.

    Ⓒ Ones in Hawaii can live around two months.

    Ⓓ They need to consume nectar to survive.

✎ **Summary Note** Fill in the blanks with the appropriate words.

Facts about Monarch Butterflies

- ❶ _____ every year
- Fly southward from August to October and northward in spring
- ❷ _____
    - one group living east of the Rocky Mountains winters in Michoacan, Mexico.
    - western group winters in central California.
- Scientists don't fully understand their migration patterns.
- Some monarchs live in ❸ _____ and don't migrate.

Exercise 6 Read the following passage and answer the questions.

🕐 Time Limit: 2 min. 30 sec.

The Development of the Typewriter

04-11

No single person invented the typewriter, but a number of people contributed to its creation. In 1714, Henry Mill received a patent for a machine similar to the typewriter. However, nothing else is known about it. Another early innovator was a man named Turri. His machine allowed the blind to write. He also invented carbon paper.

2 ➡ In 1829, William Austin Burt patented a machine called the typographer, which some consider the first typewriter. This machine was slower than writing by hand though. In 1865, Reverend Hansen created the writing ball, which was the first typewriter to go into production. Nevertheless, it was still too slow. The first machine to type faster than a human hand could write was built by Sholes and Glidden in 1867. They sold the patent to Remington. He began producing this machine in 1873.

One problem with the early typewriters was visibility. The position of the typebar blocked the page. So a typist could not see what had just been typed. In 1895, this problem was solved as "visible" typewriters started being produced. Still, older models stayed on the market as late as 1915.

4 ➡ IBM began producing the electric Selectric typewriter in the twentieth century. It featured a spherical type ball. It immediately dominated the market. The type ball was an important improvement. It eliminated jams when two keys were struck at once. Many of these machines are still used today. In the 1980s came the final major development. The type ball was replaced by the daisy wheel. The daisy wheel is simpler and cheaper than the type ball, but it wears out more quickly.

5 ➡ Today, typewriters are still sometimes used. They are useful when a computer is impractical or inconvenient. Companies such as Smith Corona, Olivetti, and Brother still make them. Generally, however, typewriters have been replaced by computers.

📖 Words & Phrases

invent v to discover or create something for the first time
carbon n an element present in all living things
visible adj able to be seen by the naked eye
dominate v to control with power
replace v to take the place of something; to substitute

1 The word "innovator" in the passage is closest in meaning to

    Ⓐ inventor   Ⓑ owner

    Ⓒ philosopher   Ⓓ typist

2 The word "It" in the passage refers to

    Ⓐ IBM

    Ⓑ The electric Selectric typewriter

    Ⓒ The twentieth century

    Ⓓ A spherical type ball

3 In paragraph 2, all of the following questions are answered EXCEPT:

    Ⓐ How much did Remington pay for Sholes and Glidden's patent?

    Ⓑ Who is said to have invented the first typewriter?

    Ⓒ What was a problem with Hansen's typewriter?

    Ⓓ What is the importance of the typographer?

4 According to paragraphs 4 and 5, which of the following is NOT true of typewriters?

    Ⓐ There are some Selectric typewriters that people still use in the present.

    Ⓑ The IBM Selectric typewriter solved the jamming problem of older models.

    Ⓒ The daisy wheel replaced the type ball since it cost less and was more durable.

    Ⓓ Some companies still produce typewriters because they are still in use.

✏ Summary Note Fill in the blanks with the appropriate words.

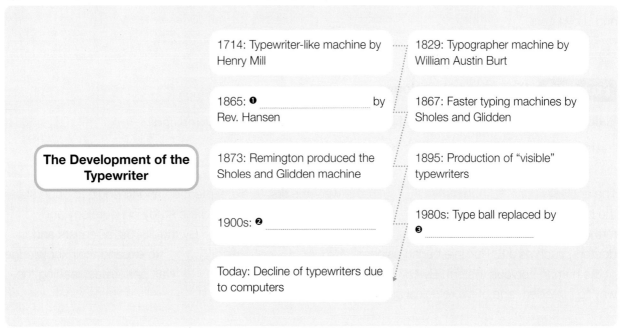

The Development of the Typewriter

1714: Typewriter-like machine by Henry Mill

1829: Typographer machine by William Austin Burt

1865: ❶ _____ by Rev. Hansen

1867: Faster typing machines by Sholes and Glidden

1873: Remington produced the Sholes and Glidden machine

1895: Production of "visible" typewriters

1900s: ❷ _____

1980s: Type ball replaced by ❸ _____

Today: Decline of typewriters due to computers

Building Summary Skills

The following summaries are based on the long passages you worked on earlier. Complete each of them by filling in the blanks with suitable words or phrases.

Exercise 1 Coral Reefs

become extinct	destructive fishing	tiny polyps
mild wave action	the tropical Indian and Pacific oceans	

Coral reefs grow best in photic tropical zones with _____. Reefs are made of the skeletons of millions of _____ that have been turned into limestone by algae. Reefs are the most common in _____. Reefs are important because they support a wide range of species that would otherwise _____. There are many threats to reefs, such as pollution, overfishing, and _____ that conservation groups are fighting against.

Exercise 2 Mass Production and the Ford Model-T

by the 1920s	moving assembly lines	the Model-T car
became lower	Henry Ford	

_____ changed the way people worked and lived in the twentieth century with his Ford Model-T and the assembly line it was produced on. After beginning the Ford Motor Company and inventing _____, Ford introduced _____ in his production plants. These were so effective that the Model-T became common around the world, and the price _____ every year. _____, there were more Model-T's on the road than any other car, and people around the world worked on assembly lines and drove cars.

Exercise 3 Pioneers in Neurology

describing its anatomy	Egyptians and Greeks	microscopes
Thomas Willis	successful brain surgery	

The ancient _____ were the first to experiment on and to begin to understand the brain. Scientists such as _____ created the study of neurology and furthered knowledge of the brain by _____. By the 1800s, scientists and doctors, such as J.E. Purkinje began using _____ to expand their knowledge of the human nervous system. By 1878, _____ was performed, leading the way to a modern age of neurological understanding and treatment.

Exercise 4　The Effects of Desert Weather

global warming	receive little precipitation	desertification
badlands	supporting life forms	

Deserts are regions that _____. _____ is the
process by which fertile land becomes desert. Many environmentalists argue that temperature increases
due to _____ are accelerating the rate of desertification around the world.
Deserts are capable of _____ that have adapted to their harsh environments.
There are six kinds of deserts, including mountain or basin deserts, hamada deserts, regs, ergs,
intermontane basins, and _____.

Exercise 5　The Migration of the Monarch Butterfly

migrate so far	alive	the same winter location
very different life spans	North America	

The monarch butterfly is found in some parts of the world, including _____.
Scientists wonder how the monarch is able to _____ every year. New
generations of monarchs return to _____ every year even though they were
not _____ at the time of the last migration. Scientists are curious about
the fact that monarchs have _____ based on their place in the seasonal
migration cycle.

Exercise 6　The Development of the Typewriter

typewriters	full of small improvements	the computer
no single person	over the years	

_____ invented the typewriter, but many people contributed to its creation
_____. The history of the typewriter is _____
made over the years. When problems such as the type bar blocking the typist's view arose,
new improvements corrected them. These days, the typewriter has been replaced by
_____. But some people still use _____, and
some companies still make them.

Chimpanzees

04-12

Chimpanzees on mangrove trees in the Congo

[1] ➡ There are two types of chimpanzees. The common chimp lives in West and Central Africa while its cousin is the bonobo or pygmy chimp, which comes from the forests of the Democratic Republic of Congo. The Congo River forms a boundary between the two species. Adult male chimps can weigh between thirty-five and seventy kilograms. They usually stand 0.9 to 1.2 meters tall. Females usually weigh twenty-six to fifty kilograms and stand 0.66 to one meter tall. Chimps rarely live past forty years old in the wild, but in captivity, they have been known to reach the age of sixty.

[2] ➡ African people have been in contact with chimps for thousands of years. The first recorded encounter between a European and a chimp occurred in the 1600s. The diary of Portuguese explorer Duarte Pacheco Pereira documented chimps and noted their use of simple tools. Chimps were brought from Angola to Europe in the 1600s. The first was given as a gift to the Prince of Orange in 1640. Scientists were fascinated by the similarities between chimps and humans. Over the next twenty years, many chimps were exported to Europe.

[3] ➡ In 1859, Charles Darwin published his theory of evolution, which spurred interest in chimps as a link to humans. Observers at the time were interested in chimp behavior, so they were searching for similarities to human behavior. Their main goal was to discover whether chimps were inherently "good." Their interest was not grounded in practical science, however. The tendency of the time was to greatly exaggerate the chimp's intelligence. At one point, plans were made to create a workforce of chimps. The idea was to make chimps fill menial labor positions such as factory work.

Chimps were treated with much more serious scientific interest in the twentieth century. Before 1960, almost nothing was known about their behavior in their natural habitat. Then, Jane Goodall went to live in Tanzania's Gombe Forest, where she lived alongside chimps and observed their habits. Her discovery of chimps making tools was groundbreaking as it was previously believed that only humans did this.

⁵➡ Common chimps sometimes attack humans. In Uganda, many children have been attacked by chimps. These attacks are usually fatal for children. One reason for these attacks is that the chimps mistake the children for a species of monkey called the Western red colobus. It is one of the common chimp's favorite foods.

Humans must be very careful around chimps because they view humans as their rivals. The average chimp also has five times the upper body strength of an adult human male. This was proven when former NASCAR (National Association for Stock Car Automobile Racing) driver Saint James Davis was attacked and almost killed by a chimp.

1 According to paragraph 1, which of the following is true of chimpanzees?
(A) West and Central Africa are home to the common chimp.
(B) The bonobo chimp lives in Madagascar.
(C) There are five different kinds of chimps.
(D) The three species of chimp are separated by the Congo River boundary.

2 According to paragraphs 1 and 2, which of the following is NOT true of chimps?
(A) Wild chimps rarely live past the age of forty.
(B) They have some similarities to humans.
(C) They were first brought to Europe in the 1600s.
(D) Adult males can be up to three meters tall.

3 The word "they" in the passage refers to
(A) chimps
(B) humans
(C) observers
(D) similarities

4 In paragraph 3, why does the author mention "a workforce of chimps"?

    (A) To show that chimps can use simple tools

    (B) To show that chimps like helping humans

    (C) To show that chimp intelligence was exaggerated

    (D) To show that chimps make excellent menial workers

5 The word "fatal" in the passage is closest in meaning to

    (A) harmful

    (B) deadly

    (C) surprising

    (D) dangerous

6 According to paragraph 5, which of the following can be inferred about chimpanzees?

    (A) They are as intelligent as humans.

    (B) They can be very dangerous.

    (C) They can do factory work if trained properly.

    (D) They are not genetically related to humans.

Glassmaking

04-13

¹ ➡ Glass is a uniform, amorphous, solid material composed mainly of silicon dioxide, which is the major raw material in sand. If the raw materials used to make glass contain as much as one-percent iron, it will come out colored. Therefore, fine glass factories enrich their silicon to make it purer.

When glass is made naturally, it tends to be colored green due to the iron content. Glassblowers can also add powdered metals to change the color of the glass. By adding sulfur and carbon, glass will become colored yellowish to black. Tin oxide can be used to create white glass while a little cobalt will color glass a deep blue. Additionally, small concentrations of selenium can yield a brilliant color known as selenium ruby.

³ ➡ Obsidian is glass that occurs naturally from hot magma flows. This glass has been used to create sharp knives, arrowheads, and tools since the Stone Age. According to history, the first glassmakers were the Phoenicians, who used glass to coat their pottery as early as 3000 B.C. Around 1500 B.C., the ancient Egyptians made glass jars and beads. The beads they created consisted of metal rods with melted glass wrapped around them. The beads were prized possessions and were believed to possess magic powers.

⁴ ➡ The Romans developed many new glassmaking techniques and also spread the use of glass as far as China and the British Isles. In Northern Europe, around 1000 A.D., a new method of glasswork was discovered. The use of soda glass was replaced with some other glass containing potash. This was important because potash was very plentiful. Potash is obtained from wood ashes. From this point on, Northern European and Mediterranean glassworks were distinguishable from each other.

In eleventh-century Germany, the techniques for making sheet glass were invented. This led to the modern methods of making the windows utilized in houses and buildings. By the fourteenth century, Venice was a center for fine glassworks where all sorts of luxury items, such as mirrors, dinnerware, and vases, were manufactured.

Hand-blown glass is still considered a commodity today. Some of the most famous fine glass artists are Dale Chihuly, Rene Lalique, and Louis Comfort Tiffany. Their works are displayed in museums such as the Smithsonian. Some of their works sell for thousands of dollars. Cold work techniques are used to transform glass into fine crystal. Crystal manufacturers such as Edinburgh Crystal and Waterford Crystal use diamond saws to cut and polish glass into beautiful designs.

7 The word "it" in the passage refers to

   Ⓐ sand

   Ⓑ glass

   Ⓒ one-percent iron

   Ⓓ their silicon

8 According to paragraph 1, glass is

   Ⓐ a uniform, amorphous, solid material

   Ⓑ silicon dioxide formed into a shape

   Ⓒ a solid material with iron content

   Ⓓ tin oxide mixed with sulfur and carbon

9 The author discusses "glass jars and beads" in paragraph 3 in order to show that

   Ⓐ glass comes from natural sources in Egypt

   Ⓑ glass was once a rare and prized object in ancient Egypt

   Ⓒ glass was used as currency in ancient Egypt

   Ⓓ glass was invented by the ancient Egyptians

10 According to paragraph 3, which of the following is NOT true of glass?

   Ⓐ Obsidian is a naturally occurring form of it.

   Ⓑ Stone Age people made weapons and tools from it.

   Ⓒ It is believed that the Phoenicians produced glass for the first time.

   Ⓓ The Phoenicians coated their pottery with glass 3,000 years ago.

11 In paragraph 4, the author implies that potash

    Ⓐ was used in glassmaking by the Romans

    Ⓑ was not used by Mediterranean people

    Ⓒ was difficult to find in some places in the past

    Ⓓ can be used in the creation of crystal

12 The word "polish" in the passage is closest in meaning to

    Ⓐ rub

    Ⓑ break

    Ⓒ bond

    Ⓓ sell

Vocabulary Check-Up

A Choose the words with the closest meanings to the highlighted words.

1 Many people enrich themselves by taking educational classes.

ⓐ damage

ⓑ improve

ⓒ help

ⓓ research

2 His business specialized in manufacturing vacuum cleaners.

ⓐ selling

ⓑ buying

ⓒ making

ⓓ fixing

3 The filmmaker tried to depict the lives of early colonists in his movie.

ⓐ laugh at

ⓑ destroy

ⓒ name

ⓓ show

4 He spent many months working on his car to modify its fuel injection system.

ⓐ change

ⓑ remove

ⓒ transfer

ⓓ resell

5 She was disappointed that she could not grow vegetables in her garden because it was so arid.

ⓐ dry

ⓑ flooded

ⓒ fertile

ⓓ ugly

6 He hoped to inherit his father's successful business.

ⓐ buy

ⓑ receive

ⓒ find

ⓓ take

7 Anybody who has seen him play the game chess has seen him dominate the board.

ⓐ lose

ⓑ win

ⓒ control

ⓓ tie

8 Their first encounter was at the birthday party of a mutual friend.

ⓐ meeting

ⓑ argument

ⓒ disagreement

ⓓ formal introduction

B Match the words with the correct definitions.

1 evaporation •   • Ⓐ a disease of the nervous system that causes victims to shake violently

2 migrant •   • Ⓑ a place where one or more species of living organisms thrives

3 scroll •   • Ⓒ a small piece

4 epilepsy •   • Ⓓ one who improves preexisting objects or solves problems practically

5 lifespan •   • Ⓔ the process by which water is turned into gas by heat

6 advent •   • Ⓕ one who goes to a new country for an extended period of time

7 habitat •   • Ⓖ an old form of paper that writing was kept on

8 fragment •   • Ⓗ the bone structure within an organism

9 innovator •   • Ⓘ the arrival of an important person or thing

10 skeleton •   • Ⓙ the expected length of life of an organism

Sentence Simplification

Overview

Introduction

Sentence Simplification questions ask you to choose a sentence that best paraphrases the original sentence in the passage. The correct answer uses different vocabulary and different grammar to restate the essential meaning of the original sentence in a simpler way. This type of question does not appear in every reading passage. In addition, there is never more than one Sentence Simplification question in a passage.

Question Types

▷ Which of the following best expresses the essential information in the highlighted sentence? *Incorrect* answer choices change the meaning in important ways or leave out essential information.

Useful Tips

- Figure out what essential information is in the original sentence.
- Do not focus on minor information such as details and examples.
- Keep in mind that incorrect answers contradict something in the original sentence or leave out important information from the original sentence.
- Make sure that your answer agrees with the main argument of the paragraph or the passage as a whole.

05-01

Q Which of the following best expresses the essential information in the highlighted sentence? *Incorrect* answer choices change the meaning in important ways or leave out essential information.

- Ⓐ The blue mussel uses special bodily structures to stay on objects.
- Ⓑ The blue mussel has strong threadlike appendages growing out of its body.
- Ⓒ The blue mussel lives on rocks and other things that grow strong thread-like strings.
- Ⓓ The blue mussel eats thread-like substances on rocks and other objects to survive.

The Blue Mussel

The blue mussel is an edible bivalve. It is commonly farmed and harvested for food around the world. It attaches itself to rocks and other objects by strong thread-like structures called byssal threads. The shell of the blue mussel is smooth with a sculpting of concentric lines but no radiating ribs. It can be purple, blue, or sometimes brown in color. Blue mussels are preyed upon by starfish and are also eaten by the dogwhelk, a carnivorous rocky-shore mollusk. The blue mussel is part of a long-term environmental monitoring program in Prince William Sound, Alaska. The study examines how the blue mussel's hydrocarbon signature helps with ecosystem recovery.

✅ Correct Answer

The essential information in the original sentence is that the blue mussel has special bodily structures and uses them to cling to objects. So the correct answer is Ⓐ.

Basic Drill

Read the passages and answer the questions.

Skill & Tip

In order to answer Sentence Simplification questions, you should choose the sentence that best paraphrases the essential information in the highlighted sentence. A good paraphrase has different words and a different sentence structure from the original sentence. It does not focus on minor information such as details and examples.

Drill 1

Folk Medicine

Folk medicine refers to traditional methods of healing. It is used to deal with illnesses and injuries. It is also used to aid with childbirth and to maintain wellness. It is a body of knowledge distinct from scientific medicine, but both types of medicine may coexist in the same culture. It is usually unwritten and transmitted orally until someone collects it. Within a culture, elements of folk medicine may be known by many adults. It is gathered and applied by healers and shamans. Midwives, witches, and dealers in herbs also use it. This medicine is not always collected into a system. Many treatments may seem to contradict one another.

05-02

Q Which of the following best expresses the essential information in the highlighted sentence?

    Ⓐ Many people in cultural groups think folk medicine is good.

    Ⓑ Folk medicine is part of a culture known to many grown-ups.

    Ⓒ Within some cultures, only adults practice folk medicine.

    Ⓓ Adults treat themselves with folk medicine in some cultures.

Drill 2

Jury Selection

In the United States, the criminal justice system and some civil cases require a jury. These people are selected at random from the adult population in the same district served by the court concerned. A person who is serving on a jury is known as a juror. The number of jurors is usually six or twelve. They are chosen based on their ability to consider the trial fairly. There is always the possibility of jurors not completing the trial for health or other reasons, so some alternate jurors may be nominated. They also follow the trial but do not take part in deciding the verdict.

05-03

Q Which of the following best expresses the essential information in the highlighted sentence?

    Ⓐ The people on a jury are randomly chosen from the same jurisdiction.

    Ⓑ The adult population in the same area randomly selects the people in a jury.

    Ⓒ The jury is made up of the entire adult population in the same jurisdiction.

    Ⓓ There is a random selection of jury members by the adult population.

Oak Trees

05-04

The term *oak* can be used to name hundreds of species of trees and shrubs. Oaks are native to the Northern Hemisphere. They include deciduous and evergreen species and extend from cold latitudes to tropical Asia and the Americas.

Oaks have spirally arranged leaves with a lobed margin in many species while some have serrated leaves or entire leaves with a smooth margin. The flowers are catkins and are produced in spring. The fruit is a nut called an acorn, which is borne in a cup-like structure. Each acorn contains one seed and takes six to eighteen months to mature. The length of time depends upon the species. Oaks with evergreen leaves are called "live oaks," but they are not a distinct group. Their members are typically scattered among other sections.

Q   Which of the following best expresses the essential information in the highlighted sentence?

Ⓐ All the deciduous and evergreen trees in Asia and the Americas are oaks.

Ⓑ Deciduous and evergreen oaks are found in cold and hot parts of Asia and the Americas.

Ⓒ Oaks are deciduous or evergreen trees found in both cold and hot regions.

Ⓓ Deciduous and evergreen species of oaks survive best at cold or hot latitudes.

The Lumber Industry

05-05

Trees felled to make wood are called timber, and wood cut into boards is called lumber. Lumber is supplied either rough or finished. Rough lumber is the raw material for furniture making. It is available in many species, but usually hardwoods are used. Finished lumber is supplied in standard sizes and is used mostly by the construction industry. Lumber was one of the first industries in the United States. Maine and New York were early leaders in production. Later expansion of the lumber industry occurred in Michigan, Oregon, Washington, and California. The men who cut the trees down to make lumber are known as lumberjacks. These men are often characters in early American folklore.

Q   Which of the following best expresses the essential information in the highlighted sentence?

Ⓐ The construction industry accounts for most standardized lumber use.

Ⓑ Lumber comes in standard sizes provided by the construction industry.

Ⓒ The construction industry provides most lumber in standard sizes.

Ⓓ Standard sizes in the construction industry are important for finished lumber.

Exercises with Mid-Length Passages

Exercise 1 Read the following passage and answer the questions.

⏱ Time Limit: 2 min. 50 sec.

Wheat Production

05-06

¹➡ Wheat is cultivated worldwide and is the most important human food grain. It ranks second in total production as a cereal crop behind maize while rice is third. Wheat is a staple food used to make flour for leavened, flat, and steamed breads. It is used for cookies, cakes, pasta, noodles, and couscous. In addition, it is used to make forms of alcohol such as beer and vodka. These days, it is even being used to create biofuel. The husk of the grain, separated when milling white flour, is bran. Wheat is planted to a limited extent as a forage crop for livestock. The straw can be used as fodder for livestock and as a construction material for roofing hatch.

Harvested wheat grain is classified according to grain properties for the purposes of the commodities market. Wheat buyers use these classifications to enable them to decide which wheat to purchase. Each class has special uses, and wheat producers determine which classes of wheat are the most profitable to cultivate with this system.

³➡ Wheat is widely cultivated as a cash crop because it produces a good yield per unit area. It also grows well in temperate climates, even in places with moderately short growing seasons. It yields high-quality flour that is widely used for baking. Most breads, including many breads named for the additional grains they contain, like rye and oats, are made with wheat flour. Numerous other popular foods are made from wheat flour as well. This results in a large demand for the grain, even in countries with significant food surpluses.

There are six classes of wheat grown in the United States. Durum wheat is very hard with light-colored grain, and hard red spring wheat is brownish and contains a lot of protein. Hard red winter wheat is similar and is primarily grown in Kansas while soft red winter wheat is soft and low in protein. Hard white wheat is light colored and chalky while soft white wheat has very little protein and is grown in moist temperate regions.

📖 Words & Phrases

cultivate v to grow; to farm
rank v to achieve a level or place on a list
maize n corn
staple n something that is used every day
profitable adj able to be sold for money
yield n the amount of something that is produced

1   According to paragraph 1, which of the following is true of wheat? *To receive credit, you must select TWO answers.*

    Ⓐ It is cultivated less than rice by people around the world.

    Ⓑ It can be consumed in part by animals.

    Ⓒ It is the most important cereal crop for humans.

    Ⓓ It can only be used to make baked goods.

2   According to paragraph 3, which of the following is NOT true of wheat?

    Ⓐ Temperate climates are ideal for it to grow in.

    Ⓑ Flour made from it is used in many types of bread.

    Ⓒ It can be raised in places with short growing seasons.

    Ⓓ Countries that have food surpluses do not need it.

3   Which of the following best expresses the essential information in the first highlighted sentence? *Incorrect* answer choices change the meaning in important ways or leave out essential information.

    Ⓐ Wheat is planted to increase crops and livestock.

    Ⓑ Some wheat is planted for farm animals to eat.

    Ⓒ Wheat can be found planted on farms with animals.

    Ⓓ Many farmers plant less wheat if they have animals.

4   Which of the following best expresses the essential information in the second highlighted sentence? *Incorrect* answer choices change the meaning in important ways or leave out essential information.

    Ⓐ The high productivity of wheat makes people grow a lot of it for profit.

    Ⓑ Wheat is widely grown in places where people need lots of cash.

    Ⓒ Wheat must be grown in very large fields, which costs a lot.

    Ⓓ Wheat is the most abundant cash crop in the world.

Summary Note Fill in the blanks with the appropriate words.

Used to feed livestock

Used to make bread, pasta, and alcohol

Facts about Wheat

❶ _____
commonly grown varieties

Most important
❷ _____

Cultivated as
❸ _____
because of high yield

🕐 Time Limit: 2 min. 40 sec.

Cave Ecosystems

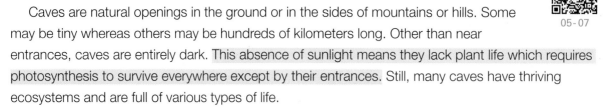

05-07

　　Caves are natural openings in the ground or in the sides of mountains or hills. Some may be tiny whereas others may be hundreds of kilometers long. Other than near entrances, caves are entirely dark. This absence of sunlight means they lack plant life which requires photosynthesis to survive everywhere except by their entrances. Still, many caves have thriving ecosystems and are full of various types of life.

²➡ Animals that live in caves can be divided into two separate categories: trogloxenes and troglobites. The former are animals that use caves but do not spend their entire lives in caves. For instance, chipmunks, mice, and bears often sleep in caves. But they find food outside caves. Bats are also trogloxenes. Most bats hunt insects for food. So while they might sleep in caves during daylight hours, they depart at night to hunt for food. Troglobites, on the other hand, are animals that live their entire lives in caves. Typically, these are small animals such as spiders, mites, and scorpions. However, various species of fish are known to live in lakes found in caves. Troglobites have usually undergone changes to make them better adapted to life in the dark. They may lack eyes but have other senses that are heightened.

³➡ Cave dwellers obtain nourishment in various ways. Trogloxenes such as bats actually provide sustenance for a lot of troglobites in the form of their guano. In fact, all kinds of creatures in caves feed on bat droppings. Other animals may eat eggs and the carcasses of animals left in caves. In many cases, water that seeps or flows into caves provides nutrients for troglobites. Flowing water may also carry a variety of foods, including fruit, berries, and nuts, into caves. These foods are then devoured by animals.

　　Overall, animals have learned to adapt to their dark environments. Some caves may therefore have thriving communities of various organisms.

📖 Words & Phrases

entirely `adv` completely; totally
lack `v` not to have something
heightened `adj` increased; improved
guano `n` solid waste produced by bats
carcass `n` the dead body of an animal
devour `v` to eat; to consume

1 According to paragraph 2, which of the following is NOT true of trogloxenes?

Ⓐ They include animals such as bears and chipmunks.

Ⓑ They do not spend all of their time inside caves.

Ⓒ They get their food in places other than in caves.

Ⓓ They can be found living in lakes inside caves.

2 According to paragraph 3, nuts and berries may get into caves because

Ⓐ they seep through the ground into caves

Ⓑ flowing water carries them there

Ⓒ they fall off trees and roll into caves

Ⓓ bats bring them there

3 Which of the following best expresses the essential information in the first highlighted sentence? *Incorrect* answer choices change the meaning in important ways or leave out essential information.

Ⓐ The entrances of caves are the only places where plants grow in them in great numbers.

Ⓑ Plants using photosynthesis live nowhere in caves other than by their entrances because they get no sunlight.

Ⓒ Because plants need photosynthesis to survive, they are never found anywhere in or around caves.

Ⓓ It is possible for some plants to survive in caves so long as they do not rely upon photosynthesis to create energy.

4 Which of the following best expresses the essential information in the second highlighted sentence? *Incorrect* answer choices change the meaning in important ways or leave out essential information.

Ⓐ Troglobites can adapt to life in the dark better than other animals.

Ⓑ It is not possible for some troglobites to survive life in the dark.

Ⓒ Animals that change to live in the dark become troglobites.

Ⓓ Many troglobites have evolved to live in the dark better.

Summary Note Fill in the blanks with the appropriate words.

Cave Ecosystems

Trogloxenes and Troglobites
- ❶ _____ do not spend their entire lives in caves
- ❷ _____ live entirely in caves

Obtaining Nourishment
- Feed on bat guano
- Eat eggs and animal carcasses
- Get nutrients from ❸ _____

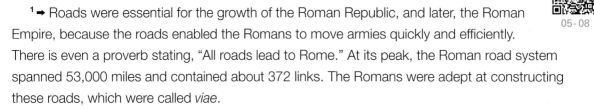

🕒 Time Limit: 2 min. 50 sec.

Road Law in Rome

05-08

1 ➡ Roads were essential for the growth of the Roman Republic, and later, the Roman Empire, because the roads enabled the Romans to move armies quickly and efficiently. There is even a proverb stating, "All roads lead to Rome." At its peak, the Roman road system spanned 53,000 miles and contained about 372 links. The Romans were adept at constructing these roads, which were called *viae*.

2 ➡ Prepared *viae* had their beginnings as the streets of Rome. The laws of the Twelve Tables, which date to approximately 450 B.C., specified that roads should be eight feet wide where straight and sixteen feet wide where curved. The tables commanded the Romans to build roads and to give wayfarers the right to pass over private land when roads are in disrepair. Therefore, building roads that would not need frequent repairs became an ideological objective.

3 ➡ Roman law defined the right to use a road as a *servitus*, or claim. The right of going established a claim to use a footpath across private land. The right of driving allowed for a carriage. A road combined both types of claims as long as it was of the proper width, which was determined by an arbiter. The default width was eight feet. In these rather dry laws, the prevalence of public domain over private can be seen, which characterized the republic.

The Romans had a preference for standardization whenever it was possible. After being made permanent commissioner of roads in 20 B.C., Augustus set up a golden milestone near the temple of Saturn. On it were listed all of the cities in the empire and the distance to them. This was later called the navel of Rome.

Roman roads were very important for maintaining the stability of the empire and for expanding it. The legions made good time on them, and some Roman roads were still used a thousand years later. During the fall of the Roman Empire, the same roads offered avenues of invasion to barbarians, which contributed to Roman military reverses.

📖 Words & Phrases

adept adj highly skilled at something
wayfarer n a traveler
in disrepair phr in a state of poor condition
arbiter n a judge or decision maker
prevalence n commonness
permanent adj everlasting; constant
stability n steadiness; firmness

1 According to paragraph 1, roads were important to the Roman Empire because
  Ⓐ they were a symbol of the Roman people
  Ⓑ they had signs that listed the distance from cities around the world to Rome
  Ⓒ they allowed the quick and efficient movement of armies
  Ⓓ they showed the Romans' eagerness for standardization

2 According to paragraphs 2 and 3, which of the following is NOT true of Roman roads?
  Ⓐ The right to use them was defined as a *servitus*.
  Ⓑ Roads were required to be eight feet wide when they were straight.
  Ⓒ Roads were called *viae*.
  Ⓓ The right to drive on them did not allow for carriages.

Mastering the Question Type

3 Which of the following best expresses the essential information in the first highlighted sentence?
Incorrect answer choices change the meaning in important ways or leave out essential information.
  Ⓐ Roman republicans believed privacy was more important than public life.
  Ⓑ The Romans separated public life from private life by law.
  Ⓒ One characteristic of the Roman republic was the strict enactment of public law.
  Ⓓ The laws of the Roman republic tended to put public life before private life.

4 Which of the following best expresses the essential information in the second highlighted sentence?
Incorrect answer choices change the meaning in important ways or leave out essential information.
  Ⓐ The Roman Empire built roads to allow barbarians to invade.
  Ⓑ The barbarians invaded Rome on those roads, leading to its downfall.
  Ⓒ The barbarians preferred to invade the Roman Empire on roads and avenues.
  Ⓓ The Roman Empire offered barbarians a chance to invade on different avenues.

✎ Summary Note Fill in the blanks with the appropriate words.

The Roads of Ancient Rome

| Were important to the empire | Gave people ❶ _____ | Were important to the republic | Were ordered to be built and repaired ❷ _____ | Distances between cities were recorded on roads |

Read the following passage and answer the questions.

Time Limit: 2 min. 40 sec.

Animal Territoriality

05-09

The term *territory* refers to any area that an animal defends. Animals that defend territories are territorial. The idea of animal territories was first introduced by Eliot Howard. He wrote of this concept in a book published in 1920. In the 1930s, the concept was developed further by Margaret Morse Nice, who elaborated on it through her studies on the song sparrow. Later, it was widely popularized by Robert Ardrey in his book *The Territorial Imperative*. The popularity of the book led to an exaggerated idea of the importance of territory. This concept was thought to be part of the field of social ecology. In fact, however, only a small number of species have territories with clear boundaries. Within these boundaries, they live and find all the resources they need.

2 ➡ The most obvious examples of territory are seen with birds and fish. These animals often develop bright colors to warn others away from their territories. The European robin and the Siamese fighting fish adopt these kinds of colors to defend their territories. These areas usually contain their nest sites and offer sufficient food for them and their young.

3 ➡ Defense rarely takes the form of overt fights. More frequently, there is a highly noticeable display. This display may be visual. An example of this is the red breast of the robin. It may also be auditory. Many bird songs and the calls of gibbons are made for this reason. It can also be olfactory. This is carried out through the deposit of scent marks. These marks may be deposited by urination or by defecation. Dogs mark their scents in these ways. Scent marks can also be placed by rubbing parts of the bodies that bear specialized scent glands against objects in a territory. Cats mark their scents by rubbing their faces and flanks against objects.

📕 Words & Phrases

exaggerate (v) to overstate
overt (adj) done or shown in an open and obvious way
auditory (adj) related to sound
olfactory (adj) related to smell
urination (n) the act of getting rid of liquid waste from the body
defecation (n) the act of getting rid of solid waste from the body

1 According to paragraph 2, animals often develop bright colors in order to

    Ⓐ attract the opposite sex

    Ⓑ mark clear territorial boundaries

    Ⓒ provide food for their young in their nests

    Ⓓ send warnings to other animals

2 In paragraph 3, the author's description of animal territories mentions all of the following EXCEPT:

    Ⓐ Animals that use scents to mark their territories

    Ⓑ A type of visual display used by animals

    Ⓒ Different auditory markings of territories

    Ⓓ How some animals use violence to defend their territories

3 Which of the following best expresses the essential information in the first highlighted sentence? *Incorrect* answer choices change the meaning in important ways or leave out essential information.

    Ⓐ In the 1930s, Margaret Morse Nice began to study the song sparrow.

    Ⓑ The concept of song sparrow territories was suggested by Margaret Morse Nice in the 1930s.

    Ⓒ Margaret Morse Nice furthered the concept of animal territories by studying song sparrows in the 1930s.

    Ⓓ Studies on the song sparrow were popularized by Margaret Morse Nice in the 1930s.

4 Which of the following best expresses the essential information in the second highlighted sentence? *Incorrect* answer choices change the meaning in important ways or leave out essential information.

    Ⓐ Rubbing particular body parts against the objects in a territory is a way to leave scent marks.

    Ⓑ Some animals have scent glands that are marked by different objects in their territories.

    Ⓒ The objects in a territory contain specialized scent marks from different body parts of different animals.

    Ⓓ With scent marks left by rubbing, animals claim different objects in their territories.

✎ **Summary Note** Fill in the blanks with the appropriate words.

Territory-Defending Methods Used by Animals

❶ _____	❷ _____	❸ _____	Fights
• Bright coloring used to scare away invaders	• Scent marks by urination, by defecation, or by rubbing body parts	• Strange noises used to scare or hurt the ears of invaders	• Rarely happen

🕐 Time Limit: 2 min. 50 sec.

The Economic Cycle

05-10

Local and national economies are constantly undergoing changes. Economists have analyzed these changes. They have determined that there are four parts of an economic cycle. They are expansion, peak, contraction, and recovery. Each phase has its own unique characteristics.

2 ➡ When an economy is undergoing expansion, economic times are good. Businesses are investing and hiring. They also typically have to offer higher salaries in order to secure the best workers. Since most consumers are employed and have plenty of money, their purchasing power is high. There is therefore high demand for consumer goods, which causes businesses to manufacture more products. Interest rates are low, too, so acquiring loans from banks is easy for both businesses and consumers.

During the peak stage, the economy reaches its highest point. Most businesses no longer need to expand, hire more employees, or make more products. Some businesses see their profits plateauing while others may begin to see lower profits. Inflation in the guise of rising prices begins to appear. Governments often increase interest rates at this time to keep the economy from overheating.

4 ➡ When contraction occurs, consumer spending and business profits both decline. Production slows or declines. The unemployment rate rises as some companies begin laying off employees as well. Production decreases, and some companies may even go out of business. In some cases, a recession, which happens when an economy declines for at least two quarters, occurs. In severe situations, a depression may happen. This is reduced economic conditions for two or more years.

At some point, the economy reaches its lowest point. Then, the final stage—recovery—can begin. Businesses start hiring again and increase production. People are able to find employment as well. Consumer demand begins to increase since people have more spending money. Interest rates become lower as inflationary pressure no longer exists.

All economies go through the four phases. However, some phases may be long while others may last a short time.

📖 Words & Phrases

analyze Ⓥ to study to determine information about something
salary Ⓝ money that an employee is paid each month or year
consumer Ⓝ a shopper; a customer
profit Ⓝ money that a person or business makes
guise Ⓝ an appearance
overheat Ⓥ to become too hot

1 In paragraph 2, all of the following questions are answered EXCEPT:

Ⓐ How do businesses treat their employees during an expansion?

Ⓑ How long does a typical expansion last?

Ⓒ How are economic times during an expansion?

Ⓓ How is demand for consumer goods during an expansion?

2 In paragraph 4, the author uses "a recession" as an example of

Ⓐ a phase that leads to a recovery

Ⓑ a period of economic expansion

Ⓒ a time that is worse than a depression

Ⓓ a feature of some contraction phases

3 Which of the following best expresses the essential information in the first highlighted sentence? *Incorrect* answer choices change the meaning in important ways or leave out essential information.

Ⓐ Interest rates get lower, so people start applying for loans.

Ⓑ Getting bank loans is simple thanks to low interest rates.

Ⓒ Businesses can get loans more easily than consumers can.

Ⓓ Low interest rates cause banks to lend more money.

4 Which of the following best expresses the essential information in the second highlighted sentence? *Incorrect* answer choices change the meaning in important ways or leave out essential information.

Ⓐ Companies begin to lose money because they do not make profits anymore.

Ⓑ Companies set records for profits while others start to lose money.

Ⓒ Companies may stop making more money or see profits go down.

Ⓓ Companies have problems making higher profits during this time.

✏️ **Summary Note** Fill in the blanks with the appropriate words.

> **The Four Phases of the Economic Cycle**

❶ _____
- Good economic times
- High demand for goods so production is high

Peak
- Economy reaches its highest point
- Interest rates increase

❷ _____
- Spending and profits decline
- Economy declines

❸ _____
- Businesses start hiring again
- Consumer demand increases

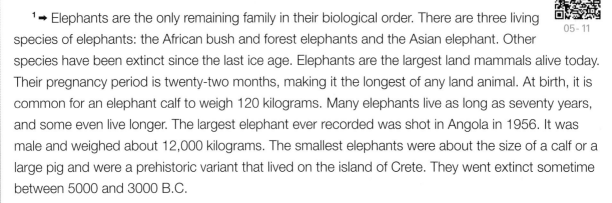

The Evolution of the Elephant

05-11

1 ➡ Elephants are the only remaining family in their biological order. There are three living species of elephants: the African bush and forest elephants and the Asian elephant. Other species have been extinct since the last ice age. Elephants are the largest land mammals alive today. Their pregnancy period is twenty-two months, making it the longest of any land animal. At birth, it is common for an elephant calf to weigh 120 kilograms. Many elephants live as long as seventy years, and some even live longer. The largest elephant ever recorded was shot in Angola in 1956. It was male and weighed about 12,000 kilograms. The smallest elephants were about the size of a calf or a large pig and were a prehistoric variant that lived on the island of Crete. They went extinct sometime between 5000 and 3000 B.C.

Elephants are increasingly threatened by humans, and human-elephant conflicts are often deadly. They kill 150 elephants and up to 100 people in Asia each year. The African elephant population went from three million in 1970 to about 600,000 in 1989. The numbers of this beast then dropped even further. By 2000, the number was down to 272,000. In recent years, efforts to save these animals have helped its numbers increase. The elephant is now protected around the world. Many restrictions have been enacted to benefit the elephant as the laws strictly limit its capture and domestic use. Trade in products such as ivory is also controlled.

3 ➡ Some scientists believe that the elephant family is distantly related to sea cows and that there is a link between elephants and hyraxes. The fossil evidence does not offer certain proof despite many people believing the genetic evidence shows this. One theory suggests that these animals spent most of their time underwater. They would have used their trunks like snorkels for breathing. Modern elephants still have this ability and are known to swim like that. They can swim distances of around fifty kilometers for approximately six hours.

📕 **Words & Phrases**

mammal Ⓝ animals that give birth to babies and feed their young with milk
prehistoric 〔adj〕 from the time before recorded human history
variant Ⓝ something that slightly differs from another thing
conflict Ⓝ fighting; a war
restriction Ⓝ a rule that limits something
enact Ⓥ to make or pass a law

1 In paragraph 1, the author's description of elephants mentions all of the following EXCEPT:

Ⓐ How long females are pregnant

Ⓑ How some species went extinct in the past

Ⓒ How many species are alive today

Ⓓ How much calves can weigh at birth

2 According to paragraph 3, which of the following is true of modern elephants?

Ⓐ They spend most of their time underwater.

Ⓑ They are the size of a calf or large pig.

Ⓒ They use their trunks like snorkels.

Ⓓ They can run up to fifty kilometers per hour.

3 Which of the following best expresses the essential information in the first highlighted sentence? *Incorrect* answer choices change the meaning in important ways or leave out essential information.

Ⓐ Laws have been passed to help protect elephants from people.

Ⓑ Laws allowing elephants to be captured and raised domestically have been passed.

Ⓒ Without laws, elephants would be captured and put in zoos.

Ⓓ The laws benefit people by allowing elephants to be captured.

4 Which of the following best expresses the essential information in the second highlighted sentence? *Incorrect* answer choices change the meaning in important ways or leave out essential information.

Ⓐ People believe what the fossil and genetic evidence shows about the link between elephants and hyraxes.

Ⓑ The fossil and genetic evidence clearly shows the link between elephants and hyraxes.

Ⓒ The genetic evidence is believed to show the link between elephants and hyraxes by supporters of the fossil evidence.

Ⓓ Unlike the fossil evidence, the genetic evidence seems to show a clear link between elephants and hyraxes.

Summary Note Fill in the blanks with the appropriate words.

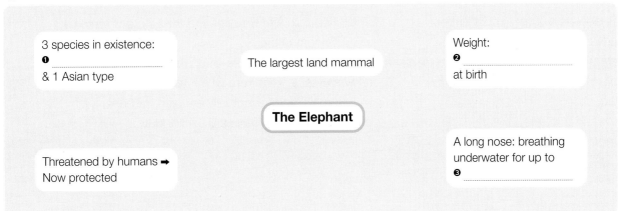

3 species in existence:
❶ _____
& 1 Asian type

The largest land mammal

Weight:
❷ _____
at birth

The Elephant

Threatened by humans ➡
Now protected

A long nose: breathing underwater for up to
❸ _____

Building Summary Skills

The following summaries are based on the long passages you worked on earlier. Complete each of them by filling in the blanks with suitable words or phrases.

Exercise 1 Wheat Production

classification system	the quality and the price	six classes
profitable crop	widely grown	

Wheat is one of the most _____ and important crops in the world. It has many important uses by humans. Wheat grain is harvested according to a _____ that determines _____. Wheat is a very _____ because it is used so widely in products that are consumed daily. There are _____ of wheat grown in the United States.

Exercise 2 Cave Ecosystems

eat bat guano	caves are dark	their entire lives
trogloxenes	chipmunks, mice, and bears	

Even though _____, they have ecosystems with animals living in them. _____ use caves but get food in other places. They can be _____. Troglobites live _____ in caves. Many cave dwellers _____. They may eat other food, too, such as food brought in by water. Many cave animals have adapted to live life in dark places.

Exercise 3 Road Law in Rome

invade and conquer	in disrepair	Roman roads
the golden milestone	building and administering laws	

Roads were a very important part of the Roman Republic and Empire, and the Romans were very advanced at _____ to control them. _____ were built to very strict measurements, and laws protected travelers when roads were not available or _____. There was even a point from which all roads to Rome led, called _____. Roman roads eventually enabled barbarians to _____ Rome, and some Roman roads still exist today.

Exercise 4 Animal Territoriality

territories	bright colors or strong smells	mark their territory
few animals	in the early twentieth century	

Animals defend areas called _____, that are important to them. This concept was introduced _____ although it was greatly exaggerated. Many animals develop _____ to protect their territories. _____ fight over territory. Many common animals _____ with their own smell.

Exercise 5 The Economic Cycle

expansion	to get better	an economy declines
four parts	the peak stage	

The economic cycle has _____: expansion, peak, contraction, and recovery. _____ happens during good economic times when people have jobs and production is high. _____ sees profits plateauing and interest rates rising. Contractions happens when _____ and people lose jobs. Recovery is when the economy starts _____.

Exercise 6 The Evolution of the Elephant

the longest pregnancy period	by humans	increase their numbers
three species	sea cows and possibly hyraxes	

There are only _____ of elephants still living today. They are the largest of all land mammals and have _____. These days, elephants are endangered _____, but efforts are being made to _____. Scientists think elephants are genetically related to _____ although there is not enough evidence to prove this.

The Development of Industry in the United States

05-12

A drawing of the cotton gin invented by Eli Whitney

¹ ➡ After the American Revolution, industry in the United States was behind Europe—but not very far behind. Several waves of inventions and growth soon hit over a period of 150 years. These advances made the American economy the largest and most modern in the world.

During the American Revolution, America had not yet entered its industrial age as most manufacturing was done in people's homes. Whereas Britain was industrialized, America had not caught on yet. Then Francis Cabot Lowell went to Britain in 1811 and memorized the secrets to constructing a power loom. After he and his associates returned to America, they founded some textile plants in Boston. The most famous was in Lowell, Massachusetts, and was built in 1822. The Lowell system employed many "mill girls" who lived in dormitories in order to run the factory. New England was the home of a growing textile industry. It was the first area of the United States to experience such rapid growth. This growth also occurred in Pennsylvania. The iron industry pushed that state along and helped it grow even faster.

³ ➡ Then, the direction of progress began to change. This new period took place between 1810 and the 1860s. Factories continued to expand. But greater strides were being taken in inventing. American manufacturing and agriculture were greatly improved. These improvements came from practical inventions. Richard Chenaworth invented the cast-iron plow. It was useful because it had replaceable parts. John Deere created the steel plow, which made farming faster because the soil did not stick to it. Eli Whitney invented the cotton gin and the jig, which resulted in the creation of a huge cotton industry in the South. Samuel Morse invented the telegraph, which began the age of long-range communication. Elisha Otis invented the passenger elevator, which led to modern-day skyscrapers. Finally, George Pullman created the sleeping car for trains, thereby allowing for long-distance travel.

⁴ ➡ From the 1850s on, industry in the United States boomed. After the victory of the North in the Civil War in the 1860s, Northern business entrepreneurs flourished. Government was eager to

see business expand. The numerous innovations caused swift and dramatic changes. Railroads were now needed to carry goods across the country. People in the South traded cotton. They sold that product to the North and to Britain. By the early 1900s, cars were needed by many people. The auto industry introduced a new dimension of growth to America. By the 1920s, Henry Ford introduced his Model-T. With it came the modern assembly line.

1   According to paragraph 1, the United States' economy became the largest and most modern in the world because

     Ⓐ the United States won the American Revolution

     Ⓑ there were many new inventions

     Ⓒ America imported many European products

     Ⓓ the economy grew steadily for more than 150 years

2   Which of the following best expresses the essential information in the highlighted sentence? *Incorrect* answer choices change the meaning in important ways or leave out essential information.

     Ⓐ New England grew more rapidly than European countries.

     Ⓑ There was rapid growth everywhere in the United States, including New England.

     Ⓒ Only one area besides New England in America experienced fast growth.

     Ⓓ Fast growth occurred in New England first in America.

3   According to paragraph 2, which of the following can be inferred about Pennsylvania's industry?

     Ⓐ It had a textile industry similar to that of Massachusetts.

     Ⓑ It often competed against Massachusetts and other states.

     Ⓒ Its iron industry was stronger than in other states.

     Ⓓ It was the richest state in the country.

4 Why does the author mention "practical inventions" in paragraph 3?

    Ⓐ To exemplify the reasons for the development of industry in America

    Ⓑ To prove that America became very rich by selling new products

    Ⓒ To illustrate how intelligent American inventors were

    Ⓓ To prove that most useful inventions came from America

5 The word "it" in the passage refers to

    Ⓐ the cast-iron plow

    Ⓑ the steel plow

    Ⓒ farming

    Ⓓ the soil

6 The word "boomed" in the passage is closest in meaning to

    Ⓐ imploded

    Ⓑ increased

    Ⓒ shrank

    Ⓓ continued

Microbes

05-13

Before the discovery of microbes, the changes that took place in foods as they aged were a mystery. Nobody knew why grapes turned into wine and milk turned into cheese. No one even thought that there were living organisms too small to be seen by the naked eye at work on foods. Then, in 1676, a Dutch scientist discovered these microscopic creatures.

We now know much more about microbes. Scientists who specialize in their study look at the various forms of these tiny creatures. These microbes can take the forms of bacteria, fungi, archaea, or eukaryotes. Viruses are not considered to be microbes since they are not alive. Microbes can be single or have multiple cells. A few single-celled microbes, known as protists, are visible to the naked eye.

Microbes are usually found in water or other liquids that are below their boiling points. Scientists have taken samples of microbes from hot springs, on the ocean floor, and even from deep within the Earth's crust. These microbes are important parts of the Earth's many ecosystems. They are responsible for recycling nutrients and are also important parts of the nitrogen cycle.

⁴➡ Scientists believe the first single-celled microbes formed around four billion years ago. These were the first life forms on the Earth and were the only ones for three billion years. Microbes reproduce quickly and vastly and are able freely to exchange genes between different species. They also mutate at an accelerated rate, which allows them to evolve swiftly in order to adapt to new environments. A problem associated with the ability of microbes to evolve so rapidly is the development of super bugs that are able to resist modern antibiotic drugs.

The simplest microbes are bacteria. They are also among the most common group of living things on the Earth. They can be found in all environments where the temperature is below 140 degrees Celsius. They are present in sea water, soil, and even the human stomach and intestines. The genome of bacteria is a single strand of DNA. Bacteria are surrounded by a cell wall. They are known to reproduce by a process called binary fission. By this process, they split again and again. Some bacteria are able to double every ten minutes under prime conditions.

Another variety of microbes is archaea. These are single-celled creatures with no nuclei. These microbes are common in all types of habitats, including extreme environments. Eukaryotes are different from bacteria and archaea. They have multi-celled structures called organelles within them. The eukaryote's DNA is housed within the nucleus.

⁷➡ One of the most interesting kinds of microbes is the extremophile. These are microbes that have adapted to highly hostile environments. These robust creatures can be found at the North and South poles, in deserts, and in the deep sea. These microbes have even been found as far as seven kilometers below the Earth's surface. Some extremophiles have survived in a vacuum and are resistant to radiation. This leads scientists to believe that it is possible for them to survive in space.

7 Which of the following best expresses the essential information in the highlighted sentence? *Incorrect* answer choices change the meaning in important ways or leave out essential information.

    Ⓐ Small living creatures that people cannot see are always in food.

    Ⓑ No one realized that foods consisted of small living organisms.

    Ⓒ People did not realize that foods held tiny, invisible living creatures.

    Ⓓ Nobody thought organisms living in food were too tiny to see.

8 The word "specialize" in the passage is closest in meaning to

    Ⓐ focus

    Ⓑ prefer

    Ⓒ examine

    Ⓓ discuss

9 In paragraph 4, why does the author mention "the first single-celled microbes formed around four billion years ago"?

    Ⓐ To show how basic they were

    Ⓑ To indicate how long they have been on the Earth

    Ⓒ To show how much they have mutated over the years

    Ⓓ To explain why they are still in existence

10 The word "reproduce" in the passage is closest in meaning to

    Ⓐ become pregnant

    Ⓑ fertilize

    Ⓒ duplicate

    Ⓓ combine

11 According to paragraph 7, where have extremophiles been found? *To receive credit, you must select TWO answers.*

    Ⓐ The moon

    Ⓑ Oceans

    Ⓒ Volcanoes

    Ⓓ Deserts

12 According to paragraph 7, which of the following can be inferred about extremophiles?

    Ⓐ Scientists have discovered simple ways to kill them.

    Ⓑ They are less resistant to influences than microbes.

    Ⓒ There are more of them in existence than microbes.

    Ⓓ Scientists will possibly find them in outer space in the future.

Vocabulary Check-Up

A **Choose the words with the closest meanings to the highlighted words.**

1 They wanted to cultivate tomatoes in their backyard.

    Ⓐ eat

    Ⓑ find

    Ⓒ use

    Ⓓ grow

2 She hoped to prevent an accident by checking the brakes on her car.

    Ⓐ help

    Ⓑ encourage

    Ⓒ stop

    Ⓓ need

3 We are almost entirely finished with this project.

    Ⓐ seriously

    Ⓑ completely

    Ⓒ steadily

    Ⓓ happily

4 He wanted to increase the pace of our walking.

    Ⓐ difficulty

    Ⓑ ease

    Ⓒ style

    Ⓓ speed

5 He was known to help wayfarers in need.

    Ⓐ people

    Ⓑ travelers

    Ⓒ stray animals

    Ⓓ vegetables

6 The popular new product was based on the designer's concept.

    Ⓐ idea

    Ⓑ work

    Ⓒ promise

    Ⓓ design

7 A mother moose will always defend her young children.

    Ⓐ hurt

    Ⓑ help

    Ⓒ protect

    Ⓓ enjoy

8 We were fascinated to view so many exotic creatures at the nature park.

    Ⓐ people

    Ⓑ scenes

    Ⓒ plants

    Ⓓ animals

B Match the words with the correct definitions.

1 prevalence •

2 heightened •

3 staple •

4 olfactory •

5 analyze •

6 inflation •

7 prehistoric •

8 profit •

9 yield •

10 boundary •

• Ⓐ to study to determine information about something

• Ⓑ a line that marks an area

• Ⓒ from the time before recorded human history

• Ⓓ a period that marks a rise in prices

• Ⓔ the amount of something that is produced

• Ⓕ increased; improved

• Ⓖ money a person or business makes

• Ⓗ something that is used every day

• Ⓘ commonness

• Ⓙ related to smell

PART II

Making Inferences

In this part, the reading comprehension questions include rhetorical purpose, inference, and insert text. The learning objectives of these comprehension questions are to understand the rhetorical function of a statement or paragraph, the logic of the passage, and the strongly implied ideas in the text.

UNIT

06

Rhetorical Purpose

Overview

Introduction

Rhetorical Purpose questions ask you to understand why and how the author uses a particular piece of information in the passage. This information can be used to argue, define, explain, or compare ideas. Because this type of question usually focuses on the logical development of the passage, you need to figure out how a word, a phrase, or information relates to the rest of the passage.

Question Types

▶ The author discusses X in paragraph Y in order to

▶ Why does the author mention "X"?

▶ The author uses X as an example of

Useful Tips

■ Read the question first and then recognize the author's purpose immediately by scanning specific phrases or paragraphs.

■ Focus on the logical links between sentences and paragraphs, not on the overall organization of the passage.

■ Familiarize yourself with the words or phrases for rhetorical functions such as *to illustrate, to criticize, to explain, to contrast, to compare,* and *to note.*

Q In the passage, why does the author mention "all celestial objects"?

   Ⓐ To name one problem regarding astrophysics

   Ⓑ To prove that astrophysics is important

   Ⓒ To explain why astrophysics is difficult

   Ⓓ To name something astrophysicists study

Astrophysics

Astrophysics looks at the makeup of outer space as a branch of astronomy. Scientists in this field consider the brightness and the density of objects in space. They examine the fabric of all celestial objects. This is a difficult science because it is purely theoretical. It is much different from the physical activity of observing the stars. None of the events that astrophysicists study can be created on the Earth. These scientists must create theoretical models from real observations. Then, they solve the problems that arise. Astrophysics is said to be the only branch of science that has never been able to obtain a single specimen.

✅ Correct Answer

The highlighted phrase concerns one of the topics that is studied by astrophysicists. So the correct answer is Ⓓ.

Basic Drill

Read the passages and answer the questions.

Skill & Tip

> Rhetorical Purpose questions ask why the author uses particular words, phrases, or sentences in certain paragraphs. These expressions can be used to define, argue, explain, illustrate, or contrast ideas. So you need to look at the logical links between ideas rather than the overall organization of the passage.

Drill 1

Comb Jelly

06-02

    The comb jelly is a sea creature but not a true jellyfish. The reason is that it lacks poison stingers. There are more than 100 species of comb jelly living in the world's oceans. They make up a large amount of plankton biomass. One species is the sea gooseberry, which is native to the North Sea. It has attained a population that is so high that it often clogs fishermen's nets, something that few other species are known to do. The fragile makeup of the comb jelly makes it very difficult to research, so data on its lifespan is not available. But it is known that the comb jelly reproduces even before adulthood, so it is assumed that its generational cycle is short.

Q   Why does the author mention "poison stingers"?

    Ⓐ To explain how the comb jelly is not fully understood by scientists

    Ⓑ To note that the comb jelly often clogs the nets of fishermen

    Ⓒ To contrast the comb jelly with species of true jellyfish

    Ⓓ To discuss how the comb jelly makes up a large amount of plankton biomass

Drill 2

White and Brown Dwarfs

06-03

    A low- or medium-mass star goes into the white dwarf stage when it dies. Stars reach this stage after entering the red giant stage and shedding their outer material. White dwarfs are approximately the size of Earth but have the density of the sun. This gives them the densest mass in the universe except for black holes and neutron and quark stars. On the other hand, brown dwarfs are different from white dwarfs because they have very low density. They are comprised mostly of gas and are frequently difficult to tell apart from large planets.

Q   The author uses "black holes" as an example of

    Ⓐ objects similar to neutron and quark stars

    Ⓑ objects with a denser mass than a white dwarf

    Ⓒ objects that are much smaller than white dwarfs

    Ⓓ objects that are created by white dwarfs

Spider Sociality

Spiders are predatory animals. In many cases, the female eats the male after mating. Some types of female spiders are also known to eat their own babies. Most spiders are solitary creatures, but a few species that build webs live together in large colonies. Although they show social behavior, they are not as well evolved as social insects such as bees and ants. The most social species are probably *Anelosimus eximius*. They can form colonies consisting of up to fifty thousand individuals. Many spiders only live one or two years. But it is common for tarantulas to live around twenty years.

06-04

Q The author uses "tarantulas" as an example of

Ⓐ spiders that typically eat their young

Ⓑ spiders that live by themselves

Ⓒ socially evolved spiders

Ⓓ spiders that live relatively long lives

Handicrafts

Handicrafts are useful and attractive devices. They are usually made by hand, but sometimes simple tools are used. The term is usually applied to traditional ways of making goods. The unique style of the items is important. Such items often have cultural and religious meanings. Items made by mass production or machines are not handicrafts. Handcrafted items are intended to be used and worn. This is what makes them different from decorative arts and crafts. They have a purpose beyond being simple decorations. Handicrafts are usually thought of as more traditional works. They are created as a part of daily life.

06-05

Q The author discusses "Handicrafts" in the passage in order to

Ⓐ explain how they are made

Ⓑ mention some specific kinds of them

Ⓒ describe how much they cost

Ⓓ note how long it takes to make them

Exercises with Mid-Length Passages

Exercise 1 Read the following passage and answer the questions.

🕐 Time Limit: 2 min. 50 sec.

Neptune

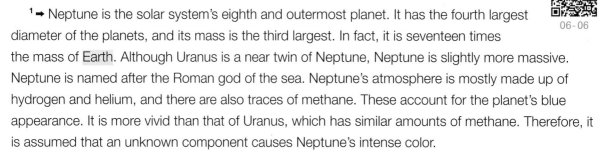
06-06

1 ➡ Neptune is the solar system's eighth and outermost planet. It has the fourth largest diameter of the planets, and its mass is the third largest. In fact, it is seventeen times the mass of Earth. Although Uranus is a near twin of Neptune, Neptune is slightly more massive. Neptune is named after the Roman god of the sea. Neptune's atmosphere is mostly made up of hydrogen and helium, and there are also traces of methane. These account for the planet's blue appearance. It is more vivid than that of Uranus, which has similar amounts of methane. Therefore, it is assumed that an unknown component causes Neptune's intense color.

2 ➡ This planet has many strange aspects that make it interesting to scientists. One such aspect is that Neptune has the strongest winds of any planet in the solar system. They can blow as fast as 2,500 kilometers per hour. There are also sixteen confirmed moons orbiting Neptune. Notable for its retrograde orbit is Triton. This moon has an atmosphere comprised of nitrogen and methane and is very cold.

The temperature at the top of Neptune's clouds remains around –210 degrees Celsius, making it one of the coldest planets in the solar system. This coldness is caused by Neptune's great distance from the sun. The temperature at the center of the planet is about 7,000 degrees Celsius due to extremely hot gases and rock in its core. This is hotter than the surface of the sun. But the planet's outermost layers are extremely cold.

4 ➡ The *Voyager 2* probe flew by Neptune in 1989 and discovered a region called the Great Dark Spot. This spot was viewed on its southern hemisphere and is comparable to the Great Red Spot on Jupiter. Additionally, faint rings have been detected around the planet. These are much smaller than Saturn's rings. These rings were discovered by Edward Guinan's research team. They were at first thought to be incomplete, fading out before they rounded the planet. But *Voyager 2* disproved this belief with photos of complete rings.

📖 **Words & Phrases**

outermost [adj] furthest from the center
component [n] a part of a whole of something
vivid [adj] very bright
notable [adj] important or interesting; noteworthy
retrograde [adj] moving backward
region [n] an area
detect [v] to discover; to notice

1   According to paragraph 1, which of the following is true of Neptune?

    Ⓐ It has the fifth largest diameter of the planets in the solar system.

    Ⓑ It was discovered by people who lived in ancient Rome.

    Ⓒ It has a blue appearance that is similar to that of Saturn.

    Ⓓ It has a very cold atmosphere containing hydrogen, helium, and methane.

2   According to paragraph 2, which of the following is NOT true of Neptune?

    Ⓐ No other planet in the solar system has stronger winds.

    Ⓑ One of its moons has an atmosphere with oxygen and nitrogen.

    Ⓒ Its moon Triton has a retrograde orbit.

    Ⓓ There are sixteen moons known to be orbiting it.

3   In paragraph 1, why does the author mention "Earth"?

    Ⓐ To explain how it was given its name

    Ⓑ To describe how large it is in diameter

    Ⓒ To point out its relative nearness to Neptune

    Ⓓ To compare its mass with that of Neptune

4   The author discusses "*Voyager 2*" in paragraph 4 in order to

    Ⓐ point out when it was first launched from Earth

    Ⓑ describe the types of pictures it took of Neptune

    Ⓒ focus on some information it learned about Neptune

    Ⓓ claim that Neptune was the last planet it visited

✎ **Summary Note** Fill in the blanks with the appropriate words.

Neptune

* Core temperature: ❶ _____
* Eighth and outermost planet in solar system
* Fourth largest diameter of all planets in solar system
* Atmosphere of ❷ _____
* Strongest winds of any planet in solar system
* Orbited by ❸ _____

🕐 Time Limit: 2 min. 50 sec.

The Metaphysics of Aristotle

06-07

1 ➡ Aristotle was one of the most influential thinkers of all time. In an age before science and technology existed, he created many fields of study, one of which was metaphysics. He argued that the causes of all things could be understood by studying their beginnings. He claimed that people have scientific knowledge when they know the cause of something. To know something's existence is to know the reason for its existence. He was the first to set the guidelines for all later causal theories. According to Aristotle's theory, all the causes may fall into several groups.

2 ➡ He defined causes by placing them in four major divisions. The material cause is the way something comes into existence from the combination of its parts. An example of this is a cheeseburger. It is assembled from meat, bread, and cheese. Alone, these do not make a cheeseburger, but together, they are the cause of its existence. The formal cause tells what a thing is. For example, the formal cause of a flood is an overabundance of water. The efficient cause describes the reason for a change. An example of this is that a fire was burning, but it was put out by rain, which caused it to end. The final cause is the reason that something is done. For instance, a country may go to war to protect its borders, which is the cause of the war.

3 ➡ The concept of substance is also examined in the metaphysics of Aristotle. He concludes that a particular substance is a combination of both matter and form. He goes on to define the five major elements. He named fire, which is hot and dry, and earth, which is cold and dry. Air is hot and wet while water is cold and wet. Finally, he named aether, the divine substance that makes up the heavenly spheres and bodies. These classifications recorded by Aristotle paved the way for the modern physical sciences. One can imagine his work as the concrete foundation upon which the building of modern physics is constructed.

📖 **Words & Phrases**

influential adj important; authoritative
metaphysics n the theoretical philosophy of being and knowing
causal adj relating to the cause of something
overabundance n an excess
border n a line that separates two distinct areas

1 According to paragraph 1, Aristotle is important to science because
- Ⓐ he wrote a large number of books about it
- Ⓑ he trained many scientists at his academy
- Ⓒ he established many of its fields of study
- Ⓓ he conducted a large amount of scientific research

2 According to paragraph 3, which of the following is NOT true of the concept of substance?
- Ⓐ Matter and form combine to make something.
- Ⓑ Aristotle classified the elements of substance into five categories.
- Ⓒ The elements earth and air are defined as having opposite characteristics.
- Ⓓ Aether is the divine substance that makes clouds.

Mastering the Question Type

3 In paragraph 2, why does the author mention "a cheeseburger"?
- Ⓐ To explain the formal cause
- Ⓑ To exemplify the material cause
- Ⓒ To illustrate the efficient cause
- Ⓓ To introduce the final cause

4 In paragraph 3, the author uses "aether" as an example of
- Ⓐ matter that can be found in the atmosphere
- Ⓑ a substance found in abundance on the Earth
- Ⓒ an element that is both hot and wet
- Ⓓ a major element named by Aristotle

✎ **Summary Note** Fill in the blanks with the appropriate words.

Aristotle's Major Causal Division

❶ _____
- The way a thing comes into existence from the combination of its parts
- Ex. a cheeseburger caused by meat, bread, and cheese

❷ _____
- What a thing is
- Ex. a flood caused by an overabundance of water

❸ _____
- The reason for a change
- Ex. rain causes a fire that was burning to be put out

❹ _____
- The reason something is done
- Ex. the cause for a country to go to war to protect its borders

Exercise 3 Read the following passage and answer the questions.

⏱ Time Limit: 2 min. 40 sec.

Sequoyah

06-08

¹➡ Sequoyah was a Cherokee Native American also known as George Gist. His main skill was as a silversmith. But he is famous for inventing the Cherokee written language. This earned him a place of honor on the list of those who invented writing systems.

²➡ Sequoyah's exact place and date of birth are unknown. The reason is that no written records exist from that time. Guesswork by historians places his birth somewhere between 1760 and 1776. Places in Tennessee, Georgia, North Carolina, Alabama, and South Carolina have been claimed as his birthplace. James Mooney, a prominent historian of the Cherokee people, quotes a cousin who said that Sequoyah and his mother spent his early years in the village of Tuskegee, Tennessee.

The name Sequoyah comes from the Cherokee word meaning "hog." This nickname may be a reference to a childhood deformity, or it could refer to later injury that left him disabled. Sequoyah's father was either white or part white and part Native American. But Sequoyah could not speak English. This may be proof that he and his mother were abandoned by his father. Sequoyah moved to Willstown, Alabama, at some point in 1809. He established his trade as a silversmith there.

⁴➡ The white settlers' writing often impressed Sequoyah. He called papers with English written on them "talking leaves." Sequoyah began working on creating a system of writing for the Cherokee language around 1809. He created eighty-five characters to represent various syllables. It took Sequoyah twelve years to complete this work. Sequoyah then taught his daughter to read and write in the new system he had created. The locals were amazed by this. But the medicine men of the tribe said he was being controlled by evil spirits. So Sequoyah taught his system to a group of warriors. Then, the other people of the tribe accepted it. The Cherokee nation fully embraced the new system by 1823. It gave them a way to record their history for future generations.

📕 **Words & Phrases**

prominent adj well known; famous
reference n a mention; an allusion
deformity n an irregularity in the body of a living thing
disabled adj not having full use of one's body
represent v to show; to describe
embrace v to accept; to adopt

1 In paragraph 2, the author's description of Sequoyah mentions which of the following?

    Ⓐ His exact date of birth

    Ⓑ His acknowledged birthplace

    Ⓒ The place where he grew up

    Ⓓ The name of his cousin

2 In paragraph 4, all of the following questions are answered EXCEPT:

    Ⓐ What did the characters in Sequoyah's alphabet look like?

    Ⓑ When was Sequoyah's writing system accepted by the Cherokee nation?

    Ⓒ How long did Sequoyah work on creating his alphabet?

    Ⓓ What was the initial reaction of people to Sequoyah's new alphabet?

3 In paragraph 1, why does the author mention "George Gist"?

    Ⓐ To refer to the founder of the Cherokee nation

    Ⓑ To give another name for Sequoyah

    Ⓒ To provide the name of an historian

    Ⓓ To name Sequoyah's father

4 The author discusses "the medicine men of the tribe" in paragraph 4 in order to

    Ⓐ describe their feelings about Sequoyah's alphabet

    Ⓑ explain how they helped create the Cherokee alphabet

    Ⓒ stress their leadership role in the Cherokee nation

    Ⓓ provide their opinions about Sequoyah and his daughter

Summary Note Fill in the blanks with the appropriate words.

The Development of the Cherokee Writing System by Sequoyah

1809
- Begins working on system of writing for Cherokee language

❶ _____
- Finishes Cherokee language writing system
- Teaches
  ❷ _____
  to read and write with new system

1823
- Teaches respected
  ❸ _____
  to read and write with new system
- Writing system is finally embraced by Cherokee nation

⏱ Time Limit: 2 min. 40 sec.

The First Transcontinental Railroad

06-09

1 ➡ The first transcontinental railroad was constructed in the United States and ran across North America. It was begun and completed in the 1860s. It linked the railway network of the eastern United States with California. The famous Golden Spike event, a ceremony to open the railway, was held on May 9, 1869. This railway created a nationwide mode of travel and changed the population and the economy of the American West. It also completed the move away from wagon trains.

2 ➡ This railroad was agreed to be built by the Pacific Railway Act of 1862 and was heavily backed by the federal government. It was the victory of a decades-long effort to build such a line. It was one of the great achievements of Abraham Lincoln and was completed four years after his death. Building the railway took huge feats of engineering and labor. The tracks ran across the plains and high mountains. The railway was comprised of the Union Pacific Railroad and the Central Pacific Railroad. The two were privately built, but both were backed by the federal government. They led westward and eastward.

3 ➡ The building of the railroad was meant to bind the country together during the strife of the American Civil War. It filled the west with white settlers. This contributed to the decline of Native Americans in these areas. Most of the Union Pacific track was built by Irish laborers. Veterans of the Union and Confederate armies and Mormons also helped build the tracks. Most of the Central Pacific track was built by Chinese laborers. At first, Chinese people were thought to be too fragile to do this type of work. But later, more people were brought over from China. Most workers were paid between one and three dollars per day, but the Chinese workers received much less. Eventually, they went on strike, which earned them a small increase in salary.

📕 **Words & Phrases**

transcontinental [adj] crossing a continent
ceremony [n] an event held to mark a special occasion
mode [n] a method or type
decade [n] a period of ten years
feat [n] an effort
strike [n] an event in which workers do not work to express their dissatisfaction

1 According to paragraph 1, which of the following is true of the Golden Spike event?

Ⓐ It was the name of the first transcontinental railroad.

Ⓑ It took place in California to celebrate the opening of the local railway.

Ⓒ It required great amounts of engineering and labor.

Ⓓ It was a ceremony held in 1869.

2 According to paragraph 3, which of the following is NOT true of the transcontinental railroad?

Ⓐ Irish laborers laid much of the Union Pacific track.

Ⓑ People thought the Chinese lacked the strength for hard work.

Ⓒ Soldiers belonging to the Confederate army helped build the track.

Ⓓ Workers typically earned three dollars or less each day.

Mastering the Question Type

3 In paragraph 2, why does the author mention "the Pacific Railway Act of 1862"?

Ⓐ To criticize it for not ensuring that workers were paid properly

Ⓑ To explain how much money it provided for the transcontinental railroad

Ⓒ To name the Congressperson responsible for passing it

Ⓓ To note the start of the effort to build the transcontinental railroad

4 In paragraph 3, the author uses "Chinese people" as an example of

Ⓐ people who provided funding for the transcontinental railroad

Ⓑ travelers who made use of the transcontinental railroad

Ⓒ laborers who worked on constructing the transcontinental railroad

Ⓓ managers responsible for designing the transcontinental railroad

🖉 **Summary Note** Fill in the blanks with the appropriate words.

> **The First Transcontinental Railroad**
>
> Connected the east and west
> coasts of the United States

❶ _____

• Built mostly by ❷ _____,
  veterans of the Union and Confederate
  armies, and Mormons

❸ _____

• Built mostly by Chinese laborers

⏱ Time Limit: 2 min. 50 sec.

Mechanization

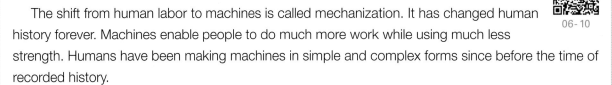

06- 10

The shift from human labor to machines is called mechanization. It has changed human history forever. Machines enable people to do much more work while using much less strength. Humans have been making machines in simple and complex forms since before the time of recorded history.

2 ➡ The simplest kind of machine is the lever, which can be a stick placed underneath an object and over a stone or other object. The object beneath the stick acts as the fulcrum, which gives the stick leverage. When a person presses down on the stick with force, it pushes off the fulcrum and lifts the object on top of the stick. In this act, the person's strength is amplified by the lever, enabling the person to employ less force to lift more weight. This is one of the guiding principles for the development of all machines. A machine does the work for a human, who exerts a minimal amount of force.

3 ➡ One important machine was the steam-powered lathe. This device increased the speed and the accuracy that metal and woodwork could be done. Another helpful machine was the steam engine, which made steamboats and steam-powered trains possible. This led to a revolution in transportation. The Colt revolver was the first machine pistol able to fire repeated shots. This device made warfare deadlier. The early twentieth century saw the mechanization of car assembly lines with the Ford system, which changed the way people worked and traveled.

The term *mechanization* is also used by military forces. This term refers to the use of tracked armored vehicles. The armored personnel carrier is one of these vehicles. It is utilized to move large numbers of troops around a battlefield very quickly and also protects them so that as few soldiers as possible are killed on the way into battle. In the past, many soldiers died before even going into battle. The mobility and fighting capability of soldiers are greatly increased by mechanization. In modern countries, all armed forces are supported by mechanized infantry.

📖 Words & Phrases

shift ⓝ a noticeable change
fulcrum ⓝ the point against which a lever is placed
leverage ⓝ the action of a lever
amplify ⓥ to make something or someone stronger
exert ⓥ to use force
lathe ⓝ a machine used in wood and metalworking
infantry ⓝ soldiers who fight on the ground

1   According to paragraph 2, which of the following is true of the level?

    Ⓐ It has few uses for humans.

    Ⓑ It was invented in modern times.

    Ⓒ It is a very simple machine.

    Ⓓ It can be operated with steam power.

2   According to paragraph 3, which of the following is NOT true of machines?

    Ⓐ The steam-powered lathe made metal and woodwork much faster.

    Ⓑ The steam engine completely changed transportation.

    Ⓒ The Colt revolver helped armies kill more soldiers.

    Ⓓ Car assembly lines relied on steam engines.

3   In paragraph 2, the author uses "the fulcrum" as an example of

    Ⓐ a simple machine

    Ⓑ a heavy weight

    Ⓒ a part of a lever

    Ⓓ a principle of a machine

4   The author discusses "The term *mechanization*" in paragraph 3 in order to

    Ⓐ provide examples of civilian uses

    Ⓑ stress its role in modern times

    Ⓒ describe its use by the military

    Ⓓ contrast its use by various inventors

✎ **Summary Note** Fill in the blanks with the appropriate words.

Mechanization

- The shift from human labor to machines ➡ more work with less strength
- ❶ _____ : the simplest machine
- Steam-powered lathe ➡ speedier and more accurate metal and woodwork
- Steam engine ➡ steamboats and steam-powered trains
- ❷ _____ : deadlier warfare
- ❸ _____ : changed the way people work and live

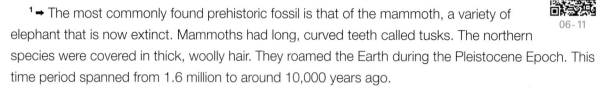

🕐 Time Limit: 2 min. 50 sec.

The Mammoth

06-11

1 ➡ The most commonly found prehistoric fossil is that of the mammoth, a variety of elephant that is now extinct. Mammoths had long, curved teeth called tusks. The northern species were covered in thick, woolly hair. They roamed the Earth during the Pleistocene Epoch. This time period spanned from 1.6 million to around 10,000 years ago.

2 ➡ The mammoth blood line is related most closely to the modern Asian elephant. The genes of the two African elephant varieties do not resemble those of the mammoth as closely. The Asian elephant and the mammoth's common ancestor split off from the African elephant's line. This divergence took place about 6.0 to 7.3 million years ago. Asian elephants and mammoths diverged from one another approximately half a million years later.

3 ➡ Scientists believe that the mammoth originally evolved in North Africa. Its origins stretch back some 4.8 million years. Bones that date back this far have been found in Chad, Libya, Morocco, and Tunisia. Sites in South Africa and Kenya have also revealed ancient remains that are thought to be the oldest of the species.

4 ➡ The African mammoth then migrated. The fossil record shows that it eventually reached Europe in the north. A new species, which is termed the southern mammoth, soon came about. This was the species that lived throughout Asia and Europe. Studies deduce that it then crossed the now-submerged Bering Strait Land Bridge. This was the frozen land structure that linked Asia and North America through present-day Siberia and Alaska. This brought the mammoth onto the North American continent.

5 ➡ Then around 700,000 years ago, the warm climate began to change. In Europe, Asia, and North America, the savannah plains became steppes which were colder and less fertile. The southern mammoths were the first variety of the species to die off. A new variety, the woolly mammoth, evolved 300,000 years ago. This beast was covered with a thick coat of woolly hair and could cope with the extreme cold of the ice ages.

📖 **Words & Phrases**

epoch ⓝ a period of history marked by notable events
diverge ⓥ to separate; to split
reveal ⓥ to uncover; to disclose
deduce ⓥ to infer
cope with phr to deal with; to survive

1 According to paragraph 1, which of the following is true of the mammoth?

Ⓐ It still exists on the Earth in some places today.

Ⓑ It was a type of elephant with tusks.

Ⓒ It evolved around 1.6 million years ago.

Ⓓ All species of it had thick, woolly hair.

2 In paragraphs 4 and 5, the author's description of the mammoth mentions all of the following EXCEPT:

Ⓐ How the woolly mammoth could survive the cold

Ⓑ Places where it migrated

Ⓒ Which species went extinct first

Ⓓ How many mammoths existed in the past

3 In paragraph 2, why does the author mention "the modern Asian elephant"?

Ⓐ To support the belief that it went extinct at the same time as the mammoth

Ⓑ To compare its physical features to those of the woolly mammoth

Ⓒ To define it as the closest genetic relative of the mammoth

Ⓓ To portray it as a common enemy of the mammoth

4 In paragraph 3, the author uses "Chad, Libya, Morocco, and Tunisia" as examples of

Ⓐ places where the mammoth never existed

Ⓑ places where remains of mammoths have been found

Ⓒ places that were too hot for the woolly mammoth

Ⓓ places where the oldest mammoths lived

Summary Note Fill in the blanks with the appropriate words.

6.0 - 7.3 million years ago
- Blood line diverged

500,000 years later
- Blood line diverged

❶ _____
- Mammoth blood line fully evolved
- Southern mammoth evolved

Mammoth Timeline

❷ _____
- Southern mammoth died off

300,000 years ago
- Woolly mammoth developed

❸ _____
- Woolly mammoth became extinct

Building Summary Skills

The following summaries are based on the long passages you worked on earlier. Complete each of them by filling in the blanks with suitable words or phrases.

Exercise 1   Neptune

a vivid blue appearance	*Voyager 2*	hot core temperature
the fourth largest	the outermost planet	

Neptune is _____ of the solar system and is _____ in diameter and the third largest in mass. Its atmosphere is composed mostly of gas, and it has _____. There are many interesting facts about the planet, such as its high winds, sixteen moons, and _____ that make it interesting to scientists. The only human probe ever to visit and collect information of Neptune was _____.

Exercise 2   The Metaphysics of Aristotle

the causes of things	four major categories	modern science
metaphysics	the substance of matter and form	

Aristotle was one of the most important thinkers of all time because he created many fields of study, one of which is _____. He created the guidelines for understanding _____, of which there are _____. He made many conclusions about _____ and also defined five major elements. His classifications laid important foundations for _____ that are used today.

Exercise 3   Sequoyah

eighty-five characters	a group of warriors	a system of writing
record their history	Cherokee Native American	

Sequoyah was a _____ who is famous for creating the first system of writing for the Cherokee people. His exact place and date of birth are unknown because his people lacked _____ for recording historical data. After twelve years of work, Sequoyah created a writing system for the Cherokee language that used _____ to represent the sounds of the language. This system was at first rejected by the Cherokee people, but they later accepted it after Sequoyah taught it to _____. This system gave the Cherokee people a way to _____ for future generations.

Exercise 4 The First Transcontinental Railroad

| the federal government | Ireland and China | Native Americans |
| President Abraham Lincoln | run across North America | |

The first transcontinental railroad to _____ was completed in
1869 and was commemorated with the famous Golden Spike event. The railroad was heavily
backed by _____ and stands as one of the great achievements of
_____. The building had many effects, such as bringing the Union states
together during the Civil War as well as leading to the decline of _____ in
the west by populating it with white settlers. Much of the railroad was built by immigrant laborers from
_____ as well as by veterans of the Union and Confederate armies and
Mormons.

Exercise 5 Mechanization

| the steam-powered lathe | warfare | mechanization |
| human history | the lever | |

_____ has been changed by the shift from human labor to
_____. A good example of a simple machine that relieves a
human of labor is _____. Some very important machines were
_____, steam-powered trains, the Colt revolver, and the mechanization of
car assembly lines. Military forces have also mechanized their forces, which results in many advantages in
_____.

Exercise 6 The Mammoth

| North Africa | climate changes | over seven million years ago |
| a prehistoric animal | the Asian variety of elephant | |

The mammoth was _____ that is now extinct and whose fossil remains are
the most commonly found. Mammoths are the most closely related to _____,
having genetically split off from the African varieties of elephant _____. Due
to fossil evidence, scientists believe the mammoth originally evolved in _____
and then migrated around the world, ending up in North America. Mammoths began to die off due to
_____ that began 700,000 years ago.

Sunspots

06-12

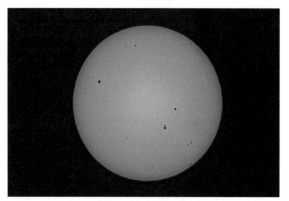

The sun and sunspots

[1] ➡ Sunspots are dark regions on the surface of the sun that have been a mystery to astronomers for thousands of years. Chinese astronomers made references to them in 28 B.C. They could see the largest spot groups, which were visible to them when the sun's glare was filtered by dust blown by the wind from the deserts of Central Asia. In the West, a large sunspot was viewed during the Middle Ages. But the mystery of this observation was not clearly understood until 1612 when Galileo explained it.

[2] ➡ Sunspots have been recorded by astronomers since the year 1700 A.D. Current scientists have been able to estimate the cycle of appearance of these sunspots back to 11,000 B.C. The most recent trend of sunspots rises upward from 1900 to the 1960s. The sun was similarly active over 8,000 years ago.

[3] ➡ Sunspot areas have lower temperatures than the areas around them and also show heightened magnetic activity. The normal convection of the sun is inhibited by this high level of magnetism. The result is the formation of low surface temperature areas. But these areas are still too bright to look at directly. Sunspots burn at temperatures as low as 4,000 degrees Kelvin. Meanwhile, the rest of the sun burns at 5,700 degrees Kelvin. This difference is the cause of the clearly visible dark spots. Similar spots observed on stars other than the sun are called starspots.

[4] ➡ It is not fully understood how sunspots come into being, but quite clear is the fact that they are the visible counterparts of magnetic flux tubes in the convective zone of the sun. The magnetic flux tubes get "wound up" by differential rotation. When the stress on the flux tubes reaches a certain limit, they curl up like a rubber band and puncture the sun's surface. At the puncture points, convection is inhibited. Then, energy flux from the sun's interior decreases, which drops the surface temperature.

The number of spots is connected to the intensity of solar radiation. This connection has been recorded since 1979, when satellite measurements of radiation became available. Since sunspots are dark, it would be natural to assume that more spots mean less solar radiation; however, the areas surrounding sunspots are brighter. The overall effect is that more spots cause the sun to burn brighter. This variation is too small to notice with the naked eye though. A period called the Maunder Minimum marked a time when there were hardly any sunspots on the sun. At this time, the Earth was believed to have cooled by up to one degree Celsius.

1   The word "it" in the passage refers to
    Ⓐ Central Asia
    Ⓑ the West
    Ⓒ a large sunspot
    Ⓓ the mystery of this observation

2   According to paragraph 1, which of the following is true of sunspots?
    Ⓐ Galileo saw them through filtered dust.
    Ⓑ Astronomers have puzzled over them for a long time.
    Ⓒ They were first observed during the Middle Ages.
    Ⓓ They are regions of the sun that have stopped burning.

3   In paragraph 2, the author's description of sunspots mentions all of the following EXCEPT:
    Ⓐ When scientists started recording them
    Ⓑ When there was a rise in the number of them
    Ⓒ What happened regarding them 8,000 years ago
    Ⓓ What causes them to form

4   According to paragraph 3, which of the following can be inferred about the normal convection of the sun?

  Ⓐ It is not inhibited by areas with low levels of magnetism.

  Ⓑ It is more inhibited by areas with low levels of magnetism.

  Ⓒ It is not affected by the level of magnetism at all.

  Ⓓ It makes sunspots larger due to low levels of magnetism.

5   The author discusses "magnetic flux tubes" in paragraph 4 in order to

  Ⓐ show that scientists do not fully understand sunspots

  Ⓑ support the theory that sunspots are areas of low magnetism

  Ⓒ explain that they are closely connected with sunspots

  Ⓓ prove that scientists fully understand sunspots

6   The word "inhibited" in the passage is closest in meaning to

  Ⓐ strengthened

  Ⓑ weakened

  Ⓒ destroyed

  Ⓓ increased

The Frequency of Thunderstorms

06-13

1 ➡ Thunderstorms are called electrical storms due to the presence of lightning and thunder. These violent storms are produced by cumulonimbus clouds, which can make heavy rain or hail. On rare occasions, these clouds can bring snow. This snow usually happens during the winter months and is called a thundersnow.

2 ➡ When heavy condensation occurs in an unstable atmosphere, thunderstorms form. This event produces a wide range of water droplets and ice crystals. A deep, upward motion supports it. It is often marked by the presence of three conditions. Sufficient moisture in the lower atmosphere is the first. This is reflected by high dewpoint temperatures. A large drop in air temperature and increasing height are the second. This is termed adiabatic lapse rate. A force such as mechanical turbulence is the third. This force occurs along the cold front and focuses its lift.

3 ➡ Thunderstorms happen all over the world and even hit the polar regions. The areas with the most storms are tropical rainforest areas. There, they may occur on a daily basis. Kampala and Tororo in Uganda are said to have more thunderstorms than any other region on the Earth. Bogor on the Indonesian island of Java is also said to be very thunderous. In temperate regions, thunderstorms happen mostly in spring. However, they can hit along with cold fronts at any time of year. Florida is the most thunderous region outside the tropics. Violent storms hit the southern and central regions of this state and often happen daily in the summer.

The United States gets the most powerful and dangerous storms. The most severe storms touch down in the Midwest and the southern states. These storms yield very large hail and also produce powerful tornadoes. Thunderstorms are uncommon on the west coast of the United States. But they do hit inland areas. Sacramento and the San Joaquin Valley of California get hit with thunderstorms. Storms in the Northwest take on similar patterns as those in the Midwest. But their frequency and severity are much less.

Early human civilizations were powerfully influenced by the frequency of thunderstorms. The Romans thought they were battles waged by Jupiter, who hurled lightning bolts forged by Vulcan. Any increase in the frequency of thunderstorms made the Romans anxious to the point that they would sacrifice many animals to appease the angry god. Native Americans believed these thunderstorms to be linked to servants of the Great Spirit. They also felt the frequency was linked to the spirit's anger. Nowadays, storm chasers head to the Great Plains of the United States and Canadian prairies every spring. They study storms and tornadoes visually and scientifically in the summer. For these thrill seekers, more frequent storms satisfy their desire for adventure.

7 According to paragraph 1, which of the following is true of thunderstorms?

Ⓐ They are created by thundersnows.

Ⓑ They are produced by heavy rain and hail.

Ⓒ They often cause snow to fall.

Ⓓ Cumulonimbus clouds cause them.

8 According to paragraph 2, which of the following is NOT true of the formation of thunderstorms?

Ⓐ They form only when the atmosphere is unstable.

Ⓑ They produce a large amount of condensation.

Ⓒ They are characterized by moisture in the lower atmosphere.

Ⓓ They may result in the air temperature rising.

9 In paragraph 3, why does the author mention "Florida"?

Ⓐ To claim that it is in a temperate region

Ⓑ To describe a place that sees few thunderstorms

Ⓒ To note that it gets more thunderstorms than most places

Ⓓ To prove that there are daily thunderstorms there all year long

10 According to paragraph 3, which of the following can be inferred about thunderstorms?

Ⓐ They occur in Europe.

Ⓑ They never occur in Australia.

Ⓒ They mostly occur in Uganda.

Ⓓ Florida has more thunderstorms than Bogor.

11 The word "severity" in the passage is closest in meaning to

(A) electricity

(B) intensity

(C) frequency

(D) danger

12 Which of the following best expresses the essential information in the highlighted sentence? *Incorrect* answer choices change the meaning in important ways or leave out essential information.

(A) The Romans thought Jupiter and Vulcan were fighting each other with lightning bolts.

(B) The Romans thought thunderstorms were caused by Jupiter throwing lightning bolts.

(C) The Romans wanted to fight gods such as Jupiter and Vulcan.

(D) The Romans thought Vulcan created thunderstorms with which to battle Jupiter.

Vocabulary Check-Up

A Choose the words with the closest meanings to the highlighted words.

1 He gave a very vivid description of the accident.

    Ⓐ graphic

    Ⓑ dim

    Ⓒ beautiful

    Ⓓ ugly

2 They were unable to detect the problem with the airplane's engine.

    Ⓐ fix

    Ⓑ hear

    Ⓒ find

    Ⓓ cause

3 He was a very prominent politician in the town.

    Ⓐ beloved

    Ⓑ famous

    Ⓒ disliked

    Ⓓ problematic

4 The teacher thought that it was an extraordinary feat for the student to win the contest.

    Ⓐ action

    Ⓑ foot

    Ⓒ trick

    Ⓓ hope

5 There was a shift in the mood of everybody in the room once the baby began to cry.

    Ⓐ change

    Ⓑ emergency

    Ⓒ break

    Ⓓ trouble

6 After completing a marathon, he was unable to exert any strength.

    Ⓐ make

    Ⓑ find

    Ⓒ use

    Ⓓ have

7 From the available evidence, the detective was able to deduce who had committed the crime.

    Ⓐ know

    Ⓑ infer

    Ⓒ imply

    Ⓓ decide

8 She was unable to cope with the cold weather and had to go inside.

    Ⓐ enjoy

    Ⓑ deal with

    Ⓒ accept

    Ⓓ block

B Match the words with the correct definitions.

1 spike •   • Ⓐ an amount that is too much of something

2 retrograde •   • Ⓑ to make something or someone stronger

3 deformity •   • Ⓒ a period of history marked by notable events

4 epoch •   • Ⓓ a large metal nail that is driven through something
                                            to fasten or hold it down

5 amplify •   • Ⓔ farthest from the center

6 infantry •   • Ⓕ a grassy plain in a tropical or subtropical region

7 savannah •   • Ⓖ soldiers who fight on the ground

8 metaphysics •   • Ⓗ moving backward

9 outermost •   • Ⓘ the theoretical philosophy of being and knowing

10 overabundance •   • Ⓙ an irregularity in the body of a living thing

07

Inference

Overview

Introduction

Inference questions ask you to understand an argument or an idea that is strongly suggested but not clearly mentioned in the passage. So you should use logical thinking in order to make an inference based on some information in the passage. You need to figure out the logical implications of the author's words as well as the surface meaning of those words.

Question Types

▷ Which of the following can be inferred about X?

▷ Which of the following can be inferred from paragraph X about Y?

▷ The author of the passage implies that

Useful Tips

■ Think logically to draw a reasonable conclusion from what is implied in the passage.

■ Remember that the correct answer does not contradict the main idea of the passage.

■ Do not choose an answer just because it is mentioned in the passage.

Q Which of the following can be inferred about the American women's suffrage movement?

   (A) Alice Paul led all of the major groups.

   (B) Its leading groups did not agree with each other's methods.

   (C) Most of the women in it used nonviolent methods.

   (D) Suffragists were unsuccessful at achieving most of their goals.

The American Women's Suffrage Movement

07-01

Suffrage is the civil right to vote and was the primary goal of many women's groups. In many Western democracies, suffrage was a major movement of the late nineteenth and early twentieth centuries. Suffragists protested strongly for many years, demanding equality with men and the right to vote. Alice Paul was a well-known suffragist who was also the leader of the American National Women's Party. There were two suffrage parties in the United States around this time. One was largely peaceful and tried to advance its cause in a peaceful manner. But the other was willing to commit acts of violence. This party once released 100 rats at a polling station in New Hampshire.

✅ Correct Answer

The passage mentions two leading suffrage parties in the United States. One was peaceful while the other group was aggressive. Each group adopted different methods to gain women's voting right. Therefore, the correct answer is (B).

Read the passages and answer the questions.

Inference questions ask you to understand an idea that is not explicitly stated in the passage. You need to use logical thinking to draw a correct conclusion from the author's words in the passage. Your conclusion must agree with the main idea of the passage.

Drill 1

Sponges

Sponges are animals that are members of the phylum Porifera. They are primitive filter feeders that dwell underwater. They pump water through their bodies to filter out particles of food matter. Sponges are among the simplest of animals. They have no true tissue and additionally lack muscles, nerves, and internal organs. There are over 5,000 known species of sponges. They can be found attached to surfaces of rocks and live in intertidal zones. They can be found at depths of 8,500 meters and deeper. The fossil record of sponges dates back to the Precambrian Era, but new species are still commonly discovered.

07-02

Q The author of the passage implies that
(A) most sponges live in the deep sea
(B) sponges are more complicated than people think
(C) sponges have been evolving since the Precambrian Era
(D) more species of sponges will be discovered in the future

Drill 2

Tenochtitlan

Tenochtitlan was the capital of the ancient Aztec Empire and is now the site of modern-day Mexico City. This ancient city was constructed over a series of islets in Lake Texcoco. The city plan was based on a symmetrical layout. Four sections divided the city into areas called *campans*. Canals interlaced the city and were useful for transportation. The city was built according to a fixed plan centering on the ritual precinct. There, the Great Pyramid of Tenochtitlan rose sixty meters above the city. Houses were made of wood and loam, and their roofs were made of reeds. But pyramids, temples, and palaces were generally made of stone.

07-03

Q According to the passage, it can be inferred that
(A) Tenochtitlan had an important role in the Aztec's religion
(B) the Aztecs constructed many large pyramids
(C) Tenochtitlan was built completely on the water
(D) many buildings from Tenochtitlan still exist today

Electronic Music

07-04

Electronic music is created through the use of devices, all of which run on electricity. They are systems that utilize low levels of power. Before electronic music, many composers wanted to use new technology. They tried to use this technology to make music. Several instruments were created that employed new electronic and mechanical designs. The Moog keyboard was one such instrument. It was used to record the music of Beethoven for the film *A Clockwork Orange* in the 1970s. This was one of the first electronic music recordings. In the late 1990s, electronic music split off into many genres. Its styles and substyles are too many to list. There are no strict rules for this kind of music.

Q The author of the passage implies that electronic music

Ⓐ is not as good as music created by real instruments

Ⓑ has greatly increased in popularity

Ⓒ should be used more often in movie soundtracks

Ⓓ needs to have strict rules

Ocean Currents

07-05

The constant motion of water flowing into the Earth's oceans creates ocean currents. Ocean currents can flow for thousands of kilometers. This happens more often in regions bordering an ocean. The Gulf Stream is one example. This current makes Northwest Europe much more temperate than other regions at the same latitude. The Hawaiian Islands are another example. The climate there is somewhat cooler than on other islands that occupy the same tropical latitudes. This is due to the California Current. Knowledge of surface ocean currents is important. The costs of shipping can be greatly reduced with such information. The reason is that the motion of currents helps move ships, so fuel costs can be greatly reduced.

Q Which of the following can be inferred about ocean currents?

Ⓐ They are typically found in the middle of the ocean.

Ⓑ They always make places cooler when they pass through.

Ⓒ They tend to move slower than other parts of the ocean.

Ⓓ They can change the temperature of areas they flow through.

Exercise 1 Read the following passage and answer the questions.

🕒 Time Limit: 2 min. 40 sec.

Bats and Echolocation

07-06

¹➡ Bats are mammals whose forelimbs have developed as wings. This makes them the only mammal in the world capable of flight. There are approximately 1,100 species of bats around the world.

²➡ Bats can be separated into two suborders: megabats and microbats. Not all megabats are larger than microbats. There are two major differences between these two kinds of bats. Microbats use echolocation to direct themselves. They also use this ability to find food. Megabats do not have this ability though. Instead, they have a claw on their second toe and forelimb. Microbats do not have this claw. Megabats are known to eat fruit, nectar, and pollen. Microbats eat insects, blood from larger animals, small mammals, and fish. The echolocation used by microbats is a form of biological sonar also used by dolphins and whales.

³➡ Echolocation is the process by which animals emit calls in the area around themselves. They listen to the echoes that return from various objects in the area. They then use these echoes to locate, range, and identify objects. Ranging is done by measuring the time delay between the animal's vocals and the echo's return. Microbats use their ears to perform this task.

⁴➡ In 1794, a scientist conducted a series of experiments on bats. He concluded that they navigated through their sense of hearing. But the scientific community rejected his findings. In 1938, another scientist described the ultrasound echolocation used by bats. Microbats use echolocation to navigate and forage in total darkness. They emerge from their caves or roosts as the sun sets and forage for insects at night. Their ability allows them to occupy a special niche. This is the time where there are many insects. They come out at night since there are often fewer predators active. There is much less competition for food at this time as well as fewer species that may prey on the bats themselves.

📖 **Words & Phrases**

separated adj divided
emit v to send out
range v to determine how far away something is
forage v to search for food
predator n an animal that hunts other animals

1 According to paragraph 1, which of the following is true of bats?

Ⓐ They have wings as well as a long tail.

Ⓑ They resemble birds but lack feathers.

Ⓒ They are the only mammals capable of flying.

Ⓓ There are fewer than 1,000 species of them.

2 According to paragraphs 2 and 3, which of the following is NOT true of microbats?

Ⓐ They use their ears to perform echolocation.

Ⓑ They feed on fruit, nectar, and pollen.

Ⓒ They are not always smaller than megabats.

Ⓓ They use a process that whales do as well.

3 Which of the following can be inferred from paragraph 2 about bats?

Ⓐ There are a number of different kinds of bats.

Ⓑ The wings of microbats and megabats look the same.

Ⓒ They all rely upon echolocation to find their food.

Ⓓ Some microbats are larger than megabats.

4 According to paragraph 4, which of the following can be inferred about research on bats?

Ⓐ It has been conducted for centuries.

Ⓑ It must always be done at night.

Ⓒ Scientists must do more experiments on them.

Ⓓ It is mostly incorrect.

✎ **Summary Note** Fill in the blanks with the appropriate words.

> **Megabats & Microbats**

Megabats
- Eat fruit, nectar, and pollen
- Have a ❶ _____ on their legs

Microbats
- Rely on ❷ _____
- Eat mostly insects, fish, and animals
- Hunt at ❸ _____

🕐 Time Limit: 3 min.

Modernism

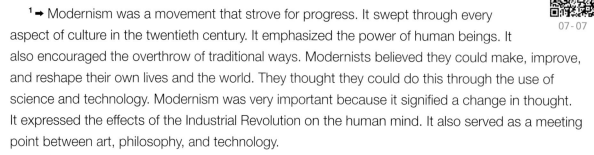

07-07

1 ➡ Modernism was a movement that strove for progress. It swept through every aspect of culture in the twentieth century. It emphasized the power of human beings. It also encouraged the overthrow of traditional ways. Modernists believed they could make, improve, and reshape their own lives and the world. They thought they could do this through the use of science and technology. Modernism was very important because it signified a change in thought. It expressed the effects of the Industrial Revolution on the human mind. It also served as a meeting point between art, philosophy, and technology.

2 ➡ The history of modernism consists of a series of movements. The members of these groups wanted to create progress. This began with painters in France in the mid-1800s. Some of the first were Impressionist painters such as Eduard Manet and Claude Monet. These painters showed that humans do not see the subject of a painting but rather the light and the shading that carries images to their eyes. Another early modernist was Gustave Eiffel. His Eiffel Tower changed people's ideas of architecture and its possibilities.

However, one major problem of modernists is that they often disclaimed the authenticity of other modernists. These conflicts usually occurred over relative issues. They would argue over who used a style first or whose style was more derivative of another popular modernist. These arguments often had no resolution. They only served to waste time and energy.

4 ➡ Some historians divide the twentieth century into modern and post-modern periods. They claim that the post-modernists used modernist styles and principles in consumer products. These styles showed up in many commercial products. Post-modern styles were used on record album cover art, postcards, and even the graphic designs of the signs for the London Underground. But others see the modernists and the post-modernists as parts of the same group. The goal is always to find anything that was holding back progress. Whatever was found to be the cause was then replaced. It was replaced with a new way of reaching the same end. Since this way was new, it was thought to be better.

📖 **Words & Phrases**

emphasize Ⓥ to stress the importance of something
signify Ⓥ to represent or symbolize something
disclaim Ⓥ to reject
resolution Ⓝ a solution; an answer
skeptically adv doubtfully

General Comprehension

1 According to paragraph 1, which of the following is true of modernists?

    Ⓐ They built on tradition to create progress.

    Ⓑ They believed in the potential of modern science.

    Ⓒ They looked at everything innocently.

    Ⓓ They usually got along well with one another.

2 According to paragraph 4, which of the following is NOT true of post-modernists?

    Ⓐ They created commercial products with modernist styles and principles.

    Ⓑ Record cover art is a common post-modernist product.

    Ⓒ The signs for the London Underground are post-modern designs.

    Ⓓ The twentieth century is divided into pre-modern and post-modern periods.

Mastering the Question Type

3 In paragraph 1, the author implies that modernism

    Ⓐ was independent of other disciplines

    Ⓑ was not particularly important

    Ⓒ was a reaction to the Industrial Revolution

    Ⓓ relied heavily upon philosophy

4 According to paragraph 2, what can be inferred about Eduard Manet?

    Ⓐ He preferred architecture to painting.

    Ⓑ He recognized the importance of light in painting.

    Ⓒ He tried to paint humans as they are seen.

    Ⓓ He was friends with Gustave Eiffel.

🖉 **Summary Note** Fill in the blanks with the appropriate words.

Was a change in thought

Looked at things
❷ _____

Emphasized
❶ _____ over
the traditional

Modernism

Sometimes followers had big arguments

Began with people who wanted to see progress

Eduard Manet, Claude Monet, and ❸ _____

Read the following passage and answer the questions.

Musical Theater

07-08

1 → Musical theater is a form of entertainment that tells stories through songs, words, and dancing. The history of this form goes back several thousand years. Some of the first musicals were developed in ancient India and Greece. The Greeks added music and dances to their popular stage plays, and some great Greek playwrights were even known to compose their own music to accompany their plays.

2 → Hundreds of years later, in 3 B.C., this form reemerged. The Roman comic writer Plautus added songs, dances, and orchestrations to his plays. To make their dance steps loud enough to be heard by audiences in large open theaters, actors put metal chips on their shoes. These were the earliest form of tap shoes. During the Middle Ages, plays became a method for the Church to spread its teachings as the liturgy was taught through religious dramas set to chants. These plays were so popular that they became a form of entertainment separate from the Church. In them, prose dialogs and liturgical chants alternated to keep audiences interested.

3 → These forms continued developing in the Renaissance and formed an Italian tradition. Silly clowns acted their way through stories known by common people. This comic entertainment form was known as opera buffa. This new tradition carried over to France in the 1600s. There, the great writer Moliere was able to convert some of his comedies into musicals which were accompanied by music written by Jean Baptiste Lully.

4 → This form of entertainment spread between countries in Europe and kept changing. In Germany and Britain, the 1700s saw the rise of two different forms of musical theater. The first was the ballad opera. The writers of this dramatic form of theater borrowed popular songs of the day and rewrote the lyrics to fit their needs. But comic operas were different in that they had original scores and plot lines full of romance.

📖 Words & Phrases

playwright Ⓝ a person who creates or writes plays
liturgy Ⓝ a kind of religious ceremony
convert Ⓥ to change
lyric Ⓝ the words of a song
plot Ⓝ a story

1 According to paragraph 2, which of the following is true of musical theater?

Ⓒ Musical theater has existed only for hundreds of years in history.

Ⓑ The Romans were the first to use tap shoes.

Ⓔ During the Middle Ages, the church used musical theater to entertain followers.

Ⓕ Musical theater disappeared during the Renaissance.

2 According to paragraph 4, which of the following is NOT true of musical theater?

Ⓒ Germany and Britain developed numerous types of musical theater in the 1700s.

Ⓑ Writers of ballad operas used songs popular at the time.

Ⓔ Comic operas had original scores and romantic plots.

Ⓕ Musical theater changed as it moved from country to country.

3 According to paragraphs 1 and 2, which of the following can be inferred about musical theater?

Ⓒ People were enthusiastic about musical theater in ancient India.

Ⓑ Roman theater had tap dancing as its main component.

Ⓔ People did not perform musical theater for a long time in history.

Ⓕ There were typically small audiences for Roman theater performances.

4 In paragraph 3, the author implies that opera buffa

Ⓒ featured dramatic stories

Ⓑ was enjoyed by ordinary people

Ⓔ could last for several hours

Ⓕ had its origins in France

Summary Note Fill in the blanks with the appropriate words.

Music Theater

- Developed in ❶ _____
- Went through many different changes
- Was used by ❷ _____
- Developed as comedies during the Renaissance
- Became more dramatic in ❸ _____

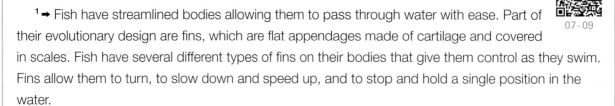

Fish Fins

07-09

1 ➡ Fish have streamlined bodies allowing them to pass through water with ease. Part of their evolutionary design are fins, which are flat appendages made of cartilage and covered in scales. Fish have several different types of fins on their bodies that give them control as they swim. Fins allow them to turn, to slow down and speed up, and to stop and hold a single position in the water.

2 ➡ The dorsal fins are located in the center of the back of a fish and can be pointed or blunt. A pointed dorsal fin increases a fish's speed while a blunt-shaped fin offers more control to small fish in strong waters. Fish can have up to three of these fins on their backs. They are supported by two kinds of cartilage rays: spiny and soft. A fin can contain either or both types of rays. Spiny rays sometimes also act as defensive weapons featuring sharp points or even poison tips.

3 ➡ The anal, pectoral, and pelvic fins of fish are additionally supported by spiny rays. These small fins give fish control over fine movements, allowing them to dart quickly with flashes of motion. By using these, fish can position themselves for feeding or in a school formation with other fish. The anal fin is located on the bottom of a fish behind its anus.

The pectoral fins are located on the sides of a fish, like wings on a bird. Their cartilage structure is parallel in design with the forelimbs of land creatures. The paired pelvic fins are located below and behind the pectoral fins and are parallel to the hindlimbs of land creatures. By flapping these fins, a fish gains momentum to propel itself through the water.

5 ➡ Tailfins, which allow for turning and thrusting through the water, are also referred to as caudal fins. Some fish able to swim very swiftly have a horizontal caudal keel fin just in front of the tailfin. This forms a kind of ridge on the tail that provides speed and stability.

📖 Words & Phrases

appendage ⓝ an external organ or part
cartilage ⓝ a substance in the body similar to bone but not as hard
dart ⓥ to move very quickly
thrust ⓥ to propel
horizontal 〔adj〕 flat; level
school ⓝ a large group of fish

1 According to paragraph 2, which of the following is NOT true of dorsal fins?
- (A) They are found on the back of a fish.
- (B) Small fish may have the blunt dorsal fins.
- (C) Fish can have a maximum of three dorsal fins.
- (D) They are mainly supported by spiny rays.

2 According to paragraph 5, which of the following is true of caudal fins?
- (A) They are made of bones and covered in scales.
- (B) They are similar to forelimbs on land animals.
- (C) They can be found on the sides of fish.
- (D) Some people call them tailfins.

3 Which of the following can be inferred from paragraph 1 about fish?
- (A) They have at least ten fins on their bodies.
- (B) They would drown without fins.
- (C) They are not constantly moving.
- (D) Every part of their bodies has fins.

4 In paragraph 3, the author implies that spiny rays
- (A) are helpful to various types of fins
- (B) can be larger than many fins
- (C) are only found on very large fish
- (D) let some fish move very quickly

✎ **Summary Note** Fill in the blanks with the appropriate words.

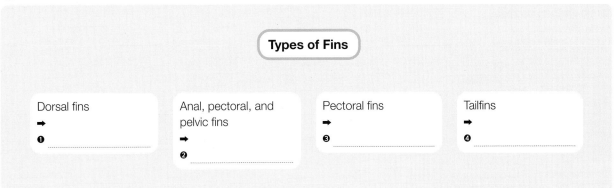

Types of Fins

Dorsal fins
➡
❶ _____

Anal, pectoral, and pelvic fins
➡
❷ _____

Pectoral fins
➡
❸ _____

Tailfins
➡
❹ _____

🕐 Time Limit: 3 min.

The Functions of the Human Brain

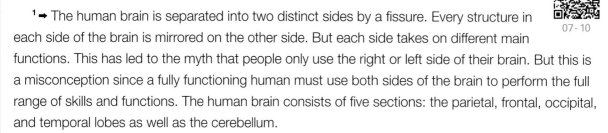

07-10

¹ ➡ The human brain is separated into two distinct sides by a fissure. Every structure in each side of the brain is mirrored on the other side. But each side takes on different main functions. This has led to the myth that people only use the right or left side of their brain. But this is a misconception since a fully functioning human must use both sides of the brain to perform the full range of skills and functions. The human brain consists of five sections: the parietal, frontal, occipital, and temporal lobes as well as the cerebellum.

² ➡ The parietal lobe is the part of the brain that combines sensory information from all of the body parts. It is also used to judge space through vision. This is the least understood region of the brain. The brain's frontal lobe contains the body's gyrus and motor cortex tissue. This is the material through which the brain can control the body's voluntary movements. The frontal lobe has also been found to govern impulse control, judgment, memory, language, motor functions, problem solving, sexual behavior, socialization, and spontaneity. A large number of the body's activities are managed through this lobe. The occipital lobe is the part of the brain which processes vision. It is the smallest of the four lobes and is located in the rear of the brain. Regions in this lobe process color, aspects of space, and motion perception. If this lobe is damaged, the ability to see can be diminished or lost.

³ ➡ The temporal lobes rest low on either side of the brain. This lobe contains the auditory cortex. It controls the body's ability to hear and process sound. It also controls high-level processing such as speech and manages such functions as comprehension, verbal memory, naming, and language. The cerebellum lies at the base of the brain at the point where it connects to the spinal cord. This region functions as the meeting point of sensory perception and muscle control through the nervous system.

📖 Words & Phrases

fissure n a crack; a break
misconception n misunderstanding
voluntary adj on purpose; willful
auditory adj of or related to hearing
spontaneity n unplanned, natural behavior
diminish v to decrease

1 According to paragraph 1, which of the following is true of the brain?

Ⓐ Humans cannot fully function without both sides of it.

Ⓑ One side of it makes up for any damage to the other side.

Ⓒ The right and left sides are asymmetrical in appearance.

Ⓓ Normal people use only one side of it.

2 In paragraph 2, the author's description of the frontal lobe mentions all of the following EXCEPT:

Ⓐ How large it is

Ⓑ What it controls

Ⓒ What it contains

Ⓓ Its importance to the body

3 In paragraph 2, the author implies that the parietal lobe

Ⓐ needs to be studied more

Ⓑ is the smallest part of the brain

Ⓒ is not particularly important

Ⓓ controls the most functions

4 According to paragraph 3, which of the following can be inferred about the temporal lobes?

Ⓐ They are connected directly to the spinal cord.

Ⓑ They are located in the direct center of the brain.

Ⓒ They can affect how people learn a foreign language.

Ⓓ They are more important to hearing than the ears are.

🖊 **Summary Note** Fill in the blanks with the appropriate words.

The Human Brain

Two separate halves
- Right brain & left brain
- Different main functions

Five different sections
- ❶ _____ : sensory information
- Frontal lobe ➡ the body's movements
- ❷ _____ : vision
- Temporal lobes ➡ hearing
- ❸ _____ : senses and muscles

Agriculture in America

07-11

1 ➡ America's foundation rests on its agriculture industry, which feeds everyone in the country and exports food to other countries around the world. However, this industry did not develop instantly. It took centuries of refinement to create an agricultural base capable of sustaining the entire population.

2 ➡ The westward movement of colonies spread farms across the United States. Settlers traveled to new areas and built farms. Their efforts created new towns and cities. The supply chains that led to these new areas became many of the roads that presently run throughout the nation. Wheat was often the crop of choice in northern regions because it is easily grown in cool places. This crop was usually planted in newly settled lands. These new areas were known as the "wheat frontier." This zone of newly settled wheat farms moved westward over the years. After these wheat farms moved on, farms with more diversified crops replaced them.

3 ➡ In the Midwest, the farming of corn and the raising of hogs were a common agricultural combination. Hogs and corn complement each other. The reason is that in the time before canals and railroads, it was difficult to get grain to market. So grain could be fed to hogs, which were much easier to transport. In the warm southern regions, cotton and herds of beef cattle were the most popular products because both flourish in the heat. Tobacco farming was also common in the South. Until the Civil War, this was done through the use of slave labor. Slaves were also used in agriculture in the Northeast up to the early 1800s. But slavery was prohibited in the Midwest by the Freedom Ordinance of 1787.

4 ➡ During the time of the Great Depression, huge areas of the Midwest were abandoned. This was due to the Dust Bowl storms that swept through the region and rendered the soil useless for farming. Many of these regions were then transformed into national forests. But in the 1940s, efforts to use these areas for farmland resumed in support of the World War II effort.

📖 **Words & Phrases**

agriculture ⓝ farming
diversified ⓐⓓⒿ having many different qualities
complement ⓥ to go well together
flourish ⓥ to grow well
render ⓥ to make

1 According to paragraph 2, why was wheat the crop of choice in northern regions?

Ⓐ It was complementary to hog farming.

Ⓑ It could be easily grown without much labor.

Ⓒ It was an ideal crop for newly settled land.

Ⓓ It grew well in regions with low temperatures.

2 According to paragraphs 3 and 4, which of the following is NOT true of American agriculture?

Ⓐ Corn and hogs were often raised together in the Midwest.

Ⓑ The farming of beef cattle was widely performed in the South.

Ⓒ Tobacco farming was done through the use of slave labor in the Northeast.

Ⓓ Many Midwestern people had to give up farming due to the Dust Bowl.

Mastering the Question Type

3 Which of the following can be inferred from paragraph 1 about agriculture?

Ⓐ It takes a long time to build up a country's agricultural base.

Ⓑ Agriculture is the most important industry in a country.

Ⓒ American agriculture cannot yet support the entire country.

Ⓓ America's economy is based on agriculture.

4 According to paragraph 3, which of the following can be inferred about the Midwest?

Ⓐ Hogs were the only animals raised there.

Ⓑ It did not have good transportation systems.

Ⓒ Many people there grew wheat instead of corn.

Ⓓ Trains were built there to transport hogs.

🖉 **Summary Note** Fill in the blanks with the appropriate words.

Agriculture in America

Was important to settlers moving across the country

❶ _____ were raised in the South

❷ _____ often raised wheat

❸ _____ were popular in the Midwest

Building Summary Skills

The following summaries are based on the long passages you worked on earlier. Complete each of them by filling in the blanks with suitable words or phrases.

Exercise 1   Bats and Echolocation

herbivorous	megabats and microbats	hunt at night
the only mammals	ultrasound echolocation	

Bats are _____ that can fly. There are two suborders of bats: _____. These bats are different from each other. Megabats have a claw on their legs and are typically _____. Microbats use _____ to get around and hunt insects, small animals, and fish. They usually _____ when there are a lot of insects, much less competition for food, and fewer enemies.

Exercise 2   Modernism

improve their lives	the twentieth century	modernism
useless arguments	Eduard Manet and Gustave Eiffel	

_____ was an important movement in _____. It encouraged people to forget about traditional ways and to try to _____. Its members, like _____, wanted to create progress. But sometimes they got into _____. Still, the effects of modernism can be seen everywhere today.

Exercise 3   Musical Theater

religious stories	ancient India and Greece	entertainment
comedies or dramas	musical theater productions	

The musical theater is a kind of _____ that is very old. It goes back to _____. Over the years, it has undergone a number of different changes. The Church in the Middle Ages used it to tell _____. Other cultures created _____ that were _____.

Exercise 4 Fish Fins

dart quickly through the water	dorsal fins	control its speed
on the sides of a fish	turn in the water	

An important evolutionary development in fish is their fins. _____ are located on the back and help a fish _____. The anal, pectoral, and pelvic fins let a fish _____. The pectoral fins _____ help give it momentum. And the tailfins let a fish _____.

Exercise 5 The Functions of the Human Brain

the body's movements	the occipital lobe	the left and the right
the senses and the muscles	the parietal lobe	

The human brain is divided into two separate halves: _____. There are five different sections: the parietal, frontal, occipital, and temporal lobes and the cerebellum. _____ controls sensory information while the frontal lobe controls _____. _____ controls vision, and the temporal lobe controls hearing. The cerebellum controls _____.

Exercise 6 Agriculture in America

moved west	crops and animals	farmed and unfarmed
agriculture	farming the land	

_____ has long been important in America for a number of reasons. As people _____ across the country, they lived by _____. Various regions in the country raised different _____, including cotton, wheat, corn, hogs, and cattle. Some parts of the country have gone back and forth between being _____.

Parasitism

07-12

A young cuckoo in the nest fed by its adoptive mother

[1] ➡ Parasitism describes a relationship between two life forms of different species. It occurs when one life form harms another. In order to be described as parasitism, the two life forms must live together for long periods of time. This does not include animals that hunt and eat their prey or the times when a mosquito feeds off its host.

There are two major kinds of parasites: endoparasites and ectoparasites. Endoparasites live inside the body of a host. An example is the hookworm, which lives in the stomach of a human or animal. Many of these parasites find their hosts by passive means. They live in the intestines. There, they lay eggs, which are passed through waste products into the outer environment. Once outside the host, they are picked up by other people or animals in unclean areas. Ectoparasites develop complex ways of finding new hosts. Some aquatic leeches locate their hosts through their motion sensors. They learn their host's identity through the temperature of the skin and chemical cues. Once they have confirmed that it is a desirable host, they use hook-like teeth to attach themselves. After they are attached, they dig through the skin and begin to suck blood.

[3] ➡ The way a parasite feeds off its host is also separated into two major distinctions, that of necrotrophs and biotrophs. Necrotrophs are parasites that consume a host's tissue until the host dies. In this relationship, the host usually dies from the loss of tissue or nutrients. Biotrophic parasites cannot survive on a host once it has died. They must keep their hosts alive to survive themselves. Many viruses are biotrophic. They use their host's genetic and cellular processes to multiply. Biotrophic parasitism is a very common way for life forms to survive. At least half of all animals go through a phase of their lives in which they are parasitic. This includes human fetuses during the time they live inside their mother's womb. This behavior is also common amongst plants and fungi. All free-living animals are host to one or more types of parasites.

Some parasites learn how to take advantage of the behavior of a social host species. Some parasitic insects like nematodes join ant or termite colonies. They are able to feed on colony members until the group is so weak that it ceases to exist. Meanwhile, many species of cuckoo bird steal food caught by their host. They even use other birds as babysitters by depositing their eggs in the nests of other birds. Cuckoo young are raised by the adults of the other bird species while adult cuckoos fend for themselves.

1 Which of the following can be inferred from paragraph 1 about parasites?
Ⓐ They can prosper while living alone.
Ⓑ All parasitic relationships involve one form harming another.
Ⓒ Many hunters have parasites.
Ⓓ Mosquitoes and hunters are advanced parasites.

2 The word "confirmed" is closest in meaning to
Ⓐ verified
Ⓑ requested
Ⓒ assumed
Ⓓ denied

3 The word "they" in the passage refers to
Ⓐ some aquatic leeches
Ⓑ their motion sensors
Ⓒ chemical cues
Ⓓ hook-like teeth

4 According to paragraph 3, which of the following is NOT true of parasites?

    Ⓐ They can be found in all animals.

    Ⓑ Almost all animals are parasites.

    Ⓒ Some of them kill their hosts.

    Ⓓ They feed in two main ways.

5 The phrase "fend for" is closest in meaning to

    Ⓐ hatch

    Ⓑ live amongst

    Ⓒ suffer

    Ⓓ take care of

6 **Directions:** Complete the table below to summarize the information about parasites. Match the appropriate statements to the characteristics of the parasites with which they are associated. *This question is worth 3 points.*

Answer Choices

1. They find new hosts in complex ways.
2. They find their hosts by passive means.
3. They feed off their hosts until the hosts die.
4. They live in the intestines of their hosts.
5. Leeches are one example of them.
6. The hookworm is a member of this group.
7. All free-living animals are this kind of parasite.

Endoparasites
-
-
-

Ectoparasites
-
-

Pangaea

07-13

¹→ Scientists in the early 1900s thought of the continental drift theory. They believed that a great number of years ago, the seven continents that exist today were a single giant continent. A scientist named Alfred Wegener named it Pangaea. The name Pangaea comes from the Greek phrase for "all Earth." This theory sparked a great controversy. The theory's timeline went against popular belief that the Earth was only a few thousand years old. People wanted to believe that God, not forces of nature, had created the Earth. Wegener argued in favor of the continental drift theory in 1920.

²→ Pangaea was a C-shaped landform that spread across the equator. The large body of water within the crescent was called the Tethys Sea. The vast ocean that flowed around the continent was called Panthalassa. The area of Pangaea would have been vast. Inland regions would have been extremely dry from a lack of water. Animals could migrate freely from the North Pole to the South Pole. There were three major phases in the breakup of Pangaea. It is believed to have begun breaking up about 180 million years ago (mya). This happened in the Jurassic Period. Over many millions of years, it broke into the seven continents presently existing.

The first phase of the breakup began about 180 mya. This change started when a large fault line ruptured. Activity would have been initiated through earthquakes and volcanic eruptions. A rift was created through Pangaea that stretched from the Tethys Ocean to the east. This was located in the area between what is now North America and Africa. The first split created two smaller continents. The southern one is known as Gondwana while the northern one is called Laurasia. The second major phase in the breakup began about 150 to 140 mya. At this time, the minor continent of Gondwana broke into four landmasses. These became Africa, South America, India, and Australia. The third major and final phase of the breakup was about sixty to fifty-five mya. North America broke free from Eurasia. This opened up the Norwegian Sea.

But proponents of this theory argue that Pangaea was not the first giant continent. They have reconstructed several other continental phases by tracing back the Earth's geological history. The most recent continent before Pangea is named Pannotia. Scientists think it formed about 600 mya. They believe it divided again about fifty million years later. An even earlier continent has been named Rodinia. Scientists think it formed about 1,100 mya and then divided 750 million years later. The earliest possible giant continent is Columbia. Scientists think it existed between 1.8 and 1.5 billion years ago.

7 The word "controversy" in the passage is closest in meaning to

Ⓐ debate

Ⓑ anger

Ⓒ research

Ⓓ interest

8 According to paragraph 1, what can be inferred about continental drift?

Ⓐ It was caused by Alfred Wegener.

Ⓑ It happened recently.

Ⓒ It was unknown before the 1900s.

Ⓓ It is named after a Greek phrase.

9 According to paragraph 2, what did Pangaea look like?

Ⓐ It looked like a sphere.

Ⓑ It resembled Africa.

Ⓒ It was shaped like Panthalassa.

Ⓓ It was shaped like a C.

10 The word "This" in the passage refers to

Ⓐ A rift

Ⓑ Pangaea

Ⓒ The Tethys Ocean

Ⓓ The east

11 The word "proponents" in the passage is closest in meaning to

Ⓐ creators

Ⓑ opponents

Ⓒ disputers

Ⓓ supporters

12 Directions: An introductory sentence for a brief summary of the passage is provided below. Complete the summary by selecting the THREE answer choices that express the most important ideas in the passage. Some answer choices do not belong in the summary because they express ideas that are not in the passage or are minor ideas in the passage. *This question is worth 2 points.*

There are various theories about the history of the Pangaea supercontinent.

-
-
-

Answer Choices

① Some people believe the Earth was created by God.

② Pangaea was an enormous continent that spread out over the equator.

③ One breakup of Pangaea occurred during the Jurassic Period.

④ Alfred Wegener was the first to call the giant continent Pangaea.

⑤ Pangaea is believed to have split into two smaller continents.

⑥ Scientists disagree over when Pangaea split up.

Vocabulary Check-Up

A Choose the words with the closest meanings to the highlighted words.

1 The small community began to flourish and became bigger.

- Ⓐ thrive
- Ⓑ build
- Ⓒ improve
- Ⓓ shrink

5 The politician tried to convert people to think the same way he did.

- Ⓐ change
- Ⓑ direct
- Ⓒ frighten
- Ⓓ encourage

2 The workers abandoned the factory because it was too old and dangerous.

- Ⓐ repaired
- Ⓑ sold
- Ⓒ left
- Ⓓ fixed

6 Mary looked at John skeptically when he told her the news.

- Ⓐ happily
- Ⓑ angrily
- Ⓒ sadly
- Ⓓ doubtfully

3 The two parties came to a resolution on the contract.

- Ⓐ disagreement
- Ⓑ solution
- Ⓒ promise
- Ⓓ problem

7 Lions are some of the top predators in Africa.

- Ⓐ animals
- Ⓑ hunters
- Ⓒ insects
- Ⓓ killers

4 The earthquake caused a fissure to appear in the ground.

- Ⓐ hole
- Ⓑ crack
- Ⓒ weakness
- Ⓓ ditch

8 The professor's explanation was beyond our comprehension.

- Ⓐ ability
- Ⓑ experience
- Ⓒ memories
- Ⓓ understanding

B **Match the words with the correct definitions.**

1 mammal   •   • Ⓐ a person who creates or writes plays

2 cartilage   •   • Ⓑ of or related to hearing

3 school   •   • Ⓒ to stress the importance of something

4 emphasize   •   • Ⓓ a warm-blooded species of animal

5 conclude   •   • Ⓔ to move very quickly or suddenly

6 diversified   •   • Ⓕ a substance in the body similar to bone but not as hard

7 dart   •   • Ⓖ a kind of religious ceremony

8 auditory   •   • Ⓗ having many different qualities

9 playwright   •   • Ⓘ a large group of fish

10 liturgy   •   • Ⓙ to determine; to reach an opinion about something

Overview

Introduction

Insert Text questions ask you to determine where the best place for a given sentence would be in the passage. In this type of question, you will see four black squares appearing in one paragraph. In either case, you need to understand the logical stream of the passage and focus on any grammatical connections between sentences, such as conjunctions, pronouns, demonstratives, and repeated words or phrases.

Question Types

▷ Look at the four squares [■] that indicate where the following sentence could be added to the passage.

[a sentence to be inserted into the passage]

Where would the sentence best fit?

Click on a square [■] to add the sentence to the passage.

Useful Tips

■ Put the sentence next to each square to see how it reads there.

■ Try to pay attention to the logical connections between sentences.

■ Be familiar with connecting words such as *on the other hand, for example, on the contrary, similarly, in contrast, furthermore, therefore, in other words, as a result,* and *finally.*

08-01

Q Look at the four squares [■] that indicate where the following sentence could be added to the passage.

It greatly increased astronomers' knowledge of the planet.

Where would the sentence best fit?

Uranus

Uranus is the seventh farthest planet from the sun and has an orbit between those of Saturn and Neptune. It is the third largest planet by diameter and has the fourth largest mass of any planet in the solar system. Uranus is named after the Greek god of the sky, who also created all of the other gods. **1** The only spacecraft to have visited the planet is NASA's *Voyager 2*. **2** *Voyager 2* was launched in 1977. **3** This unmanned probe made its closest approach to Uranus on January 24, 1986. **4** It then continued to Neptune. Uranus is the first planet discovered in modern times. It is also the first planet to be found by using the technology of a telescope. Before this, all of the other planets were discovered by the naked eye.

 **Correct Answer**

The new sentence notes that it increased the knowledge astronomers have of the planet. The "It" in the sentence refers to *Voyager 2*. So the new sentence should go in the place where **2** is.

Read the passages and answer the questions.

Skill & Tip

Insert Text questions ask you where the best place for a given sentence would be in the passage. You should understand the logical flow of the information in the passage. It is helpful to check out pronouns, linking words, demonstratives, and repeated words and phrases.

Drill 1

Molecules

A molecule is a group of two or more atoms held together by bonds. These substances are never divisible into smaller fractions of the same substance. A molecule is considered the smallest particle of a substance. **1** In this state, it still holds its composition and chemical properties. **2** It is better to consider that many substances are composed of networks of atoms or ions. **3** Scientists think of them this way instead of as molecular units. **4** The idea of molecules was first stated in 1811. It was thought up by a scientist named Avogadro.

08-02

Q Look at the three squares [■] that indicate where the following sentence could be added to the passage.

This makes the concept easier to understand.

Where would the sentence best fit?

Drill 2

Eclipse

The word *eclipse* comes from the Greek word for "to vanish." It is an astronomical event that takes place when one celestial object enters the shadow of another. **1** The term is most often used to describe a solar eclipse, which is when the moon's shadow passes over the Earth's surface. **2** There is also a lunar eclipse, which is when the moon enters the Earth's shadow. **3** It may refer to events outside the Earth-moon system and can be used to describe a planet passing through the shadow cast by one of its moons. **4** It could be a moon passing into the shadow cast by the planet it orbits, or it could even be a moon going into the shadow of another moon.

08-03

Q Look at the three squares [■] that indicate where the following sentence could be added to the passage.

However, there are also eclipses throughout the solar system.

Where would the sentence best fit?

Jazz

08-04

Jazz is a musical art form that comes from the United States. It was first played in New Orleans around the start of the twentieth century. Its roots come from African-American music. **1** It was later combined with Western music techniques and theory. **2** Jazz employs blue notes, swing, call and response, and improvisation. **3** After beginning in African-American communities, these styles spread throughout the United States in the 1920s. **4** They influenced many other musical styles. The instruments used in marching and dance bands at the turn of the century became the basic instruments of jazz. Bass, reeds, and drums were used with the Western 12-tone scale. Where or who the word *jazz* came from is uncertain.

Q Look at the three squares [■] that indicate where the following sentence could be added to the passage.

But it has many other influences.

Where would the sentence best fit?

Sophocles

08-05

Sophocles was one of the three great tragic playwrights in ancient Greece. One document recorded that he wrote 123 plays, and he also won more first prizes in dramatic competitions than any other playwright. Submissions to dramatic festivals included four plays. **1** Three were tragedies, and the final one was called a satyr play. **2** He also placed second in all the other competitions he entered. **3** He won his first victory in 468 B.C. although scholars now think this may not have been the first time that he competed. **4** Only seven of Sophocles' tragedies have survived in their complete form. The most famous of these are the three plays concerning Oedipus and Antigone, which are known as the *Oedipus Cycle*.

Q Look at the three squares [■] that indicate where the following sentence could be added to the passage.

It was a more comical entry and not a drama.

Where would the sentence best fit?

Exercises with Mid-Length Passages

Exercise 1 Read the following passage and answer the questions.

🕐 Time Limit: 3 min. 10 sec.

The Observatories at Mauna Kea

08-06

1 ➡ Eleven research stations sit atop Mauna Kea, which is the best place to look at stars in the world. *Mauna Kea* means "white mountain" in Hawaiian. This mountain is a dormant volcano on the island of Hawaii and is the highest point in the Pacific Basin. It is also the highest island-mountain in the world. Mauna Kea rises 9,750 meters above the ocean floor. It reaches an altitude of 4,205 meters above sea level. Its summit is above forty percent of the Earth's atmosphere.

2 ➡ The atmosphere above Mauna Kea is extremely dry and clear. This situation is due to a cloud layer that floats below the summit. These clouds isolate the upper atmosphere from the lower moist maritime air. This ensures that the summit skies are pure and dry. The clouds keep the air around the summit free from pollutants. This clarity makes Mauna Kea an ideal place for studying the stars. The number of clear nights is the highest in the world. The seeing factor is also very high here. Another factor that makes the stars so clear is the mountain's distance from city lights. A strong island-wide lighting law ensures an extremely dark sky.

The Astronomy Precinct on Mauna Kea was established in 1967. **A1** The Astronomy Precinct is located on protected land. **A2** This land is protected because of its sacred place in Hawaiian culture. **A3** This precinct was built to be an international center for astronomers to come to study stars. **A4** The dorms for scientists are located below the summit. They are at about 3,000 meters above sea level. A visitor information station is located a hundred meters farther below. Scientists and other visitors are told to stay at the lower level for thirty minutes. They do this to acclimate themselves before reaching the summit. This prevents altitude sickness.

4 ➡ Twelve telescopes are located at the summit. They are funded by companies and agencies of various nations. The University of Hawaii controls two telescopes. Two twin telescopes are run by the Keck Observatory. Subaru owns and administers another telescope. **B1** The United Kingdom has an infrared telescope while Canada and France have a joint-effort telescope. **B2** Another is owned and operated by California Technical University. **B3** The groups that make up this effort help mankind better understand outer space. **B4**

📖 Words & Phrases

dormant a not active
isolate v to separate something
seeing factor phr the ability to see something in a certain place
sacred adj holy
acclimate v to become used to something

1 According to paragraphs 1 and 2, which of the following is true of Mauna Kea?

    Ⓐ It is the highest point in the Atlantic Basin.

    Ⓑ The moist sea air makes it a good place for studying the stars.

    Ⓒ There are eleven telescopes located at its summit.

    Ⓓ Its summit skies are dry and pollutant-free.

2 According to paragraph 4, which of the following is NOT true of the telescopes at Mauna Kea?

    Ⓐ Two telescopes are run by the University of Hawaii.

    Ⓑ There is a telescope that is owned together by Canada and France.

    Ⓒ An infrared telescope is owned and administrated by Subaru.

    Ⓓ The Keck Observatory controls a couple of twin telescopes.

3 Look at the four squares [■] that indicate where the following sentence could be added to the passage.

It has been in existence for more than fifty years.

Where would the sentence best fit?

4 Look at the four squares [■] that indicate where the following sentence could be added to the passage.

The rest are operated by other various entities.

Where would the sentence best fit?

✎ **Summary Note** Fill in the blanks with the appropriate words.

(**Observatories at Mauna Kea**)

Located high on the mountain	❶ _____
❷ _____	❸ _____
Very dark in the area	Are run by different countries and corporations

🕒 Time Limit: 3 min. 20 sec.

The Element Naming Controversy

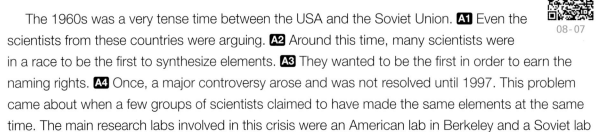
08-07

The 1960s was a very tense time between the USA and the Soviet Union. **A1** Even the scientists from these countries were arguing. **A2** Around this time, many scientists were in a race to be the first to synthesize elements. **A3** They wanted to be the first in order to earn the naming rights. **A4** Once, a major controversy arose and was not resolved until 1997. This problem came about when a few groups of scientists claimed to have made the same elements at the same time. The main research labs involved in this crisis were an American lab in Berkeley and a Soviet lab in Dubna.

2 ➡ When Soviet scientists synthesized element 104, they named it after Igor Kurchatov, the father of the Soviet atomic bomb. The Americans strongly objected to this. They did not want to refer to an element named after an enemy who created a weapon that could destroy their country. But they were called hypocrites since they had named an element after Einstein, who had also worked on atomic weapons.

3 ➡ Then, members of the International Union of Pure and Applied Chemistry objected to the American name for 106, seaborgium. The reason was that scientist Glenn T. Seaborg was still alive. **B1** He was handing out periodic tables signed with his name. **B2** This went against the union's rules. **B3** In 1994, the union proposed a new set of names. **B4** It was attempting to resolve the dispute. It tried to do this by replacing the name for 104 with a name after the Soviet Dubna Research Center. It also proposed not to name 106 after Seaborg.

4 ➡ This solution was objected to by the American Chemical Society. It felt that the society should have the right to propose the name for 106. The name should be whatever the society wanted. The international union decided that credit for element 106 should be shared between Berkeley and Dubna. But the Dubna group had not yet proposed a name. In addition, many American books already used the earlier names.

Finally, in 1997, the names were agreed on. But prior to his death in 1999, Seaborg was still disputing the name change for 105. It had been changed from hahnium to dubnium. He said that the Dubna group had not really discovered the element for which it had been credited. But the Dubna group refused to remove its claim. Some scientists at Berkeley still refer to 105 as hahnium.

📙 **Words & Phrases**

tense [adj] worrisome; nervous
synthesize [v] to create; to make
controversy [n] an argument; a dispute
hypocrite [n] a person who says one thing but does the opposite

1 According to paragraph 2, Igor Kurchatov was

    Ⓐ a coworker of Einstein's

    Ⓑ the discoverer of elements 104 and 106

    Ⓒ the creator of a Soviet atomic weapon

    Ⓓ an opponent of the name change for element 105

2 According to paragraphs 3 and 4, which of the following is NOT true of the controversy between the USA and the Soviet Union?

    Ⓐ The Americans did not want element 106 named after the Dubna Research Center.

    Ⓑ Some scientists objected to the American name for element 106.

    Ⓒ The American and Soviet labs were recommended to share credit for element 106.

    Ⓓ The Soviet group from Dubna offered some alternative names for elements 104 and 106.

3 Look at the four squares [■] that indicate where the following sentence could be added to the passage.

This was in the middle of the Cold War.

Where would the sentence best fit?

4 Look at the four squares [■] that indicate where the following sentence could be added to the passage.

So the union refused to allow this to be the element's name.

Where would the sentence best fit?

Summary Note Fill in the blanks with the appropriate words.

The Element Naming Controversy

1960s: American and Soviet scientists claimed to have discovered the same elements at the same time	Soviets wanted to name ❶ _____ after Igor Kurchatov ➡ Objection by Americans	Americans named ❷ _____ after Glenn T. Seaborg ➡ Canceled by the International Union of Pure and Applied Chemistry
1997: Decided that credit for element 106 would be shared by Soviets and Americans		1999: Seaborg still disputed the Soviet name for ❸ _____

Plato

08-08

¹ ➡ Plato was born during the golden age of ancient Greece. His real name was Aristocles, but historians think he was given the nickname Plato because of his broad stature. In Greek, *plato* means "broad." It is also said that Plato had a wide, broad forehead. His parents were influential citizens in Athens. **A1** Plato began his career as a student of Socrates. **A2** When his master died, Plato studied in Egypt and Italy. **A3** He then returned to Athens and started his own school. **A4** There, Plato tried to pass on the Socratic style of thinking. He guided his students toward the discovery of truth.

Plato tried to convey Socrates's teachings. He did this by writing down his master's conversations. These dialogues are the primary source of historical information about Socrates. Early dialogues look at a single issue. But they rarely come to conclusions about these issues. The *Euthyphro*, one of Plato's dialogues, points out a dilemma about any appeal to authority in defense of moral judgments. The *Apology* offers a description of the philosophical life. This description is presented as Socrates makes his own defense before an Athenian jury.

The dialogues of Plato use Socrates as a fictional character. But the middle dialogues express Plato's own views about philosophical issues. **B1** In the *Meno*, Plato reports the Socratic notion that no one knowingly does wrong. **B2** He also introduces the doctrine of recollection. **B3** This is done in an attempt to discover whether or not virtue can be taught. **B4** The *Phaedo* continues the development of Platonic notions. It presents the doctrine of the forms. These arguments show that the immortality of the human soul exists.

The masterpiece among the middle dialogues is the *Republic*. It begins with a conversation about the nature of justice. It then proceeds directly to an extended discussion of justice, wisdom, courage, and moderation. He looks at the ways in which these appear to individual human beings and in society as a whole. The allegory of the cave captures the powerful image of the possibilities for human life. The dialogue concludes with a review of various forms of government. In it is an explicit description of the ideal state. It is one in which only philosophers are fit to rule. There is also an attempt to show that justice is better than injustice.

📖 **Words & Phrases**

influential adj able to affect many things
convey v to transmit; to teach
doctrine n a form of teaching
immortality n everlasting life; eternity
allegory n a story that uses symbols to convey meaning

1 According to paragraph 1, which of the following is true of Plato?

    Ⓐ He was born in the golden age of ancient Rome.

    Ⓑ He started his own school to separate from Socrates's teachings.

    Ⓒ He studied in places other than Greece.

    Ⓓ He is best known for being the teacher of Socrates.

2 The word "one" in the passage refers to

    Ⓐ a review

    Ⓑ government

    Ⓒ an explicit description

    Ⓓ the ideal state

3 Look at the four squares [■] that indicate where the following sentence could be added to the passage.

He was greatly influenced by his master's thoughts and ideas.

Where would the sentence best fit?

4 Look at the four squares [■] that indicate where the following sentence could be added to the passage.

They do not depict Socrates as the main character.

Where would the sentence best fit?

Summary Note Fill in the blanks with the appropriate words.

Plato

- Real name: ❶ _____
- A student of Socrates
- Founded his own school
- Wrote many works of philosophy
- Used Socrates as a character in ❷ _____ ➡ the *Euthyphro* & the *Apology*
- Middle dialogues didn't use Socrates ➡ the *Meno* & the *Phaedo*
- ❸ _____ : the greatest middle dialogue

🕐 Time Limit: 2 min. 40 sec.

Loie Fuller

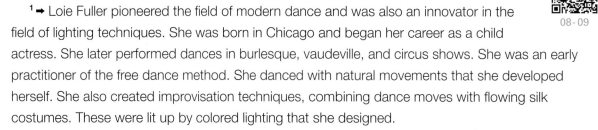
08-09

¹ ➡ Loie Fuller pioneered the field of modern dance and was also an innovator in the field of lighting techniques. She was born in Chicago and began her career as a child actress. She later performed dances in burlesque, vaudeville, and circus shows. She was an early practitioner of the free dance method. She danced with natural movements that she developed herself. She also created improvisation techniques, combining dance moves with flowing silk costumes. These were lit up by colored lighting that she designed.

² ➡ Fuller became famous in the United States. She was known for works such as the Serpentine Dance. **A1** But she felt unhappy that she was not taken seriously by the public. **A2** She felt they still saw her as an actress. **A3** The people of Paris received her warmly. **A4** She remained in France to continue her work. She was a regular performer at the Folies Bergere. There, she performed such works as the Fire Dance. She became the embodiment of the Art Nouveau movement.

Many French artists and scientists were attracted to Fuller's groundbreaking work. Her fans included greats such as Jules Cheret, Henri de Toulouse-Lautrec, and Marie Curie. **B1** Fuller also filed many patents related to stage lighting. **B2** This included chemical compounds for creating color gel. **B3** She was even a member of the French Astronomical Society. **B4**

Fuller arranged many tours of Europe for early modern dancers. She was known as the first American modern dancer to perform in Europe. She also introduced Isadora Duncan to the audiences of Paris. She is famous for causing modern dance to be accepted as a serious art form.

Fuller returned to the United States occasionally. She came back to stage performances by her students, who were called the Fullerets or Muses. But she was in Paris at the end of her life. Breast cancer took her in 1928. She was cremated, and her ashes were buried in Paris.

📖 Words & Phrases

pioneer ⓥ to be the leader in something
improvisation ⓝ creativeness; the act of creating new things
embodiment ⓝ an ideal; a perfect model
groundbreaking ⓐⓓⓙ new; innovative
cremate ⓥ to burn a dead body to turn it into ashes

1 According to paragraph 1, which of the following is NOT true of Loie Fuller?
  Ⓐ She created many techniques for stage lighting.
  Ⓑ She danced with unnatural movements.
  Ⓒ She used to dance while wearing silk outfits.
  Ⓓ She started out as a child actress.

2 According to paragraph 2, Loie Fuller was not happy because
  Ⓐ she felt unappreciated as a dancer in the United States
  Ⓑ not many French people were attracted to her work
  Ⓒ she had to perform dances in vaudeville
  Ⓓ her Serpentine Dance was severely criticized

3 Look at the four squares [■] that indicate where the following sentence could be added to the passage.
  However, she felt different in Europe.
  Where would the sentence best fit?

4 Look at the four squares [■] that indicate where the following sentence could be added to the passage.
  But she also had many fans who were just regular people.
  Where would the sentence best fit?

Summary Note Fill in the blanks with the appropriate words.

Loie Fuller

Was a pioneer in the field of ❶ _____

Created many ❷ _____

Became famous in America and Europe

Had many famous ❸ _____

Helped other dancers tour through Europe

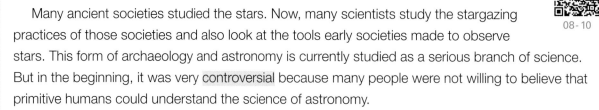

Exercise 5 Read the following passage and answer the questions.

🕐 Time Limit: 2 min. 50 sec.

Ancient Astronomy

Many ancient societies studied the stars. Now, many scientists study the stargazing practices of those societies and also look at the tools early societies made to observe stars. This form of archaeology and astronomy is currently studied as a serious branch of science. But in the beginning, it was very controversial because many people were not willing to believe that primitive humans could understand the science of astronomy.

At the end of the nineteenth century, astronomer Norman Lockyer was active in this field. **A1** His studies covered Stonehenge and the pyramids of Egypt. **A2** He tried to bring this field into wide acceptance as a serious branch of science. **A3** But on the British Isles, interest in this field waned. **A4** Then, in the 1960s, there was new interest that was revived by astronomer Gerald Hawkins. He proposed that Stonehenge was a Stone Age computer. This unique concept made people interested again.

Around the same time, an engineer named Alexander Thom published the results of a study. His article stated that there was a widespread practice of accurate astronomy in ancient cultures. He claimed that Stonehenge was used on the British Isles during ancient times. **B1** Hawkins's claims were widely dismissed. **B2** But Thom's analysis posed a problem. **B3** This challenged the historical academic beliefs at that time. **B4** A reevaluation of Thom's fieldwork by Clive Ruggles tried to show that his claims were not supportable. But there was evidence of widespread interest in astronomy at these Stone Age sites.

⁴➡ Only one scientist, Euan Mackie, agreed that Thom's theories needed to be tested. This man went to the Kintraw standing stone site in Argyllshire in 1970 and 1971. There, he checked whether Thom's prediction about the accuracy of the observation platform above the stone was correct. He checked the alignment of the platform with the stone and found that it was correct. Thom's conclusions were accepted and published in new prehistoric accounts of Britain. These persistent scientists proved that people from long ago did study the stars with accurate results. History was changed forever.

📙 **Words & Phrases**

primitive (adj) early in the history of the world or of humankind
revive (v) to renew
wane (v) to decrease; to become less
pose (v) to present
alignment (n) the placement of something
persistent (adj) constant; unrelenting

212 Part **II**

1 The word "controversial" in the passage is closest in meaning to

    Ⓐ skeptical

    Ⓑ intellectual

    Ⓒ fascinating

    Ⓓ divisive

2 According to paragraph 4, which of the following is NOT true of Euan Mackie?

    Ⓐ In 1970 and 1971, he went to the Kintraw standing stone site.

    Ⓑ He checked on the accuracy of an observation platform above a stone.

    Ⓒ He found that the alignment of a platform was not correct.

    Ⓓ The results of his test helped rewrite early history.

3 Look at the four squares [■] that indicate where the following sentence could be added to the passage.

People simply were not interested in studying it.

Where would the sentence best fit?

4 Look at the four squares [■] that indicate where the following sentence could be added to the passage.

His conclusions startled many people.

Where would the sentence best fit?

✎ **Summary Note** Fill in the blanks with the appropriate words.

Ancient Astronomy

❶ _____
- Studied it seriously
- Studied Stonehenge and the pyramids of Egypt

❷ _____
- Studied Stonehenge
- Revived people's interest in ancient astronomy

❸ _____
- Studied Stonehenge
- Challenged the historical academic beliefs

❹ _____
- Proved Thom's conclusions were correct

A serious branch of science now

⏱ Time Limit: 3 min. 10 sec.

Melvin Calvin

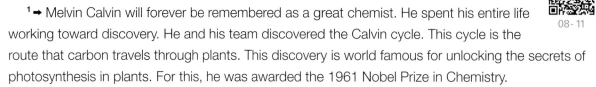

08- 11

¹ ➡ Melvin Calvin will forever be remembered as a great chemist. He spent his entire life working toward discovery. He and his team discovered the Calvin cycle. This cycle is the route that carbon travels through plants. This discovery is world famous for unlocking the secrets of photosynthesis in plants. For this, he was awarded the 1961 Nobel Prize in Chemistry.

² ➡ Calvin joined the faculty at the University of California at Berkeley in 1937. **A1** By 1963, he was named Professor of Molecular Biology. **A2** He was the founder and director of the Chemical Biodynamics Lab. **A3** He was also the associate director of the Berkeley Radiation Lab at the same time. **A4**

According to legend, on the day of the Japanese surrender in World War II, the head of the laboratory came to Calvin. He said, "Now is the time to do something useful with radioactive carbon." He was referring to the isotope of carbon that had been discovered in 1940. This isotope had been used in the atomic bombs that were dropped on Japan. In response, Calvin organized a team of Rad Lab researchers. They began to study the photosynthetic process. This is the process by which green plants convert energy from the sun into chemical energy.

Calvin and his team used the carbon-14 isotope as a tracer. They mapped the complete route that carbon travels through a plant. The path starts from its intake as carbon dioxide from the air to the point where it changes into carbohydrates. **B1** In doing so, the Calvin group showed that sunlight acts on the chlorophyll in a plant. **B2** It fuels the creation of organic compounds. **B3** Before this discovery, sunlight was believed to act only on the carbon dioxide within a plant. **B4**

Calvin's work led to a lifelong interest in energy production. He also spent many years testing the chemical evolution of life. He wrote a book on the subject that was published in 1969. Calvin actively pursued scientific research into his old age. He studied the use of oil-producing plants. He looked at them as renewable sources of energy. Calvin even analyzed moon rocks. He was a man who loved science. It was more important to him than the many awards he received.

📙 **Words & Phrases**

faculty Ⓝ all the teachers at a school
founder Ⓝ a person who establishes some kind of organization
organize Ⓥ to gather together; to form something
convert Ⓥ to change
pursue Ⓥ to chase after

1 According to paragraphs 1 and 2, which of the following is NOT true of Melvin Calvin?

    Ⓐ He won the Nobel Prize in 1961 for first discovering photosynthesis.

    Ⓑ He established the Chemical Biodynamics Lab at U.C. Berkeley in 1963.

    Ⓒ He studied the photosynthesis process of plants.

    Ⓓ He was employed as a professor at a university.

2 The word "pursued" in the passage is closest in meaning to

    Ⓐ widened

    Ⓑ accomplished

    Ⓒ continued

    Ⓓ followed

3 Look at the four squares [■] that indicate where the following sentence could be added to the passage.

He quickly became an important professor there.

Where would the sentence best fit?

4 Look at the four squares [■] that indicate where the following sentence could be added to the passage.

But now scientists understand this process much better.

Where would the sentence best fit?

✎ Summary Note Fill in the blanks with the appropriate words.

Won a Nobel Prize in Chemistry

Discovered ❶ _____

Discovered the secret of ❷ _____

Melvin Calvin

Was a member of the UC Berkeley faculty

Used ❸ _____ as a tracer

Mapped the route of carbon through plants

Building Summary Skills

The following summaries are based on the long passages you worked on earlier. Complete each of them by filling in the blanks with suitable words or phrases.

Exercise 1 The Observatories at Mauna Kea

Mauna Kea in Hawaii	twelve telescopes	the air quality
very dark and clear	1967	

There are many research stations located on _____. These observatories are located there because of _____ and the fact that the night skies are _____. The Astronomy Precinct there was established in _____. There are _____ located there that are run by different countries or corporations.

Exercise 2 The Element Naming Controversy

American scientists	in the 1960s	the Soviet name
naming controversies	the Unite States and the Soviet Union	

_____, tensions between _____ even caused problems between scientists. There were _____ over various elements that different laboratories created. The Americans objected to _____, and the Soviets objected to the American name. Finally, an agreement on the name was arrived at, but some _____ still use the old name.

Exercise 3 Plato

his early dialogues	Greek philosopher	the *Republic*
Plato's own thoughts	the Socratic method of philosophy	

Plato was a great _____ who lived in Athens and studied with Socrates. After Socrates died, Plato opened his own school and tried to imitate _____. Many of _____ looked at single issues but never came up with answers. His middle dialogues stopped using Socrates as a character and expressed _____. _____ was one of Plato's greatest works.

Exercise 4 Loie Fuller

modern dance	helped other artists	important French fans
improvisation	felt unappreciated	

Loie Fuller was a pioneer in the field of _____. She created many new dance movements through _____. She became famous in America, but she _____, so she moved to France, where she had many fans. She had many _____, including Jules Cheret, Henri de Toulouse-Lautrec, and Marie Curie. She toured Europe and also _____ do so.

Exercise 5 Ancient Astronomy

Alexander Thom	Stonehenge	the stargazing practices
Thom's conclusions	Norman Lockyer	

Nowadays, many scientists study _____ of ancient societies. _____ was an early scholar who looked into these practices. Gerald Hawkins also looked at _____ and noticed how it was connected to astronomy. Most people discounted Hawkins's work, but _____ produced new evidence to support it. Euan Mackie went to Stonehenge and proved that _____ were correct.

Exercise 6 Melvin Calvin

the secrets of photosynthesis	the Calvin cycle	a great chemist
the carbon-14 isotope	U.C. Berkeley	

Melvin Calvin was _____ who won a Nobel Prize. He discovered _____, which helped unlock _____. He worked at _____, where he was a professor. He used _____ to trace the route of carbon through the plant. He studied many different things through the course of his life.

The Potlatch Ceremony

08-12

¹➡ A potlatch was a religious ceremony held by some American Indian tribes. This ceremony was extremely important to their social structure. These tribes were from regions along the Pacific Northwest coast. These regions ranged from the United States to British Columbia, Canada. Some of the tribes were the Haida, the Nuxalk, the Salish, and the Tlingit.

The name *potlatch* is derived from the Chinook language. Every group that participated in the ceremony has a different way of saying it. The Chinook word sounds like the English words "pot" and "latch." But it has nothing to do with these things. Originally, the potlatch was held to commemorate important events. It could be the death of a highly respected person or a new child being born. Social ranks in American Indian societies were limited. So when a person changed his rank to a higher one, it had to be witnessed in order for people to accept it.

The potlatch took the form of a ceremonial feast. **1** It traditionally featured seal meat or salmon. **2** During the feast, relationships of hierarchy between groups were created and strengthened through the exchange of gifts, dance performances, and other ceremonies. **3** The host family made great efforts to demonstrate their wealth by giving away their possessions. **4** This prompted prominent guests to return the favor by holding their own potlatch ceremonies.

Before the arrival of the Europeans, potlatch gifts might be preserved food, boats, or human slaves. The influx of new sorts of goods such as blankets and copper caused a negative change in the potlatch in the late eighteenth and nineteenth centuries. Some groups used the potlatch as an arena for battle. At this arena, highly competitive contests of status took place. In some cases, gifts were destroyed after being received.

⁵➡ Potlatching was made illegal in Canada in 1885 and outlawed in the United States in the late nineteenth century because missionaries and government agents desired this. They thought it was a foolish custom. In their view, it was wasteful, unproductive, and bad for the people who did it. Despite the ban, potlatching continued secretly for many years. Years later, numerous tribes begged the government to repeal the ban. They compared the potlatch to Christmas. They said the potlatch was a feast where friends exchanged gifts, like Christmas. Potlatching became less of an issue in the twentieth century, so the ban was dropped.

Today, many ethnographers study the potlatch. They are fascinated by this festive event. The sponsors of a potlatch hand out many valuable items and earn prestige in return. This prestige increases with the richness of the potlatch.

1 In paragraph 1, which of the following tribes is NOT mentioned as practicing the potlatch?

(A) The Haida

(B) The Cherokee

(C) The Salish

(D) The Tlingit

2 The word "it" in the passage refers to

(A) the name *potlatch*

(B) every group

(C) the ceremony

(D) a different way

3 The word "witnessed" is closest in meaning to

(A) studied

(B) practiced

(C) enjoyed

(D) viewed

4 The word "influx" is closest in meaning to

(A) arrival

(B) export

(C) possibility

(D) interest

5 In paragraph 5, the author implies that the potlatch

Ⓐ was always a friendly occasion

Ⓑ was restarted by missionaries

Ⓒ is a tradition that continues today

Ⓓ stopped in Canada after 1885

6 Look at the four squares [■] that indicate where the following sentence could be added to the passage.

But there were also many other special foods.

Where would the sentence best fit?

Literary Criticism

08-13

Students around the world study great literature at school. But sometimes they need the help of experts to better understand what they have read. It is the job of literary critics to study and discuss the works of authors. They think about and decide what the author meant. This kind of work is based on literary theory. However, it is important to note that not all critics are theorists.

2 ➡ These days, literary criticism often comes in an essay or book format. Academic critics teach classes on this subject and also write their findings in academic journals. Ironically, their writings are sometimes longer than the books they are writing about. More popular critics have their work printed in magazines. Some popular magazines that print literary criticism are *The New York Times Book Review, The Nation,* and *The New Yorker.*

3 ➡ As long as literature has been around, there have been critics to discuss it. Aristotle and Plato wrote works that were highly critical of Greek poetry. **1** In the Middle Ages, classical critics focused on religious texts. **2** But around this time, it was dangerous to criticize the Holy Bible. **3** Critics' comments on holy books such as this were usually made with the official opinions of church leaders in mind. **4** During the Renaissance, many new ideas about writing were formed. These ideas about form and content led to a new group of critics. These critics claimed that writing was at the center of all culture. They claimed that poets and authors were protectors of a long literary tradition. Some of these noble poets began restoring great works of the past. One classic work that was rescued was Aristotle's *Poetics.*

4 ➡ More new ideas about literature were brought to the field of literary criticism by the British Romantic movement. These critics of the early nineteenth century thought that the object of writing did not always have to be beautiful. They had no problem with it being common, gritty, or ugly. They thought that the act of creating literature itself could raise a common subject. The highest level a work could attain was that of the "sublime." Then, in the early twentieth century, a new group of critics began to publish their work. These critics, who came from Britain and America, called their work the New Criticism. These critics thought the most important way to study writing was to read it very closely. They encouraged people to focus on the words themselves. This method is still a very popular way of reading.

The New Criticism was the most common method of studying writing until the late 1960s. Around this time, university professors became highly influenced by Continental Philosophy. This new way of thinking led to a new style of criticism. Both this philosophy and method of criticism focus on the form of information. They look very closely at the way it is presented. The critic must go through a process of taking a work apart. This process is called deconstruction.

7 The word "Ironically" in the passage is closest in meaning to

    Ⓐ Amusingly

    Ⓑ Groundlessly

    Ⓒ Hypocritically

    Ⓓ Scarily

8 According to paragraph 2, where is literary criticism commonly found?

    Ⓐ On television

    Ⓑ In books

    Ⓒ In magazines

    Ⓓ In newspapers

9 The author discusses "Aristotle's *Poetics*" in paragraph 3 in order to

    Ⓐ describe a work of criticism from the Renaissance

    Ⓑ exemplify ancient criticism

    Ⓒ illustrate the restoration efforts of critics in the Renaissance

    Ⓓ highlight an important work of criticism

10 According to paragraph 4, what can be inferred about the New Criticism?

    Ⓐ It was founded by a single individual.

    Ⓑ It was based on the works of Plato and Aristotle.

    Ⓒ It was similar to deconstruction.

    Ⓓ It did not form in only one place.

11 The word "it" in the passage refers to

Ⓐ this philosophy

Ⓑ criticism

Ⓒ the form

Ⓓ information

12 Look at the four squares [■] that indicate where the following sentence could be added to the passage.

So these people were taking a big risk by engaging in criticism.

Where would the sentence best fit?

Vocabulary Check-Up

A Choose the words with the closest meanings to the highlighted words.

1 The engineer created a very primitive model for his experiment.

 Ⓐ excessive
 Ⓑ basic
 Ⓒ advanced
 Ⓓ complicated

2 The founder of the organization finally retired after thirty-five years as president.

 Ⓐ president
 Ⓑ manager
 Ⓒ creator
 Ⓓ discoverer

3 Bill Gates is a pioneer in the field of software.

 Ⓐ engineer
 Ⓑ discoverer
 Ⓒ opportunist
 Ⓓ leader

4 Everyone looked tense while they were waiting for the results to come in.

 Ⓐ upset
 Ⓑ disinterested
 Ⓒ nervous
 Ⓓ pleased

5 The question poses many potential problems for people.

 Ⓐ presents
 Ⓑ answers
 Ⓒ asks
 Ⓓ manages

6 Jerusalem is a sacred city to people of several different religions.

 Ⓐ holy
 Ⓑ fascinating
 Ⓒ capital
 Ⓓ popular

7 We did not dispute what the man accused us of doing.

 Ⓐ agree with
 Ⓑ do
 Ⓒ argue
 Ⓓ state

8 Donald made it to the summit of the mountain after climbing for several hours.

 Ⓐ base
 Ⓑ bottom
 Ⓒ cliff
 Ⓓ top

B **Match the words with the correct definitions.**

1 alignment   •

2 improvisation   •

3 seeing factor   •

4 hypocrite   •

5 dilemma   •

6 allegory   •

7 archaeology   •

8 legend   •

9 acclimate   •

10 synthesize   •

• Ⓐ the ability to see something in a certain place

• Ⓑ a very big problem

• Ⓒ a story from the past that may or may not be true

• Ⓓ the placement of something

• Ⓔ to create; to make

• Ⓕ creativeness; the act of creating new things

• Ⓖ the science of studying ancient cultures

• Ⓗ to become used to something

• Ⓘ a person who says one thing but does the opposite

• Ⓙ a story that uses symbols to convey meaning

PART III

Reading to Learn

In this part, the reading comprehension questions include prose summary and fill in a table. The learning objectives of these comprehension questions are to recognize the major ideas and the relative importance of information in a passage and to organize the main ideas and other important information in the appropriate categories.

Overview

Introduction

In Prose Summary questions, you will be asked to complete a summary chart by choosing the three most important ideas from six choices. In order to solve Prose Summary questions, you should understand the overall theme of the passage and distinguish important ideas from minor ones in the passage.

Question Types

▷ **Directions:** An introductory sentence for a brief summary of the passage is provided below. Complete the summary by selecting the THREE answer choices that express important ideas in the passage. Some sentences do not belong in the summary because they express ideas that are not presented in the passage or are minor ideas in the passage. *This question is worth 2 points.*

> Drag your answer choices to the spaces where they belong.
> To remove an answer choice, click on it. To review the passage, click on **View Text**.

[An introductory sentence]

-
-
-

Answer Choices

1 XXXXXXXXXXXXXXXXXXXXXX   4 XXXXXXXXXXXXXXXXXXXXXX

2 XXXXXXXXXXXXXXXXXXXXXX   5 XXXXXXXXXXXXXXXXXXXXXX

3 XXXXXXXXXXXXXXXXXXXXXX   6 XXXXXXXXXXXXXXXXXXXXXX

Useful Tips

- Try to understand the overall structure of the passage.
- Write down the main idea of each paragraph on scratch paper.
- Distinguish major points from minor details in the passage.
- Incorrect answer choices usually deal with minor points of the passage or are not mentioned in the passage.

09-01

Pennsylvania's Coal

Coal is an enormous source of energy which countries have spent vast amounts of money getting at the coal they have. The eastern United States has a tradition of mining coal, such as the one that exists in Pennsylvania. It is the source of so much coal, but it is also the home of a great mining disaster.

There are two primary ways to get at coal in the ground. The first way is to dig a hole below the surface of the earth as miners make tunnels that can be miles long. The second way is called open mining, during which miners remove the surface of the earth over a huge area until they reach what they want.

Centralia, Pennsylvania, has very high-quality coal which burns hotter than most other kinds of coal, and numerous open mines are in that town. Sadly, the town garbage dump was near an old open mine pit which, in 1962, caught on fire and then additionally set the open mine on fire. The fire started burning underground, where it was impossible to put out. The fine quality of the coal made the disaster even worse. The fire has been burning underground for more than sixty years. No one knows how to stop it, and experts claim that it will burn for approximately 250 years.

Q   **Directions:** An introductory sentence for a brief summary of the passage is provided below. Complete the summary by selecting the THREE answer choices that express the most important ideas in the passage. Some answer choices do not belong in the summary because they express ideas that are not in the passage or are minor ideas in the passage. *This question is worth 2 points.*

Pennsylvania has a great mining tradition and a sad history.

-
-
-

Answer Choices

1 The town garbage dump was near an old, open mine.

2 The coal near a town caught fire and has been burning for decades.

3 The town of Centralia has many open mines.

4 Pennsylvania uses open mining to get coal from the ground.

5 The fire will burn for around 250 years.

6 There is high-quality coal in Pennsylvania.

✓ Correct Answer

Choices 2, 4, and 6 are correct because they represent major ideas in the passage: Pennsylvania's open mining and the long-lasting burning fire. Choices 1, 3, and 5 are just minor ideas.

Read the passages and answer the questions.

Skill & Tip

Prose Summary questions ask you to complete a summary chart with the most important ideas from the passage. The topic sentence will be given for the summary. You need to understand the overall theme of the passage first and then distinguish major points from minor ideas in the passage.

Drill 1

Portrait Painting

09-02

The painting of portraits is a kind of art whose intent is to show a visual image of the subject, which is usually a person. The portrait is expected to show the true form of the subject. Portraitists create their portraits for someone who hires and pays them. They are sometimes inspired by strong feelings they have for the subject. Self-portraits are pictures in which artists portray themselves. Portraits can show a subject's entire body, half of a person's body, or a bust, which covers from the shoulders to the top of the head. Animals, pets, and even houses are sometimes chosen to be subjects of portraits.

Q **Directions:** Complete the summary by selecting the TWO answer choices that express the most important ideas in the passage.

This passage discusses the characteristics of portrait painting.

-
-

Answer Choices

1 A portraitist is someone who paints portraits for money.

2 Portraits are created to show the true form of the subject.

3 Some people prefer self-portraits for the strong feelings they experience.

4 The subjects of portraits include humans, animals, and buildings.

5 A portrait of a bust shows the subject from the shoulders to the top of the head.

Flatworms

Flatworms are a group of simple life forms with very soft bodies and no spine. They are found in saltwater and freshwater environments as well as moist places. Most of them are free-living forms, but some species are parasitic and live on other animals. There are four classes of flatworm: Tematoda, Cestoda, Monogenea, and Turbellaria. A flatworm's soft body is ribbon shaped. Flatworms are the simplest animals with organs formed out of three germ layers. There are outer and inner layers and a middle layer between them. These worms have no true body cavity except for their gut. The insides of their bodies are filled with loosely spaced tissue.

09-03

Q **Directions:** Complete the summary by selecting the TWO answer choices that express the most important ideas in the passage.

Flatworms' bodies are very basic.

-
-

Answer Choices

1. Flatworms live in watery places.

2. Flatworms have ribbon-shaped soft bodies without spines.

3. Flatworms have three germ layers to develop a body cavity.

4. Flatworms are classified into four different kinds according to their size.

5. Flatworms cannot survive without a supply of nutrients from other animals.

Deltas

09-04

A delta is a landform that occurs where a river flows into an ocean, sea, desert, or lake. This flow builds a deltaic deposit in the outward direction of the flow. A delta is formed by sediment carried by a river. This sediment is deposited as the water current dissipates. Deltaic deposits of larger rivers that are heavy with sediment divide river channels into multiple streams. These streams divide and come together again to form a system of active and inactive channels. A deposit at the mouth of a river forms a shape that is roughly triangular. The blocking of the river mouth by silt causes the shape and the increased width at the base of the delta.

Q **Directions:** Complete the summary by selecting the TWO answer choices that express the most important ideas in the passage.

This passage describes how deltas are formed.

-
-

Answer Choices

1. Sediment carried by a river creates deltas.

2. Rivers are often divided into multiple streams.

3. Deltas are triangular in shape.

4. The mouth of a river is blocked by silt deposits.

5. Deltaic deposits build in the inward direction of a river flow.

Social Psychology

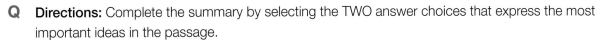

09-05

The field of social psychology is an ongoing study of how people behave in groups. It focuses on how they perceive, influence, and relate to others. Gordon Allport is credited with the classic definition of this study. He said it is an attempt to understand and explain how people are influenced by others. This can include their ways of dealing with the imagined or implied presence of other people. Much of the research done in this field is completed through the observation of small groups. These groups are assembled and given tasks to complete. Researchers observe the group interactions as they attempt to complete the assigned tasks.

Q **Directions:** Complete the summary by selecting the TWO answer choices that express the most important ideas in the passage.

Social psychology examines the group dynamics of people.

-
-

Answer Choices

[1] Social psychologists publish their research in various journals.

[2] Social psychology explains how people are influenced by others.

[3] Researchers often observe small groups of people doing tasks.

[4] Social psychology was first defined by Gordon Allport.

[5] Social psychology is a subfield of psychology and sociology.

Exercise 1 Read the following passage and answer the questions.

⏱ Time Limit: 2 min. 40 sec.

Estuaries

09-06

[1] ➡ An estuary forms at the tidal mouth of a river. It is a semi-enclosed coastal body of water that has a free-flowing connection to the open sea. The main feature of an estuary occurs within this connection when sea water mixes with fresh water. The combining of sea water and fresh water from a stream or river creates a supply of brackish water. A tide must be present to create motion at the point where the two waters meet. In seas without a tide, rivers naturally form deltas.

The tidal mouth of a river is the usual location of an estuary. An estuary typically contains many sediment deposits that consist of silt carried from runoff from the land. Estuaries occur more frequently on sunken coasts, where the land is situated lower because the sea level has risen. Valleys are flooded by this process, which creates forms such as rias and fjords. If there is a stream or river flowing into them, they can become estuaries.

Brackish water created in estuaries is not as salty as sea water. But it is saltier than fresh water. This kind of water allows estuaries to harbor thriving ecosystems. One of the best-known estuaries is the River Thames, which flows through London. It reaches the town of Teddington, a few miles west of London. This area marks the limit of the tidal part of the Thames. But as far west as Battersea, it is still a freshwater river.

The fauna in that part of the Thames consists mostly of freshwater species. There are many fish found there, such as roach, dace, carp, perch, and pike. Between Battersea and Gravesend, the Thames becomes brackish. A limited number of freshwater and marine species populate this area. The salinity increases a little further east, and marine species completely replace freshwater fish.

📖 Words & Phrases

sediment [n] dirt and silt from the bottom of a river
runoff [n] rainwater that forms a stream rather than going into the ground
sunken [adj] beneath the water level
brackish [adj] somewhat salty
thrive [v] to become successful or strong; to flourish
fauna [n] animals living in a particular area
populate [v] to live in a certain place

1 According to paragraph 1, a tide must be present at an estuary in order to

    Ⓐ build sediment deposits

    Ⓑ mix fresh and salty water into brackish water

    Ⓒ form a delta naturally

    Ⓓ maintain a thriving ecosystem

2 The word "harbor" in the passage is closest in meaning to

    Ⓐ contain

    Ⓑ hide

    Ⓒ destroy

    Ⓓ create

3 **Directions:** An introductory sentence for a brief summary of the passage is provided below. Complete the summary by selecting the THREE answer choices that express the most important ideas in the passage. Some answer choices do not belong in the summary because they express ideas that are not in the passage or are minor ideas in the passage.

An estuary has many different features.

    •

    •

    •

Answer Choices

① Freshwater species mostly live in estuaries.

② The River Thames is one of the most studied estuaries.

③ Estuaries have lots of sediment deposits.

④ Many different types of fish live in the River Thames.

⑤ Valleys can flood near sunken coasts.

⑥ Estuaries are a combination of fresh water and sea water.

🖉 **Summary Note** Fill in the blanks with the appropriate words.

Form at ❶ _____

Are a combination of ❷ _____

Estuaries   Have a lot of sediment deposits

Have mostly freshwater species

Can have ❸ _____ closer to the ocean

🕐 Time Limit: 3 min.

The Embryo

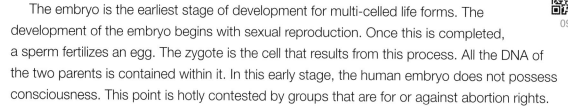

09-07

The embryo is the earliest stage of development for multi-celled life forms. The development of the embryo begins with sexual reproduction. Once this is completed, a sperm fertilizes an egg. The zygote is the cell that results from this process. All the DNA of the two parents is contained within it. In this early stage, the human embryo does not possess consciousness. This point is hotly contested by groups that are for or against abortion rights.

2 ➡ For human embryos, there are three major stages of development. From weeks one to four, the embryo begins to search for a place to attach to the wall of the uterus. It finds the right place and implants itself there. The mother and the embryo then start forming their connections. The umbilical cord forms during this time. During weeks five and six, the embryo puts out chemicals that cause the woman's menstrual cycle to cease. The brain begins to develop, and around the sixth week, brainwave activity begins. Additionally, the heart begins to beat around this time. Stubs where arms and legs will grow later become visible, and all of the main organs start developing. Between weeks seven and eight, the embryo's blood type is established, the embryo can move, and its eyes form. Most organs are fully developed or are in the process of developing. At the end of the eighth week, the embryonic stage ends, which marks the beginning of the fetal stage.

Much controversy and argumentation have revolved around the topic of human embryos. The question is at which point an embryo becomes a human with a consciousness and a soul. This question is central to the abortion issue in the United States. Many believe that the embryo is a human life and should be protected. They want abortion and scientific testing on embryos to be illegalized as a form of murder. But opponents believe that the embryo is merely undeveloped tissue and claim that women should be able to make their own decisions on whether or not to abort a human embryo before it enters the fetal stage.

📖 Words & Phrases

fertilize Ⓥ to make pregnant
consciousness Ⓝ awareness; realization
contest Ⓥ to dispute
abortion Ⓝ a surgical process that terminates the life of a fetus
illegalize Ⓥ to make something unlawful

1 The author discusses "human embryos" in paragraph 2 in order to

Ⓐ question the way that they form

Ⓑ describe how they develop over time

Ⓒ compare them with fetuses

Ⓓ explain how they are formed

2 The word "opponents" in the passage is closest in meaning to

Ⓐ allies

Ⓑ helpers

Ⓒ murderers

Ⓓ enemies

3 **Directions:** An introductory sentence for a brief summary of the passage is provided below. Complete the summary by selecting the THREE answer choices that express the most important ideas in the passage. Some answer choices do not belong in the summary because they express ideas that are not in the passage or are minor ideas in the passage.

The human embryo develops over the course of three stages.

-
-
-

Answer Choices

① Main organs, such as limbs and eyes, start developing relatively early.

② In the early stage, the embryo attaches itself to the mother's womb.

③ The question of when a fetus becomes a baby is important to the abortion issue.

④ The fetal stage begins as soon as the embryonic stage ends.

⑤ Before a baby is born, the eyes are fully developed.

⑥ The brain and the heart begin to activate in the middle stage.

Summary Note Fill in the blanks with the appropriate words.

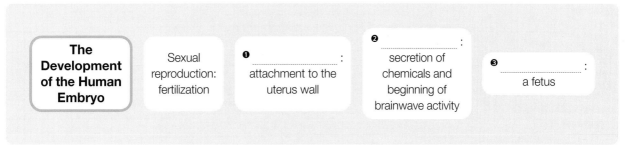

| The Development of the Human Embryo | Sexual reproduction: fertilization | ❶ _____ : attachment to the uterus wall | ❷ _____ : secretion of chemicals and beginning of brainwave activity | ❸ _____ : a fetus |

🕐 Time Limit: 2 min. 40 sec.

Johannes Gutenberg and Metal Type

09-08

Johannes Gutenberg was an inventor. He achieved fame for his invention of a printing press with movable type. His press had a type metal alloy, oil-based inks, and a mold for casting type. This invention led to the book becoming an item commonly used by regular people.

The exact origin of Gutenberg's first press is unknown. Tradition credits him with inventing movable type in Europe. It was an improvement on the block printing already in use there. By combining these components into a production system, he enabled the rapid printing of written materials, which led to an information explosion in across Renaissance Europe. Gutenberg moved from his native town of Mainz to Strasbourg around 1430. He began experimenting with metal type after he moved. He knew that wood-block type involved a great deal of time and expense to produce because everything had to be hand carved. Gutenberg concluded that metal type could be reproduced much more quickly since it could be done once a single mold had been fashioned.

In 1455, Gutenberg made a demonstration of his printing press by selling copies of a two-volume Bible for just 300 German florins each. This was the same amount of money as three year's wages for an average clerk, but it was much cheaper than a handwritten Bible. One of those books normally took a single monk twenty years to write by hand. Gutenberg had a partner named Johann Fust. The money Gutenberg earned from his press was not enough to repay Fust for his investment. Fust sued Gutenberg in court and won. The court's ruling bankrupted Gutenberg and also awarded control of the movable type and his printing equipment to Fust. Gutenberg ran a small print shop until shortly before his death. But Fust became the first printer to publish a book with his name on it.

📖 Words & Phrases

mold ⓝ a shape or form
fashion ⓥ to make or create
demonstration ⓝ a practical illustration of how something works
wage ⓝ the money one receives for work; a salary
ruling ⓝ a decision by an authority
award ⓥ to give on the basis of a legal decision

1 The word "fashioned" in the passage is closest in meaning to

Ⓐ planned

Ⓑ shaped

Ⓒ broken

Ⓓ decorated

2 The word "it" in the passage refers to

Ⓐ a small print shop

Ⓑ the first printer

Ⓒ a book

Ⓓ his name

Mastering the Question Type

3 **Directions:** An introductory sentence for a brief summary of the passage is provided below. Complete the summary by selecting the THREE answer choices that express the most important ideas in the passage. Some answer choices do not belong in the summary because they express ideas that are not in the passage or are minor ideas in the passage.

Gutenberg's press influenced printing practices and society in important ways.

-
-
-

Answer Choices

① Movable type was invented in 1455.

② Books became available to regular people because of the printing press.

③ It used to take a monk around twenty years to copy the entire Bible.

④ Johann Fust was Gutenberg's partner.

⑤ Metal type cut down on the amount of time and money spent on printing.

⑥ The circulation of information increased rapidly over a short period of time.

✎ **Summary Note** Fill in the blanks with the appropriate words.

Invented movable metal type, which was better than wooden blocks

Led to ❶ _____ in the Renaissance

Gutenberg's Printing Press

Printed Bibles at a lower cost than handwritten ones

Enabled regular people to ❷ _____

Johann Fust ❸ _____ Gutenberg for the right to the printing press

Gutenberg died in poverty

🕐 Time Limit: 2 min. 50 sec.

Transgenic Plants

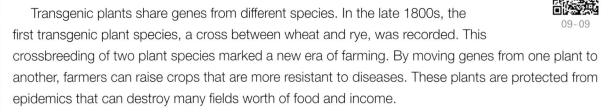

09-09

Transgenic plants share genes from different species. In the late 1800s, the first transgenic plant species, a cross between wheat and rye, was recorded. This crossbreeding of two plant species marked a new era of farming. By moving genes from one plant to another, farmers can raise crops that are more resistant to diseases. These plants are protected from epidemics that can destroy many fields worth of food and income.

In the 1930s, E.S. McFadden bred a variety of wheat that had a transgene from wild grass. This variety was called Hope and was resistant to a stem rust disease that was threatening to destroy the entire American wheat crop. This new kind of wheat saved farmers from ruin. Many people were also shielded from famine. The growth of transgenic plants began through normal crossbreeding methods. But by the 1970s, scientists were performing DNA transplants between plant and even animal species. In 1985, a laboratory in Belgium created a genetically engineered tobacco plant that had an insect tolerance by adding genes encoded with proteins that could kill insects.

This development opened up the field of transgenic recombinant plants. This field has been the subject of controversy between several international bodies. These warring groups promote and oppose genetically modified crops and foods. This battle over the use of plant DNA has resulted in the creation of a new biological class. Members of this class are known as genetically modified organisms (GMOs).

⁴➡ One example of a useful transgenic plant is golden rice. This version of rice was created in a laboratory. It contains twenty-three times more vitamin A than regular white rice. Vitamin A is an important form of nourishment that is scarce in many parts of the world. This version of rice was created as a humanitarian tool to help people in these areas. But due to opposition from various groups that are against transgenic foods, this rice is not available in certain places.

📖 Words & Phrases

cross ⓝ a combination of two things
resistant adj unaffected by
epidemic ⓝ a disease that spreads quickly among many people
nourishment ⓝ sustenance; nutrition
scarce adj rare; insufficient
humanitarian adj helpful to humans

1 The word "shielded" in the passage is closest in meaning to

Ⓐ chased

Ⓑ subjected

Ⓒ needed

Ⓓ protected

2 In paragraph 4, the author uses "golden rice" as an example of

Ⓐ an expensive GMO that farmers want to grow

Ⓑ the most popular transgenic plant in the world

Ⓒ a transgenic plant with nutritional benefits

Ⓓ a GMO known to be harmful to people

3 **Directions:** An introductory sentence for a brief summary of the passage is provided below. Complete the summary by selecting the THREE answer choices that express the most important ideas in the passage. Some answer choices do not belong in the summary because they express ideas that are not in the passage or are minor ideas in the passage.

Scientists have developed many different transgenic plants.

-
-
-

Answer Choices

1. A Belgian laboratory has made tobacco plants that can resist insects.

2. Some transgenic plants are causing controversy with different groups.

3. Transgenic plants are those that share characteristics with other species.

4. A strain of wheat called Hope helped save many American farmers.

5. Golden rice created in the laboratory is more nutritious than regular rice.

6. Since the 1970s, scientists have been creating transgenic plants.

✎ **Summary Note** Fill in the blanks with the appropriate words.

> (**Transgenic Plants**)
>
> - Share genes with other species
> - Are more resistant to ❶ _____
> - Are more nutritious
>
> - A cross between wheat and rye
> - ❷ _____ called Hope
> - Insect-resistant tobacco plants
> - Golden rice
>
> - ❸ _____ about transgenic plants
> - Some groups oppose to GMOs

Sigmund Freud

09-10

Sigmund Freud was an Austrian neurologist who was the founder of a new kind of psychology. He is best known for his theories about sexual desire and dreams. He is additionally famous for his studies of repression and the unconscious mind. He has been called by many "the father of psychoanalysis."

Freud was born in Freiberg in 1856. His family lived in a crowded apartment. But his parents made an effort to foster his intellect. He ranked first in his class in six of his eight years of schooling. He attended the University of Vienna at the age of seventeen. Freud opened his own practice for patients with nervous and brain disorders. He tried using hypnotism with his most hysterical and neurotic patients, but he eventually gave up this practice. He found that he could get his patients to talk by an easier method. He put them on a couch and encouraged them to say whatever came to their minds. This process was termed "free association."

In his forties, Freud felt that he had many mental problems. He began to explore his own dreams. He also examined his own memories and the dynamics of his personality. During this self-analysis, he came to realize the hostility he felt toward his father. He also recalled his childhood feelings for his mother, who was attractive, warm, and protective. Scholars who have studied Freud consider this time of emotional difficulty to be the most creative time in his life.

⁴ ➡ Freud's theories and research methods were controversial during his life. A paper by Lydiard H. Horton called Freud's dream theory "dangerously inaccurate." Another of Freud's critics was Juliet Mitchell. She suggested that Freud's basic claim that our conscious thoughts are driven by unconscious fears and desires should be rejected. She said this because it challenges the possibility of making universal and objective claims about the world. Many critics think that Freud's ideas were a byproduct of his heavy cocaine use.

📖 Words & Phrases

repression Ⓝ the stopping of some action or feeling
hysterical ⓐⓓⱼ frantic; in a panic
neurotic ⓐⓓⱼ unstable; nervous
association Ⓝ the connecting or combining of ideas
hostility Ⓝ hatred; unfriendliness
controversial ⓐⓓⱼ divisive; contentious
byproduct Ⓝ a result; an effect

1 The word "foster" in the passage is closest in meaning to

Ⓐ promote

Ⓑ destroy

Ⓒ hide

Ⓓ popularize

2 In paragraph 4, the author implies that Sigmund Freud's theories

Ⓐ enabled him to become very wealthy

Ⓑ are the subjects of a large number of books

Ⓒ were disproven by Juliet Mitchell

Ⓓ were rejected by many individuals

3 **Directions:** An introductory sentence for a brief summary of the passage is provided below. Complete the summary by selecting the THREE answer choices that express the most important ideas in the passage. Some answer choices do not belong in the summary because they express ideas that are not in the passage or are minor ideas in the passage.

Sigmund Freud made many advances in the field of psychology.

-
-
-

Answer Choices

1 He introduced the free association method.

2 He used drugs to get insight into dreams.

3 He almost always ranked at the top of his class.

4 He theorized about sexual desires and unconsciousness.

5 He opened and pioneered the field of psychoanalysis.

6 He treated his physical illness through self-analysis.

✎ **Summary Note** Fill in the blanks with the appropriate words.

Was the father of ❶ _____

Used hypnotism on hysterical and neurotic patients

Sigmund Freud   Developed the ❷ _____ method

Looked at his relationships with his parents through self-analysis

Criticized by many scholars as ❸ _____

Time Limit: 2 min. 50 sec.

The History of Cartography

09- 11

The study and practice of making maps or globes is called cartography and has been an important part of human history as far back as can be traced. The first known maps were of the constellations of stars rather than the Earth. The night sky was found mapped out as dots dating to 16,500 B.C. These were found on the walls of Lascaux Cave in France. Three bright stars, Vega, Deneb, and Altair, were included on these walls. The Pleiades star cluster was also mapped in these cave paintings.

2 ➡ In ancient Babylon, maps were made by using very accurate surveying techniques. A clay tablet found in 1930 at Ga-Sur, near modern-day Kirkuk in northern Iraq, shows a map that is a good example. It features a river valley between two hills. An inscription on this tablet shows that the plot of land belonged to someone named Azala. Scholars date this tablet to between 2500 and 2300 B.C. In ancient Egypt, maps were quite rare, but those which survived show a focus on geometric calculation and survey techniques. The Turin Papyrus, which is dated to 1300 B.C., depicts mountains east of the Nile, which were an important area where gold and silver were mined.

An early revolution in mapmaking occurred during the time of Claudius Ptolemy, who lived in the Hellenic Egyptian city of Alexandria from 90 to 168 A.D. He began depicting the Earth as a sphere and outlined the concepts of parallels of latitude and meridians of longitude that are utilized today. Throughout the Middle Ages, mapmaking advanced. By the time of the Renaissance, cartographers from Portugal were making nautical charts for the navigation of ships. The oldest known nautical chart was made by Pedro Reinel in 1485. This chart had a scale of latitudes on it.

By 1569, a Flemish geographer named Gerardus Mercator published the first map based on his Mercator projection. This is an accurate map of the world in which the sphere of the globe is stretched out on a plane. During the 1900s, maps became more abundant due to improvements in printing and photography. These factors made the production of maps cheaper and easier. Airplanes additionally made it possible to photograph large areas at a time and are credited with giving people a chance to view the Earth from a greater altitude than ever before possible.

📖 Words & Phrases

trace [v] to detect or find
constellation [n] a group of stars which form a pattern
accurate [adj] correct; exact
nautical [adj] related to the sea
abundant [adj] plentiful; available in large or great numbers

1 According to paragraph 2, which of the following is true of the history of mapmaking?

    Ⓐ The practice of making maps and globes is called choreography.

    Ⓑ Accurate surveying techniques were used to make maps in ancient Babylon.

    Ⓒ The practice of mapmaking was invented by the ancient Egyptians.

    Ⓓ The first map made by the Egyptians is dated at around 2300 B.C.

2 The word "depicting" in the passage is closest in meaning to

    Ⓐ erasing   Ⓑ studying

    Ⓒ characterizing   Ⓓ referring to

3 **Directions:** An introductory sentence for a brief summary of the passage is provided below. Complete the summary by selecting the THREE answer choices that express the most important ideas in the passage. Some answer choices do not belong in the summary because they express ideas that are not in the passage or are minor ideas in the passage.

Maps have been made by people for a long time.

-
-
-

Answer Choices

① Maps became widely used by photographers in the 1900s.

② Some maps on cave walls show various stars.

③ A map in Babylon from 2500 B.C. shows some land ownership.

④ Maps were common in ancient Egypt.

⑤ Mercator published a map using the projection he had invented.

⑥ Mapmaking was not allowed during the Middle Ages.

Summary Note Fill in the blanks with the appropriate words.

The History of Cartography

Maps in Lascaux Cave showing stars and constellations

A Babylonian map showing ❶ _____

Egyptian maps showing the location of gold and silver mines

Ptolemy's concept of ❷ _____ in second century A.D.

❸ _____ in the Renaissance

Mercator's world map using the Mercator projection around 1569

Better and more maps thanks to better printing technology, photography, and airplanes in the 1900s

Building Summary Skills

The following summaries are based on the long passages you worked on earlier. Complete each of them by filling in the blanks with suitable words or phrases.

Exercise 1   Estuaries

marine species	the tidal mouth of a river	the River Thames
somewhat salty	both salt water and fresh water	

Estuaries are semi-enclosed bodies of water that form near _____. They combine _____. The water formed is _____. Mostly freshwater species live in estuaries, but _____ live in them closer to the ocean. _____ is among the most famous estuaries in the world.

Exercise 2   The Embryo

three major stages	eight weeks	abortion rights
the organ forming stage	multi-celled life forms	

The embryo is the earliest stage of development for _____. There are _____ of development in the human embryo. These stages include the connection forming stage, the brain forming stage, and _____. This marks the point at which the embryo becomes a fetus. After _____, the fetal stage begins. There is a lot of controversy around the development of the embryo because of _____.

Exercise 3   Johannes Gutenberg and Metal Type

metal type	an information explosion	handwritten ones
Johann Fust	moveable type	

Johannes Gutenberg invented _____. This revolutionized Europe and led to _____. He used _____ instead of wood-block type. In 1455, he sold copies of a two-volume Bible that were much cheaper than _____. However, Gutenberg's partner _____ sued him and took the rights to his invention. Gutenberg died in poverty.

Exercise 4 Transgenic Plants

modified	the genes of other species	transfer genes
more nutritious	genetically modified organisms	

Transgenic plants share _____. Scientists _____
from one plant to another to give the plants better resistance to diseases or insects or to make them
_____. Wheat, tobacco, rice, and even animals have had their genes
_____. Some people are opposed to transgenic plants, which they call
_____.

Exercise 5 Sigmund Freud

his parents	the father of psychoanalysis	many critics
psychology	a neurologist	

Sigmund Freud was _____ who founded a new kind of
_____. He is often referred to as _____. He had
his own practice and soon began to use free-association methods with his patients. He also interpreted
his dreams and his relationships with _____. He did, however, have
_____ during his life and afterward.

Exercise 6 The History of Cartography

stars and constellations	the Renaissance	cartography
Babylon and Egypt	accuracy and efficiency	

Making maps or globes is called _____, and people have been making them
for thousands of years. Early maps just showed _____ as in the wall paintings
in Lascaux Cave. There were also early maps in _____. Mapmaking improved
in the Middle Ages and _____. Later mapmakers showed lines of latitude and
longitude and made maps for sailors. By the 1900s, advancements in photography as well as the advent
of airplanes and later, satellites, led to giant leaps forward in the _____ of
mapmaking.

Ancient Greek Pottery

09-12

Scholars have knowledge of ancient Greek art through the pottery that survives from that culture. While little else in the way of Greek painting or artwork still exists, there are more than 100,000 extant Greek vases. Many are adorned with paintings of Greek characters and scenes. These vases were common in every level of Greek society because the Greeks produced vases to be used for everyday needs such as drinking and cooking.

2 ➡ In the early periods of Greek civilization, small city-states produced their own pottery. But later, Corinth and Athens became the two great producers of these vases. Pottery from these cities became the standard all over the Greek world and was so widely exported that it put an end to local varieties.

3 ➡ Two of the major periods of pottery in ancient Greece were the black-figure period and the red-figure period. The black-figure period began around 700 B.C. and originated in the city of Corinth. By this method, vases were made of pale iron-rich clay. When fired, they became a reddish-orange color. The designs were outlined on the surface of the vase. Refined clay was then used to paint the figures that had been drawn. Finer details were added with an engraving tool, after which the vase was fired again. The second firing process left the painted designs a glossy black color.

Red-figure pottery was developed around 530 B.C. It became such a popular style that it was used over black-figure pottery. Even today, this style is thought to be the height of Greek pottery craftsmanship. The most highly valued surviving Greek vases are of this style. The process that resulted in a finished piece of this type of pottery required close cooperation between a potter and a painter. In this process, the painter would create a design on the vase before it was fired. Since the vase was unfired, the paint and the clay were the same color, and the painter had to create the design without being able to see it. After the potter fired the vase, the design would become visible. This process required the painter to work very quickly and precisely, relying only on memory.

The painters of these vases rarely signed their names. So the only ways scholars of modern times can identify these artists are by the images they repeatedly painted. For example, one of the greatest vase painters is known as "Achilles Painter" since his most common subject choice was the Greek character of that name. Another way painters are identified is by the name of the potter they worked for. Potters often signed their names on the vases, so the painter who worked for Kleophrades is identified as "Kleophrades Painter."

1 The word "adorned" in the passage is closest in meaning to
- Ⓐ etched
- Ⓑ decorated
- Ⓒ scribbled
- Ⓓ portrayed

2 According to paragraph 2, what can be inferred about ancient Greek pottery?
- Ⓐ Corinth and Athens made the best pottery.
- Ⓑ Vases from Athens were the most expensive in Greece.
- Ⓒ People from Corinth invented the art of Greek pottery.
- Ⓓ The names of some vase makers from Athens are known today.

3 According to paragraph 3, which of the following is true of the black-figure period?
- Ⓐ The pottery looked black due to iron-rich clay.
- Ⓑ The period concluded around 700 B.C.
- Ⓒ It first started in Corinth.
- Ⓓ The pottery had to be fired three times.

4 The word "process" in the passage is closest in meaning to
- Ⓐ method
- Ⓑ delivery
- Ⓒ analysis
- Ⓓ instructions

5 The word "it" in the passage refers to

(A) the paint

(B) the clay

(C) the same color

(D) the design

6 **Directions:** An introductory sentence for a brief summary of the passage is provided below. Complete the summary by selecting the THREE answer choices that express the most important ideas in the passage. Some answer choices do not belong in the summary because they express ideas that are not in the passage or are minor ideas in the passage. *This question is worth 2 points.*

Greek pottery often had many different paintings and pictures on it.

-
-
-

Answer Choices

1. In red-figure pottery, a painter created a design before a pot was fired.

2. Corinth and Athens produced high-quality pottery.

3. Many city-states in ancient Greece made their own pottery.

4. Ancient Greek painters used refined clay to paint figures on pottery.

5. Many different characters were often painted on Greek pottery.

6. Achilles Painter was one of the greatest painters in ancient Greece.

Cliffs and Erosion

09-13

The cliffs of Moher in Ireland

¹➡ A cliff is a geographic feature consisting of a sharply vertical rock exposure. Cliffs are created by the processes of erosion and weathering. They are most common on coasts and in mountainous areas. The strong bases of cliffs are usually formed by rock resistant to erosion and weathering. Sedimentary rocks such as sandstone, limestone, chalk, and dolomite are most likely to form cliffs. Cliffs comprised of igneous rocks, such as granite and basalt, can also be found.

Erosion is described as the displacement of solids by the agents of wind, water, or ice. These solids can be soil, mud, rock, and other particles. The process of erosion occurs by down-slope movement in response to gravity. It can also be caused by living organisms, which is called bioerosion. Erosion is different from weathering, which is the breakdown of rock and particles through processes where no motion is involved. However, these two processes can occur at the same place and time.

³➡ Erosion is a process that occurs naturally. But it is increased by human land use in many places. Cutting down trees and allowing animals to overgraze are poor land use practices that lead to faster erosion. Unmanaged construction activity and road or railroad building also fall into this category. Erosion can be limited by improved land use practices. Activities such as terrace building and tree planting can help rebuild damaged areas.

⁴➡ A type of cliff formed by the movement of a geologic fault or a landslide is called a scarp. Most cliffs have a talus slope at their bases. These are usually exposed jumbles of fallen rock in arid areas or under high cliffs. A soil slope may obscure the talus in areas with more water in the air. Waterfalls and rock shelters also occur as features on cliffs. A cliff sometimes peters out at the end of a ridge, which might leave tea tables or other types of rock columns behind. A cliff does not have to be exactly vertical to be classified as such. So there can be some ambiguity about whether a slope is actually a cliff or not.

There are unique cliffs to be found all over the world. The highest cliff is said to be the east face of Great Trango. It exists in the Karakoram Mountains of northern Pakistan and is about 1,340 meters high. Kalaupapa, Hawaii, is home to the highest sea cliffs, which measure 1,010 meters high. Mount Thor on Baffin Island in Arctic Canada has the highest vertical drop at 1,370 meters in total. It has the longest purely vertical drop on the Earth, which is 1,250 meters.

7 The word "vertical" in the passage is closest in meaning to
Ⓐ upright
Ⓑ high
Ⓒ unique
Ⓓ elevated

8 According to paragraph 1, which of the following is true of cliffs?
Ⓐ They are always found along rivers.
Ⓑ They cannot be formed by igneous rocks.
Ⓒ They may be formed through erosion.
Ⓓ They are not particularly vertical.

9 In paragraph 3, the author implies that humans
Ⓐ are the only reason erosion occurs
Ⓑ create cliffs by cutting down trees
Ⓒ can cause erosion to occur faster
Ⓓ rarely utilize good land practices

10 Why does the author mention "waterfalls and rock shelters" in paragraph 4?
Ⓐ To claim that they only appear on cliffs
Ⓑ To exemplify some features that cliffs sometimes have
Ⓒ To explain why they are eroding forces on cliffs
Ⓓ To emphasize how important they are to cliffs

11 The phrase "peters out" in the passage is closest in meaning to

    (A) increases in size

    (B) becomes more dangerous

    (C) stops eroding

    (D) comes to an end

12 **Directions:** An introductory sentence for a brief summary of the passage is provided below. Complete the summary by selecting the THREE answer choices that express the most important ideas in the passage. Some answer choices do not belong in the summary because they express ideas that are not in the passage or are minor ideas in the passage. *This question is worth 2 points.*

Cliffs have many different features that are a product of forces of nature such as erosion.

-
-
-

Answer Choices

① The highest cliff in the world is the east face of Great Trango.

② The bases of cliffs are usually formed by erosion-resistant rocks.

③ Cliffs tend to peter out at the end of a ridge, leaving behind columns of rock.

④ Scarps are formed by the movement of glaciers.

⑤ There is sometimes ambiguity over whether or not a slope is a cliff.

⑥ Erosion can sometimes be slowed down by people using improved land use practices.

Vocabulary Check-Up

A Choose the words with the closest meanings to the highlighted words.

1 There was a cluster of students gathered around the table.

- (A) lot
- (B) class
- (C) group
- (D) room

2 This was the central part of the project.

- (A) secondary
- (B) next
- (C) confusing
- (D) important

3 The businessman earned a lot of money last month.

- (A) made
- (B) spent
- (C) borrowed
- (D) used

4 Some trees are highly resistant to storm damage.

- (A) destroyed
- (B) exhausted
- (C) resilient
- (D) informal

5 Dr. Park's theory was very controversial.

- (A) original
- (B) divisive
- (C) educational
- (D) scholarly

6 The river carried sediment down to the delta.

- (A) water
- (B) mud
- (C) sand
- (D) silt

7 All the students' answers on the test were accurate.

- (A) exceptional
- (B) correct
- (C) mistaken
- (D) wrong

8 The plane was traveling at a very rapid speed.

- (A) fast
- (B) moderate
- (C) slow
- (D) incredible

B **Match the words with the correct definitions.**

1 brackish • • Ⓐ important parts of the body such as the heart, the liver, and the lungs

2 fertilize • • Ⓑ helpful to humans

3 mold • • Ⓒ a person who studies the nerves and the nervous system

4 hysterical • • Ⓓ to detect or find

5 humanitarian • • Ⓔ related to the sea

6 constellation • • Ⓕ to make pregnant

7 neurologist • • Ⓖ a design that stars make in the sky

8 trace • • Ⓗ a shape or form

9 organ • • Ⓘ somewhat salty

10 nautical • • Ⓙ frantic; in a panic

Overview

Introduction

Fill in a Table questions ask you to identify and organize major ideas and important supporting information from across the passage. Then, you should classify them into the appropriate categories. Passages used for this type of question usually have particular types of organization such as compare and contrast, cause and effect, or problem and solution. A five-answer table is worth 3 points, and a seven-answer table is worth 4 points.

Question Types

▶ **Directions:** Complete the table below to summarize the information about X discussed in the passage. Match the appropriate statements to the categories with which they are associated. TWO of the answer choices will NOT be used. *This question is worth 3 points.*

> Drag your answer choices to the spaces where they belong.
> To remove an answer choice, click on it. To review the passage, click on **View Text**.

Answer Choices

1. X X X X X X X X X X X X X X X X X X X X
2. X X X X X X X X X X X X X X X X X X X X
3. X X X X X X X X X X X X X X X X X X X
4. X X X X X X X X X X X X X X X X X X X
5. X X X X X X X X X X X X X X X X X X X
6. X X X X X X X X X X X X X X X X X X
7. X X X X X X X X X X X X X X X X X X

Category 1
-
-
-

Category 2
-
-

Useful Tips

■ Look at the categories of information in the table first.

■ Using scratch paper, make an outline of the passage according to these categories.

■ Distinguish between major and minor information in the passage.

■ Wrong answers usually include information that is not mentioned in the passage or that is not directly relevant to the categories in the table.

10-01

The Opossum

Marsupials are mammals that have a pouch. The female keeps her babies in the pouch until they are old enough to live outside it. The only marsupial residing in North America is the opossum.

The opossum is about the size of a large cat, its fur is gray, and it has a pink nose, feet, and tail. This marsupial has large black eyes for seeing at night, which is when it is the most active. Even though it has fifty very sharp teeth, it is a very gentle animal that tries to avoid fights and conflicts.

The opossum is extremely adaptable and can live in many places, including trees and underground. It consumes all kinds of food, both plants and animals, such as insects, mice, small snakes, grass, leaves, and berries.

The opossum has a variety of defenses, one of which is being mostly immune to snake venom. It typically does not get rabies, a nasty disease, because of the temperature of its blood. Its most famous defense, however, is playing dead. Because most animals do not consume dead things, this is an effective defense. When playing dead, an opossum turns on its back, shows its teeth, and then produces a bad smell near its tail. Usually, the other animal departs.

Q   Directions: Complete the table below to summarize the information about the adaptability and defenses of the opossum. Match the appropriate statements to the categories with which they are associated. TWO of the answer choices will NOT be used. *This question is worth 3 points.*

Answer Choices

1 It has a variety of homes.

2 It is not affected by snake venom.

3 Its blood temperature prevents rabies.

4 It is as large as a cat.

5 It avoids fights.

6 It can eat many different things.

7 It sometimes plays dead.

Adaptability
-
-

Defenses
-
-
-

✓ Correct Answer

Choices 1 and 6 are concerned with the adaptability of the opossum, and choices 2, 3, and 7 are about its defenses. Choices 4 and 5 are not relevant to either category.

Read the passages and answer the questions.

Skill & Tip

Fill in a Table questions ask you to recognize and organize the important ideas of the passage into table categories. You need to understand what type of organization the passage uses: for example, compare/contrast, cause/effect, or problem/solution.

Drill 1

Classism

10-02

The term "classism" refers to a form of prejudice and takes place against people who are in lower social classes. It is a form of social elitism. Individual classism is practiced by people and happens when wealthy people disregard those who make less money than they do. It additionally happens when the rich receive advantages over the middle class and the poor. Structural classism occurs in institutions when actions are taken in such a way as to exclude people from lower classes. Many people see this type of classism in American politics because people who make the largest campaign contributions seem to have more influence in the government. This practice excludes the working class from having an equal level of influence.

Q **Directions:** Complete the table below by matching FOUR of the six answer choices with the appropriate types of individual and structural classism.

Answer Choices

① Rich people ignore those people with lower incomes.

② People from lower classes cannot find decent jobs.

③ Bigger political campaign donors have more influence in the government.

④ The rich receive advantages that the middle class and the poor do not get.

⑤ The children of the rich receive better gifts than the children of the poor.

⑥ People from lower classes cannot participate in making decisions.

Individual Classism

-
-

Structural Classism

-
-

Mesopotamia

Mesopotamia is called the "cradle of civilization" because the first human societies began in this area. The region is located in a fertile zone between two rivers, which made it possible for humans to grow crops. Their prosperity led to the rise of cities. Once cities existed, many discoveries were made. For instance, the first writing system was developed, and the people of these cities also invented metal working. They were some of the first Bronze Age people. They used copper, bronze, and gold to decorate their palaces and temples. They also used astronomy. By studying the stars, they were able to calculate the length of an Earth year. This led to the accurate sixty-minute hour and the twenty-four-hour day that is still utilized today.

10-03

Q **Directions:** Complete the table below by matching FOUR of the six answer choices with the appropriate causes and effects of Mesopotamian discovery and innovation.

Answer Choices

1. Mesopotamians engaged in farming.
2. Cities thrived in Mesopotamia.
3. Mesopotamia was surrounded by a big river.
4. A unique calculating system was invented.
5. Mesopotamians were good astronomers.
6. A day was divided into twenty-four hours.

Causes
-
-

Effects
-
-

The Green Revolution

The term Green Revolution is used to describe a large change in farming which took place in many developing nations between the 1940s and the 1960s. It led to a large increase in cereal production. This change was the result of programs of agricultural research. The Green Revolution has had positive and negative impacts on society and the Earth. One positive impact is that famines were avoided. But this led to the negative effect of overpopulation in some areas. The Green Revolution is also credited with the success of large-scale farming. But this success has made it very difficult for small-scale farmers to profit. This shift in economics greatly hurt the socialist movement.

10-04

Q Directions: Complete the table below by matching FOUR of the six answer choices with the positive and negative effects of the Green Revolution.

Answer Choices

① Agricultural research was widely encouraged.

② Fewer people suffered from hunger.

③ Some areas experienced a rapid increase in population.

④ Large-scale farming took root in some countries.

⑤ It became difficult for small-scale farmers to survive.

⑥ Cereal production increased substantially in a few countries.

Positive Effects
-
-

Negative Effects
-
-

Natural Phenomena

A natural phenomenon is an event that is not caused by humans but instead occurs in nature. However, it can affect humans. Some natural phenomena can be described by physics, so they are called physical phenomena. Lightning is an example of this type of event. The orbit of the planets due to gravity is another example. Natural disasters that come from within the Earth are considered geological phenomena. A common example is a volcanic eruption. A tsunami, a large, fast-moving wave, is also this type of event. These events cannot be controlled. Humans do not create them and cannot stop them. But these events can be understood through science.

10-05

Q **Directions:** Complete the table below by matching FOUR of the six answer choices with the appropriate types of physical and geological phenomena.

Answer Choices

1. A wildfire is caused by humans.
2. A flash of lightning strikes across the sky.
3. A tsunami occurs in the ocean.
4. A volcano explodes and spews hot lava.
5. Gravity makes planets move in their orbits.
6. An earthquake is simulated in a laboratory.

Physical Phenomena
-
-

Geological Phenomena
-
-

Exercises with Mid-Length Passages

Exercise 1 Read the following passage and answer the questions.

🕐 Time Limit: 3 min. 20 sec.

Emergence

10-06

¹➡ The concept of emergence describes the way in which a complex pattern forms. This pattern arises from its basic parts. An emergent property comes from the relationships between these parts. This is a constantly changing process that may occur over a long period of time. The evolution of the human body is a good example. Its form emerged over thousands of generations. The human body is very complex, but it is formed by millions of tiny cells, which are not.

Emergence occurs on disparate-size scales. An example is between neurons and the human brain. Interactions between many neurons produce a human brain which is capable of thought. But none of the neurons that made it is capable of thought. The single brain that results from many neurons is much bigger than any of the single neuron parts that created it.

A common way of looking at emergence in nature is through structures. They can come from organic or inorganic sources. A good example of a living structure is a flock of birds. The flock takes a shape and has behavioral characteristics, but these properties are not exhibited by individual birds. Another example of an organic emergent structure is an ant colony. The ant colony is emergent because no single ant, including the queen, could organize such an effective colony of workers. Yet collectively, a colony structure arises. An example of an inorganic emergent structure is a hurricane. This storm system forms as a result of various factors, some of which are pressure, temperature, and humidity. They combine to form a violent storm. But any single factor would not form the same storm by itself.

Emergence also occurs in human culture. One place this kind of emergence has occurred on a large scale is in the stock market. As a system, it regulates the prices of companies around the world. But there is no single leader that controls the entire market. Agents only know of a limited number of companies and must follow strict rules of the market. Through these interactions, the complexity of the market as a whole emerges. Another type of this emergence occurs with regard to the World Wide Web. In this case there is no central website, yet links between major and minor websites create the complex that is known as the World Wide Web.

📖 Words & Phrases

property (n) a characteristic
evolution (n) the process by which organisms develop
disparate (adj) essentially different and distinct
colony (n) a group of organisms

1 According to paragraph 1, emergence is

Ⓐ the way in which a number of small units interact to form a very large structure

Ⓑ the way in which simple components combine to form a complex system

Ⓒ the way in which a complex organic system emerges from its basic parts

Ⓓ the way in which various single units interlock to form a large system

2 The word "regulates" in the passage is closest in meaning to

Ⓐ controls

Ⓑ limits

Ⓒ raises

Ⓓ maintains

3 **Directions:** Complete the table below by matching FIVE of the seven answer choices with structural and cultural emergence.

Answer Choices

1. A queen bee is fed by workers many times a day.
2. A flock of birds exhibits a shape and certain behavior.
3. Small and large websites are linked to create the World Wide Web.
4. The human brain is composed of numerous thinking neurons.
5. A hurricane is the result of various climatic factors.
6. The stock market forms a complex pattern.
7. Ants build an effective colony collectively.

Structural Emergence
-
-
-

Cultural Emergence
-
-

✎ **Summary Note** Fill in the blanks with the appropriate words.

Emergence

The way a complex pattern forms from lesser parts

Structural Emergence
- The human body and brain
- ❶ _____
- ❷ _____
- A hurricane storm system

Cultural Emergence
- The stock market
- ❸ _____

Exercise 2 **Read the following passage and answer the questions.**

⏱ Time Limit: 2 min. 50 sec.

The Media Influence Theory

10-07

1 ➡ The American entertainment industry has been heavily criticized. Critics are unhappy with the amount of pretend violent acts it shows. The Media Influence Theory explains this problem. It suggests that the rise in the rates of real violent acts is linked to entertainment. This theory considers many acts of violence. High school shootings are the most common. It claims they are caused by the high number of violent acts in the media. This takes on various forms in popular entertainment.

The basis of the theory lies in the assumption that many people are exposed to a high level of violent content in media outlets. A small percentage of these people have trouble separating fantasy and reality about the violence they see. These people think that it is okay to commit violent acts. The most frequent targets of the theory's advocates are video game companies. These companies produce many first-person shooter games. Most feature a high amount of violence and gore. Advocates say these games make life seem cheap because these games reward players for committing acts of violence.

Advocates also target musicians who sing hateful lyrics. They claim these artists incite violence. Violent movies do not avoid accusations either. People claim these kinds of movies make violence look glamorous. All of these are forms of entertainment, and people want companies to take more responsibility for their products. People want them to label products that are extremely violent. They also want minors to have limited or no access to these products.

However, critics of this theory say that government should not regulate media. They say that it would harm American citizens' right to free speech. They compare statistics of violence between the United States and other countries. Some of these other countries have the same kind of violent media. But there are much fewer violent acts being committed. So these critics claim that the problem of violence in America is not due to the media. They say it is caused by the availability of weapons.

📖 Words & Phrases

criticize Ⓥ to find fault with; to judge
pretend adj not real; imagined
assumption Ⓝ a supposition; a belief
advocate Ⓝ a supporter
incite Ⓥ to provoke; to encourage

1 In paragraph 1, the author uses "High school shootings" as an example of
Ⓐ violence mainly caused by young people
Ⓑ violence covered by the media
Ⓒ the most common violent acts in some countries
Ⓓ violent acts connected to entertainment

2 The word "them" in the passage refers to
Ⓐ forms of entertainment
Ⓑ companies
Ⓒ their products
Ⓓ people

3 **Directions:** Complete the table below by matching FIVE of the seven answer choices with the appropriate claims made by advocates or critics of the Media Influence Theory.

Answer Choices

① Artists who sing hateful lyrics incite violence.
② High school punishment can lead teenagers to be violent.
③ Alcohol abuse causes people to shoot guns.
④ Media should not be controlled by the government.
⑤ Violent movies make violence look glamorous.
⑥ Violent video games cheapen human life.
⑦ Violence is caused by weapons being available.

Advocates
·
·
·

Critics
·
·

✏ **Summary Note** Fill in the blanks with the appropriate words.

The Media Influence Theory

Advocates
• Some cannot tell imaginary violence from reality
• Video games, music with hateful lyrics, and violent movies responsible for violence in society
• ❶ _____ should be more responsible
• Government should ❷ _____

Critics
• Reason for rising levels of violence:
  ❸ _____
• Government should not control the entertainment industry
• Other countries have similar violence in media but fewer real violent acts

⏱ Time Limit: 2 min. 40 sec.

The Great Chicago Fire

10-08

The Great Chicago Fire burned from October 8 to 10, 1871. It had terrible effects. Hundreds of people were killed by the inferno, and much of the city turned into ashes. It was one of the largest disasters in the United States during the nineteenth century. But the people of Chicago began to rebuild their city immediately, which led to Chicago's status as one of the most economically important American cities.

[2]→ The fire began around 9 PM on Sunday, October 8. It started in a small shed in an alley off DeKoven Street. The most commonly believed reason for the fire starting is that a cow kicked over a lantern in a barn which was owned by Patrick and Catherine O'Leary. It is now known that Mrs. O'Leary was used as a scapegoat. Historians believe she was blamed for the fire because she was a woman, immigrant, and Catholic. All of these groups suffered persecution at this time in American history. The *Chicago Tribune*'s first post-fire issue claimed that Mrs. O'Leary's negligence was the cause. Later, however, the reporter who wrote the story admitted that he made it up and said he did that because he thought it was a colorful story.

[3]→ Richard Bales is an amateur historian who believes the fire was started by Daniel Sullivan. He was the man who first reported the fire. Bales offered the theory that this man ignited some hay in the barn. He says Sullivan did it while trying to steal some milk. But Anthony DeBartolo recently reported some new evidence to the *Chicago Tribune*. He put forth the suggestion that a gambler named Louis M. Cohn may have started the fire. DeBartolo claims that Cohn did this during a craps game. According to a book by Alan Wykes, a lost will by Cohn includes a confession that he started the fire.

📖 **Words & Phrases**

destroy Ⓥ to ruin; to demolish; to wreck
shed Ⓝ a small structure used for storage
scapegoat Ⓝ a whipping boy; a fall guy
persecution Ⓝ cruel and unfair treatment
craps game Ⓝ a dice game that is usually played for money

1 The word "ignited" in the passage is closest in meaning to

Ⓐ lit up

Ⓑ set fire to

Ⓒ blew up

Ⓓ put out

2 According to paragraphs 2 and 3, which of the following is true of the Great Chicago Fire?

Ⓐ It burned all the barns in the city to the ground.

Ⓑ An amateur historian suggested that it was started by a gambler.

Ⓒ There are several theories about how it started.

Ⓓ People believe it was caused by Patrick O'Leary.

3 **Directions:** Complete the table below by matching FIVE of the seven answer choices with the reported causes and effects of the Great Chicago Fire.

Answer Choices

① It killed hundreds of people.

② A lantern in a barn was kicked over by a cow.

③ Daniel Sullivan burned the barn while stealing some milk.

④ A milk thief kicked a torch and started the fire.

⑤ Many parts of Chicago were destroyed.

⑥ Anthony DeBartolo found new evidence concerning how the fire started.

⑦ A gambler started the fire during a craps game.

Reported Causes

-
-
-

Effects

-
-

✎ **Summary Note** Fill in the blanks with the appropriate words.

The Great Chicago Fire of 1871

- Happened from
  ❶ _____
- Destroyed much of Chicago
- Killed many people

- A false story in the *Chicago Tribune*
  ➡ ❷ _____
  kicked over a lantern in a barn

- Richard Bales
  ➡ Daniel Sullivan set fire to hay in barn while stealing milk

- Antony DeBartolo
  ➡ ❸ _____
  started fire during a game of craps

Exercise 4 Read the following passage and answer the questions.

Time Limit: 2 min. 50 sec.

Differences in the Concept of Family

10-09

A family consists of a group of people who live together and are linked by birth or marriage. They can also be linked by other legal ties, some of which are domestic partnerships and adoption.

[2]→ Many people think families are only related by blood. But many social scientists say that the notion of blood should be taken metaphorically. Many societies define family through other concepts. Article 16 of the Universal Declaration of Human Rights calls family the natural group unit of society. It states that the family is entitled to protection by society and the state. The structure of families is based on ties between parents and children and is also based on links between spouses. Or it can be based on both.

There are three major types of families. A matrifocal family consists of a mother and her children. The children are usually the mother's biological offspring. But this does not rule out adoption. This type usually occurs in places where the woman has enough resources to raise a family alone. A consanguineal family can be found in various forms. The most common form consists of a mother and her children and the family of the mother. Fathers are often not present. This is especially true when property is passed down through inheritance. When men own property, this type of family may include members of the husband's family. A conjugal family is made up of one or more mothers and their children. It also includes one or more fathers. This kind of family is linked to the existence of a division of labor. Both men and women must do different types of labor in this form. Families in this situation have high mobility.

The nuclear family is a sub-group of the conjugal family type. This type has one woman and one husband. Together, they raise their children. This type of family is the most common in modern industrialized society.

📖 Words & Phrases

adoption (n) taking legal responsibility for parenting
notion (n) an idea; a thought; a concept
be entitled to (phr) to deserve something
spouse (n) a husband or wife
inheritance (n) a legacy
mobility (n) the ability to move easily

1 According to paragraph 2, which of the following is NOT a criterion by which the structure of families is defined?

Ⓐ Links between husband and wife
Ⓑ Blood or legal ties
Ⓒ Spousal links and ties between parents and children
Ⓓ Parent-children ties

2 The phrase "rule out" in the passage is closest in meaning to

Ⓐ illegalize　　　　　　　　Ⓑ omit
Ⓒ allow　　　　　　　　　 Ⓓ exclude

3 **Directions:** Complete the table below by matching SEVEN of the nine answer choices with the types of families.

Answer Choices

① Fathers are often absent from this type of family.
② There is usually a division of labor in this type of family.
③ This kind of family has only children and no parents.
④ This type usually happens when a mother can support a family by herself.
⑤ The nuclear family belongs to this type.
⑥ A mother and her children and the family of the mother are the most common form of this type.
⑦ This type is composed of a mother and her children.
⑧ This type includes the husband's parents when he is poor.
⑨ There are one or more mothers or fathers in this type of family.

Matrifocal Family
•
•

Consanguineal Family
•
•

Conjugal Family
•
•
•

Summary Note Fill in the blanks with the appropriate words.

Types of Families

❶ _____
• A mother and her children
• Children are biological offspring
• Does not rule out adoption
• Woman has resources to raise family alone

❷ _____
• A mother and her children and the family of the mother
• No fathers
• May include members of the husband's family when men own property

❸ _____
• One or more mothers and their children; includes one or more fathers
• Linked to division of labor
• High mobility
• Nuclear family included as a sub-group

🕐 Time Limit: 2 min. 50 sec.

Bioethics

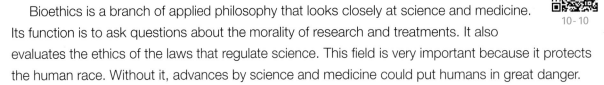

10-10

Bioethics is a branch of applied philosophy that looks closely at science and medicine. Its function is to ask questions about the morality of research and treatments. It also evaluates the ethics of the laws that regulate science. This field is very important because it protects the human race. Without it, advances by science and medicine could put humans in great danger.

The study of bioethics affects many laws. Many scientists react blindly against those who practice bioethics for this reason. These scientists believe that their work is ethical by nature. Bioethics is an academic area that shows rapid growth. Its history as a formal study is around forty years old. Many academic centers now offer degrees in bioethics. In the 1990s, a group of social scientists created a mode of discourse. This established the method of research about ethical issues which attempts to resolve these issues with society. This data compiled by bioethicists is subject to the same peer review as other social sciences.

There are some major questions about bioethics. Its validity as an area of academic inquiry is doubted. Why must it exist apart from philosophy? Is everyone not an ethicist? These questions are answered by the needs of institutions. Bioethicists put to work the enormous body of research and history. They apply it to questions of bioethics. They do it in a fair, honest, and intelligent way. They share a commitment to this goal.

Bioethicists research many topics. They often focus on issues that cause controversy in society. They compile data and publish reports which are used to form public opinion. They also form policy. Some of the topics which bioethicists deal with concern abortion and cloning. They also cover the use of embryos in stem cell research. These are difficult ethical problems. They arise from questions about human life. Bioethicists try to educate lawmakers and others with power. These are the ones who draw boundaries. They decide what is acceptable in medicine and science.

📖 Words & Phrases

morality ⓝ the state of being good or bad
evaluate ⓥ to look at closely based on a set of criteria
blindly 〔adv〕 without considering, examining, looking, or thinking
rapid 〔adj〕 fast
resolve ⓥ to solve

1 The word "resolve" in the passage is closest in meaning to
- Ⓐ settle
- Ⓑ avoid
- Ⓒ discuss
- Ⓓ examine

2 The word "These" in the passage refers to
- Ⓐ Ethical problems
- Ⓑ Questions about human life
- Ⓒ Bioethicists
- Ⓓ Lawmakers and others with power

3 **Directions:** Complete the table below by matching FIVE of the seven answer choices with the topics examined by bioethicists and the functions of bioethicists.

Answer Choices

1. They examine the use of embryos in stem cell research.
2. They compile data about social sciences.
3. They examine the morality of research and treatments.
4. They evaluate ethics of laws that regulate science.
5. They express their opinions about abortion.
6. They look at the ethics of cloning.
7. They protect people from the development of science and medicine.

Topics
- •
- •
- •

Functions
- •
- •

🖊 **Summary Note** Fill in the blanks with the appropriate words.

Bioethics

Functions
- Looks closely at science and technology
- Examines the
  ❶ _____ of research and treatments
- Evaluates ethics of laws that regulate science and medicine

Topics
- Embryonic stem cell research
- ❷ _____
- Abortion

Activities
- Research, compilation, and publication of reports
- Education of lawmakers and people in power
- Formation of
  ❸ _____ and opinion

🕐 Time Limit: 2 min. 50 sec.

Paleoanthropology

10-11

The study of human and pre-human fossils is called paleoanthropology. It is a branch of physical anthropology that focuses on tracing the evolution of humans through the ages. Scientists in this field examine anatomic, behavioral, and genetic linkages. These links show how humans developed from pre-humans. Scientists use these links to reconstruct a timeline for the rise of man. This timeline spans from prehistoric to modern times.

Paleoanthropologists are able to study early hominids by digging up fossil remains. They scour the earth and dig up small traces. These bits they find give them impressions of ancient life. Preserved bones, tools, and footprints provide this type of fossil evidence.

Paleoanthropology began in the late 1800s when a few important discoveries were made that led to the study of human evolution. The first was made in 1856. A Neanderthal man was discovered in Germany. This was an important event. It led to the emergence of this science. Other notable events were the publication of two important books on this subject. The first was Thomas Huxley's *Evidence as to Man's Place in Nature*. The second important book was Charles Darwin's *The Descent of Man*.

[4] ➡ Some of the most important discoveries in this field were made by the Leakey family. Their long list of important fossil discoveries began with Louis Leakey. He began digging in the Olduvai Gorge in Kenya, Africa. In 1959, he and his wife found the remains of an early hominid skull.

[5] ➡ After Louis's death in 1972, his wife Mary Leakey continued his research. One of her most notable discoveries was the Laetoli footprints. She found these in Tanzania in 1976. These footprints were preserved in volcanic ash. They dated back to 3.7 million years ago. They represent the most conclusive proof that early pre-humans walked on two legs. The Leakey's son Richard is also credited with some important fossil discoveries. In 1972, his group found the skull of a *Homo habilis* in Tanzania. Later, in 1975, his group also found the skull of a *Homo erectus* in Kenya.

📖 **Words & Phrases**

anthropology [n] the study of people and their culture
trace [v] to track down; to find
anatomic [adj] relating to the body of an organism
linkage [n] something that connects two separate things
conclusive [adj] convincing; without doubt

1 The word "scour" in the passage is closest in meaning to

Ⓐ spoil

Ⓑ explore

Ⓒ search

Ⓓ study

2 According to paragraphs 4 and 5, which of the following is true of the Leakey family?

Ⓐ They published many important books about pre-humans.

Ⓑ They discovered a Neanderthal man fossil in Germany.

Ⓒ They created the field of paleoanthropology.

Ⓓ They made some important fossil discoveries.

3 **Directions:** Complete the table below by matching FIVE of the seven answer choices with the places where major discoveries were made.

Answer Choices

1 The remains of an early hominid skull were found in 1959.

2 Preserved prehistoric tools were discovered in the 1800s.

3 The remains of a Neanderthal man were discovered in 1856.

4 The skull of a *Homo habilis* was found in 1972.

5 Fossil bones of a hominid were found in 1852.

6 The skull of a *Homo erectus* was discovered in 1975.

7 The Laetoli footprints were found in 1976.

Kenya

•

•

Tanzania

•

•

Germany

•

✎ **Summary Note** **Fill in the blanks with the appropriate words.**

1856
• Neanderthal man discovered

The late 1800s
• *Evidence as to Man's Place in Nature* by Thomas Huxley
• *The Descent of Man* by Charles Darwin

1959
• Louis and Mary Leakey found
❶ ....

Important Discoveries in the Field of Paleoanthropology

1976
• Mary Leakey discovered
❷ ....

1975
• Richard Leakey's team unearthed skull of
❸ ....

Building Summary Skills

The following summaries are based on the long passages you worked on earlier. Complete each of them by filling in the blanks with suitable words or phrases.

Exercise 1   Emergence

cultural	the World Wide Web	organic and inorganic structures
a complex pattern	ant colonies and flocks of birds	

Emergence is the concept that describes how _____ forms from lesser parts. It is evident in all forms of _____. Scientists who study emergence look at the characteristics of organic emergent structures such as _____ and at inorganic structures such as hurricanes. Another form of emergence is _____, in which some form of human organization results in a highly complex structure that is more than the sum of its parts. _____ and the stock market are prime examples of the sort of phenomenon in which simple components combine to form a complex whole.

Exercise 2   The Media Influence Theory

reality	the availability of weapons	regulated by the government
many acts of violence	rising levels of violence	

The Media Influence Theory states that _____ in society are attributable to individuals who see violence depicted in entertainment and are unable to distinguish it apart from _____. Advocates of this theory target video games, music with hateful lyrics, and movies as being responsible for _____. They want to see these forms of entertainment heavily _____. On the other hand, critics of this theory think that the government should not control the entertainment industry and that rising levels of violence are due to _____.

Exercise 3   The Great Chicago Fire

a female Catholic immigrant	steal some milk	1871
a game of craps	Mrs. O'Leary's cow	

From October 8 to 10, _____, the Great Chicago Fire burned down much of the city and killed hundreds of people. The fire was originally blamed on _____ kicking down a lantern in the barn. But the reporter who wrote this story later said he made it up because it sounded interesting, so this led people to believe that Mrs. O'Leary was made a target because she was _____. Some other possible causes of the fire were Daniel Sullivan, who may have started it while trying to _____, and Louis M. Cohn, who is said to have started it during _____.

Exercise 4 Differences in the Concept of Family

the conjugal family	conjugal	blood relation
the nuclear family	genetic or other types of bonds	

A family consists of people who live together and are linked by _____.
Although _____ defines many families, it is not the only thing that
can link people together. There are three major types of families: matrifocal, consanguineal, and
_____. The most common type of family in modern society is a sub-group of
_____ called _____.

Exercise 5 Bioethics

the human race	public opinion	the ethics of scientific
politicians	bioethics programs	

Bioethics is a branch of applied philosophy that looks closely at _____ and
medical practices. This field is very important because it asks questions about and examines policies and
treatments that greatly affect _____. It is also an area of academic growth,
as many universities have created _____. Although bioethicists' roles are
often questioned, they do many activities such as researching and compiling reports that greatly affect
_____ and the policies made by _____.

Exercise 6 Paleoanthropology

the late 1800s	the skull of a hominid	the Leakeys
the Laetoli footprints	a *Homo habilis* and a *Homo erectus*	

The study of human and pre-human fossils is paleoanthropology. This field began with several important
discoveries and publications in _____, including the discovery of Neanderthal
man fossils. Some of the most important discoveries in this field have been made by a family named
_____. Their long list of discoveries began in the 1950s when Louis and Mary
Leakey found _____ in Kenya. But Mary Leakey's most important discovery
came after her husband's death, when she found _____ in 1976. These
footprints offered conclusive evidence that early man walked upright on two legs. Their son, Richard, also
found the skulls of _____.

Partnerships in Business

10-12

1 ➡ A partnership is a type of business in which two or more partners share profits and losses. Partners are people who have united to take part in the same business. This form of business is good for people who want to work with their friends or people they trust. It is also useful for two or more people who have different specialties. By forming a partnership, they can combine their skills. A partnership can also be made between existing companies.

2 ➡ Partners may have a partnership agreement, or they may make a declaration of partnership. In some jurisdictions, such agreements must be registered. After doing this, they are made available for public inspection. In many countries, a partnership is a legal entity. Partnerships are often favored over corporations for taxation purposes. This makes a partnership more useful for businesses that face heavy taxation. A partnership structure may eliminate the dividend tax. This tax is levied on profits made by the owners of a corporation.

A general partnership is the most basic form. In this style, all partners manage the business, and everyone is personally liable for the company's debts. There are two other forms of partnership as a business. One of them is the limited partnership. With this style, certain limited partners give up their ability to manage the business. They trade this ability in order to receive limited liability for the partnership's debts. The other kind is a limited liability partnership. In this style, all partners accept some degree of liability.

According to the Partnership Act 1958, there are four criteria for a partnership to exist. The first is a valid agreement between the parties, and the second is for them to carry on a business. This is defined in the agreement as any trade, occupation, or profession. The third is that they must be in common. This means there must be some mutuality of rights. This includes interests and obligations. Finally, there must be a view to profit. This is the reason charities cannot be partnerships.

The businesspeople who are going to form a partnership must choose which form best suits them. Some partners may want more control. They may be willing to risk greater liability. Others may want to lessen their liability. They may be willing to forego some ability to control the business. The balance between control, profit, and liability must be found by the new partners. But the most important ingredient for a successful relationship between them is trust.

1 According to paragraph 1, which of the following is true of a partnership?

   Ⓐ It is not a very good form of business because it is outdated.

   Ⓑ People who want to work with their friends find this form of business useful.

   Ⓒ A partnership can only be established between people with the same college degrees.

   Ⓓ It is used by people opening businesses such as bakeries and pubs.

2 The word "levied" in the passage is closest in meaning to

   Ⓐ saved

   Ⓑ pointed at

   Ⓒ imposed

   Ⓓ exempted

3 According to paragraph 2, which of the following is NOT true of a partnership?

   Ⓐ A partnership agreement may exist between partners.

   Ⓑ A declaration of partnership may be made between partners.

   Ⓒ A partnership cannot be available for public inspection.

   Ⓓ A partnership is a legal entity in many countries.

4 Which of the following best expresses the information in the highlighted sentence? *Incorrect* answer choices change the meaning in important ways or leave out essential information.

   Ⓐ People about to start a partnership must decide which form they like best.

   Ⓑ Partners must always think about the possible forms of business.

   Ⓒ Partners must make many choices about their new business.

   Ⓓ Business partners should always make choices together.

5   The word "them" in the passage refers to

Ⓐ the businesspeople

Ⓑ others

Ⓒ control, profit, and liability

Ⓓ the new partners

6   **Directions:** Complete the table below by matching SEVEN of the nine answer choices with the appropriate forms of partnership and the criteria for a partnership to exist. TWO of the answer choices will NOT be used. *This question is worth 3 points.*

Answer Choices

① The partners must have known each other for at least ten years.

② A general partnership is the most basic kind.

③ There must be a valid agreement between parties.

④ A view to profit is necessary.

⑤ The ability to manage the business is given up by limited partners.

⑥ Unknown partners are not aware of each other's existence.

⑦ A business must be carried on.

Criteria

•

•

•

Forms

•

•

The Anasazi Architecture of Cliff Palace

10-13

Cliff Palace in Colorado, United States

1 ➡ The largest cliff dwelling in North America is an ancient Pueblo structure named Cliff Palace. It is located in Mesa Verde National Park, which is in the southwest corner of Colorado. It was an ancient home to the Anasazi people.

2 ➡ Cliff Palace is a large ruin that many people find amazing. It was built into an empty space in a sandstone cliff. This alcove is approximately forty meters deep and twenty-five meters high while the stone structure is about 130 meters long. Cliff Palace has 150 rooms, but not all of them had hearths. A hearth used for building fires shows that a room was a living space for people. Only approximately twenty-five to thirty of Cliff Palace's rooms have these. The remaining rooms were probably used for storage.

Cliff Palace has numerous open areas and rooms whose functions are still not understood. Nine storage rooms were constructed high on the upper level, where they were safe from moisture and pests. The surplus harvest was almost surely stored here. Removable ladders allowed people access to these rooms. Archaeologists have made approximations as to how many people lived there. They based their estimates on the number of rooms with hearths and concluded that Cliff Palace was home to between 100 to 150 Anasazi.

At Cliff Palace, there are a few towers which are square, round structures that rise a few stories. Some of the finest stonework in the ruin is contained in these towers. The interior of a four-story tower at the south end of the complex contains some abstract designs painted on original plaster within the tower.

Cliff Palace additionally contains round sunken rooms of ceremonial importance called kivas. One kiva is located in the center of the ruin. The entire structure at this point is partitioned by a series of walls. It has no doorways or other access portals. The walls of this kiva were plastered with one color on one side and a different color on the opposing side. **1** Archaeologists have studied this strange structure. **2** They have concluded that two communities lived here. **3** This kiva may have been used to integrate the two communities. **4**

6 ➡ Archaeologists can tell the age of Cliff Palace through tree ring dating. This indicates that the construction and refurbishing of Cliff Palace was continuous and took place from 1190 to 1260. They also figure that a major portion of the building was done during a time span of twenty years. Cliff Palace was abandoned by 1300 for reasons that are still unknown.

7 In paragraph 1, the author's description of Cliff Palace mentions which of the following?
  (A) When it became a national park
  (B) How it looks
  (C) Where it can be found
  (D) Why it was constructed

8 According to paragraph 2, which of the following is NOT true of Cliff Palace?
  (A) It occupies a space in an empty sandstone cliff.
  (B) There were probably about 120 storage rooms.
  (C) Not every room in it had a hearth.
  (D) Some Anasazi people still live there.

9 The word "partitioned" in the passage is closest in meaning to
  (A) separated
  (B) distinguished
  (C) formalized
  (D) constructed

10 In paragraph 6, the author mentions "tree ring dating" in order to

    Ⓐ show that much of Cliff Palace was made with wood

    Ⓑ determine approximately when Cliff Palace was built

    Ⓒ argue that Cliff Palace is not as old as people believe

    Ⓓ prove Cliff Palace is the oldest structure in the region

11 Look at the four squares [■] that indicate where the following sentence can be added to the passage.

Another possibility suggested by some archaeologists familiar with the mysterious structure is that it was used to hold prisoners.

Where would the sentence best fit?

12 **Directions:** Complete the table below by matching FIVE of the seven choices with the appropriate characteristics of a storage room, a tower, and a kiva in Cliff Palace. TWO answer choices will NOT be used. *This question is worth 3 points.*

Answer Choices

① It was built high to be safe from moisture and pests.

② The structure is partitioned by walls.

③ This room has a self-heating bathtub.

④ There is no way to access it through doorways or portals.

⑤ This place contains some abstract designs.

⑥ People accessed this room with a removable ladder.

⑦ This room has a beautiful view of the surrounding area.

Storage Room
-
-

Kiva
-
-

Tower
-

Vocabulary Check-Up

A Choose the words with the closest meanings to the highlighted words.

1 Scientists examined several properties of the strange phenomenon.

ⓐ characteristics
ⓑ vehicles
ⓒ owners
ⓓ colors

2 His dream was to move to New Mexico to join an art colony.

ⓐ house
ⓑ school
ⓒ group
ⓓ list

3 He had a poor reaction after viewing some pretend violence.

ⓐ real
ⓑ necessary
ⓒ negative
ⓓ imaginary

4 She was a strong advocate of the Media Influence Theory.

ⓐ critic
ⓑ supporter
ⓒ not sure
ⓓ enemy

5 The police found many linkages between the crime scene and the suspect.

ⓐ fingerprints
ⓑ witnesses
ⓒ similarities
ⓓ connections

6 She suddenly got the notion that he wanted to ask her out on a date.

ⓐ hope
ⓑ expectation
ⓒ idea
ⓓ worry

7 The morality club engaged in a discourse about current issues.

ⓐ questioning
ⓑ argument
ⓒ fighting
ⓓ ethics

8 The doctors were able to reconstruct his nose after the accident.

ⓐ rebuild
ⓑ help
ⓒ replace
ⓓ remove

B Match the words with the correct definitions.

1 anthropology •

• Ⓐ someone who is blamed for a problem, usually unjustly

2 surname •

• Ⓑ cells that process and transmit information in the brain

3 scapegoat •

• Ⓒ the visual aspect of blood or murder

4 assumption •

• Ⓓ a certificate of accreditation from a university or college

5 evolution •

• Ⓔ the practice of parents raising a child that is not genetically theirs

6 adoption •

• Ⓕ objects or money passed from someone who dies to someone else

7 inheritance •

• Ⓖ the study of people and their culture

8 neurons •

• Ⓗ the process by which organisms develop

9 gore •

• Ⓘ the name shared by family members or people who are related

10 degree •

• Ⓙ a belief that is created by looking at various information

Actual Test

Actual Test

01

CONTINUE

Reading Section Directions

This section measures your ability to understand academic passages in English. You will have **35 minutes** to read and answer questions about **2 passages**. A clock at the top of the screen will show you how much time is remaining.

Most questions are worth 1 point but the last question for each passage is worth more than 1 point. The directions for the last question indicate how many points you may receive.

Some passages include a word or phrase that is <u>underlined</u> in blue. Click on the word or phrase to see a definition or an explanation.

When you want to move to the next question, click on **Next**. You may skip questions and go back to them later. If you want to return to previous questions, click on **Back**. You can click on **Review** at any time, and the review screen will show you which questions you have answered and which you have not answered. From this review screen, you may go directly to any question you have already seen in the Reading section.

Click on **Continue** to go on.

11-01

The Periodic Table

The periodic table of the elements

Humans have always known about certain elemental substances, such as gold and silver, that occur in nature and cannot be broken down into other substances. Other chemical elements were discovered gradually beginning in 1669. That was when a German merchant, Hennig Brand, accidentally found phosphorus while attempting to find a way to create gold out of more common metals. By 1809, the number of known elements had increased to forty-seven. Chemists studying the elements began to notice patterns in the way chemicals reacted. The first modern chemistry textbook was written in 1789 by Antoine-Laurent de Lavoisier. He listed the known elements, which he classified into metals and nonmetals. But his list omitted the gases. It also included some things that were not substances, such as light and calories. Thus, it was not accepted as an accurate organizing system.

An important trait of elements is their periodicity: similarly acting elements tend to occur at regular intervals when arranged by their atomic weight, the number of protons plus neutrons in the nucleus. A French geologist, Alexandre-Emile Beguyer de Chancourtois, was the first to notice this periodicity. He designed a **precursor** to the periodic table. It was called the telluric helix. His system arranged the elements on a spiral-shaped cylinder in order of their atomic weight. Elements with similar physical properties appeared vertically on the cylinder. But because Chancourtois's 1862 paper used geological terms and did not include drawings, his periodic system was not accepted by those in the field of chemistry.

New elements were discovered throughout the first half of the 1800s. So chemists confirmed the regular repetition of the physical properties of the elements. Chemists studied ways to classify the elements to reflect this periodicity. In 1863, an English chemist, John Newlands, divided the fifty-six known elements into groups, each sharing the same characteristics. As each group seemed to contain eight elements, he referred to his system as the Law of Octaves. He named it after the eight keys in an octave on the piano. But Newlands's idea was ridiculed and his theory dismissed. Not until 1919 did it become accepted that the elements should be grouped by eights.

The underlying concept of the periodicity of the elements was adapted to better effect in 1869 by the Russian chemist Dmitri Mendeleev. His great breakthrough was to see that the two key characteristics of an element—atomic weight and atomic number, which is the number of protons in the nucleus— could be combined in a single table. His table came to be called the periodic table. Mendeleev's table was inspired by the card game solitaire, in which cards are arranged horizontally by suit and vertically by number. Borrowing the same patterns, Mendeleev arranged the elements in groups of seven. He grouped them horizontally by their atomic number in ascending order and vertically by their similar qualities in groups of seven. Thus, similar metals such as gold, silver, and copper appear in the same vertical column. Similarly reacting gases such as helium, argon, and neon appear in another column. The most common elements—hydrogen, helium, and lithium—have lower atomic numbers and thus appear near the beginning of the table in the first horizontal row. The rarest elements—uranium and plutonium—have the greatest number of protons in their nuclei. They are ordered near the end of the table.

In Mendeleev's time, only sixty-three elements had been discovered. The **brilliance** of his periodic table, however, was that it predicted new elements would be found to fit into the missing slots in his original table. Today, the table shows 120 elements, ninety-two naturally occurring ones and twenty-eight created in laboratories. Scientists believe many more will be found. The periodic table has been called "the most elegant organizational chart ever devised." Mendeleev's chart remains valid today. But it has been modified by the continual discovery and manufacture of new elements. And in 1914, Henry Mosely discovered a relationship between an element's X-ray wavelength and its atomic number. Thus, he rearranged the elements by electric charge. Another important improvement was suggested by Glenn T. Seaborg in 1945. He proposed adding a vertical group of certain heavy elements called the actinide series.

📖 *Glossary*
precursor: something that comes before another thing
brilliance: great intelligence or skill

1 The word "it" in the passage refers to

   Ⓐ the first modern chemistry textbook

   Ⓑ his list

   Ⓒ light

   Ⓓ an accurate organizing system

2 Which of the following best expresses the essential information in the highlighted sentence? *Incorrect* choices change the meaning in important ways or leave out essential information.

   Ⓐ Elements with the same number of protons do not react with one another.

   Ⓑ Periodicity refers to an element's tendency to gain an extra proton at times.

   Ⓒ An element has protons and neutrons in the nucleus of its atoms.

   Ⓓ The properties of elements tend to reoccur at fixed intervals of their atomic weights.

The Periodic Table

Humans have always known about certain elemental substances, such as gold and silver, that occur in nature and cannot be broken down into other substances. Other chemical elements were discovered gradually beginning in 1669. That was when a German merchant, Hennig Brand, accidentally found phosphorus while attempting to find a way to create gold out of more common metals. By 1809, the number of known elements had increased to forty-seven. Chemists studying the elements began to notice patterns in the way chemicals reacted. The first modern chemistry textbook was written in 1789 by Antoine-Laurent de Lavoisier. He listed the known elements, which he classified into metals and nonmetals. But his list omitted the gases. It also included some things that were not substances, such as light and calories. Thus, it was not accepted as an accurate organizing system.

An important trait of elements is their periodicity: similarly acting elements tend to occur at regular intervals when arranged by their atomic weight, the number of protons plus neutrons in the nucleus. A French geologist, Alexandre-Emile Beguyer de Chancourtois, was the first to notice this periodicity. He designed a **precursor** to the periodic table. It was called the telluric helix. His system arranged the elements on a spiral-shaped cylinder in order of their atomic weight. Elements with similar physical properties appeared vertically on the cylinder. But because Chancourtois's 1862 paper used geological terms and did not include drawings, his periodic system was not accepted by those in the field of chemistry.

📖 *Glossary*

precursor: something that comes before another thing

3 According to paragraphs 2 and 3, the first chemist to notice periodicity was

   Ⓐ Mendeleev

   Ⓑ Chancourtois

   Ⓒ Lavoisier

   Ⓓ Newlands

4 In paragraph 3, why does the author mention "the Law of Octaves"?

   Ⓐ To point out that it was an incorrect theory

   Ⓑ To name the people who believed it was incorrect

   Ⓒ To explain how a chemist grouped the elements

   Ⓓ To compare it with the keys on a piano

2 ➡ An important trait of elements is their periodicity: similarly acting elements tend to occur at regular intervals when arranged by their atomic weight, the number of protons plus neutrons in the nucleus. A French geologist, Alexandre-Emile Beguyer de Chancourtois, was the first to notice this periodicity. He designed a **precursor** to the periodic table. It was called the telluric helix. His system arranged the elements on a spiral-shaped cylinder in order of their atomic weight. Elements with similar physical properties appeared vertically on the cylinder. But because Chancourtois's 1862 paper used geological terms and did not include drawings, his periodic system was not accepted by those in the field of chemistry.

3 ➡ New elements were discovered throughout the first half of the 1800s. So chemists confirmed the regular repetition of the physical properties of the elements. Chemists studied ways to classify the elements to reflect this periodicity. In 1863, an English chemist, John Newlands, divided the fifty-six known elements into groups, each sharing the same characteristics. As each group seemed to contain eight elements, he referred to his system as the Law of Octaves. He named it after the eight keys in an octave on the piano. But Newlands's idea was ridiculed and his theory dismissed. Not until 1919 did it become accepted that the elements should be grouped by eights.

📖 *Glossary*

precursor: something that comes before another thing

5 According to paragraph 4, Mendeleev's main discovery was that

Ⓐ some elements have similar physical properties that reoccur at regular intervals of their atomic weights

Ⓑ an element's atomic weight and number can be shown in a single table

Ⓒ similarly acting elements always appear in groups of eight

Ⓓ the rarest elements tend to have the lowest atomic weights

6 According to paragraph 4, which of the following can be inferred about hydrogen?

Ⓐ Its atomic number is less than that of uranium.

Ⓑ It appears in a vertical row on the table of elements.

Ⓒ It reacts with helium to form various compounds.

Ⓓ Its atomic weight is greater than that of lithium.

⁴ ➡ The underlying concept of the periodicity of the elements was adapted to better effect in 1869 by the Russian chemist Dmitri Mendeleev. His great breakthrough was to see that the two key characteristics of an element—atomic weight and atomic number, which is the number of protons in the nucleus—could be combined in a single table. His table came to be called the periodic table. Mendeleev's table was inspired by the card game solitaire, in which cards are arranged horizontally by suit and vertically by number. Borrowing the same patterns, Mendeleev arranged the elements in groups of seven. He grouped them horizontally by their atomic number in ascending order and vertically by their similar qualities in groups of seven. Thus, similar metals such as gold, silver, and copper appear in the same vertical column. Similarly reacting gases such as helium, argon, and neon appear in another column. The most common elements—hydrogen, helium, and lithium—have lower atomic numbers and thus appear near the beginning of the table in the first horizontal row. The rarest elements—uranium and plutonium—have the greatest number of protons in their nuclei. They are ordered near the end of the table.

7 The word "valid" in the passage is closest in meaning to

- (A) studied
- (B) misleading
- (C) legal
- (D) accurate

8 According to paragraph 5, which of the following is NOT true of the periodic table of the elements?

- (A) It is constantly changing as new elements are found.
- (B) It originally predicted that more elements would be discovered.
- (C) It will never contain more than 120 elements.
- (D) It includes the elements that have been created artificially.

⁵ ➡ In Mendeleev's time, only sixty-three elements had been discovered. The **brilliance** of his periodic table, however, was that it predicted new elements would be found to fit into the missing slots in his original table. Today, the table shows 120 elements, ninety-two naturally occurring ones and twenty-eight created in laboratories. Scientists believe many more will be found. The periodic table has been called "the most elegant organizational chart ever devised." Mendeleev's chart remains valid today. But it has been modified by the continual discovery and manufacture of new elements. And in 1914, Henry Mosely discovered a relationship between an element's X-ray wavelength and its atomic number. Thus, he rearranged the elements by electric charge. Another important improvement was suggested by Glenn T. Seaborg in 1945. He proposed adding a vertical group of certain heavy elements called the actinide series.

📖 *Glossary*

brilliance: great intelligence or skill

9 Look at the four squares [■] that indicate where the following sentence could be added to the passage.

But no one had succeeded in organizing the elements in a format that showed those patterns.

Where would the sentence best fit?

Click on a square [■] to add the sentence to the passage.

Humans have always known about certain elemental substances, such as gold and silver, that occur in nature and cannot be broken down into other substances. Other chemical elements were discovered gradually beginning in 1669. **1** That was when a German merchant, Hennig Brand, accidentally found phosphorus while attempting to find a way to create gold out of more common metals. **2** By 1809, the number of known elements had increased to forty-seven. **3** Chemists studying the elements began to notice patterns in the way chemicals reacted. **4** The first modern chemistry textbook was written in 1789 by Antoine-Laurent de Lavoisier. He listed the known elements, which he classified into metals and nonmetals. But his list omitted the gases. It also included some things that were not substances, such as light and calories. Thus, it was not accepted as an accurate organizing system.

10 **Directions:** An introductory sentence for a brief summary of the passage is provided below. Complete the summary by selecting the THREE answer choices that express the most important ideas in the passage. Some answer choices do not belong in the summary because they express ideas that are not in the passage or are minor ideas in the passage. *This question is worth 2 points.*

Drag your answer choices to the spaces where they belong.
To remove an answer choice, click on it. To review the passage, click on **View Text**.

This passage explores the history of the periodic table.

-
-
-

Answer Choices

1 Chancourtois was the first to notice the periodicity of elements.

2 The periodic table is constantly changing as new elements and new ways of classifying them are discovered.

3 Lavoisier's list of elements included light and calories.

4 By 1809, there were forty-seven elements that were known to humans.

5 The most common elements appear near the end of the table while the least common are near the beginning.

6 Mendeleev organized the elements into a table based on their atomic weight.

11 - 02

The History of Counting

The earliest signs of counting have been found in ancient hunting artifacts. <u>Notches</u> in animal bones from 30,000 B.C. may have been a tallying system. Tallies were used to keep track of things. A sheepherder would put a pebble in a pile each time a sheep was let out to graze. When the sheep returned at night, the owner would remove the pebble. Any pebbles that remained represented missing sheep. But such tallying was not true counting. It merely compared two sets of objects.

Egypt was one of the first civilizations to adopt a real number system. Beginning around 3000 B.C., Egyptians expressed numbers with pictographs, or symbols to represent numbers. Thus, the numbers from one to nine were combinations of vertical strokes. Ten was an inverted U, 100 was a coiled rope, and 1,000 was a lotus flower. Different cultures used different base numbers for their counting systems. Many, such as the Egyptians, used a base 10, a reflection of the numbers of fingers on both hands. Others, like the Babylonians, used a base 60. But that system was awkward because it required either separate symbols for each number up to 60 or clusters of 10 numbers. But the base of 60 survives today in geometry—60 seconds and minutes of angular measurement, 360 degrees in a circle, and 180 degrees in a rectangle—and in timekeeping—60 seconds in a minute and 60 minutes in an hour.

The first great advance in numbering was the place-value concept. Invented by the Babylonians, place values were needed to show the value of each digit in a numeric <u>notation</u>. For example, without place values, the number 236 was complicated to write in most systems because it required multiple symbols and strokes. But with a value assigned to each place in a system based on 10, we know that the digit 6 represents 6 ones, the digit 3 represents 3 tens, and the digit 2 represents 2 hundreds. For place value to accurately reflect a number, a "zero" was needed to eliminate any confusion over, for example, whether the digits 236 were intended to represent 236 or 2,360 or 2,036 or 2,306. The zero or "empty" place value was originally indicated by leaving a gap between numbers, as in 23_6 to mean 2306. Eventually, a special symbol was designed to show zero, the 0 digit that is used today. That symbol was invented for the Arabic counting system and was in common use by about 650 A.D.

For zero and place values to be useful in mathematics, it was necessary to invent a symbol for each number up to the base figure. Different symbols for one through nine were therefore adopted with zero added after each symbol to reflect another 10: 10, 20, 30, 40, and so on. And multiple zeros were added to represent even larger numbers such as 100, 1000, and 10,000.

Arabic numerals ultimately replaced the Roman numerals that had dominated Western European history until the seventeenth century. Those are the numerals used in most of the world today. Early forms of Arabic numbers appeared in India by 200 B.C. Indian mathematicians found that a place-value system which included a symbol for zero allowed them to perform mathematical operations by writing down and manipulating numerals. That was faster than the abacus, a mechanical device that had been the principal means of counting. Using written numerals to calculate did not become known outside India until the ninth century, when an Arab mathematician, Al-Khwarizmi, wrote a treatise about numbers. But his work was not translated into Latin until the twelfth century and thus did not become known in Europe until then. An Italian, Leonardo Fibonacci, popularized the Arabic numbering system, called algorism, by writing books about it that were read by bookkeepers and merchants. They started to use the system in their commercial transactions.

For a few hundred years after Fibonacci, scholars and merchants debated the merits of algorism versus the abacus. With the invention of printing, books about algorism became widely known, leading to it becoming the accepted method from about 1500. By about 1600, Roman numerals had been supplanted by Arabic numerals for performing most computations.

📖 *Glossary*

notch: a small cut or nick in a surface
notation: a series of signs or symbols used to represent information

11 According to paragraph 1, the first signs of counting were found in

- Ⓐ tallies
- Ⓑ sheep
- Ⓒ rocks
- Ⓓ animal bones

12 According to paragraph 2, Egypt's counting system used which of the following to show numbers?

- Ⓐ Tallies
- Ⓑ Pictographs
- Ⓒ Place values
- Ⓓ An inverted U

The History of Counting

1 ➡ The earliest signs of counting have been found in ancient hunting artifacts. **Notches** in animal bones from 30,000 B.C. may have been a tallying system. Tallies were used to keep track of things. A sheepherder would put a pebble in a pile each time a sheep was let out to graze. When the sheep returned at night, the owner would remove the pebble. Any pebbles that remained represented missing sheep. But such tallying was not true counting. It merely compared two sets of objects.

2 ➡ Egypt was one of the first civilizations to adopt a real number system. Beginning around 3000 B.C., Egyptians expressed numbers with pictographs, or symbols to represent numbers. Thus, the numbers from one to nine were combinations of vertical strokes. Ten was an inverted U, 100 was a coiled rope, and 1,000 was a lotus flower. Different cultures used different base numbers for their counting systems. Many, such as the Egyptians, used a base 10, a reflection of the numbers of fingers on both hands. Others, like the Babylonians, used a base 60. But that system was awkward because it required either separate symbols for each number up to 60 or clusters of 10 numbers. But the base of 60 survives today in geometry—60 seconds and minutes of angular measurement, 360 degrees in a circle, and 180 degrees in a rectangle—and in timekeeping—60 seconds in a minute and 60 minutes in an hour.

📖 *Glossary*

notch: a small cut or nick in a surface

13 In paragraph 3, the author mentions "the number 236" in order to

(A) illustrate the importance of the zero in the place-value system

(B) explain how the Arabs invented Arabic numerals

(C) identify the first numeral that was written with place values

(D) show a number that does not contain a zero

14 In paragraph 4, the author implies that zero

(A) was not easily accepted by people in ancient times

(B) was invented by people in several different cultures

(C) helped lead to the creation of other written numbers

(D) did not take its present form until centuries after being invented

³ ➡ The first great advance in numbering was the place-value concept. Invented by the Babylonians, place values were needed to show the value of each digit in a numeric notation. For example, without place values, the number 236 was complicated to write in most systems because it required multiple symbols and strokes. But with a value assigned to each place in a system based on 10, we know that the digit 6 represents 6 ones, the digit 3 represents 3 tens, and the digit 2 represents 2 hundreds. For place value to accurately reflect a number, a "zero" was needed to eliminate any confusion over, for example, whether the digits 236 were intended to represent 236 or 2,360 or 2,036 or 2,306. The zero or "empty" place value was originally indicated by leaving a gap between numbers, as in 23_6 to mean 2306. Eventually, a special symbol was designed to show zero, the 0 digit that is used today. That symbol was invented for the Arabic counting system and was in common use by about 650 A.D.

⁴ ➡ For zero and place values to be useful in mathematics, it was necessary to invent a symbol for each number up to the base figure. Different symbols for one through nine were therefore adopted with zero added after each symbol to reflect another 10: 10, 20, 30, 40, and so on. And multiple zeros were added to represent even larger numbers such as 100, 1000, and 10,000.

📖 *Glossary*

notation: a series of signs or symbols used to represent information

15 In paragraph 5, why does the author mention "the abacus"?

(A) To contrast it with written numbers regarding speed of calculating

(B) To give an example of a means of counting used after the year 1600

(C) To describe how sheepherders used to keep track of their sheep

(D) To mention a device that was invented by Al-Khwarizmi

16 In paragraph 5, all of the following questions are answered EXCEPT:

(A) What did Al-Khwarizmi do?

(B) What type of numbers replaced Roman numerals?

(C) How did Fibonacci invent the algorism system?

(D) When did Arabic numbers first appear in India?

17 According to paragraph 5, Al-Khwarizmi's treatise was unknown in Europe until the twelfth century because

(A) it was not yet translated into Latin

(B) printing was not invented until then

(C) Arab mathematicians wanted to keep it secret

(D) Europeans were not interested in other counting systems

18 The word "supplanted" in the passage is closest in meaning to

(A) revised

(B) replaced

(C) reinforced

(D) resurrected

⁵ ➡ Arabic numerals ultimately replaced the Roman numerals that had dominated Western European history until the seventeenth century. Those are the numerals used in most of the world today. Early forms of Arabic numbers appeared in India by 200 B.C. Indian mathematicians found that a place-value system which included a symbol for zero allowed them to perform mathematical operations by writing down and manipulating numerals. That was faster than the abacus, a mechanical device that had been the principal means of counting. Using written numerals to calculate did not become known outside India until the ninth century, when an Arab mathematician, Al-Khwarizmi, wrote a treatise about numbers. But his work was not translated into Latin until the twelfth century and thus did not become known in Europe until then. An Italian, Leonardo Fibonacci, popularized the Arabic numbering system, called algorism, by writing books about it that were read by bookkeepers and merchants. They started to use the system in their commercial transactions.

For a few hundred years after Fibonacci, scholars and merchants debated the merits of algorism versus the abacus. With the invention of printing, books about algorism became widely known, leading to it becoming the accepted method from about 1500. By about 1600, Roman numerals had been supplanted by Arabic numerals for performing most computations.

19 Look at the four squares [■] that indicate where the following sentence could be added to the passage.

It had been used since at least 2300 B.C. and was known to people in Europe, Egypt, and Asia in ancient times.

Where would the sentence best fit?

> Click on a square [■] to add the sentence to the passage.

Arabic numerals ultimately replaced the Roman numerals that had dominated Western European history until the seventeenth century. Those are the numerals used in most of the world today. Early forms of Arabic numbers appeared in India by 200 B.C. Indian mathematicians found that a place-value system which included a symbol for zero allowed them to perform mathematical operations by writing down and manipulating numerals. That was faster than the abacus, a mechanical device that had been the principal means of counting. **1** Using written numerals to calculate did not become known outside India until the ninth century, when an Arab mathematician, Al-Khwarizmi, wrote a treatise about numbers. **2** But his work was not translated into Latin until the twelfth century and thus did not become known in Europe until then. **3** An Italian, Leonardo Fibonacci, popularized the Arabic numbering system, called algorism, by writing books about it that were read by bookkeepers and merchants. **4** They started to use the system in their commercial transactions.

20 Directions: Complete the table below to summarize the information about the two ideas that permitted counting with written numerals discussed in the passage. Match the appropriate statements to the idea with which they are associated. TWO of the answer choices will NOT be used. *This question is worth 3 points.*

Drag your answer choices to the spaces where they belong.
To remove an answer choice, click on it. To review the passage, click on **View Text**.

Answer Choices

1. Computation required that a number show the value of each digit.

2. Tallying was used to keep records.

3. Numbers were complicated to write.

4. A special symbol was needed to show an empty place value.

5. The idea was first invented by the Babylonians.

6. Roman numerals were replaced by Arabic numerals.

7. The symbol was first used by the Arabs.

Place Value
-
-
-

Zero
-
-

Actual Test

02

CONTINUE

Reading Section Directions

This section measures your ability to understand academic passages in English. You will have **35 minutes** to read and answer questions about **2 passages**. A clock at the top of the screen will show you how much time is remaining.

Most questions are worth 1 point but the last question for each passage is worth more than 1 point. The directions for the last question indicate how many points you may receive.

Some passages include a word or phrase that is <u>underlined</u> in blue. Click on the word or phrase to see a definition or an explanation.

When you want to move to the next question, click on **Next**. You may skip questions and go back to them later. If you want to return to previous questions, click on **Back**. You can click on **Review** at any time, and the review screen will show you which questions you have answered and which you have not answered. From this review screen, you may go directly to any question you have already seen in the Reading section.

Click on **Continue** to go on.

11-03

Minerals

Minerals are naturally occurring solid substances formed by geologic movements in the Earth. Their main defining characteristics are that they are inorganic and composed of nonliving matter, they have a crystal structure, and they have a unique chemical composition. The type of mineral is determined both by its crystal structure and its chemical composition. A crystal structure occurs when the atoms inside a mineral are ordered in a geometric pattern that repeats itself throughout the mineral. All crystal structures fit into one of fourteen possible lattices—regular patterns—which are arrangements of atoms. These lattices can be detected by X-rays.

A mineral's physical traits are influenced by its crystal form. For example, both diamond and graphite are composed of the same element, carbon, but the former is the hardest mineral while the latter is soft. The reason is that graphite's crystal structure arranges the carbon atoms in sheets that can slide past one another while diamond's carbon atoms are arrayed in a strong, interlocking network. Two minerals with identical crystal structures can have different chemical compositions. Thus, halite and galena share the same crystal structure but are composed of different chemicals. Conversely, two minerals with the same chemical ingredients can differ in their crystal structure. For example, pyrite and marcasite both are made of iron sulfide. However, the arrangement of their atoms differs.

According to the International Mineralogical Association, 4,000 minerals have been identified to date. Only about 150 of them are plentiful. About fifty are classified as "occasional." The remainder are rarely found. Some of these consist only of small grains of rock. Minerals are often found as components of rocks, which may contain organic matter as well. Some rocks consist wholly of one mineral, such as calcite in limestone rock. Other rocks may host many minerals. Almost all of the rocks visible today contain one or more of a group of about fifteen minerals. Among them are quartz, mica, and felspar.

The kinds of minerals found in any given rock are determined by three factors. First, the rock's chemical composition must be **hospitable** to a particular mineral. For example, rocks containing silicon will likely contain quartz. Second, the conditions under which the rock was formed will influence the kinds of minerals found in it. Thus, rock born from volcanic movements at high temperatures and pressures may contain granite. Third, mineral distribution is affected by the geological stages through which the rock passed before reaching its present state. For example, exposure to moisture and acids may decay some minerals and cause others to take their place. During the changes from one ecological stage to another, the rock may disintegrate into sand or soil.

Mineralogists classify minerals according to either physical properties or chemical composition. Minerals have numerous measurable physical properties. Hardness is measured on the Mohs scale. It ranks hardness from one to ten. Any mineral can be cut or marked by a mineral with a higher ranking on the Mohs scale. A diamond, with a rank of ten, can therefore cut into quartz, with a rank of seven. Luster measures the reflection of light by the surface of the mineral. Metals have a higher luster than gypsum, which has a porous surface. Cleavage refers to the way a mineral splits apart along its natural grain. Fracture refers to its breakage against its natural cleavage planes. Streak is the color of the residue left by a mineral as it is rubbed across a special plate. Specific gravity measures the density of the mineral. It is computed by comparing the mass of the mineral to the mass of an equal volume of water.

Minerals can also be classified by their chemical characteristics. The most frequently occurring minerals are called silicates because of their large shares of silicon and oxygen. Almost all rocks fit this category. The second most common minerals are carbonates. They contain carbon and oxygen. Carbonates are found on the ocean floor as deposits of decayed plankton. Another grouping, halides, are found where water has evaporated. They can be found in dried lake beds and landlocked seas such as the Great Salt Lake in Utah. Other common classes include sulfates, oxides, sulfides, and phosphates.

📖 *Glossary*

hospitable: welcoming to guests or visitors
residue: a small amount of something that remains after a part is removed

1   According to paragraph 1, which of the following is a characteristic of minerals?

    Ⓐ Having a crystal structure

    Ⓑ Being comprised of organic matter

    Ⓒ Being harder than other objects

    Ⓓ Possessing a smooth surface

2   Which of the following best expresses the essential information in the highlighted sentence? *Incorrect* answer choices change the meaning in important ways or leave out essential information.

    Ⓐ The sheets of graphite's carbon atoms slide past the sheets of diamond's carbon atoms.

    Ⓑ Graphite contains a network of carbon atoms that create a strong crystal structure.

    Ⓒ Diamond is harder than graphite because of its carbon atoms' interlocking structure.

    Ⓓ The networks of carbon atoms in diamond and graphite make each mineral very hard.

3   According to paragraph 2, two minerals with the same crystal structure can be different because

    Ⓐ they have different specific gravities

    Ⓑ they are found in different locations

    Ⓒ they were formed by different geologic processes

    Ⓓ they have different chemical compositions

Minerals

[1] → Minerals are naturally occurring solid substances formed by geologic movements in the Earth. Their main defining characteristics are that they are inorganic and composed of nonliving matter, they have a crystal structure, and they have a unique chemical composition. The type of mineral is determined both by its crystal structure and its chemical composition. A crystal structure occurs when the atoms inside a mineral are ordered in a geometric pattern that repeats itself throughout the mineral. All crystal structures fit into one of fourteen possible lattices—regular patterns—which are arrangements of atoms. These lattices can be detected by X-rays.

[2] → A mineral's physical traits are influenced by its crystal form. For example, both diamond and graphite are composed of the same element, carbon, but the former is the hardest mineral while the latter is soft. The reason is that graphite's crystal structure arranges the carbon atoms in sheets that can slide past one another while diamond's carbon atoms are arrayed in a strong, interlocking network. Two minerals with identical crystal structures can have different chemical compositions. Thus, halite and galena share the same crystal structure but are composed of different chemicals. Conversely, two minerals with the same chemical ingredients can differ in their crystal structure. For example, pyrite and marcasite both are made of iron sulfide. However, the arrangement of their atoms differs.

4 In paragraph 3, which of the following is mentioned about the International Mineralogical Association?

   Ⓐ The number of minerals that it has identified

   Ⓑ The year when it was founded

   Ⓒ The role it currently plays in the field of geology

   Ⓓ The places where it prefers to look for rocks

5 In paragraph 4, why does the author discuss "volcanic movements"?

   Ⓐ To give an example of one of the Earth's geologic forces

   Ⓑ To identify a factor that determines what kinds of minerals are found in rocks

   Ⓒ To explain why some rocks are known to contain large amounts of silicon

   Ⓓ To criticize the theory that minerals are created only by chemical reactions

6 The word "disintegrate" in the passage is closest in meaning to

   Ⓐ decompose

   Ⓑ imbed

   Ⓒ pressurize

   Ⓓ decline

³ ➡ According to the International Mineralogical Association, 4,000 minerals have been identified to date. Only about 150 of them are plentiful. About fifty are classified as "occasional." The remainder are rarely found. Some of these consist only of small grains of rock. Minerals are often found as components of rocks, which may contain organic matter as well. Some rocks consist wholly of one mineral, such as calcite in limestone rock. Other rocks may host many minerals. Almost all of the rocks visible today contain one or more of a group of about fifteen minerals. Among them are quartz, mica, and felspar.

⁴ ➡ The kinds of minerals found in any given rock are determined by three factors. First, the rock's chemical composition must be **hospitable** to a particular mineral. For example, rocks containing silicon will likely contain quartz. Second, the conditions under which the rock was formed will influence the kinds of minerals found in it. Thus, rock born from volcanic movements at high temperatures and pressures may contain granite. Third, mineral distribution is affected by the geological stages through which the rock passed before reaching its present state. For example, exposure to moisture and acids may decay some minerals and cause others to take their place. During the changes from one ecological stage to another, the rock may disintegrate into sand or soil.

📖 *Glossary*

hospitable: welcoming to guests or visitors

7   According to paragraph 5, which of the following can be inferred about minerals on the Mohs scale?

   Ⓐ Graphite is softer than gypsum.

   Ⓑ Quartz can cut a mineral with a rank of 8.

   Ⓒ Diamond can cut a mineral with a rank of 9.

   Ⓓ The hardest minerals are metals.

8   According to paragraph 5, which of the following is NOT a property of minerals?

   Ⓐ Cleavage

   Ⓑ Luster

   Ⓒ Streak

   Ⓓ Weight

⁵ ➡ Mineralogists classify minerals according to either physical properties or chemical composition. Minerals have numerous measurable physical properties. Hardness is measured on the Mohs scale. It ranks hardness from one to ten. Any mineral can be cut or marked by a mineral with a higher ranking on the Mohs scale. A diamond, with a rank of ten, can therefore cut into quartz, with a rank of seven. Luster measures the reflection of light by the surface of the mineral. Metals have a higher luster than gypsum, which has a porous surface. Cleavage refers to the way a mineral splits apart along its natural grain. Fracture refers to its breakage against its natural cleavage planes. Streak is the color of the **residue** left by a mineral as it is rubbed across a special plate. Specific gravity measures the density of the mineral. It is computed by comparing the mass of the mineral to the mass of an equal volume of water.

Minerals can also be classified by their chemical characteristics. The most frequently occurring minerals are called silicates because of their large shares of silicon and oxygen. Almost all rocks fit this category. The second most common minerals are carbonates. They contain carbon and oxygen. Carbonates are found on the ocean floor as deposits of decayed plankton. Another grouping, halides, are found where water has evaporated. They can be found in dried lake beds and landlocked seas such as the Great Salt Lake in Utah. Other common classes include sulfates, oxides, sulfides, and phosphates.

📖 *Glossary*

residue: a small amount of something that remains after a part is removed

9 Look at the four squares [■] that indicate where the following sentence could be added to the passage.

As a result, specialized equipment is required to detect any of them.

Where would the sentence best fit?

Click on a square [■] to add the sentence to the passage.

According to the International Mineralogical Association, 4,000 minerals have been identified to date. Only about 150 of them are plentiful. About fifty are classified as "occasional." **1** The remainder are rarely found. **2** Some of these consist only of small grains of rock. **3** Minerals are often found as components of rocks, which may contain organic matter as well. **4** Some rocks consist wholly of one mineral, such as calcite in limestone rock. Other rocks may host many minerals. Almost all of the rocks visible today contain one or more of a group of about fifteen minerals. Among them are quartz, mica, and felspar.

10 Directions: An introductory sentence for a brief summary of the passage is provided below. Complete the summary by selecting the THREE answer choices that express the most important ideas in the passage. Some answer choices do not belong in the summary because they express ideas that are not in the passage or are minor ideas in the passage. *This question is worth 2 points.*

> Drag your answer choices to the spaces where they belong.
> To remove an answer choice, click on it. To review the passage, click on **View Text**.

This passage explores the structure and composition of minerals.

-
-
-

Answer Choices

1. When a mineral is exposed to moisture and acid, it may decay and allow a new mineral to form.

2. Minerals are classified by their physical properties and chemical composition.

3. The kind of mineral is defined by its crystal structure and its chemical composition.

4. Carbonates are deposits of dead plankton that are found on the ocean floor.

5. Minerals are often found in rocks, and each rock may host one or many minerals.

6. Cleavage is the property of minerals that concerns the way it breaks along its natural cleavage planes.

11-04

The Whitetail and Blacktail Deer

A male whitetail deer in a field

Of all of North America's large animals, the most numerous is the whitetail deer. This species of deer is known for its habit of raising and flopping its tail over its back. This action reveals its white underside and buttocks. People often observe this telltale marking as the deer runs away from them. When the tail is down, it is brown with a white fringe. Varying with the seasons, the color of the whitetail deer is reddish in summer and grayish in winter. An adult male, which is known as a buck, grows to over a meter at shoulder height. It also weighs about 110 kilograms. Males grow antlers, which occasionally become entangled with those of another male. This **dooms** each animal to a slow death.

Also known as the Virginia deer, the whitetail deer inhabits most of the continental United States. It can be found in southern Canada, Mexico, Central America, and the northern countries of South America. It has also been introduced into northern Europe. The whitetail is highly adaptable. Though it most often lives in densely forested areas, it can also adapt to live in open savannas. These include the plains of Texas and the Venezuelan llanos. Mating season is in the fall. Bucks attempt to mate with as many females—called does—as possible. Does give birth to one or two fawns in late spring. A doe leaves her fawn alone for hours at a time, as its natural camouflage—a spotted coat and the absence of scent—makes it invisible to most predators. It returns periodically to feed the fawn.

With sufficient food and shelter, whitetail deer populations grow rapidly. But they can grow too rapidly at times. It often becomes a nuisance to farmers, whose crops serve as food for the deer. It also frequently collides with cars as it bounds across roadways. This causes the death of the deer and injury or death to human drivers. Regulated hunts are scheduled to thin out excessive populations. In addition, deer hunting is a significant cultural ritual in many areas. It even serves as an important boost to some local economies. The cutting down of forests to make way for commercial development has deprived many herds of their natural habitat, leading to their starvation or increased **vulnerability** to highway collisions.

The blacktail deer descended from its whitetail relative millions of years ago. Scientists believe that it migrated down the east coast of the North American continent. It crossed Mexico and went up the California coast. There, it ultimately evolved into the blacktail deer. Their common ancestry explains why the two species resemble each other both in physical appearance and psychological traits. Indeed, the two are often hard to distinguish. Though the blacktail's tail is black, it shares the whitetail's habit of raising its tail. This lets it display some white coloring underneath. And the males of both species have similar antlers. But the blacktail is found only along the western edge of the continent. Its range extends from British Columbia in Canada to southern California. Moreover, the blacktail is slightly smaller than its white-tailed cousin.

Until recently scientists believed that the blacktail deer was a subspecies of the mule deer. But DNA testing has proved that it is a separate species. The mule deer evolved into a distinct species from breeding with the whitetail and the blacktail. Experienced hunters report that the blacktail is the hardest deer species to hunt. One reason is that blacktails inhabit a much hotter climate. Daytime temperatures reach around 100 degrees Fahrenheit in the summer during archery season in California. In that heat, blacktail bucks stay quiet during the day. They move only under the protective cover of darkness. In the rainy season, the blacktail is active during the day. But few hunters want to venture out in bad weather. Blacktail hunting is further complicated by the fact that the hunting season in western states ends before the mating season. That is when many bucks are most active while searching for females. Thus, they are the most accessible at a time when deer hunting is not permitted by the state.

📖 *Glossary*
doom: to make certain of the failure or destruction of
vulnerability: the state of being easily hurt or attacked

11 According to paragraph 1, the best way to identify a whitetail deer is to

- Ⓐ observe the spots on its entire body
- Ⓑ notice how it runs away from humans
- Ⓒ see it lift its tail to show its underside
- Ⓓ pay attention to how much it weighs

12 The word "adapt" in the passage is closest in meaning to

- Ⓐ adjust
- Ⓑ submit
- Ⓒ reconcile
- Ⓓ move

13 According to paragraph 2, does can leave fawns alone at times because

- Ⓐ fawns have no natural predators
- Ⓑ fawns are hard to see or smell
- Ⓒ fawns are born when other animals are hibernating
- Ⓓ fawns can run faster than any predators

The Whitetail and Blacktail Deer

1 ➡ Of all of North America's large animals, the most numerous is the whitetail deer. This species of deer is known for its habit of raising and flopping its tail over its back. This action reveals its white underside and buttocks. People often observe this telltale marking as the deer runs away from them. When the tail is down, it is brown with a white fringe. Varying with the seasons, the color of the whitetail deer is reddish in summer and grayish in winter. An adult male, which is known as a buck, grows to over a meter at shoulder height. It also weighs about 110 kilograms. Males grow antlers, which occasionally become entangled with those of another male. This **dooms** each animal to a slow death.

2 ➡ Also known as the Virginia deer, the whitetail deer inhabits most of the continental United States. It can be found in southern Canada, Mexico, Central America, and the northern countries of South America. It has also been introduced into northern Europe. The whitetail is highly adaptable. Though it most often lives in densely forested areas, it can also adapt to live in open savannas. These include the plains of Texas and the Venezuelan llanos. Mating season is in the fall. Bucks attempt to mate with as many females—called does—as possible. Does give birth to one or two fawns in late spring. A doe leaves her fawn alone for hours at a time, as its natural camouflage—a spotted coat and the absence of scent—makes it invisible to most predators. It returns periodically to feed the fawn.

📖 *Glossary*

doom: to make certain of the failure or destruction of

14 The word "nuisance" in the passage is closest in meaning to

- Ⓐ competitor
- Ⓑ obligation
- Ⓒ attraction
- Ⓓ annoyance

15 Which of the sentences below best expresses the essential information in the highlighted sentence? *Incorrect* choices change the meaning in important ways or leave out essential information.

- Ⓐ As humans move into the deer's natural habitat, deer are able to adapt to the changing environment.
- Ⓑ Humans have caused the whitetail deer almost to become extinct.
- Ⓒ The needs of the increasing human business activities take away the deer's food sources and safe habitats.
- Ⓓ Humans cut down forests in order to make it easier for them to hunt deer.

With sufficient food and shelter, whitetail deer populations grow rapidly. But they can grow too rapidly at times. It often becomes a nuisance to farmers, whose crops serve as food for the deer. It also frequently collides with cars as it bounds across roadways. This causes the death of the deer and injury or death to human drivers. Regulated hunts are scheduled to thin out excessive populations. In addition, deer hunting is a significant cultural ritual in many areas. It even serves as an important boost to some local economies. The cutting down of forests to make way for commercial development has deprived many herds of their natural habitat, leading to their starvation or increased vulnerability to highway collisions.

The blacktail deer descended from its whitetail relative millions of years ago. Scientists believe that it migrated down the east coast of the North American continent. It crossed Mexico and went up the California coast. There, it ultimately evolved into the blacktail deer. Their common ancestry explains why the two species resemble each other both in physical appearance and psychological traits. Indeed, the two are often hard to distinguish. Though the blacktail's tail is black, it shares the whitetail's habit of raising its tail. This lets it display some white coloring underneath. And the males of both species have similar antlers. But the blacktail is found only along the western edge of the continent. Its range extends from British Columbia in Canada to southern California. Moreover, the blacktail is slightly smaller than its white-tailed cousin.

📖 *Glossary*

vulnerability: the state of being easily hurt or attacked

16 The word "it" in the passage refers to

- Ⓐ the blacktail deer
- Ⓑ the mule deer
- Ⓒ DNA testing
- Ⓓ a separate species

17 The phrase "venture out" in the passage is closest in meaning to

- Ⓐ get into trouble
- Ⓑ manage to survive
- Ⓒ start a business
- Ⓓ go outside

18 According to paragraph 5, which of the following can be inferred about hunting blacktail deer?

- Ⓐ It is too difficult to be very popular with hunters.
- Ⓑ It is better for the economy than whitetail hunting.
- Ⓒ It is permitted only in the daytime during hunting season.
- Ⓓ It occurs only during the winter months each year.

5 → Until recently scientists believed that the blacktail deer was a subspecies of the mule deer. But DNA testing has proved that it is a separate species. The mule deer evolved into a distinct species from breeding with the whitetail and the blacktail. Experienced hunters report that the blacktail is the hardest deer species to hunt. One reason is that blacktails inhabit a much hotter climate. Daytime temperatures reach around 100 degrees Fahrenheit in the summer during archery season in California. In that heat, blacktail bucks stay quiet during the day. They move only under the protective cover of darkness. In the rainy season, the blacktail is active during the day. But few hunters want to venture out in bad weather. Blacktail hunting is further complicated by the fact that the hunting season in western states ends before the mating season. That is when many bucks are most active while searching for females. Thus, they are the most accessible at a time when deer hunting is not permitted by the state.

19 Look at the four squares [■] that indicate where the following sentence could be added to the passage.

As a result, the fawn is safe while its mother looks for food.

Where would the sentence best fit?

Click on a square [■] to add the sentence to the passage.

Also known as the Virginia deer, the whitetail deer inhabits most of the continental United States. It can be found in southern Canada, Mexico, Central America, and the northern countries of South America. It has also been introduced into northern Europe. The whitetail is highly adaptable. Though it most often lives in densely forested areas, it can also adapt to live in open savannas. These include the plains of Texas and the Venezuelan llanos. Mating season is in the fall. Bucks attempt to mate with as many females—called does—as possible. **1** Does give birth to one or two fawns in late spring. **2** A doe leaves her fawn alone for hours at a time, as its natural camouflage—a spotted coat and the absence of scent—makes it invisible to most predators. **3** It returns periodically to feed the fawn. **4**

20 **Directions:** An introductory sentence for a brief summary of the passage is provided below. Complete the summary by selecting the THREE answer choices that express the most important ideas in the passage. Some answer choices do not belong in the summary because they express ideas that are not in the passage or are minor ideas in the passage. *This question is worth 2 points.*

> Drag your answer choices to the spaces where they belong.
> To remove an answer choice, click on it. To review the passage, click on **View Text**.

This passage describes two major species of North American deer.

-
-
-

Answer Choices

① A whitetail fawn has natural protection such as its spotted coat and lack of scent.

② The whitetail and blacktail deer are difficult to distinguish from each other because of their common ancestry.

③ Male whitetail deer die when their antlers get entangled with another's.

④ Whitetail deer inhabit most of the continental United States while the blacktail deer is limited to the west coast of North America.

⑤ Deer hunting serves as a means of curtailing excessive populations and also stimulates the local economy.

⑥ DNA testing shows that the blacktail deer is a subspecies of the mule deer.

Appendix

Mastering Word List

This part provides lists of important vocabulary words in each unit. They are essential words for understanding any academic texts. Many of the words are listed with their derivative forms so that students can expand their vocabulary in an effective way. These lists can be used as homework assignments.

UNIT 01 Vocabulary

Step A

- [ ] affection
- [ ] analysis
- [ ] author
- [ ] banish
- [ ] consensus
- [ ] conservation
- [ ] constant
- [ ] constitution
- [ ] despot
- [ ] distinct
- [ ] drought
- [ ] ennoble
- [ ] era
- [ ] execute
- [ ] expel
- [ ] flourish
- [ ] genre
- [ ] hereditary
- [ ] initiative
- [ ] intestine
- [ ] launch
- [ ] microbe
- [ ] mob
- [ ] monarchy
- [ ] nonrenewable
- [ ] notorious
- [ ] opulence
- [ ] overthrow
- [ ] perspective
- [ ] population
- [ ] precede
- [ ] predictability
- [ ] prominent
- [ ] proponent
- [ ] rampant
- [ ] ratify
- [ ] reign
- [ ] sham
- [ ] smash
- [ ] sovereign
- [ ] treason

Step B

- [ ] *n.* abundance
- [ ] *v.* abound
- [ ] *adj.* abundant
- [ ] *adv.* abundantly

- [ ] *n.* adherence
- [ ] *v.* adhere
- [ ] *adj.* adhesive
- [ ] *adv.* adhesively

- [ ] *n.* anatomy
- [ ] *v.* anatomize
- [ ] *adj.* anatomical
- [ ] *adv.* anatomically

- [ ] *n.* circulation
- [ ] *v.* circulate
- [ ] *adj.* circulative / circulatory

- [ ] *n.* colony
- [ ] *v.* colonize
- [ ] *adj.* colonial
- [ ] *adv.* colonially

- [ ] *n.* consideration
- [ ] *v.* consider
- [ ] *adj.* considerate
- [ ] *adv.* considerately

- [ ] *n.* execution
- [ ] *v.* execute

- [ ] *n.* identification
- [ ] *v.* identify
- [ ] *adj.* identifiable
- [ ] *adv.* identifiably

- [ ] *n.* inspiration
- [ ] *v.* inspire
- [ ] *adj.* inspiring
- [ ] *adv.* inspiringly

- [ ] *n.* oppression
- [ ] *v.* oppress
- [ ] *adj.* oppressive
- [ ] *adv.* oppressively

- [ ] *n.* patron
- [ ] *v.* patronize
- [ ] *adj.* patronizing
- [ ] *adv.* patronizingly

- [ ] *n.* prediction
- [ ] *v.* predict
- [ ] *adj.* predictable
- [ ] *adv.* predictably

- [ ] *n.* stability
- [ ] *v.* stabilize
- [ ] *adj.* stable
- [ ] *adv.* stably

- [ ] *n.* consequence
- [ ] *adj.* consequential
- [ ] *adv.* consequentially

- [ ] *n.* transformation
- [ ] *v.* transform
- [ ] *adj.* transformable

UNIT 02 Reference

Step A

- [ ] abnormal
- [ ] affect
- [ ] approximately
- [ ] biodiversity
- [ ] carnivorous
- [ ] catastrophic
- [ ] condense
- [ ] corpse
- [ ] deadly
- [ ] decline
- [ ] ecology
- [ ] ecosystem
- [ ] equatorial
- [ ] estuary
- [ ] exotic
- [ ] fend for
- [ ] fungus
- [ ] hibernate
- [ ] impose
- [ ] indigenous
- [ ] inertia
- [ ] inhale
- [ ] meteorology
- [ ] momentum
- [ ] nutrient

□ offspring
□ opaque
□ parasite
□ parched
□ phenomenon
□ unprecedented
□ unrestrained

Step B

□ *n.* accumulation
□ *v.* accumulate
□ *adj.* accumulative
□ *adv.* accumulatively

□ *n.* aggression
□ *v.* aggress
□ *adj.* aggressive
□ *adv.* aggressively

□ *n.* condition
□ *v.* condition
□ *adj.* conditional
□ *adv.* conditionally

□ *n.* deduction
□ *v.* deduce
□ *adj.* deductive
□ *adv.* deductively

□ *n.* deprivation
□ *v.* deprive
□ *adj.* deprivable
□ *adv.* deprivably

□ *n.* dissipation
□ *v.* dissipate
□ *adj.* dissipative / dissipated
□ *adv.* dissipatively / dissipatedly

□ *n.* diversity
□ *v.* diversify
□ *adj.* diverse
□ *adv.* diversely

□ *n.* domination
□ *v.* dominate
□ *adj.* dominant
□ *adv.* dominantly

□ *n.* epidemic
□ *adj.* epidemic / epidemical
□ *adv.* epidemically

□ *n.* estimation
□ *v.* estimate
□ *adj.* estimative
□ *adv.* estimably / estimable

□ *n.* evaporation
□ *v.* evaporate
□ *adj.* evaporative
□ *adv.* evaporatively

□ *n.* falsification
□ *v.* falsify
□ *adj.* falsifiable
□ *adv.* falsifiably

□ *n.* fertilization
□ *v.* fertilize
□ *adj.* fertile
□ *adv.* fertily

□ *n.* need
□ *v.* necessitate
□ *adj.* necessary
□ *adv.* necessarily

□ *n.* precipitation
□ *v.* precipitate
□ *adj.* precipitate
□ *adv.* precipitately

□ *n.* regulation
□ *v.* regulate
□ *adj.* regulative / regulatory
□ *adv.* regulatively / regulatorily

□ *n.* sustenance
□ *v.* sustain
□ *adj.* sustainable
□ *adv.* sustainably

UNIT 03 Factual Information

Step A

□ acrobatics
□ assassinate
□ awareness
□ bounce
□ cede
□ civic

□ centennial
□ disfavor
□ drastic
□ establish
□ glacial
□ hygiene
□ integrity
□ internal
□ majestic
□ massacre
□ monument
□ nitrogen
□ optical
□ propaganda
□ refined
□ requirement
□ sleet
□ splice
□ sulfur
□ summon
□ supreme
□ thereof
□ tuberculosis
□ transparent
□ treaty
□ unrest

Step B

□ *n.* absorption
□ *v.* absorb
□ *adj.* absorptive
□ *adv.* absortively

□ *n.* commemoration
□ *v.* commemorate
□ *adj.* commemorative
□ *adv.* commemoratively

□ *n.* conclusion
□ *v.* conclude
□ *adj.* conclusive
□ *adv.* conclusively

□ *n.* controversy
□ *v.* controvert
□ *adj.* controversial
□ *adv.* controversially

□ *n.* corruption

□ *v.* corrupt
□ *adj.* corruptive
□ *adv.* corruptively

□ *n.* deduction
□ *v.* deduct
□ *adj.* deductive
□ *adv.* deductively

□ *n.* delight
□ *v.* delight
□ *adj.* delightful
□ *adv.* delightfully

□ *n.* eruption
□ *v.* erupt
□ *adj.* eruptive
□ *adv.* eruptively

□ *n.* exaggeration
□ *v.* exaggerate
□ *adj.* exaggerative
□ *adv.* exaggeratively

□ *n.* immigration / immigrant
□ *v.* immigrate
□ *adj.* immigrant
□ *adv.* immigrantly

□ *n.* incorporation
□ *v.* incorporate
□ *adj.* incorporative
□ *adv.* incorporatively

□ *n.* induction
□ *v.* induct
□ *adj.* inductive
□ *adv.* inductively

□ *n.* inscription
□ *v.* inscribe
□ *adj.* inscriptive
□ *adv.* inscriptively

□ *n.* proclamation
□ *v.* proclaim
□ *adj.* proclamatory
□ *adv.* proclamatorily

□ *n.* repeal
□ *v.* repeal
□ *adj.* repealable

□ *n.* symbol

□ *v.* symbolize
□ *adj.* symbolic
□ *adv.* symbolically

□ *n.* transmission
□ *v.* transmit
□ *adj.* transmissive
□ *adv.* transmissively

UNIT 04 Negative Factual Information

Step A

□ annual
□ arid
□ array
□ camouflage
□ carbon
□ caterpillar
□ commodity
□ comprise
□ circadian
□ crude
□ current
□ deposit
□ epilepsy
□ evaporation
□ fertile
□ fragment
□ habitat
□ manufacture
□ metabolism
□ nectar
□ neurology
□ photic
□ physiologist
□ precipitation
□ reputation
□ specimen
□ spherical
□ vegetation

Step B

□ *n.* assembly
□ *v.* assemble
□ *adj.* assembled

□ *n.* assumption
□ *v.* assume
□ *adj.* assumptive
□ *adv.* assumptively

□ *n.* competition
□ *v.* compete
□ *adj.* competitive
□ *adv.* competitively

□ *n.* conversion
□ *v.* convert
□ *adj.* convertible
□ *adv.* convertibly

□ *n.* domination
□ *v.* dominate
□ *adj.* dominant
□ *adv.* dominantly

□ *n.* elimination
□ *v.* eliminate
□ *adj.* eliminative
□ *adv.* eliminatively

□ *n.* externalization
□ *v.* externalize
□ *adj.* external
□ *adv.* externally

□ *n.* generation
□ *v.* generate
□ *adj.* generative
□ *adv.* generatively

□ *n.* illustration
□ *v.* illustrate
□ *adj.* illustrative
□ *adv.* illustratively

□ *n.* inherence
□ *v.* inhere
□ *adj.* inherent
□ *adv.* inherently

□ *n.* inheritance
□ *v.* inherit
□ *adj.* inheritable
□ *adv.* inheritably

□ *n.* invention
□ *v.* invent
□ *adj.* inventive

□ *adv.* inventively

□ *n.* migration / migrant
□ *v.* migrate
□ *adj.* migrant
□ *adv.* migrantly

□ *n.* modification
□ *v.* modify
□ *adj.* modifiable

□ *n.* obtainment
□ *v.* obtain
□ *adj.* obtainable
□ *adv.* obtainably

□ *n.* replacement
□ *v.* replace
□ *adj.* replaceable
□ *adv.* replaceably

□ *n.* reproduction
□ *v.* reproduce
□ *adj.* reproductive
□ *adv.* reproductively

□ *n.* visibility
□ *v.* view
□ *adj.* visible
□ *adv.* visibly

UNIT 05 Sentence Simplification

Step A

□ adept
□ auditory
□ binary
□ carcass
□ concentric
□ conflict
□ deciduous
□ defecation
□ devour
□ edible
□ entirely
□ entrepreneur
□ harvest
□ heightened

□ in disrepair
□ inflation
□ latitude
□ lumber
□ maize
□ mammal
□ mollusk
□ olfactory
□ overt
□ permanent
□ protein
□ rank
□ salary
□ shaman
□ staple
□ temperate
□ territory
□ tropical
□ urination
□ variant
□ wayfarer
□ whereas

Step B

□ *n.* analysis
□ *v.* analyze
□ *adj.* analyzable

□ *n.* alternation
□ *v.* alternate
□ *adj.* alternate
□ *adv.* alternately

□ *n.* consumer
□ *v.* consume
□ *adj.* consumable

□ *n.* contradiction
□ *v.* contradict
□ *adj.* contradictory
□ *adv.* contradictorily

□ *n.* cultivation
□ *v.* cultivate
□ *adj.* cultivatable

□ *n.* domestication
□ *v.* domesticate
□ *adj.* domestic
□ *adv.* domestically

□ *n.* elaboration
□ *v.* elaborate
□ *adj.* elaborate
□ *adv.* elaborately

□ *n.* enactment
□ *v.* enact
□ *adj.* enactive

□ *n.* extinction
□ *v.* extinguish
□ *adj.* extinct / extinctive
□ *adv.* extinctively

□ *n.* mutation
□ *v.* mutate
□ *adj.* mutational
□ *adv.* mutationally

□ *n.* prevalence
□ *v.* prevail
□ *adj.* prevalent
□ *adv.* prevalently

□ *n.* profit
□ *v.* profit
□ *adj.* profitable
□ *adv.* profitably

□ *n.* radiation
□ *v.* radiate
□ *adj.* radiational

□ *n.* reference
□ *v.* refer
□ *adj.* referent / referential
□ *adv.* referentially

□ *n.* restriction
□ *v.* restrict
□ *adj.* restrictive
□ *adv.* restrictively

□ *n.* tradition
□ *adj.* traditional
□ *adv.* traditionally

UNIT 06 Rhetorical Purpose

Step A

- [ ] accuracy
- [ ] amplify
- [ ] aspect
- [ ] astronomy
- [ ] causal
- [ ] celestial
- [ ] cope with
- [ ] component
- [ ] confederate
- [ ] decade
- [ ] disabled
- [ ] epoch
- [ ] feat
- [ ] fulcrum
- [ ] embrace
- [ ] magnetic
- [ ] infantry
- [ ] metaphysics
- [ ] outermost
- [ ] predatory
- [ ] probe
- [ ] prominent
- [ ] region
- [ ] retrograde
- [ ] shift
- [ ] solitary
- [ ] transcontinental
- [ ] vivid

Step B

- [ ] *n.* ceremony
- [ ] *adj.* ceremonial
- [ ] *adv.* ceremonially

- [ ] *n.* civilization
- [ ] *v.* civilize
- [ ] *adj.* civilizational
- [ ] *adv.* civilizationally

- [ ] *n.* condensation
- [ ] *v.* condense
- [ ] *adj.* condensable

- [ ] *n.* contribution
- [ ] *v.* contribute

- [ ] *adj.* contributive
- [ ] *adv.* contributively

- [ ] *n.* convection
- [ ] *v.* convect
- [ ] *adj.* convective
- [ ] *adv.* convectively

- [ ] *n.* deformity
- [ ] *v.* deform
- [ ] *adj.* deformative

- [ ] *n.* divergence
- [ ] *v.* diverge
- [ ] *adj.* divergent
- [ ] *adv.* divergently

- [ ] *n.* exertion
- [ ] *v.* exert
- [ ] *adj.* exertive

- [ ] *n.* filter
- [ ] *v.* filter
- [ ] *adj.* filtered

- [ ] *n.* foundation
- [ ] *v.* found
- [ ] *adj.* foundational
- [ ] *adv.* foundationally

- [ ] *n.* influence
- [ ] *v.* influence
- [ ] *adj.* influential
- [ ] *adv.* influentially

- [ ] *n.* inhibition
- [ ] *v.* inhibit
- [ ] *adj.* inhibitive

- [ ] *n.* intensity / intensification
- [ ] *v.* intensify
- [ ] *adj.* intense
- [ ] *adv.* intensely

- [ ] *n.* notability
- [ ] *v.* note
- [ ] *adj.* notable
- [ ] *adv.* notably

- [ ] *n.* representation
- [ ] *v.* represent
- [ ] *adj.* representative
- [ ] *adv.* representatively

- [ ] *n.* revelation
- [ ] *v.* reveal
- [ ] *adj.* revealing
- [ ] *adv.* revealingly

- [ ] *n.* theory
- [ ] *v.* theorize
- [ ] *adj.* theoretical
- [ ] *adv.* theoretically

- [ ] *n.* transportation
- [ ] *v.* transport
- [ ] *adj.* transportable

UNIT 07 Inference

Step A

- [ ] agriculture
- [ ] appendage
- [ ] aquatic
- [ ] cartilage
- [ ] cerebellum
- [ ] complement
- [ ] complex
- [ ] dart
- [ ] disclaim
- [ ] echolocation
- [ ] fissure
- [ ] forage
- [ ] geological
- [ ] horizontal
- [ ] lyric
- [ ] mechanical
- [ ] misconception
- [ ] niche
- [ ] parallel
- [ ] parasite
- [ ] playwright
- [ ] pollen
- [ ] render
- [ ] rupture
- [ ] sensory
- [ ] skeptically
- [ ] spontaneity
- [ ] suffrage
- [ ] symmetrical

□ temporal
□ thrust
□ verbal

Step B

□ *n.* accompaniment
□ *v.* accompany
□ *adj.* accompanying

□ *n.* attachment
□ *v.* attach
□ *adj.* attachable / attached

□ *n.* confirmation
□ *v.* confirm
□ *adj.* confirmative
□ *adv.* confirmatively

□ *n.* diminishment
□ *v.* diminish
□ *adj.* diminishing
□ *adv.* diminishingly

□ *n.* distinction
□ *v.* distinguish
□ *adj.* distinct
□ *adv.* distinctly

□ *n.* diversification
□ *v.* diversify
□ *adj.* diverse / diversifiable
□ *adv.* diversely

□ *n.* emergence
□ *v.* emerge
□ *adj.* emergent
□ *adv.* emergently

□ *n.* emphasis
□ *v.* emphasize
□ *adj.* emphatic
□ *adv.* emphatically

□ *n.* emission
□ *v.* emit
□ *adj.* emissive

□ *n.* impulse
□ *v.* impel
□ *adj.* impulsive
□ *adv.* impulsively

□ *n.* initiation
□ *v.* initiate
□ *adj.* initiatory
□ *adv.* initiatorily

□ *n.* perception
□ *v.* perceive
□ *adj.* perceptive
□ *adv.* perceptively

□ *n.* prohibition
□ *v.* prohibit
□ *adj.* prohibitive
□ *adv.* prohibitively

□ *n.* resolution
□ *v.* resolve
□ *adj.* resolute
□ *adv.* resolutely

□ *n.* separation
□ *v.* separate
□ *adj.* separate
□ *adv.* separately

□ *n.* significance
□ *v.* signify
□ *adj.* significant
□ *adv.* significantly

□ *n.* volunteer
□ *v.* volunteer
□ *adj.* voluntary
□ *adv.* voluntarily

UNIT 08 Insert Text

Step A

□ acclimate
□ alignment
□ allegory
□ burlesque
□ carbohydrate
□ diameter
□ dispute
□ doctrine
□ dormant
□ embodiment

□ ensure
□ entity
□ explicit
□ faculty
□ fictional
□ groundbreaking
□ hypocrite
□ influx
□ legend
□ maritime
□ notion
□ observatory
□ pioneer
□ primitive
□ proceed
□ radioactive
□ repeal
□ revive
□ sacred
□ submission
□ summit
□ telescope
□ tense
□ unmanned
□ vanish
□ wane

Step B

□ *n.* attainment
□ *v.* attain
□ *adj.* attainable
□ *adv.* attainably

□ *n.* conveyance
□ *v.* convey
□ *adj.* conveyable

□ *n.* cremation
□ *v.* cremate
□ *adj.* crematory

□ *n.* criticism
□ *v.* criticize
□ *adj.* critical
□ *adv.* critically

□ *n.* division
□ *v.* divide
□ *adj.* divisible

□ *n.* derivation
□ *v.* derive
□ *adj.* derivative
□ *adv.* derivatively

□ *n.* hierarchy
□ *adj.* hierarchical
□ *adv.* hierarchically

□ *n.* immortality
□ *v.* immortalize
□ *adj.* immortal
□ *adv.* immortally

□ *n.* improvisation
□ *v.* improvise
□ *adj.* improvisational
□ *adv.* improvisationally

□ *n.* isolation
□ *v.* isolate
□ *adj.* isolated
□ *adv.* isolatedly

□ *n.* moderation
□ *v.* moderate
□ *adj.* moderate
□ *adv.* moderately

□ *n.* organization
□ *v.* organize
□ *adj.* organizational
□ *adv.* organizationally

□ *n.* persistence
□ *v.* persist
□ *adj.* persistent
□ *adv.* persistently

□ *n.* pursuit
□ *v.* pursue
□ *adj.* pursuable

□ *n.* recollection
□ *v.* recollect
□ *adj.* recollective
□ *adv.* recollectively

□ *n.* synthesis
□ *v.* synthesize
□ *adj.* synthetic
□ *adv.* synthetically

Step A

□ adorn
□ ambiguity
□ brackish
□ byproduct
□ calculation
□ cartography
□ consciousness
□ constellation
□ craftsmanship
□ delta
□ epidemic
□ embryo
□ engraving
□ era
□ estuary
□ famine
□ fauna
□ fetus
□ geometric
□ germ
□ granite
□ hostility
□ humanitarian
□ hysterical
□ inscription
□ mold
□ nautical
□ navigation
□ neurotic
□ objective
□ obscure
□ organ
□ pottery
□ ruling
□ runoff
□ scarce
□ sediment
□ spine
□ trace
□ transplant
□ triangular
□ umbilical
□ vertical

□ zygote

Step B

□ *n.* abortion
□ *v.* abort
□ *adj.* abortive
□ *adv.* abortively

□ *n.* association
□ *v.* associate
□ *adj.* associative
□ *adv.* associatively

□ *n.* assignment
□ *v.* assign
□ *adj.* assignable
□ *adv.* assignably

□ *n.* erosion
□ *v.* erode
□ *adj.* erosive
□ *adv.* erosively

□ *n.* demonstration
□ *v.* demonstrate
□ *adj.* demonstrative
□ *adv.* demonstratively

□ *n.* displacement
□ *v.* displace
□ *adj.* displaceable

□ *n.* illegalization
□ *v.* illegalize
□ *adj.* illegal
□ *adv.* illegally

□ *n.* nourishment
□ *v.* nourish
□ *adj.* nourishing
□ *adv.* nourishingly

□ *n.* opposition
□ *v.* oppose
□ *adj.* opposing
□ *adv.* opposingly

□ *n.* portrayal
□ *v.* portray
□ *adj.* portrayable

□ *n.* promotion
□ *v.* promote

- adj. promotive
- adv. promotively

- n. recombination
- v. recombine
- adj. recombinant
- adv. recombinantly

- n. repression
- v. repress
- adj. repressive
- adv. repressively

- n. resistance
- v. resist
- adj. resistant
- adv. resistantly

UNIT 10 Fill in a Table

Step A

- anatomic
- collectively
- commitment
- conjugal
- corporation
- disparate
- dividend
- entitle
- evolution
- flock
- glamorous
- gore
- hominid
- humidity
- impact
- incite
- jurisdiction
- levy
- liability
- linkage
- metaphorically
- mobility
- morality
- outlet
- paleoanthropology
- prejudice

- property
- refurbish
- scapegoat
- scour
- skull
- span
- spouse
- statistics
- surplus
- validity

Step B

- n. adaptation
- v. adapt
- adj. adaptable

- n. adoption
- v. adopt
- adj. adoptive
- adv. adoptively

- n. advocacy
- v. advocate
- adj. advocative
- adv. advocatively

- n. compilation
- v. compile
- adj. compilatory

- n. definition
- v. define
- adj. definitive
- adv. definitively

- n. descent
- v. descend
- adj. descendent
- adv. descendently

- n. exhibition
- v. exhibit
- adj. exhibitive
- adv. exhibitively

- n. evaluation
- v. evaluate
- adj. evaluative
- adv. evaluatively

- n. ignition
- v. ignite

- adj. ignitable

- n. immunization
- v. immunize
- adj. immune
- adv. immunely

- n. impression
- v. impress
- adj. impressive
- adv. impressively

- n. integration
- v. integrate
- adj. integrative
- adv. integratively

- n. persecution
- v. persecute
- adj. persecutive / persecutory

- n. pretense
- v. pretend
- adj. pretended / pretending
- adv. pretendedly / pretendingly

- n. prosperity
- v. prosper
- adj. prosperous
- adv. prosperously

- n. reconstruction
- v. reconstruct
- adj. reconstructive
- adv. reconstructively

MEMO

How to
Master Skills for the
TOEFL® iBT

READING

| Answers and Translations

Second Edition

Intermediate

How to
Master Skills for the

TOEFL® iBT

READING Intermediate

▌ Answers and Translations

🔲 DARAKWON

UNIT 01 Vocabulary

Basic Drill p.14

Drill 1 Ⓑ

해석

바카족

바카족은 카메룬, 콩고, 가봉, 중앙아프리카공화국의 열대 우림에서 생활하는 유목 민족이다. 평균 신장은 1.5미터이고 피그미족으로도 불린다. 그러나 이들은 그러한 이름을 싫어하며 자신들의 부족명인 바카족으로 불리기를 원한다.

바카족은 수렵 채집민이다. 이들은 오두막으로 이루어진 임시 거처를 만드는데, 오두막은 나뭇가지로 만들어지고 커다란 나뭇잎으로 덮여 있다. 남성은 독을 묻힌 화살과 창을 사용해서 숲에서 동물을 사냥한다. 여성은 과일과 견과류를 채집한다. 또한 양봉과 자녀의 양육도 담당한다. 무리는 자치적으로 운영되며 모든 결정은 만장일치에 의해 이루어진다.

Drill 2 Ⓑ

해석

박테리아

박테리아는 모든 생물 중에서 가장 흔한 생물이다. 토양과 수중에서 서식한다. 또한 다른 생물의 몸속에서 발견될 수도 있다. 일반적으로 대부분의 박테리아는 크기가 대단히 작기 때문에 육안으로 관찰되지 않는다. 하지만 거대 박테리아는 0.5mm 이상으로 자랄 수도 있다. 이들에게는, 식물이나 균류의 세포와 같이, 세포벽이 있다. 많은 박테리아는 편모라고 불리는 펄럭이는 수족을 사용하여 몸을 움직인다.

박테리아는 인간과 동물에 유익할 수도 있고 해로울 수도 있다. 일부 박테리아는 콜레라나 나병과 같은 끔찍한 질병을 일으킨다. 그러나 인간의 장 속에 사는 박테리아는 해로운 병균이 자라지 못하도록 하기 때문에 유익하다. 이들은 병균을 분해시켜 병균의 성장을 막는다.

Drill 3 Ⓓ

해석

가뭄

가뭄은 건조한 날씨가 비정상적으로 오래 지속되는 것을 말한다. 이때에는 농장, 도시, 혹은 환경에 필요한 물이 충분하지 않게 된다. 가뭄은 보통 오랜 기간 동안 정상적인 경우보다 강수량이 낮은 시기를 가리킨다. 하지만 순환되는 물의 양을 감소시키는 어떠한 요인에 의해서라도 가뭄은 일어날 수 있다.

인간은 날씨를 조종할 수 없기 때문에 가뭄을 일으키는 원인을 막을 수 없다. 가뭄의 가장 일반적인 원인은 물 부족과 더운 날씨이다. 많은 과학자들은 최근의 가뭄이 지구 온난화 때문에 발생했다고 생각한다. 그들은 오존층에 가해지는 피해를 줄일 수 있다면 가뭄도 줄어들 것이라고 주장한다.

Drill 4 Ⓒ

해석

은유

은유란 관련이 없는 두 가지 대상을 직접적으로 비교하는 수사법 중 하나이다. 은유는 첫 번째 대상을 어떤 측면에서 두 번째 대상과 동일하다고 설명한다. 은유에는 혼합 은유, 활성 은유, 그리고 사은유와 같은 다양한 종류가 있다. 혼합 은유는 흔히 사용되는 두 가지 은유를 결합해서 터무니없는 하나의 이미지를 만들어 낸다. 이에 대한 예로 "그는 행동에 나서서 정면으로 문제에 맞섰다."를 들 수 있다. "당신은 나의 태양이다."와 같은 활성 은유는 일상에서 잘 쓰이지 않는다. 사은유는 "어색함을 깨다."와 같은 진부한 은유적인 표현을 설명할 때 사용된다.

Drill 5 Ⓒ

해석

엘리자베스 1세 여왕

엘리자베스 1세 여왕은 잉글랜드와 아일랜드를 통치했다. 그녀는 1558년부터 1603년까지 왕위에 있었다. 또한 프랑스의 여왕으로 간주되기도 했지만, 그곳에서는 아무런 권력을 갖지 못했다. 그녀는 튜더 왕조의 다섯 번째이자 마지막 군주였다. 엘리자베스 여왕은 결혼을 한 적이 없었기 때문에 "처녀 여왕(Virgin Queen)"으로 불렸다.

엘리자베스 여왕의 통치 기간은 엘리자베스 시대라고 불린다. 통치 기간 동안 여러 위대한 업적이 이루어졌다. 셰익스피어가 희곡을 썼고, 프란시스 드레이크 경은 세계를 일주했다. 영국은 북아메리카를 식민지로 삼았다. 그녀가 죽은 직후에 버지니아라는 미국 식민지가 만들어졌다. 처녀 여왕을 기리기 위해 그와 같은 이름이 붙여진 것이었다.

Drill 6 Ⓐ

해석

짚신벌레

짚신벌레는 짚신처럼 생겼기 때문에 짚신벌레라고 알려진 생물이다. 짚신벌레는 섬모충이라고 불리는 단세포 생물을 대표한다. 그 이유는 이들의 신체가 섬모, 즉 가느다란 꼬리처럼 생긴 수족으로 덮여 있기 때문이다. 섬모가 계속 움직이기 때문에 짚신벌레는 이동을 할 수 있다. 이 세포는 깊은 구구를 가지고 있다. 이는 일종의 입이라 할 수 있는데, 이 역시 섬모로 덮여 있다. 입은 수분을 분출하는데 사용된다. 짚신벌레는 보통 담수 지역, 특히 거품 안에서 찾아볼 수 있다. 이들은 산성을 좋아한다.

Exercises with Mid-Length Passages

Exercise 1   1 Ⓒ   2 Ⓒ   3 Ⓑ   4 Ⓑ   p.18

해석

유럽의 군주제

군주제란 한 명의 통치자가 국가의 수반이 되는 정부 형태이다. 이는 세계에서 가장 오래된 정치 형태 중 하나이다. 일반적으로 군주는 왕이나 여왕이다. 그러나 이들은 족장, 황제, 혹은 또 다른 이름으로도 불릴 수 있다. 일본과 같은 일부 국가에서는 군주가 단지 상징적인 의미만 갖는다. 이들은 실질적인 권력을 전혀 갖지 않는 명목상의 군주이다. 하지만 군주가 상당한 권력을 행사하는 나라들도 있다. 현재 전 세계적으로 25개 이상의 군주제 국가들이 존재한다.

세습 군주제는 가장 일반적 형태의 왕위 계승 방법이다. 이러한 방식은 전 세계 대부분의 군주들에 의해 시행되고 있다. 이 경우 모든 왕과 여왕은 동일한 가문 출신이다. 일정 기간 동안 통치를 하는 가문은 왕조라고 불린다. 왕좌는 그 가문 출신의 한 사람에게서 그 가문 출신의 또 다른 사람에게로 세습된다. 세습제는 안정성, 연속성, 그리고 예측 가능성이라는 이점을 갖는다. 가족간의 애정과 충성심 역시 안정감을 가져다 주는 요인이다.

수 세기 동안 대부분의 유럽 국가들은 군주에 의해 통치되었다. 영국, 덴마크, 그리고 노르웨이는 여전히 입헌 군주국이다. 입헌 군주국에서는 왕이나 여왕이 통치를 하지만 국가의 헌법을 반드시 준수해야 한다. 이러한 형태의 정부에서는 군주의 권력이 크게 제한된다.

17세기에 영국은 입헌 군주국이 되었다. 찰스 1세가 협정에 서명했다. 그는 새로운 세금을 부과하거나 새로운 법률을 제정하려고 할 때, 그리고 전쟁을 하고자 할 때 반드시 영국 의회의 승인을 얻어야 했다. 협정에 서명한 후 찰스 1세는 협정을 무시했다. 그는 절대 권력을 행사하려고 했기 때문에 반역죄로 처형되었다. 입헌 군주제라는 새로운 시대가 시작된 것이었다.

러시아 제국은 유럽의 절대 군주국이었다. 첫 번째 통치자는 피터 1세였다. 그는 로마노프 가문 출신이었다. 그는 1692년에 짜르가 되었다. *짜르*란 "황제"를 뜻하는 러시아 말이다. 로마노프 가문은 1917년 2월 혁명 때까지 이 제국을 다스렸다. 그 해에 러시아인들은 혁명을 일으켰다. 그 당시 통치를 했던 짜르인 니콜라스 2세는 강제로 왕좌에서 물러나야 했다. 1918년 니콜라스 2세와 그의 가족들은 총살을 당했다.

> ### 📝 Summary Note
> ❶ Absolute
> ❷ Symbolic
> ❸ Constitutional

Exercise 2 1 Ⓐ 2 Ⓒ 3 Ⓑ 4 Ⓑ p.20

해석

대체 에너지원

화석 연료는 많은 문제를 일으킨다. 지구 온난화로 이어지는 심각한 오염을 유발한다. 많은 전쟁들이 유전과 가스전을 차지하기 위해 일어난다. 화석 연료는 또한 재생이 불가능한 에너지원이기 때문에 언젠가는 고갈될 것이다. 연료가 부족한 상황이 발생하면 세계 각국이 고통을 겪는다.

어떤 사람들은 태양 에너지가 화석 연료를 완전히 대체할 수 있을 것으로 생각한다. 태양 에너지는 깨끗하고 안전하며 저렴하다. 하지만 태양 에너지만으로 화석 연료를 대체할 수 있다는 생각은 전적으로 비현실적이다. 현재 태양 전지 기술은 충분히 발전해 있지 않다. 태양 전지는 신뢰할 수 없다. 구름이 끼거나 비가 오는 날에는 사용할 수 없고, 밤에도 마찬가지이다. 또한 공간을 너무 많이 차지한다. 마지막으로 충분한 양의 전력도 만들어 내지 못한다.

연성 에너지 경로는 화석 연료 의존에 대한 좋은 대안이 된다. 연성 에너지 경로는 에너지 보존 계획이다. 경성 에너지 경로에 대한 대안이다. 경성 에너지는 유해하고 재생 불가능한 에너지로 정의된다. 화석 연료와 원자력이 경성 에너지로 분류된다. 반면에 연성 에너지는 재생이 가능하고 환경에 안전한 에너지로 정의된다. 태양 에너지와 풍력이 연성 에너지의 예이다. 바이오 연료 및 지열 에너지 역시 연성 에너지에 속한다.

많은 이들이 연성 에너지 경로를 지지한다. 이들은 새로운 에너지 생산 방식에 해결책이 있다고 믿는다. 첫 번째 단계는 경성 에너지 기술을 사용하면서 보존에 세심한 주의를 기울이는 것이다. 이후 연성 에너지 기술이 발전을 하면 다수의 새로운 연성 에너지원들이 단계적으로 사용될 것이다.

일부 비판가들은 그렇게 되면 모든 에너지 생산에 피해가 발생할 것이라고 주장한다. 그들은 화석 연료가 중요하다고 생각한다. 그들은 석유 생산을 최대한 많이 조절하고자 한다. 화석 연료의 소비가 산업에 이롭다고 생각한다.

캐나다 및 스웨덴 같은 나라는 연성 에너지 경로를 택하고 있다. 캐나다는 현재 휘발유에 대한 의존도를 줄이고 있다. 몇 년 후에는 캐나다에서 판매되는 모든 휘발유에 일정량의 바이오 연료가 포함될 예정이다. 스웨덴은 석유 의존도를 40%까지 감소시키기로 했다. 스웨덴 정부는 향후 몇 년 이내에 그러한 일이 가능할 것이라고 주장한다.

> ### 📝 Summary Note
> ❶ Hard-energy path
> ❷ Soft-energy path

Exercise 3 1 Ⓓ 2 Ⓑ 3 Ⓐ 4 Ⓒ p.22

해석

19세기의 공상 과학 소설

공상 과학 소설은 현재 존재하지 않는 과학을 이용한 소설로 정의될 수 있다. 서사시인 *길가메시*와 같은 옛날 작품들도 공상 과학 소설이라고 주장하는 사람들도 있다. 하지만 대부분의 사람들은 이 장르가 19세기에 시작되었다고 생각한다.

공상 과학 소설로 널리 인정받은 최초의 작품은 1818년 메리 셸리에 의해 쓰여진 *프랑켄슈타인: 현대의 프로메테우스*였다. 여기에서는 전기를 이용하여 죽은 자를 되살린 과학자가 등장하는데, 소설은 이 살아난 남자의 행동이 가져온 결과를 다루었다. 그녀의 소설은 막대한 인기를 얻었고, 처음 출시된 이후부터 지금까지 계속해서 시판되고 있다.

1880년대의 또 다른 유명 작가인 쥘 베른의 여러 소설들도 공상 과학 소설의 요소들을 갖추고 있었다. 분명 이러한 소설 중 가장 잘 알려져 있는 것은 *해저 2만리*로, 이는 전 세계 바다의 해저를 탐험 중인 네모 선장과 그의 최첨단 잠수함 노틸러스 호의 이야기를 다루고 있다. 베른의 첫번째 공상 과학 소설 중 하나는 *20세기 파리*였다. 이는 베른이 생각한 미래의 파리 모습을 다루고 있다. 그는 또한 *지구에서 달까지*와 *5주간의 열기구 여행*이라는 소설도 썼다.

이 시기에 인기가 있었던 또 다른 공상 과학 소설은 로버트 루이스 스티븐슨이 쓴 *지킬 박사와 하이드 씨*였다. 소설에서 지킬 박사는 자신을, 그의 또 다른 자아인 하이드 씨로 바꾸는 약물을 만든다. H.G. 웰스는 여러 권의 공상 과학 소설을 출간했다. 그는 *타임머신*이라는 책을 썼는데, 이 책은 한 사람이 과거의 지구로 돌아가고, 또한 먼 미래로 가는 여정을 말해 준다. *우주 전쟁*은 화성의 외계인들이 지구를 공격하는 내용이다. 웰스는 또한 *투명 인간*이라는 소설도 썼는데, 이는 다른 사람들에 보이지 않는 한 남자에 관한 이야기이다.

이러한 작품들 모두 공상 과학 소설의 인기 상승에 기여했다. 1900년대에 공상 과학 소설이 가장 인기 있는 문학 장르 중 하나가 되었다.

Exercise 4 1 Ⓐ, Ⓓ 2 Ⓓ 3 Ⓑ 4 Ⓑ p.24

해석

인간 게놈 프로젝트

인간 게놈 프로젝트(HGP)는 과학 분야에서 대단히 중요한 시도였다. 이는 게놈 지도를 만들고 인간 게놈의 서열을 알아내기 위한 시도였다. 인간 게놈에는 30억 개의 코드가 존재한다. 이들은 모두 확인되었다. 하지만 아직 서열은 규명되지 않았다. 또한 이 프로젝트는 인간의 신체에 존재하는 모든 유전자를 밝혀내고자 했다.

국제 인간 게놈 프로젝트는 1986년 찰스 델리시에 의해 시작되었다. 1987년에 발표한 한 보고서에는 "이러한 노력의 궁극적인 목표는 인간 게놈을 이해하기 위한 것이다. 해부학이 있어서 현재의 의학이 존재할 수 있었듯이 인간 게놈에 대한 지식은 의학 및 기타 보건 과학의 지속적 발전에 필요한 것이다."라고 적혀 있었다. 30억 달러짜리인 이 프로젝트는 1990년에 공식적으로 시작되었다. 완성되기까지 15년이 걸릴 것으로 예상되었다. 전 세계의 유전학자들이 국제 컨소시엄에 참여했다.

수 년간의 연구 후 2003년에 게놈 지도가 완성되었다는 주장이 제기되었다. 하지만 당시 HGP에서는 인간 게놈의 약 92% 정도에 대해서만 지도가 완성되어 있었다. 그 결과 프로젝트 연구는 계속되었다. 지도 제작 및 서열 분석과 관련된 기술이 향상됨에 따라 나머지 8%에 대한 발전이 꾸준히 이루어졌다. 그럼에도 불구하고 각 염색체의 중심부에는 매우 반복적인 DNA 서열이 나타난다. 당시 기술로 이들의 순서를 밝히는 일은 매우 어려웠다. 마침내 2022년에 연구가 끝났고, 인간 게놈의 지도가 완성되었다.

HGP이 제공한 인간 게놈에 대한 이처럼 명확한 지도는 의사들에게 많은 중요한 정보를 제공해 줄 것이다. 이로써 의학적인 진보가 이루어질 것이다. 이러한 지식은 예컨대 유방암의 초기 진단에 중요한 진전을 가져다 줄 것이다. 또한 간질환이나 알츠하이머를 다루는 의사들의 능력도 향상될 것이다. 게놈의 분석으로 인류 진화에 대한 연구도 분명 새 지평을 맞이하게 될 것이다. 인간 DNA의 서열은 인터넷에 저장되어 있다. 유전자 은행(Genebank)이라는 데이터베이스에 들어 있다. 이 데이터는 누구나 이용이 가능하다.

Exercise 5 1 Ⓒ 2 Ⓑ 3 Ⓑ 4 Ⓒ p.26

해석

군중 심리

사람들은 개인으로서 독특한 방식으로 행동한다. 따라서 다른 사람들과 똑같이 행동하지 않는다. 하지만 사람들이 커다란 무리를 지어 있을 때에는 이러한 점이 바뀔 수 있다. 그렇게 되면 사람들의 행동은 다른 사람들에 의해 결정되거나 다른 사람들로부터 영향을 받을 수 있다. 그런 다음에는 군중 심리라는 것이 나타난다. 기본적으로 무리의 심리가 사람들을 지배하게 되고, 사람들은 주위의 다른 사람들과 비슷하게 행동하기 시작한다. 이는 종종 부정적인 결과로 이어질 수 있다.

군중 심리는 삶의 여러 측면에서 찾아볼 수 있다. 예를 들어 교실에 있는 어린 학생들은 다른 학생들이 떠드는 경우 자신들도 떠들기 시작할 수 있다. 마찬가지로 회의 중인 직장인들도 때때로 군중 심리를 나타낸다. 제기된 주장에 동의하지 않는 사람들이 있을 수 있다. 하지만 그룹 내 다른 사람들이 이에 동의하는 모습을 보이면, 그들은 발언을 삼가고 대신 군중들과 뜻을 같이하게 된다. 스포츠 경기의 팬들은, 다른 많은 사람들이 구호를 외치거나 환호성을 지르는 경우, 환호하기 시작할 수 있다. 이들은 모두 무해한 군중 심리의 사례이다.

안타깝게도 군중 심리가 폭력 사태 및 기타 문제들로 이어지는 경우가 많다. 미국에서는 어떤 스포츠 팀이 우승하면 승리한 팀의 팬들이 거대한 무리를 형성하는 경우가 많다. 그러면 폭력적이 될 수가 있다. 건물 유리창을 부술 수도 있고, 자동차를 박살낼 수도 있으며, 도심에 불을 지를 수도 있다. 일부 경우, 군중 심리가 지배해서 총격 사건이 발생한 적도 있다.

과거로 거슬러 가면 가장 악명 높은 군중 심리의 사례 중 하나는 1700년대 후반 프랑스 대혁명 때 일어났다. 혁명 와중인 1793년부터 1794년까지 공포 정치가 이루어졌다. 이때 수만 명의 사람들이 군중에 의해 처형되었다. 대부분의 경우 귀족이거나 혹은 혁명 정신이 부족하다는 이유로 참수를 당했다. 공포 정치 기간 동안 노동자 계급들은 종종 뭉쳐 다니며 다양한 사람들을 재판에 세웠다. 이러한 사람들은, 또 다시, 모의 재판을 받고 신속히 처형되는 경우가 많았다. 이러한 일은 군중들이 지쳐서 대량 살상을 멈추기 전까지 이루어졌다.

Exercise 6 1 Ⓒ 2 Ⓒ 3 Ⓓ 4 Ⓐ p.28

해석

아메리칸 크래프트맨 스타일

아메리칸 크래프트맨 스타일은 디자인의 일종이다. 1900년부터 1930년대까지 인기를 끌었다. 이는 미국의 건축 양식을 바꾸어 놓았다.

크래프트맨 스타일은 유럽에서 처음 시작되었다. 1860년대에 브리티시 아트 앤 크래프트 스타일이 생겨났다. 이 운동의 독특한 디자인들은 평범한 사람의 품격을 높여 주고자 했다. 대량 생산된 제품에 비해 수공으로 만든 제품들이 더 나은 것으로 여겨졌기 때문에 수제품이 선호되었다. 하지만 이 브리티시 스타일은 여전히 빅토리아식이었고, 가장 부유한 고객들만을 위한 것이었다.

1897년에 보스턴의 건축가들이 이러한 수제 스타일을 미국에 소개했다. 이들은 수제품 전시회를 기획했는데, 이는 엄청난 성공을 거두었다. 그들은 잠재성을 깨닫고 1897년 6월 28일에 아트 앤 크래프트 협회를 설립했다. 이 협회의 슬로건은 "보다 수준 높은 수공예품의 기준을 마련하고 이를 장려는 것"이었다. 이러한 아메리칸 스타일은 빅토리아 시대가 끝나자 시작되었다. 이는 수제품을 강조했고 독창성과 단순성을 높이 평가했다. 인근 지역에서 나는 재료와 수제품의 품질이 매우 중시되었다. 이러한 특성들은 중산층의 소박한 주택을 우아하게 만들기 위한 것이었다.

이 간결한 디자인은 해당 지역에서 생산되는 유리와 나무를 사용했다. 또한 매우 우아했다. 금속 제품은 빅토리아 시대의 풍요함에 대한 반발이었다. 대량 생산되는 주거 용품의 확산은 거부되었다. 아메리칸 크래프트맨 스타일은 뚜렷한 선을 사용했으며 견고한 구조에 기반했다. 가능한 경우 이러한 주택에는 항상 천연 자재가 사용되었다. 이 양식은 평균적인 미국 가정에 많은 변화를 가져다 주었다. 하인이 없는 가족을 위한 새로운 디자인들이 만들어졌다. 이는 새로운 중산층의 특징이었다. 부엌은 숨겨진 공간이 아니라 눈에 잘 띄는 공간으로 바뀌었다. 또 다른 발전은 간이 식사 코너였다. 이 새로운 공간은 가족들에게 하루 중 언제든지 모일 수 있는 장소를 제공해 주었다.

또한 셰이커 앤 미션 디자인도 크래프트맨 스타일에 영감을 주었다. 아메리칸 크래프트맨 스타일은 1930년대 아르데코 운동으로 이어졌다.

📝 Summary Note
❶ Mass-produced items
❷ middle class
❸ Locally produced materials

Building Summary Skills
p.30

Exercise 1 Monarchy in Europe

Monarchy is a form of government in which there is a single ruler. Some forms of monarchy are symbolic, absolute, and constitutional. In a symbolic monarchy, the ruler has no power. In an absolute monarchy, the ruler has total power. In a constitutional monarchy, the ruler must follow the laws of the constitution.

Exercise 2 Alternative Energy Sources

Fossil fuels cause many problems, such as pollution and wars. But solar-cell technology is not currently advanced enough to replace fossil fuels. Many proponents say societies should adopt the soft-energy path. This is a plan for reducing fossil-fuel consumption while adopting new clean-energy technologies as they emerge. Some countries are already adopting the soft-energy path.

Exercise 3 Nineteenth-Century Science-Fiction Novels

Most people say the science-fiction genre began in the nineteenth century. The first work of science fiction was Mary Shelley's *Frankenstein: or, The Modern Prometheus*, a popular work about a scientist who reanimated the dead. Jules Verne wrote *Twenty Thousand Leagues under the Sea* and other science-fiction novels. Robert Louis Stevenson and H.G. Wells also wrote science-fiction works in the 1800s.

Exercise 4 The Human Genome Project

The Human Genome Project is an important effort to identify and sequence the human genome. After working on it for more than twenty years, the project is now complete. This project is very important, so work on it had to be completed.

Knowledge of the genome is expected to lead to many advances in medicine.

Exercise 5 Mob Mentality

Mob mentality causes people to act similarly to others in groups. In many cases, it can be harmless. For instance, students in a class might make noise with others. But it can be violent, such as when mobs cause problems after sporting events. The Reign of Terror in the French Revolution was a notorious example of mob mentality.

Exercise 6 The American Craftsman Style

The American Craftsman style was the American version of the British Arts and Crafts Movement. It was brought to North America by prominent architects. This movement sought to create a unique, simple, and elegant American style of home. It introduced many design changes to middle-class homes of the time. This style influenced a later style as well.

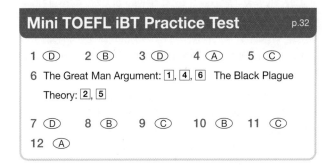

Mini TOEFL iBT Practice Test
p.32

1 Ⓓ　　2 Ⓑ　　3 Ⓓ　　4 Ⓐ　　5 Ⓒ
6 The Great Man Argument: ①, ④, ⑥　The Black Plague Theory: ②, ⑤

7 Ⓓ　　8 Ⓑ　　9 Ⓒ　　10 Ⓑ　　11 Ⓒ
12 Ⓐ

해석

[1-6]

이탈리아 르네상스 미술

르네상스는 유럽 역사의 한 시대였다. 중세 시대 이후부터 종교 개혁 이전까지의 시기였다. 이 시기는 대략 14세기부터 16세기 정도에 해당된다.

르네상스의 특징은 예술 분야에서의 새로운 기법에서 찾을 수 있다. 이탈리아가 이러한 변화의 중심에 있었으며, 피렌체가 이러한 계몽의 시대의 중심지였다. 피렌체의 문화는 고전주의적인 것이었다. 예술가들은 아테네와 로마의 공화주의적 이상을 재현하고 싶어했다. 루첼라이는 자신이 위대한 시대에 살고 있다고 글을 썼다. 레오나르도 브루니의 *피렌체 찬가*도 비슷한 느낌을 표현했다.

이 시기에는 조각 미술이 크게 발전했다. 조각가들은 고전주의적인 주제로 로마의 모델들을 사용했다. 인간의 존엄성을 담은 누드 조각들이 넘쳐났다. 회화 또한 번성했다. 지오토와 프라 안젤리코 같은 화가들에 의해 엄청난 발전이 이루어졌다. 교회가 이러한 화가들의 주요 고객이었던 탓에 주제는 대부분 종교적인 것이었다. 하지만 순전히 조형적인 주제들도 존재했다.

일반적인 주제들은 종종 신화적인 또는 종교적인 표현을 통해 다루어졌다. 예를 들어 화가들은 성경 속 인물인 아담과 이브를 이용해서 남녀의 나체를 표현하는 경우가 많았다. 이는 도덕적으로 용인되었다. 성기를 가리기 위해 종종 무화과 잎이 사용되기도 했다. 원근법의 사용 역시 눈에 띄기 시작했다. 바로 이때부터 회화가 공간으로 들어가는 창으로 여겨지기 시작했다. 이로써 건물들도 보다 사실적으로 표현될 수 있었다. 화가들은 보다 통일된 구성 요소들을 사용하게 되었다. 인쇄기도 이 시기에 등장했다. 플라톤과 아리스토텔레스가 작성한 많은 인본주의 철학서들이 출판되어 읽혀졌다. 이로 인해 르네상스의 지적인 풍조가 마련되었다.

르네상스의 발생을 설명하는 여러 가지 주장이 존재한다. 한 가지 이론은 막강한 메디치 가문 때문에 이 시기가 나타났다는 것이다. 이 가문은 피렌체의 많은 예술가들을 후원했다. 하지만 비평가들은 메디치 가문이 권력을 잡기 전인 1400년대 초에 르네상스가 시작되었다고 주장한다. 또 다른 이론은 위인론이라고 불리는 것이다. 이는 천재적인 개인들이 이러한 위대한 시기를 낳았다고 주장한다. 도나텔로와 브루넬레스키와 같은 위대한 예술가들이 선구적인 역할을 했다. 피렌체의 화가들은 레오나르도 다빈치와 미켈란젤로의 도움을 받았다. 하지만 이러한 순환성 주장은 왜 이러한 천재들이 다른 시대의 천재들과는 달랐는지 설명하지 못한다.

또 다른 주장으로 흑사병 이론이 있다. 14세기에 흑사병으로 인해 유럽 전체 인구의 3분의 1 이상이 감소했다. 이로 인해 가난한 사람들뿐만 아니라 왕과 성직자들도 사망했다. 기독교 신앙은 이러한 역병으로부터 그 누구도 지켜 주지 못했다. 이로 인해 기독교적인 세계관이 흔들렸고, 사람들은 내세보다 인생에 대해 더 많이 생각하기 시작했다.

[7-12]
프랑스 혁명

프랑스 혁명은 서구 문명사에서 중요한 시기였다. 이 시기에 프랑스의 절대군주제가 공화제로 바뀌었다. 로마 카톨릭 교회는 상당한 권력을 포기해야만 했다. 프랑스는 혁명이 끝난 후 75년 동안 공화정과 제국, 그리고 군주국 사이를 왔다 갔다 했다. 하지만 이 사건은 민주주의 시대의 주요한 전환기로서 여겨지고 있다.

여러 가지 정치적, 사회적, 경제적 요인들로 인해 혁명이 일어났다. 기존 통치자들은 경직성으로 인해 몰락했다. 신흥 중산층이 노동자 계급 및 빈민층과 손을 잡았다. 이들은 계몽주의 사상의 영향을 받았다. 혁명이 일어나기 전 수개월 동안 식량이 부족했다. 빵 가격이 크게 올라 노동자들은 빵을 사 먹을 수 없었다. 실업이 만연했다. 도둑질을 하다가 잡힌 사람들은 단두대에서 처형되는 위험을 떠안아야 했다. 루이 16세는 이러한 문제들을 효과적으로 해결하지 못했다.

혁명이 진행되면서 루이 16세는 관리들과 싸우기 시작했는데, 이로써 많은 유혈 사태가 발생했다. 국가 부채는 통제 불능 상태였고 세금은 너무 높았다. 이 시기에 루이 16세는 국민의회를 해산하려고 했다. 그래서 의원들은 테니스장에서 회의를 열고 프랑스에 헌법이 생길 때까지 휴회하지 않기로 맹약했다. 1789년 7월 11일에 루이 16세는 개혁주의자였던 총리 네커를 추방하려고 했다. 많은 파리 시민들이 공공연히 폭동에 가담했다. 7월 14일, 시민들은 바스티유 감옥으로 몰려가 수비 대장을 살해했다. 그들은 죄수들을 풀어 주고 파리 시장을 처단했다. 공포에 질린 왕은 헌법을 제정하겠다는 협정에 서명했다. 이로써 왕은 한동안 목숨을 부지할 수 있었다.

혁명의 슬로건은 "자유, 평등, 우애가 아니면 죽음을 달라"였다. 이 슬로건은 아직까지도 사용된다. 이는 억압적인 정부를 타도하려는 사람들이 부르짖는 구호가 되었다. 프랑스 귀족들도 안전하지 않았다. 많은 귀족들이 프랑스를 떠났고, 일부는 하인의 옷을 입기도 했다. 많은 변화가 일어났다. 도시에서는 무거운 세금을 거둘 수 없었고, 교회는 권력과 토지를 잃었다. 1793년 루이 16세는 사형을 선고 받았다. 그는 대중의 자유와 사회 안전에 반하는 공모죄로 기소되었다. 1월 21일 그는 단두대에서 참수되었다. 10월 16일에는 마리 앙투아네트 왕비가 그의 뒤를 따랐다.

1795년에 새 헌법이 인준되었다. 이로써 총재정부라는 명칭의 새로운 입법부가 만들어졌다. 이는 500명의 대표로 구성되었다. 이 시기에 나폴레옹 보나파르트라는 장군이 막대한 권력을 획득했다. 그는 1799년에 쿠데타를 일으켰고 5

년 뒤 스스로 황제가 되었다. 이로써 프랑스 혁명의 공화정 시기는 종말을 맞이했다.

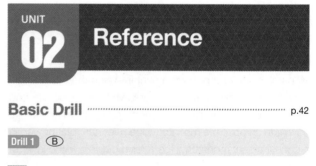

Vocabulary Check-Up   p.38

Ⓐ 1 Ⓑ   2 Ⓓ   3 Ⓒ   4 Ⓓ   5 Ⓑ
    6 Ⓐ   7 Ⓒ   8 Ⓑ

Ⓑ 1 Ⓗ   2 Ⓒ   3 Ⓐ   4 Ⓘ   5 Ⓖ
    6 Ⓙ   7 Ⓓ   8 Ⓑ   9 Ⓕ   10 Ⓔ

UNIT 02 Reference

Basic Drill   p.42

Drill 1 Ⓑ

해석

안개의 형성

안개는 지면과 맞닿아 있는 구름이다. 이는 지표면과 접촉해 있다는 점에서 다른 구름들과는 다르다. 대부분의 안개는 지면의 상대 습도가 100%에 도달할 때 형성된다. 안개는 갑자기 형성될 수도 있고, 기온이 이슬점의 어느 쪽에 있는지에 따라 빠르게 사라질 수도 있다. 안개의 두 가지 종류로 증발 안개와 강우 안개를 들 수 있다. 전자는 수분이 매우 빠르게 기체로 변할 때 만들어지며, 다른 하나는 수분이 방출될 때 만들어진다.

지구에서 가장 안개가 심한 지역은 캐나다 뉴펀드랜드의 그랜드 뱅크스이다. 이 지역에서는 북쪽에서 오는 래브라도 해류와 남쪽에서 오는 훨씬 더 따뜻한 걸프 해류가 만나기 때문에 안개가 자주 낀다.

Drill 2 Ⓐ

해석

잠자리

잠자리는 360도를 볼 수 있는 커다란 다면체의 눈을 가진 곤충이다. 두 쌍의 튼튼하고 투명한 날개와 기다란 몸통을 지니고 있다.

잠자리는 보통 모기, 파리, 그리고 기타 작은 곤충들을 잡아먹는다. 이러한 해충들을 잡아먹기 때문에 많은 사람들이 잠자리를 좋아한다. 잠자리는 호수, 연못, 시내, 습지 근처에서 서식하며, 약충이라고 불리는 잠자리의 유충은 수중에서 산다.

알에서 시작해 어미 잠자리로서 죽음을 맞기까지 잠자리의 일생은 6개월부터 길게는 6-7년에 이를 수 있다. 이러한 일생의 대부분은 유충 상태로 보내는데, 이때 약충은 아가미를 이용해서 호흡을 하며 올챙이나 물고기를 잡아먹는다.

Drill 3 Ⓑ

해석

생태학

생태학이란 서식지에 분포하는 생물들을 연구하는 학문이다. 이는 생물들이 특정 지역에 서식하는 이유와 얼마나 많은 종들이 그러한 곳에서 살 수 있는지를 연구한다. 종들과 다른 생물 간의 상호 작용 또한 관찰한다.

생물의 환경에는 다양한 물리적인 요소가 포함된다. 일부 요소로서 햇빛이나 기후 같은 것을 들 수 있다. 지질도 또 다른 요소이다. 서식지를 공유하는 다른 생물들 또한 또 다른 요소이다.

생태학은 범위가 넓은 과학이다. 한 가지 분야는 행동생태학인데, 이는 한 생물체가 서식지에 적응하는 방법을 관찰한다. 개체군생태학은 하나의 종을 연구한다. 생태학에는 그밖에도 훨씬 더 많은 분야들이 존재한다.

Drill 4 Ⓓ

해석

가설

가설이란 아직 과학으로 입증되지 못한 현상에 대해 설명을 제시한 것이다. 가설은 논리적인 방식으로 두 가지 이상의 현상 사이에 연관성이 있을 수 있다고 주장한다. 과학자들은 가설에 기반하여 관찰을 하거나 이론을 세운다.

과학적인 방법에서는 가설을 검증할 수 있어야 한다. 과학계의 많은 사람들이 가설은 반증이 가능해야 한다고 주장한다. 이는 가설이 틀렸다고 입증될 수 있다는 점을 의미한다.

잘 알려진 한 가지 예로 어떤 남자가 새로운 나라에 가서 흰색 양들만 본다고 하자. 그는 이 나라에 있는 모든 양이 하얗다는 가설을 세운다. 그러나 한 마리의 검은색 양이 보이는 경우, 그 가설은 틀린 것으로 판명될 것이다.

Drill 5 Ⓑ

해석

뉴턴의 운동 법칙

뉴턴의 운동 법칙은 세 개의 물리 법칙이다. 제1법칙을 이해하기 위해 식탁 위에 사과가 있다고 가정하자. 만약 손과 같은 힘이 사과를 민다면 사과는 관성을 얻어 움직이기 시작할 것이다.

제2법칙의 경우, 똑같은 사과를 손으로 부드럽게 밀면 사과가 서서히 움직이기 시작할 것이다. 만약 힘을 줘서 손으로 밀면 그로 인해 사과는 사과에 가해진 힘에 따른 방향과 힘에 의해 벽에 부딪칠 것이다.

뉴턴의 제3법칙에 대한 예는 사과가 벽에 부딪힌 이후 일어나는 반작용이다. 모든 작용은 크기는 같고 방향은 반대인 반작용을 필요로 하는데, 위 경우, 벽이 움푹 들어가거나 사과가 터지는 것이 반작용일 수 있다.

Drill 6 Ⓑ

해석

생물계

1735년에 카롤루스 린내우스가 생물계에 대한 책을 발표했다. 책에서 그는 생물계를 두 개의 계, 즉 동물계와 식물계로 분류했다. 지구상의 모든 생물은 두 가지 중 하나의 카테고리에 포함되었다. 이후 그는 세 번째 계인 광물계를 만들었다.

수 년이 지난 후 박테리아가 발견되었다. 생물학자들은 박테리아가 이들 세 가지 계 중 어디에도 속하지 않는다는 것을 알게 되었다. 이들을 위한 또 하나의 계가 명명되었다. 이는 모네계라고 불렸다.

과학이 발전해서 생물에 대해 더 많은 것을 알게 되자 새로운 계가 필요해졌다. 1969년 로버트 휘태커가 다섯 번째 계를 발견했다. 이 계는 균류라 명명되었다. 1980년경에 또 다른 계가 명명되었다. 이는 다양한 미생물들을 분류하기 위해 명명되었다.

Exercises with Mid-Length Passages

Exercise 1 1 Ⓓ 2 Ⓒ 3 Ⓒ 4 Ⓓ   p.46

해석

엘니뇨와 라니냐

엘니뇨와 라니냐는 전 지구적 차원에서 해양과 대기 사이에 일어나는 현상이다. 이 기간에는 열대 태평양의 표층수에서 급격한 기온 변화가 나타난다. 엘니뇨는 섭씨 0.5도 이상의 온도 상승을 가리키며, 라니냐는 동일한 수준으로 온도가 내려가는 것을 가리킨다. 이러한 변화가 엘니뇨나 라니냐로 불리기 위해서는 5개월 이상 지속되어야 한다.

이러한 기후 변화의 영향을 받는 많은 국가들이 남아메리카와 아프리카의 개발도상국이다. 이들의 경제는 주로 농업과 어업에 의존해 있다. 이러한 산업들은 식량 공급, 고용, 국제 무역의 주된 기반이다. 따라서 이러한 변화를 예측할 수 있는 새로운 방법이 마련되면 이들 국가에 커다란 사회 경제적 영향을 미칠 수 있을 것이다.

엘니뇨와 라니냐 현상은 보통 불규칙적으로 일어난다. 최근에는 2-7년마다 일어났다. 대부분 1년에서 2년 정도 지속된다. 엘니뇨는 매우 광범위한 지역에 영향을 미친다. 여러 지역에서 정상적인 기후와 반대되는 날씨가 나타난다. 일부 지역에서는 폭우로 인해 엄청난 홍수가 발생하기도 한다. 또한 극심한 가뭄으로 산불도 많이 발생한다. 반면에 라니냐는 전 세계에 영향을 미친다. 라니냐가 발생하면 무역풍이 매우 심해지고 정상적인 수온보다 차가운 물이 중앙태평양 및 동태평양에 비정상적으로 모이게 된다.

대양 대기 시스템에서 태평양의 정상적인 패턴은 적도풍이 모인 다음에 따뜻한 물이 서쪽으로 모이는 것이다. 차가운 물이 남아메리카 해안을 따라 올라온다. 이로써 어류들이 해안가로 몰려들어 인근 어업 경제가 활성화되는데, 그 이유는 어류들이 차갑고 영양분이 풍부한 물을 따라다니기 때문이다. 엘니뇨가 발생하면 따뜻한 물이 남아메리카 해안으로 흘러든다. 차가운 물이 올라오지 않기 때문에 바다가 따뜻해진다. 따라서 어류들이 해안을 따라다니는 대신 먼 바다로 나가 버린다. 이러한 상황은 지역 어업에 심각한 타격을 가져다 준다.

엘니뇨와 라니냐의 원인은 아직 밝혀지지 않았다. 그러나 많은 과학자들이 이 전 지구적인 기상 현상을 보다 잘 이해하기 위해 노력 중이다.

Summary Note

❶ El Nino

❷ La Nina

Exercise 2 1 Ⓑ 2 Ⓓ 3 Ⓒ 4 Ⓒ p.48

해석

생물 다양성의 감소

생물 다양성이란 한 지역에 서식하는 생물의 다양성을 뜻한다. 지난 100년간 과학자들은 생물 다양성의 급격한 감소를 목격해 왔다. 이는 지구의 관리자인 인간에게 막대한 손실을 의미한다.

일부 연구에 따르면 지구상에 존재하는 식물종 중 1/8이 멸종 위기에 처해 있다. 매년 14만 종의 식물들이 사라지고 있다고 추정된다. 이는 지속 불가능한 생태학적 관행들 때문이다. 이렇게 사라진 식물들 중 다수가 질병 퇴치를 위한 신약 개발에 매우 유용하게 쓰일 수 있는 것들이었다.

지난 1,000년간 멸종된 생물들은 대부분 인간 때문에 멸종되었다. 열대 우림의 벌목이 주된 이유이다. 이러한 서식지는 목초지, 농경지, 그리고 과수원으로 바뀌고 있다. 이러한 파괴는 주로 육우를 위한 목초지를 확보하기 위해 이루어진다. 또한 인간의 소비를 위해 농부들이 곡물이나 과수를 재배하기 위해서도 이루어진다.

외래종의 유입은 또 다른 위협이 된다. 외래종이 어떤 서식지로 유입되면 이들은 자급자족 개체군을 형성하려고 한다. 이는 자생종들에게 위협이 된다. 이들 외래종들은 포식자나 기생 동식물이 될 수도 있다. 또는 공격적일 수도 있다. 이들은 자생종에게서 양분을 빼앗아간다. 자생종은 진화할 기회를 갖지 못했기 때문에 방어 수단을 갖고 있지 않은 경우가 많고, 외래종들을 상대로 경쟁을 할 수가 없다.

전 세계에 다양한 생물들이 존재하는 유일한 이유는 경계가 있기 때문이다. 주요 경계는 바다와 해양이다. 자연적인 방법으로는 절대로 이들 경계를 넘어갈 수 없다. 하지만 인간이 선박과 비행기를 발명했기 때문에 현재에는 종들이 만나는 일이 가능해졌다. 이 종들이 적응할 시간 없이, 인간은 계속해서 여러 지역의 종들을 모이게 하고 있다. 곧 지구의 생태계는 공격성이 강한 극소수의 슈퍼 종들이 지배하게 될 것이다.

이러한 문제를 해결하기 위해서는 사람들이 소비를 최소한으로 줄여야 한다. 쇠고기 및 자연 환경에 해를 끼치는 기타 제품들의 소비를 줄여야 한다. 또한 정부는 자연 서식지 파괴 및 외래종 유입 행위를 엄격히 규제해야 한다.

Summary Note

❶ rainforests

❷ exotic

❸ Decline

Exercise 3 1 Ⓑ 2 Ⓒ 3 Ⓑ 4 Ⓑ p.50

해석

조력 발전소

조력 발전은 전기를 생산하는 한 가지 방법이다. 조력 발전 시스템은 조수로 다량의 물이 움직일 때 물에 들어 있는 에너지를 모은다. 이러한 방식의 생태학적인 효과는 여전히 연구 중으로, 전 세계에서 가동 중인 조력 발전소의 수는 극

소수에 불과하다. 하지만 많은 정부들이 더 많은 조력 발전소 건설을 계획 중이다. 현재 미국, 멕시코, 그리고 캐나다에서 몇 개의 조력 발전소가 세워질 계획이다.

랑스 조력 발전소는 조력 에너지로 가동되는 세계 최초의 발전소였다. 이 발전소는 프랑스 브레타뉴의 랑스강에 위치해 있다. 이 발전소를 건설하기 위해서는 주변 지역에 배수 시설이 필요했다. 2년에 걸쳐 두 개의 댐이 건설되었다. 실제 발전소 건설은 1963년 7월 20일에 시작되었다. 당시 랑스강은 두 개의 댐에 의해 완전히 막혀 있었다. 발전소는 1966년에 완공되었다. 1967년 12월 4일에는 프랑스 전국 전력망에 연결되었다. 발전소 건설 비용은 약 5억 2천 4백만 유로였다. 이는 현재 브레타뉴 지역에서 소비되는 전력의 3%를 생산하고 있다. 프로젝트에 엄청난 비용이 들었지만 그 만큼의 수익을 거두었다. 이곳에서 생산되는 전력이 원자력 발전을 이용하는 경우보다 훨씬 저렴하기 때문이다.

이 발전소의 댐 때문에 랑스강의 생태계에 점점 더 많은 토사가 쌓이고 있다. 양미리와 가자미가 사라졌다. 하지만 농어와 오징어는 강으로 돌아왔다. 여전히 강어귀에는 조수가 흐르고 있다. 발전소 관리자들은 생물학적인 영향을 최소화시키기 위해 지금도 노력하고 있다.

북아메리카 최초의 조력 발전소는 안나폴리스 로열 조력 발전소였다. 이곳은 캐나다의 아나폴리스 로열에 위치해 있었다. 처음에는 전력 생산을 위한 대안을 살펴보기 위해 1984년에 건설되었지만, 2019년에 해체되었다. 하지만 지역 환경에 변화를 가져다 주었다. 해당 지역의 수온과 기온이 변했다. 뿐만 아니라 강에 토사가 쌓이는 패턴도 바뀌었으며, 댐 양쪽에 있는 강둑의 크기도 커졌다.

Summary Note

❶ electricity

❷ nuclear power

❸ The Rance Tidal Power Plant

Exercise 4 1 Ⓒ 2 Ⓑ 3 Ⓐ 4 Ⓐ p.52

해석

코모도 도마뱀

코모도 도마뱀은 세계에서 가장 큰 도마뱀이다. 평균적으로 2-3미터까지 길이로 자란다. 야생 상태에서 성체의 몸무게는 70kg 정도이다. 코모도 도마뱀은 왕도마뱀과에 속한다. 코모도 도마뱀은 인도네시아의 여러 섬에서 서식한다. 이들에 대한 목격담은 1910년 유럽인들에게 처음 보고되었다. 널리 알려지게 된 것은 자바 보고르의 동물 박물관 관장인 피터 우웬스가 이 생물에 대한 논문을 발표한 1912년 이후였다. 1980년에는 이 도마뱀들의 개체수를 보호하기 위해 코모도 국립공원에 자금이 지원되었다.

코모도 도마뱀은 육식 동물이다. 죽은 동물의 살점도 좋아하기는 하지만 살아 있는 상태의 먹이를 사냥한다. 살금살금 다가간 후 순식간에 먹이를 공격한다. 이때의 속도는 시속 20km에 이를 수 있다.

코모도 도마뱀에게 독이 있다고 알려져 있지는 않지만, 이빨에는 50종 이상의 박테리아가 살고 있다. 먹이가 처음에 한 번 물렸다고 해서 죽지는 않지만 치명적인 감염으로 인해 일주일 이내에 먹이는 죽게 될 것이다. 그러면 코모도 도마뱀이 사체의 냄새를 따라가 이를 찾아낸 다음 사체의 살점을 먹는다. 코모도 도마뱀은 또한 어렸을 때부터 커다란 발톱을 사용한다. 이를 사용하여 나무에 올라 보다 나이가 많은 코모도 도마뱀의 이빨로부터 몸을 피한다. 하지만 나이가 들면 발톱은 주로 무기로 사용된다.

코모도 도마뱀의 먹이는 다양해서 돼지, 염소, 사슴, 물소 등이 여기에 포함된다. 야생에서는 이들이 덩치가 작은 다른 코모도 도마뱀도 잡아먹는 것이 관찰되

었다. 때로는 인간을 잡아먹거나 인간의 시체를 먹기도 한다. 지난 100년간 12명 이상이 코모도 도마뱀에 물려 목숨을 잃었다.

코모도 도마뱀은 취약종으로서 현재 6,000마리 정도가 살고 있다. 짝짓기는 5월과 8월 사이에 이루어지며 9월에 알을 낳는다. 암컷은 땅이나 나무의 구멍에 알을 낳는데, 이로써 알이 보호를 받는다. 한 번에 평균적으로 20개 정도의 알을 낳는다. 태어난 후 다 자라기까지 약 5년이 걸리며, 이들은 보통 30년 정도 산다.

✎ Summary Note
❶ Largest lizard
❷ islands in Indonesia
❸ 6,000

Exercise 5 1 ⓓ 2 ⓐ 3 ⓓ 4 ⓒ   p.54

p.54

해석

나노 기술

나노 기술은 비교적 새로운 분야의 응용 과학이다. 나노 단위의 초소형 기계를 제작하기 위한 노력이다. 나노는 10의 −9제곱을 의미하는 측정 단위이다. 이는 매우 작은 것을 설명하는데 사용된다. 나노 기술이 현재 사용되고 있는 한 예로서 폴리머 제작을 들 수 있다. 이들은 분자 구조에 기반해 있다. 또 다른 예로 컴퓨터 칩 레이아웃의 설계를 들 수 있다. 이들은 표면 과학에 기반해 있다.

나노 사이즈 수준에서는 많은 물질의 특성이 변한다. 예를 들어 구리는 불투명하지 않고 투명하다. 순금은 실온에서 액체 상태가 된다. 실리콘 같은 절연체는 전도체가 된다. 이런 모든 활동들은 다수의 잠재적인 위험성을 수반한다. 상태 변화로 인해 나노 입자들의 운동성이 증가한다. 또한 다른 물질과 반응할 가능성도 커진다. 나노 입자가 인간의 신체로 들어갈 수 있는 방법은 네 가지이다. 들이마시거나, 삼키거나, 피부를 통해 흡수하거나, 혹은 주사를 맞음으로써 들어올 수 있다. 이러한 입자들은 신체에 들어오면 운동성이 크게 증가한다.

사실 이러한 입자들이 생물의 체내에서 반응하는 방식은 아직 완벽하게 이해되지 못하고 있다. 하지만 과학자들은 이러한 작은 물체들이 방어적인 세포에 지나친 부담을 줄 수 있다고 생각한다. 이로써 질병에 대한 신체의 방어 능력이 약화될 수 있다. 인간은 이 정도 크기의 입자를 통제하지 못할 수 있다. 그렇게 되면 대규모 전염병이 발생해서 질병의 확산과 인명 피해를 야기하게 될 것이다.

나노 기술과 관련된 또 다른 우려 사항은 환경적인 위험이다. 한 보고서는 회색의 끈적거리는 물질로 지구가 뒤덮이는 재앙에 대해 상세히 다루고 있다. 이러한 끔찍한 사태의 원인은 무분별한 미세 로봇의 자기 복제에 있다. 이 로봇은 나노봇으로 불리며 자기 제어가 가능하다. 따라서 나노봇 제작 및 출시를 허가받기 위해서는 과학자들이 훨씬 더 많은 데이터를 수집해야 한다. 라이센스가 있는 과학자들만이 안전한 실험을 할 수 있도록 과학자들에게 엄격한 법률이 적용되어야 할 것이다.

✎ Summary Note
❶ Uses
❷ Risks

Exercise 6 1 ⓐ 2 ⓒ 3 ⓒ 4 ⓒ   p.56

p.56

해석

더스트 볼

더스트 볼은 1930년대 중반부터 후반까지 미 중부와 캐나다에서 발생했던 일련의 먼지 폭풍이었다. 그 원인은 극심한 가뭄과 수십 년 동안 지속된 부적절한 농법에 있었다. 땅을 일구는 과정에서 풀이 제거되자 대평원의 비옥한 토양이 노출되었다. 가뭄이 진행되는 동안 토양은 메말라 흙먼지가 되었고, 그 결과 바람에 흩어졌다. 바람으로 인해 먼지는 대규모의 검은 구름 형태로 동쪽으로 이동했다. 구름 때문에 시카고까지의 하늘이 온통 검게 보였다. 마침내 대서양을 넘어가면서 흙먼지는 사라졌다.

더스트 볼은 1934년에 시작되어 1939년까지 계속되었다. 1933년 11월 11일 매우 강력한 먼지 폭풍이 메마른 사우스 다코다의 농경지의 표토를 쓸어갔다. 이는 그해 있었던 끔찍한 먼지 폭풍 중 하나에 불과했다. 이후 1934년 5월 11일 더스트 볼의 최악의 폭풍 중 하나로서 이틀간의 강력한 폭풍이 발생하여 대평원의 막대한 표토가 쓸려가 버렸다. 또 다시 시카고까지 먼지 구름이 불었고, 시카고에서는 먼지가 눈처럼 쏟아져 내렸다. 1935년 4월 14일은 블랙 선데이로 알려져 있다. 이때가 더스트 볼 기간 중 최악의 "검은 폭풍"이 발생한 때였다. 이로 인해 광범위한 피해가 발생했고, 낮이 밤으로 변했다. 목격자들에 따르면 어떤 지점에서는 불과 1.5미터 앞도 보이지 않았다고 한다.

밀 농사로 자생 잔디가 없었던 탓에 수백만 에이커에 이르는 땅의 표토가 쓸려 갔다. 대규모 물소 떼는 더 이상 남아 있는 자생 잔디에 양분을 공급해 주지 못했다. 이러한 생태계적 재앙으로 텍사스, 아칸소, 오클라호마, 그리고 대평원 주변 지역에서 대이동이 일어났다. 50만 명 이상의 미국인들이 집을 잃었다. 이들 이재민 중 다수가 일자리를 찾아 서쪽으로 이동했다. 이 사람들은, 오클라호마 출신이 아닌 경우에도, 오키라고 불렸다.

✎ Summary Note
❶ November 11, 1933
❷ May 11, 1934
❸ April 14, 1935

Building Summary Skills   p.58

p.58

Exercise 1 El Nino and La Nina

El Nino and La Nina cause major temperature changes that affect a large portion of the world's climate. The economies of many nations in South America and Africa are strongly affected by these changes in the climate. El Nino and La Nina occur irregularly and can cause some damaging effects such as drought, flooding, and forest fires. These changes also affect the migratory patterns of fish, which affects the fishing industry. Scientists do not fully understand El Nino and La Nina yet, but they are studying them very closely.

Exercise 2 The Decline of Biodiversity

Biodiversity, which describes the range of living things, has been declining rapidly over the past century. Many species of plants are becoming extinct because of unsustainable environmental practices. Humans are the biggest cause of these environmental problems mainly because they chop down so many parts of rainforests. Another threat to biodiversity is the introduction of foreign species, which overtake local species. Humans need to take strong steps to stop the decline of biodiversity.

Exercise 3 Tidal Power Plants

Tidal power plants are a method of generating electricity through the power of moving water and are gaining popularity around the world. The Rance Tidal Power Plant in France was the first power plant in the world to use this method. The construction of the Rance Tidal Power Plant took a lot of time and money, but it has generated enough power to cover its costs. Tidal power plants do affect the local ecosystem, and scientists are still studying how. The first tidal power plant in North America was in Annapolis Royal in Canada.

Exercise 4 The Komodo Dragon

Komodo dragons are the largest lizards in the world today. They live on some islands in Indonesia. They eat meat, which they kill by a bite that infects their prey and kills it over a period of days. Komodo dragons eat a wide range of other animals, including their own species. Today, the population of Komodo dragons is not very large.

Exercise 5 Nanotechnology

Nanotechnology is the risky science of building microscopic machines. This technology could be very useful, but it is unpredictable since the properties of many materials change at the microscopic level. Some scientists worry that machines this small could easily enter human bodies and cause effects that nobody can predict. Another concern is that self-replicating nanobots could damage the environment on a very large and unexpected scale. Experiments with nanotechnology should be done in a very cautious fashion as regulated by the government.

Exercise 6 The Dust Bowl

The Dust Bowl was a series of terrible storms in the 1930s that damaged the farming industries in the United States and Canada. Farming was damaged because the fertile layer of topsoil was blown away by powerful winds, leaving only dusty, infertile ground. Some of these storms were so bad that the sky turned black, and no one could see the sun. Many farmers were made homeless by this natural disaster and were forced to travel west to look for work.

Mini TOEFL iBT Practice Test   p.60

1 ⓒ	2 ⓒ	3 ⓑ	4 ⓑ	5 ⓐ
6 ⓓ				
7 ⓐ	8 ⓑ	9 ⓓ	10 ⓑ	11 ⓑ
12 ⓑ				

해석

[1-6]

기상학

기상학은 지구의 대기를 연구하는 학문이다. 기상학은 날씨의 형성 과정 및 기상 현상에 대한 예측과 설명에 초점을 맞춘다. 이러한 현상들은 기온, 기압, 그리고 수증기와 같이 대기 안에 존재하는 요인들에 의해 일어난다. 이러한 요인들이 상호 작용을 통해 기후 패턴을 만든다. 기상학이라는 용어는 기원전 350년에 아리스토텔레스에 의해 만들어졌다. 그는 물이 증발하는 과정을 최초로 관찰하고 기록한 인물이었다. 그는 뜨거운 태양이 물을 안개로 만든 후 그 다음날 다시 땅으로 돌려보내는 과정에 주목했다.

1607년, 갈릴레오가 온도를 측정할 수 있는 최초의 도구를 만들었다. 몇 년이 지난 후 그의 조수는 최초의 기압계를 만들었다. 1648년 무렵 파스칼은 높이가 높을수록 기압이 떨어진다는 사실을 발견했다. 그는 또한 대기 위는 진공 상태일 것이라고 추측했다. 1667년 로버트 후크는 풍속을 측정할 수 있는 장치를 만들었다. 이후 에드먼드 헤일리는 선원들을 위한 무역풍 지도를 제작했다. 그는 또한 대기의 변화가 태양열에 의해서 일어난다고 추측했다. 20세기에는 중요한 많은 기상 현상들이 과학적으로 이해되기 시작했다. 아마도 가장 중요한 개념은 지구의 자전이 대기의 흐름에 영향을 미치는 방법이었을 것이다. 이 거대한 힘은 코리올리 효과라고 명명되었다.

1904년, 한 노르웨이 과학자가 자연 법칙에 근거한 계산을 통해 날씨를 예상하는 일이 가능하다고 주장했다. 이로써 현대의 기상 예보가 탄생했다. 1950년대에는 기상 예보관들이 컴퓨터를 사용하기 시작했다. 이 초창기의 기기들은 실험을 하는데 도움을 주었다. 최초의 기상 예보는 고온과 저온의 모델을 사용해 이루어졌다. 약 10년이 흐른 뒤 최초의 기상 위성이 발사되었다. 이로 인해 전 지구적인 날씨 정보의 시대가 열렸다. 위성은 산불에서부터 엘니뇨에 이르기까지 모든 것을 연구하는데 중요한 도구가 되었다. 위성 덕분에 과학자들은 지구를 전체적으로 바라볼 수 있었다.

오늘날에는 기후 모델을 사용해 과거의 기상 데이터와 비교한다. 과거의 데이터를 현재 상태와 비교하는 것이다. 이를 통해 과학자들은 장기적인 기후 변화 연구에 필요한 데이터를 얻을 수 있다. 지구 온난화와 같은 현상도 보다 잘 이해되고 있다. 현재에는 강력한 신형 슈퍼컴퓨터가 사용되고 있다. 이 컴퓨터 덕분에 대기의 작동 모델을 만드는 것도 가능하다.

인간에 의한 여러 기상 예측 방법들도 사용된다. 이러한 방법은 기상 예보관들의 능력과 판단에 달려 있다. 이들 방법 중 다수가 50% 이상의 정확도를 나타낸다. 현재 기상 예보의 시대에서는 많은 사람들이 날씨 정보에 의존한다. 이로써 성공적으로 식량 생산량이 증가하고 있다. 또한 자연 재해가 발생했을 때 인명 피해도 줄일 수 있다. 기상을 예측하는 인간의 능력은 전례 없는 정확도를 자랑하고 있다.

[7-12]

얼룩 다람쥐

지구는 수백만 종의 동물들로 뒤덮여 있으며, 각각은 정교한 지구 생태계에서 중요한 자리를 차지하고 있다. 얼룩 다람쥐는 크기는 작지만 서식지의 건강 상태

10

에 대단히 중요하다. 얼룩 다람쥐는 북아메리카와 아시아의 숲에 서식하는 작은 설치류이다. 25종의 얼룩 다람쥐가 있다. 그중 다수는 적갈색 털을 지니며, 흰색과 검정색의 줄무늬가 이들의 몸을 덮고 있다.

다른 여러 설치류와는 달리 얼룩 다람쥐는 일 년에 두 번 새끼를 낳는다. 첫 번째 시기는 2월에서 4월까지이고, 두 번째 시기는 6월에서 8월까지이다. 얼룩 다람쥐는 한 번에 평균적으로 네 마리를 낳지만, 최소 한 마리에서 최대 아홉 마리까지의 새끼를 낳을 수도 있다. 어미는 새끼들이 자라서 스스로 돌볼 수 있을 때까지 6주 동안 이들을 지하에 숨겨서 키운다. 이들의 천적으로는 고양이, 개, 독수리, 매, 여우, 코요테, 늑대 등을 들 수 있다. 야생에서 얼룩 다람쥐의 수명은 보통 1년 정도이지만, 일부는 최고 5년까지 사는 것으로 알려져 있다.

짝짓기 시기를 제외하고 얼룩 다람쥐는 대부분의 시간을 혼자서 집을 짓고 먹이를 찾고 포식자로부터 몸을 숨기는데 사용한다. 종종 먹이를 찾아 나무를 오르는 모습이 목격되곤 한다. 얼룩 다람쥐는 본래 음식을 저장하는 동물이다. 긴 겨울 동안 굶어 죽지 않고 동면을 하기 위해 봄과 여름 동안 견과류, 씨앗, 곤충, 딸기류 열매, 그리고 기타 식량들로 굴을 채운다. 다른 먹이로 균류, 새 알, 곡식, 벌레를 들 수 있다.

얼룩 다람쥐의 가장 눈에 띄는 특징 중 하나는 볼이다. 얼룩 다람쥐의 양쪽 볼에는 늘려서 음식물을 채울 수 있는 주머니가 달려 있다. 주머니가 채워지는 경우, 각각의 뺨은 얼룩 다람쥐의 머리만큼 커질 수 있다. 이러한 능력 덕분에 얼룩 다람쥐는 손쉽게 많은 양의 먹이를 굴로 운반할 수 있다.

얼룩 다람쥐는 몸집이 작은 다른 설치류들과 마찬가지로 유포 동물로 알려져 있다. 이들은 씨앗, 균류, 그리고 기타 종류의 식물들을 유포한다. 종종 얼룩 다람쥐는 굴로 가져온 먹이를 남겨 두기도 하고, 가지고 오는 도중에 먹이를 흘리기도 한다. 이들이 자라기 시작하면 또 다시 서식지 내의 다른 동물들에게 먹이가 공급되고 은신처가 마련된다. 씨앗을 유포시키든 다른 동물의 먹이가 되건 간에, 얼룩 다람쥐는 서식지의 중요한 부분이다. 이들은 자연에 존재하는 끊임없이 반복되는 순환에서 매우 중요한 존재이다.

Vocabulary Check-Up
p.66

Ⓐ 　1 Ⓑ　 2 Ⓒ　 3 Ⓐ　 4 Ⓒ　 5 Ⓓ
　　 6 Ⓑ　 7 Ⓐ　 8 Ⓓ

Ⓑ 　1 Ⓓ　 2 Ⓘ　 3 Ⓔ　 4 Ⓑ　 5 Ⓐ
　　 6 Ⓒ　 7 Ⓙ　 8 Ⓕ　 9 Ⓗ　 10 Ⓖ

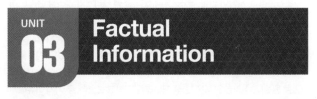

UNIT 03 Factual Information

Basic Drill
p.70

Drill 1　Ⓒ

해석

의견

의견이란 보유자에게 중요한 어떤 것에 대한 생각이나 사고를 뜻한다. 이는 사실이 아니기 때문에 옳거나 그르다고 판명될 수 없다. 하지만 미 대법원의 경우, "의견"이라는 단어는 다른 의미를 지닌다. 미 대법원에서 의견은 하나의 결정으로서, 이는 추후에 법이 따르게 될 방식을 정한다. 미 대법원은 1971년 로우 대 웨이드 사건에서 낙태가 합법이라는 의견을 제시했다. 이로 인해 미국의 임산부들이 낙태를 하는 것이 가능해졌다. 이것은 논쟁을 불러일으킨 의견의 한 예이다. 이러한 논쟁은 이슈가 된 이후 여러해 동안 계속되고 있다.

Drill 2　Ⓐ

해석

퀼트 짜기

전통적으로 퀼트는 따뜻한 이불로서 침대를 덮는 용도로 사용되었다. 하지만 요즘에는 많은 퀼트들이 예술품으로 간주되며, 전시용으로 벽에 걸려있다. 식민지 시대에는 많은 여성들이 천을 짜거나 옷을 만들며 시간을 보냈다. 이러한 여성들은 퀼팅비라고 불리는 모임을 형성했다. 퀼트는 종종 결혼이나 출생과 같은 중요한 사건을 기념하기 위해 만들어진다. 퀼트를 만드는 사람들은 바느질을 이용하여 퀼트에 중요한 날짜나 이름을 새긴다. 또한 사람 옷이나 중요한 깃발의 조각으로 퀼트로 만들어 역사적인 기록을 남기기도 한다.

Drill 3　Ⓓ

해석

의학의 역사

1960년, 의학과 관련한 최초의 증거가 선사 시대 사람의 무덤에서 발견되었다. 시신 옆에는 8종의 식물이 있었다. 이 식물들은 모두 치료 효과 때문에 현재에도 사용되고 있다. 전 세계 문화권에서 의학은 서로 다르게 발전해 왔다. 중국 한의학에서는 의사가 몸을 따라 움직이는 에너지의 흐름을 변화시켜 치료를 한다. 인도에서는 의사가 정신과 육체, 그리고 영혼 사이의 조화를 복원시켜 치료를 한다. 서양 의학은 유럽에서 처음 발전했다. 의사들은 건강을 회복시키기 위해 주로 식단과 위생에 초점을 맞춘다. 현재, 기술이 발달하고 세계가 좁아짐에 따라, 의사들은 전 세계의 의학 중 가장 좋은 측면만을 이용하고 있다.

Drill 4　Ⓑ

해석

출판 저널리즘

출판 저널리즘은 몇 가지 카테고리로 나눌 수 있다. 신문, 뉴스 잡지, 그리고 일반 잡지이다. 또한 무역 및 취미와 관련된 잡지들도 있다. 마지막으로 뉴스레터, 개인 출판물, 온라인 뉴스, 그리고 블로그도 존재한다.

출판 저널리즘은 역피라미드 방식을 이용한다. 이 방식은 특집 기사 보도보다 직설적인 혹은 딱딱한 뉴스의 보도에 사용된다. 글로 이루어진 딱딱한 뉴스 보도에서는 단어를 아껴 써야 하고 중요한 정보를 먼저 제시해야 한다. 공간이 충분하지 않은 경우에는 아래에서부터 기사 내용을 자른다. 특집 기사는 보다 여유로운 방식으로 작성된다.

| Exercise 1 | 1 Ⓐ | 2 Ⓑ | 3 Ⓒ | 4 Ⓓ | p.72 |

해석

광섬유

광섬유는 유리나 플라스틱으로 만들어진 가늘고 투명한 섬유이다. 광섬유는 정보나 빛을 이동시킬 수 있는 광신호를 보내기 위해 사용된다. 광섬유는 일반적으로 통신 시스템에서 사용된다.

광섬유 및 광섬유의 쓰임에 대한 연구는 섬유 광학이라고 불린다. 광섬유는 완전 내부 반사라는 과학적 원리에 의해 빛을 전송한다. 이 원리에 따르면 광섬유의 바깥층이 중심보다 더 두꺼운 경우 빛이 광섬유 안에서 계속 튀어 오른다.

섬유 광학의 역사는 빅토리아 시대의 영국에서 시작되었다. 당시 과학자들은 공공 분수의 물 흐름에 빛을 비추기 위해 완전 내부 반사 원리를 이용했다. 20세기 중반에는 의사들이 광섬유를 사용했다. 위내시경이라는 장비가 만들었다. 이로써 의사들은 환자의 위와 대장 안을 볼 수 있게 되었다. 1977년에는 전화 회사들이 광섬유 케이블을 사용하기 시작했다. 그들은 광섬유를 이용해서 매우 먼 곳까지 전화 신호를 보낼 수 있었다.

과거에는 구리선을 사용해서 전기 신호를 보냈다. 하지만 광섬유가 구리선을 뛰어넘는 몇 가지 장점을 가지고 있기 때문에 이들이 보다 널리 사용된다. 광섬유는 낮은 손실률로 매우 먼 거리까지 신호를 보낼 수 있다. 또한 구리선보다 훨씬 무게가 가볍다. 단 7kg의 광섬유가 20톤의 구리선을 대신할 수 있다. 이는 항공기에서 매우 유용하다. 광섬유의 유일한 단점은 단거리에서 찾아볼 수 있다. 광섬유는 적은 양을 사용할 경우 구리선보다 훨씬 더 많은 비용이 들 수 있다. 또한 꼬기도 힘들며, 신호와 함께 전력을 보낼 수도 없다.

현재의 컴퓨터 시대에서는 대역폭에 대한 필요성이 점점 커지고 있다. 광섬유는 엄청난 양의 데이터를 먼 곳으로 보낼 수 있다. 섬유 광학이 그 어느 때보다 유용하다.

Summary Note
❶ Long distances
❷ lighter than copper
❸ Cheaper

| Exercise 2 | 1 Ⓒ | 2 Ⓑ | 3 Ⓑ | 4 Ⓐ | p.74 |

해석

미국 독립 혁명

미국 독립 혁명으로 북아메리카에서 영국의 식민지 통치는 끝이 났다. 전쟁이 끝난 후 그 결과로서 미국이 탄생했다. 미국 독립 혁명은 이데올로기의 변화와 함께 시작되었다. 미국인들은 영국의 군주제를 못마땅하게 생각했다. 토머스 제퍼슨과 사무엘 애덤스 같은 건국의 아버지들이 새로운 사고를 이끌어 냈다. 전 계층의 사람들이 정부에서 발언권을 갖기를 원했다. 부패는 가장 큰 죄악으로 비춰졌다. 시민의 미덕이 최대의 선으로 여겨졌다. 가족의 지위가 더 이상 사회 내 개인의 위치를 결정하지 못하게 되었다.

혁명 전쟁으로 이어진 불안은 세 가지 사건과 연관지을 수 있다. 첫째, 1765년에 영국 의회가 인지 조례를 통과시켰다. 종이 제품에 대한 이 세금은 미국 내 주둔 중이던 영국군을 지원하기 위해 보내졌다. 식민지 주민들은 이미 영국군 주둔을 위한 세금을 내고 있었기 때문에 불만을 표현했다. 이로 인해 시위와 불복

종 운동이 시작되었다. 인지 조례는 철회되었다.

두 번째 사건은 1767년에 시작되었다. 의회가 타운센드 법을 통과시켰다. 이 법은 유리, 페인트, 그리고 종이와 같은 제품에 세금을 부과했다. 식민지 주민들은 이들 제품에 대한 불매 운동을 벌였다. 보다 많은 군대가 보스턴에 도착했고 폭력 사태가 발생했다. 영국 군대는 성난 군중들에게 발포를 했고 다섯 명의 식민지 주민들이 사망했다. 이 일은 보스턴 학살이라고 불렸다.

독립 혁명을 낳은 세 번째 사건은 1773년에 일어났다. 영국 정부가 타운센드 법을 철회했지만, 차에 대한 세금은 그대로 남아 있었다. 성난 보스턴 주민들이 영국 선박에 올라 탔다. 그들은 배에 실려 있던 차를 모두 항구에 던져버렸다. 이 사건은 보스턴 차 사건이라고 불렸다.

영국 정부와 미국의 식민지 주민들은 관계를 회복할 수 없었다. 1775년, 렉싱턴에서 전쟁이 일어났다. 1776년에는 미국 독립 선언서가 통과되었다. 전쟁은 1781년에 끝이 났고, 영국은 미국에서 철수했다.

Summary Note
❶ Boston Massacre
❷ Boston Tea Party
❸ Declaration of Independence

| Exercise 3 | 1 Ⓓ | 2 Ⓒ | 3 Ⓑ | 4 Ⓐ | p.76 |

해석

19세기 미국의 신문

1844년에는 전보가 널리 사용되었다. 전보 덕분에 신문은 먼 지역으로부터 제보를 받을 수 있었다. 뉴스를 모으기 위해 연합 통신(AP, Associated Press)이라는 뉴스 통신사가 출범했다. 매일 생생한 뉴스를 전하는 지역 신문들이 생겨났다. 하지만 뉴스 산업의 중심지는 뉴욕시였다.

미 전역의 신문들은 성장의 시대에 들어섰다. 이런 현상은 1861년 남북 전쟁이 발발하기 전까지 계속되었다. 이 기간 동안에 신문이 발전했다. 인쇄와 운송 기술이 완벽해졌고, 기사 작성 및 보도도 보다 명확하고 신선해졌다. 사무엘 보울즈 및 호레이스 그릴리와 같은 논설 위원들은 사설의 인기를 다시 올려 놓았다. 당시 사설은 인기를 잃고 있었다. 대부분의 사람들은 사설이 정당의 정책을 선전하기 위한 도구일뿐이라고 생각했다. 그릴리는 자신의 사설을 통해 노예제를 반대하는 주요 인사가 되었다.

1851년, 헨리 J. 레이몬드가 뉴욕 *타임즈*를 발행했다. 이 신문은 다른 신문들을 크게 뛰어넘었다. 사람들은 그릴리의 뉴욕 *트리뷴*이 너무 정치적이라고 생각했다. 그와 정반대로 제임스 G. 베닛의 뉴욕 *헤럴드*는 겉모습과 매출 증대에만 관심을 가졌다. 그러나 뉴욕 *타임즈*는 언론의 고결성과 시각적 조건을 모두 만족시켰다. 새로운 차원의 탁월함을 갖추었다. 뉴욕 *타임즈*는 미국에서 가장 인정받는 신문이 되었다.

1895년경 두 사람이 언론 제국을 지배했다. 조셉 퓰리처와 윌리엄 랜돌프 허스트 두 사람이 미 전역 도시의 신문사들을 보유하고 있었다. 뉴욕에서는 퓰리처의 뉴욕 *월드*와 허스트의 뉴욕 *저널*이 독자를 확보하기 위한 전쟁을 벌이고 있었다. 두 신문 모두 범죄 및 사망 기사에 초점을 맞춘다는 비난을 받았다. 사람들은 이들의 헤드라인들이 과장되었다고 생각했다. 이들은 독자의 호기심을 자극하기만을 원했다. 이러한 관행은 "황색 저널리즘"이라고 불렸다. 두 가지 이유에서 그렇게 불렸다. 한 가지 이유는 두 신문 모두 옐로우 키드라는 이름의 동일한 유명 캐릭터에 대한 만화를 게재했기 때문이었다. 또 다른 이유는 비겁하고 부정직한 것을 묘사할 때 노란색이 사용되었기 때문이다. 많은 사람들은 이러한 문제가 오늘날에도 여전히 존재한다고 생각한다.

Summary Note

❶ the telegraph
❷ *New York Times*
❸ Yellow journalism

Exercise 4 1 Ⓐ 2 Ⓒ 3 Ⓓ 4 Ⓑ p.78

해석

자유의 여신상과 자유의 종

미국에는 미국이 소중히 여기는 자유의 이상을 상징하는 두 가지 기념물이 존재한다. 자유의 여신상과 자유의 종이 각기 다른 방식으로 자유를 표현하고 있다. 자유의 여신상은 미국 땅을 밟는 이주민들에게 자유에 대한 희망을 안겨 준다. 자유의 종은 과거 미국에서 일어났던 자유를 위한 투쟁을 기념한다.

과거에는 배를 타고 미국에 들어올 때 가장 먼저 눈에 띄는 것이 자유의 여신상이었다. 이 조각상은 높이가 45m 이상이다. 이 조각상은 1885년 프랑스가 미국에게 선물로 준 것이었다. 날짜는 미국 독립 100주년을 기념하기 위해 선정되었다.

조각상은 동으로 만들어져 있다. 내부 구조는 귀스타브 에펠이 설계했는데, 그는 자신의 이름이 들어간 파리의 유명한 탑도 설계했다. 이 조각상은 뉴욕항의 리버티 아일랜드에 있다. 오른손으로는 횃불을 들고 있다. 이는 미국 전역에 자유의 길을 밝히기 위한 것이다. 왼손에는 1776년이라는 숫자가 새겨진 판을 들고 있다. 이것은 미국이 영국으로부터의 독립을 선언한 해를 기념하기 위한 것이다. 조각상 안에 들어갈 수도 있다. 많은 사람들이 계단을 올라 머리와 횃불 속으로 들어가는 것을 좋아한다.

자유의 종은 펜실베이니아주의 필라델피아에 있으며 1776년 7월 8일에 울린 것으로 가장 유명하다. 이 종은 독립 선언서 선포를 위해 시민들을 불러모을 목적으로 타종되었다. 또한 1774년 최초의 대륙 회의의 시작을 공포하기 위해서도 타종이 이루어졌다. 종 안쪽에는 성서의 레위기 25장 10절이 새겨져 있다. "너희 땅에 사는 모든 이에게 자유를 선포할지니"라고 적혀 있다. 자유의 종은 1752년에 처음 만들어졌다. 처음 타종이 이루어졌던 1753년에 그 유명한 균열이 생겼다.

1965년, 자유의 여신상과 자유의 종을 파괴하려던 테러리스트들의 계획을 FBI가 밝혀냈다. 자유의 상징물들에 대한 이러한 공격 시도는 신속히 차단되었다.

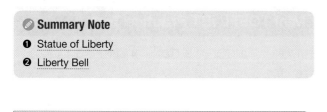

Summary Note

❶ Statue of Liberty
❷ Liberty Bell

Exercise 5 1 Ⓓ 2 Ⓓ 3 Ⓑ 4 Ⓒ p.80

해석

산성비

산성비는 황과 질소 가스가 대기 중으로 방출될 때 생긴다. 이 화학 물질은 대기 내에서 비구름에 의해 흡수된다. 오염된 물방울이 비, 눈, 혹은 진눈깨비로 땅에 떨어진다. 이로써 토양의 산성도가 증가한다. 또한 호수 및 시내의 화학적 균형도 영향을 받는다.

미국 환경 보호청에 따르면 산성비는 미국 및 캐나다의 넓은 지역에 영향을 미치는 심각한 문제이다. 강, 시내, 호수, 그리고 숲에 피해를 입힌다. 산성비의 증가를 확인할 수 있는 가장 좋은 방법은 빙하를 살펴보는 것이다. 과학자들은 산도의 급격한 상승을 확인할 수 있다. 이러한 변화는 산업 혁명 이후 계속되어 왔다.

산업화로 인한 산성비는 중국, 동유럽, 그리고 러시아에서도 심각한 문제이다. 이들 지역에서 불어오는 바람을 받는 한국 및 일본과 같은 지역들도 부정적인 영향을 받고 있다. 산성비는 영국 맨체스터에서 처음 보고되었다. 이곳은 영국의 산업 혁명 시기에 중요한 도시였다. 하지만 산성비 문제는 1960년대 후반에 이르러서야 면밀히 연구되기 시작했다. 해롤드 하비라는 캐나다 과학자가 최초 "죽은" 호수를 연구했다. 1990년대에는 *뉴욕 타임즈*가 산성비의 효과에 대한 기사를 보도했다. 이로 인해 산성비에 대한 대중의 관심이 일기 시작했다.

산성비는 화산 폭발과 같은 자연 현상에 의해서 생길 수도 있다. 하지만 산성비의 주된 원인은 화석 연료의 연소와 산업에 있다. 공장, 자동차, 발전 시설 등이 이러한 문제를 일으키는 주범이다. 산성비는 조류, 어류, 그리고 곤충과 같은 다양한 생물들을 죽게 만든다. 또한 건물에도 피해를 준다. 심지어 인간의 건강에도 부정적인 영향을 미치는 것으로도 생각된다. 뿐만 아니라 산성비는 토양에도 피해를 끼친다. 이로써 농작물 재배가 힘들어진다.

과학자들은 산성비의 효과를 반전시킬 수 있는 방법을 찾고 있다. 이러한 전 지구적 문제를 해결하기 위한 국제 협약들이 존재한다. 그러한 협약 중 하나가 대기 오염 물질의 장거리 이동에 관한 협약으로, 이는 대기 오염으로부터 인간 환경을 보호하기 위해 체결되었다.

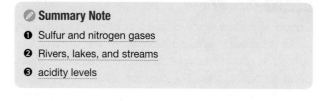

Summary Note

❶ Sulfur and nitrogen gases
❷ Rivers, lakes, and streams

❸ acidity levels

Exercise 6 1 Ⓑ 2 Ⓒ 3 Ⓐ 4 Ⓑ, Ⓓ p.82

해석

보드빌

라디오, 영화, 그리고 텔레비전이 나오기 전에는 많은 사람들이 버라이어티 극장을 찾았다. 미국에서 이러한 유흥용 극장은 보드빌이라고 불렸다. *보드빌*이라는 말은 불어인 *voix de ville*에서 나온 것인데, 이는 "도시의 소리"라는 뜻이다. 5센트만 내면 사람들은 공연을 즐길 수 있었다. 인기가 있었던 공연으로는 음악 공연, 희극, 마술쇼, 동물 공연, 곡예를 들 수 있으며, 심지어 강연도 인기가 높았다.

전형적인 보드빌 공연은 통상 곡예나 자전거 묘기와 같은 유치한 공연으로 시작되었다. 이 때문에 관객들은 늦게 도착해서 자리를 찾았다. 공연의 절정은 인기 배우가 나오는 중간 부분으로, 이때가 보통 공연의 최고조를 이루었다. 공연은 체이서 공연으로 막을 내렸는데, 이는 못 볼 정도는 아니었지만 지루했기 때문에 관객들은 이때 극장을 떠나기도 했다.

1880년과 1920년 사이에 보드빌은 대단한 인기를 끌었다. 미국에서는 경제가 성장하고 있었기 때문에 유흥에 쓸 수 있는 돈이 충분해졌다. 많은 극장들이 중산층 고객을 끌어 모으기 위해 친절하고 가족 지향적으로 보이기 위해 크게 노력했다. 공연하는 사람이 욕을 하는 일은 허용되지 않았다. 심지어 "제길"과 같은 단어조차 말해서도 안 되었다. 하지만 공연하는 사람들은 종종 이러한 규칙을 따르지 않았는데, 이 때문에 관객은 즐거워했다.

성공한 극장 소유주들은 자신의 극장이 화려하고 호화롭게 보여야 한다고 생각했다. 커튼과 의자는 최고급 레드 카펫으로 장식되었고, 멋진 목공예품에 금박이 입혀졌다. 극장을 궁궐처럼 보이게 만들었다. 그러면서도 그들은 개 저글링과 같은 유치한 공연을 했다. 1890년대에 보드빌은 전성기를 맞이했다. 교회 및 학교와 같은 인기를 누렸다. 보드빌은 사람들이 모이기에 훌륭한 장소였다.

보드빌의 시대가 언제 끝났는지는 정확하지 않다. 하지만 1910년에 영화관이 문을 열었다. 영화관은 보다 낮은 비용으로 영화를 즐길 수 있게 해 주었다. 보드빌의 관객들은 서서히 줄어들었다. 아이러니컬하게도 영화가 처음 상영된 곳이 보드빌 극장이었다. 1930년대에 미국은 대공황을 겪어야 했고 보드빌은 자취를 감추었다.

미국의 많은 유명 영화 배우와 텔레비전 스타들이 보드빌 무대에서 시작했다. 쓰리 스투지스, 막스 브라더스, 버스터 키튼, 주디 갈랜드 모두 보드빌 극장에서 데뷔했다.

> **✎ Summary Note**
> ❶ chaser
> ❷ movie theaters
> ❸ The Great Depression

Building Summary Skills
p.84

Exercise 1 Optical Fiber

Optical fibers are made of glass or plastic and are very useful for sending light and information. The study of fiber optics has shown that light can be bounced continuously down an optical fiber. The concept behind optical fibers was discovered in England and later adapted for medical equipment. Optical fibers have many advantages over copper cables. In this age of information, optical fibers are very useful.

Exercise 2 The American Revolution

The American Revolution was the war that ended British rule over some of its colonies in North America and established the United States as a country. The revolution began with a shift in ideology that was led by great men such as Thomas Jefferson and Samuel Adams. Three main events led up to the Revolutionary War. These events were the Stamp Act of 1765, the Townshend Acts of 1767, and the Boston Tea Party in 1773. By 1781, the fighting ended, and the British withdrew from the American colonies.

Exercise 3 American Newspapers in the Nineteenth Century

In the middle of the 1800s, the wide use of the telegraph enabled newspapers to get reports from far away. This led to a new age of growth in the newspaper industry. During this time, everything from the writing and visual presentation to the delivery of newspapers improved. New York was the most competitive place, and the *New York Times* emerged as the most respected newspaper in the country. Meanwhile, two newspaper owners, William Randolph Hearst and Joseph Pulitzer, battled to win readers, giving rise to the unethical practice of yellow journalism.

Exercise 4 The Statue of Liberty and the Liberty Bell

Two monuments are the best symbols of America's ideal of freedom: the Statue of Liberty and the Liberty Bell. The Statue of Liberty was given to the United States by France as a gift in 1885 to mark the 100-year birthday of the United States. It was designed by Gustave Eiffel and stands about forty-five meters tall in New York Harbor. The Liberty Bell is located in Philadelphia, Pennsylvania, and was most famously rung on July 8, 1776, to announce the first public reading of the Declaration of Independence. It has a crack which was made when it was rung for the first time.

Exercise 5 Acid Rain

Acid rain is a pollution problem caused by the release of sulfur and nitrogen gases into the air. This problem has been observed in many industrialized countries. Acid rain causes many problems such as poisoning bodies of water, killing animals, damaging soil, and harming the health of humans. Scientists are searching for ways to reduce this problem.

Exercise 6 Vaudeville

Vaudeville was a form of inexpensive live entertainment that was very popular in the United States in the late 1800s and the early 1900s. Vaudeville entertained the audience with a variety of acts, including trained animals, acrobats, magic, comedy, musical performances, and lecturers. A typical vaudeville show began with an opener, peaked with a headliner, and closed with a chaser. At the height of its popularity, vaudeville theaters were among the most popular places for people to gather. By the early 1900s, movie theaters and the Great Depression caused vaudeville to disappear.

Mini TOEFL iBT Practice Test
p.86

1 Ⓑ	2 Ⓐ	3 Ⓒ	4 Ⓑ	5 Ⓐ
6 Ⓑ				
7 Ⓐ	8 Ⓓ	9 Ⓒ	10 Ⓓ	11 Ⓒ
12 Ⓐ				

해석

[1-6]

앤드류 잭슨 대통령

앤드류 잭슨은 미국의 일곱 번째 대통령이자 플로리다의 초대 주지사였다. 잭슨은 매우 강인한 군인으로 알려져 있었기 때문에 그의 별명은 단단한 나무의 이름을 딴 "올드 히커리"였다.

잭슨은 13세 때 미국 독립 전쟁에서 영국과 싸우기 위해 육군에 입대했다. 그와 그의 형은 포로로 잡혔다. 한 영국 군인의 군화 닦기를 거부한 탓에 그는 영국 군인으로부터 얼굴과 손에 상처를 입었고, 이로써 그는 언제나 영국인을 경멸하게 되었다. 포로에서 풀려난 후 잭슨의 형은 사망했고, 잭슨은 집으로 돌아왔지만 자신의 어머니와 나머지 가족들이 사망했다는 사실을 알게 되었다.

1815년 뉴올리언즈 전투에서 잭슨은 6,000명의 군사를 이끌고 12,000명의 영국군과 맞서 싸워 승리를 거두었다. 잭슨의 부하 중 사망자는 단 8명이었던 반면 영국군의 경우 2,000명이 사망했다. 1817년 잭슨은 군대를 이끌고 플로리다에 가서 스페인군 및 세미놀 인디언들과 전투를 벌여 세미놀족을 격파했다. 이후 그는 스페인으로 하여금 플로리다의 권력을 미국에게 넘겨 주도록 했고, 그는 최초의 플로리다 주지사가 되었다.

앤드류 잭슨은 1824년 대통령 선거에 출마했다. 토머스 제퍼슨을 포함하여 많은 사람들은 그가 대통령이 되기에는 너무 법을 무시한다고 생각했다. 잭슨은 선거에서 존 퀸시 애덤스에게 패했다. 잭슨은 1828년 선거에 재출마했다. 그는 애덤스를 꺾고 대통령이 되었다. 잭슨의 대통령직 수행에 있어서 가장 논란이 컸던 부분은 미 원주민들에 대한 처우였다. 1830년 그는 인디언 강제 이주법을 제정했다. 당시 45,000명의 체로키 인디언들이 강제로 자신들의 땅을 포기하고 서쪽으로 이동해야 했다. "눈물의 행로"라고 불린 행렬에서 수천 명이 목숨을 잃었다. 한 역사가는 이 시기를 "미국 역사상 가장 불행했던 순간"이라고 불렀다. 1835년 1월 30일, 리처드 로렌스가 잭슨 대통령 암살을 시도했다. 이 정신이상자는 잭슨에게 다가가 잭슨을 겨냥해 두 자루의 권총을 발사했다. 총알은 잭슨을 빗나갔고 대통령은 들고 있던 지팡이로 로렌스를 공격했다.

앤드류 잭슨은 레이첼이라는 여성과 결혼했는데, 이때 그녀는 첫 번째 남편과 이혼한 후였다. 이후 많은 사람들이 그녀의 명예를 훼손시키려 하자 잭슨은 아내의 명예를 지키기 위해 103번의 결투를 했다. 그처럼 많은 결투를 했지만 잭슨은 찰스 디킨슨이라는 한 사람만 살해했다. 그는 잭슨의 아내를 모욕했고 그래서 둘이 결투를 하게 되었다. 디킨슨이 먼저 총을 쏘았고 그의 총알은 잭슨의 갈비뼈를 맞추었다. 그 다음에 잭슨이 총을 쏘자 디킨슨은 사망했다. 잭슨은 수많은 결투에 따른 상처들을 많이 가지고 있었는데, 이 상처들 때문에 그는 나머지 일생 동안 고통을 겪었다. 종종 피를 토하기도 했다. 그는 78세 때 결핵과 심장 마비로 사망했다.

[7-12]
아리스토텔레스와 고대 그리스 과학의 발전

서양의 과학은 고대 그리스에서 시작되었는데, 아리스토텔레스는 이 시대의 위대한 사상가였다. 최초의 과학자나 철학자는 아니었지만 그는 가장 영향력이 컸던 인물이었다. 그는 플라톤의 제자였고, 알렉산더 대왕의 스승이었다.

18세에서 37세까지 그는 학생이었다. 아카데미라고 불렸던 플라톤의 학교에 다녔다. 그 후에는 몇 년 동안 여행을 다니면서 여러 섬에서 생물학을 공부했다. 이후 마케도니아의 필립 왕이, 당시 13세였던 자신의 아들 알렉산더를 교육시키기 위해 아리스토텔레스를 불러들였다. 몇 년 후 알렉산더는 아리스토텔레스를 떠나 아시아 정복길에 올랐다. 아리스토텔레스는 아테네로 돌아와서 리케이온이라는 학교를 열고 이곳에서 학자들을 가르쳤다.

아리스토텔레스는 여러 주제에 관한 책을 썼다. 그의 저서들은 모든 주제를 다루었다. 그는 과학에서부터 예술에 이르기까지 모든 방면에 정통했다. 그의 저서 중 어느 것도 완벽한 상태로 남아 있는 것은 없다. 하지만 아리스토텔레스의 연구는 서구의 철학 및 과학의 기초가 되었다. 아리스토텔레스는 오감을 통해 얻은 지식을 소중히 여겼다. 그는 감각과 변증술을 이용해 진실을 찾고자 했다. 변증술은 플라톤에서 비롯되었지만 아리스토텔레스가 발전시켰다. 아리스토텔레스의 변증술은 논리에 기반했다. 질문으로 또 다른 질문의 답을 하는 식이었다. 답들을 이용하여 진리를 찾을 수 있었다. 이러한 방법은 귀납법과 연역법이라고

불린다.

아리스토텔레스의 논리에 기반한 과학적 방법이 등장했다. 과학적 방법은 과학자들이 사용하는 과정이다. 먼저 가설을 만든 다음 실험으로 이를 증명한다. 과학적 방법은 현대 서양의 과학에서 가장 중요한 방법이다. 아리스토텔레스가 직접 많은 실험을 한 것은 아니었지만 그의 논리 체계를 이용해 다른 사람들이 많은 것을 발견했다. 아이작 뉴턴과 갈릴레오도 과학적 방법을 이용했다. 그들의 발견은 아리스토텔레스의 영향을 받은 것 중 하나였다. 아리스토텔레스는 또한 범주라는 개념을 만들었다. 그는 가능한 모든 분야의 과학을 연구했고, 그런 다음 이들을 서로 다른 그룹으로 나누었다. 그는 동물학에서부터 지질학에 이르기까지 모든 주제를 섭렵했다. 그의 저작물은 그리스 지식에서 엄청난 부분을 차지한다.

아리스토텔레스를 비판하는 사람들도 많다. 일부 학자들은 그가 여성을 존중하지 않았다고 생각하며, 그의 연구가 너무 혼란스럽다고 믿는 사람들도 있다. 그가 종종 자신의 논리 규칙을 따르지 않는 것처럼 보이기도 한다. 그리고 중세 시대에는, 오류가 없는 것으로 보였던 그의 연구가 사람들을 억압하는데 사용되기도 했다. 하지만 아리스토텔레스의 연구는 수천 년 동안 인용되어 왔다. 그의 연구는 현대 사회를 지탱하는 기둥 중 하나이다.

Vocabulary Check-Up　　　p.92

A
| 1 Ⓑ | 2 Ⓒ | 3 Ⓓ | 4 Ⓐ | 5 Ⓑ |
| 6 Ⓐ | 7 Ⓒ | 8 Ⓐ | | |

B
| 1 Ⓔ | 2 Ⓘ | 3 Ⓗ | 4 Ⓙ | 5 Ⓐ |
| 6 Ⓓ | 7 Ⓑ | 8 Ⓖ | 9 Ⓒ | 10 Ⓕ |

UNIT 04　Negative Factual Information

Basic Drill　　　p.96

Drill 1　Ⓒ

해석

모충

모충은 나비나 나방의 유충을 말한다. 모충의 몸은 길고 체절로 이루어져 있으며 부드럽다. 이 때문에 많은 양의 먹이를 먹으면서 풍선처럼 빠른 속도로 성장할 수 있다. 모충은 번데기 단계로 들어갈 준비를 하기 때문에 엄청난 양을 먹어 치운다.

모든 곤충들과 마찬가지로 모충 또한 입으로 호흡을 하지 않고 몸의 측면에 있는 관을 통해 호흡을 한다. 이들은 시력이 매우 나쁘기 때문에 더듬이를 이용하여 먹이를 찾는다. 모충은 새나 다른 동물로부터 자신을 방어하기 위한 여러 가지 방어 수단을 가지고 있다. 이들의 신체는 위장을 이용할 수 있기 때문에 일

부 모충은 뱀이나 나뭇잎처럼 보이기도 한다. 또한 일부 모충은 독이 든 잎을 먹고 독성을 나타내기도 한다.

Drill 2　Ⓑ

해석

냉장고

인간의 일상 생활을 바꾼 한 가지 발명품은 냉장고이다. 냉장고가 나오기 전에는 사람들이 신선한 식품을 구하느라 매일 많은 시간을 썼다. 음식을 차갑게 유지시키는 유일한 방법은 커다란 얼음 덩어리를 집으로 배달시키는 것인데, 이는 비용도 비싸고 불편한 일이었다.

최초의 가정용 냉장고는 1911년에 출시되었다. 이때 냉장고의 가격은 신차 가격의 거의 2배에 이르렀다. 초기 모델들은 가정에서 너무 많은 공간을 차지해서 때로는 방 두 개가 필요하기도 했다. 1927년에 제너럴 일렉트릭사에서 모니터 탑 냉장고를 선보였다. 이것이 널리 보급된 최초의 냉장고로, 이는 오늘날까지 여전히 사용되고 있다.

Drill 3　Ⓐ

해석

바람의 종류

바람은 지표면 위에서의 공기의 이동으로 대기가 균일하지 않게 가열되기 때문에 발생한다. 바람에 영향을 미치는 두 가지 주요 요인은 적도와 극지방 사이의 가열과 지구의 자전이다.

바람의 종류를 구분하는 한 가지 방법은 그것을 일으키는 힘에 있다. 무역풍, 편서풍, 그리고 제트 기류와 같은 우세풍은 전 지구적인 순환에 의해 발생한다. 종관풍은 온난 전선과 한랭 전선의 충돌로 발생하며, 중간 규모의 바람은 뇌우에 의해 만들어진다. 미소 바람은 갑자기 일어나는, 매우 짧게 지속되는 바람이다. 바람은 매일매일 사람들의 삶과 지구에 영향을 미치는 가장 흔하면서도 강력한 힘 중 하나이다.

Drill 4　Ⓒ

해석

벌새

벌새는 초당 15번에서 80번 정도로 날개를 빠르게 퍼덕여서 공중에 떠 있을 수 있는 능력으로 잘 알려져 있다. 이러한 동작을 통해 벌새는 꽃의 꿀을 빨아먹으면서도 자세를 유지할 수 있다. 벌새는 날개가 퍼덕일 때 나는 윙윙거리는 소리 때문에 벌새라는 이름이 붙여졌다.

꿀벌새는 세상에서 가장 작은 새로 무게가 1.8g이 나가는 반면, 갈색 벌새는 보다 전형적인 벌새로 3g의 무게가 나간다. 큰벌새의 무게는 24g 정도까지 나간다. 벌새는 곤충을 제외하고 대사율이 가장 높은 동물이다. 심장은 분당 1,260번이나 뛸 수 있다. 이처럼 빠른 박동을 유지하기 위해, 벌새는 매일 자기 체중 이상의 먹이를 섭취해야만 한다.

Exercises with Mid-Length Passages

Exercise 1　1 Ⓑ　2 Ⓒ　3 Ⓓ　4 Ⓐ　p.98

해석

산호초

산호초는 물속으로 충분한 빛이 들어오는 열대 바다의 투광층에서 자란다. 산호가 살아남기 위해서는, 산호를 부서뜨릴 정도로 강하지 않은, 약한 파도가 치는 장소에 있어야 한다. 하지만 파도의 움직임이 물을 휘저어 먹이와 산소를 공급해 줄 수 있을 정도로는 강해야 한다.

산호초는 폴립이라는 작은 동물에서 나오는 수백만 개의 뼈로 만들어진다. 폴립이 죽으면 파도와 물고기들이 뼈를 분해시킨다. 그러면 그 조각들이 산호에 떨어져 산호를 성장시킨다. 해조류가 뼈에 붙어 자라면서 뼈는 석회석으로 바뀌는데, 이 석회석이 산호 위에 쌓이면 추후에 보호막이 형성된다. 이러한 해조류는 깨끗하고 얕은 물에서 가장 잘 자란다.

전 세계 산호의 대부분이 태평양과 인도양의 열대 바다에 서식한다. 남북아메리카와 아프리카의 서쪽 해안에는 산호초가 거의 없다. 이들 지역의 해류가 강하고 차갑기 때문이다. 산호초는 엄청난 규모의 생물 다양성에 도움을 준다. 여러 종의 어류와 식물들이 번식할 수 있는 서식처를 제공해 준다. 산호초가 없다면 이러한 종 중 다수가 멸종 위기에 처할 것이다.

현재 전 세계 산호에 위협이 되는 몇 가지 요인들이 존재한다. 공장 및 농장에서 유출되는 여러 오염 물질들이 산호초를 죽이고 있다. 이러한 지역의 수질은 종종 독성을 띠며, 산호초 및 그 주변에 서식하는 생물들을 죽이고 있다.

산호초에 가해지는 또 다른 위협은 인간의 과도하고 파괴적인 어업 활동이다. 관상용 물고기를 잡는 많은 어부들이 물고기를 기절시키기 위해 시안화물을 사용한다. 이러한 방식은 잡힌 물고기들의 수명도 단축시키고 산호초도 오염시킨다. 다이너마이트를 이용한 어업 방식도 산호 생태계를 해치는 또 다른 요인이다. 이 방법은 건강한 산호초의 서식처가 되는 산호를 죽게 만든다. 많은 환경 보호 단체들이 전 세계의 산호초를 보호하기 위해 적극적으로 노력하고 있다.

> 🖉 **Summary Note**
> ❶ Photic zones
> ❷ Mild wave action
> ❸ Threats

Exercise 2　1 Ⓒ　2 Ⓒ　3 Ⓐ　4 Ⓐ　p.100

해석

대량 생산과 포드의 모델 T

조립 라인에서 엄청난 양의 제품을 생산하는 것을 대량 생산이라고 부른다. 20세기에 생산 라인이 들어서면서 사람들의 작업 방식과 생활 방식이 바뀌었다. 이러한 방법은 1908년 헨리 포드의 포드 자동차 회사가 모델 T 자동차를 생산하기 시작하면서 일반화되었다.

헨리 포드는 이 차의 발명가이자 회사의 사장이었다. 그는 항상 보다 효율적인 생산 방법을 찾으려 했다. 1913년에 그는 자신의 생산 시설에 움직이는 조립 라인을 도입했다. 1914년 포드의 조립 라인은 매우 효율적이어서 모델 T 한 대를 만드는데 93분 밖에 걸리지 않았다. 조립 라인에서 3분 마다 한 대씩 나왔다. 포드는 모든 경쟁 상대들을 합친 것보다 더 많은 자동차를 만들었다.

뿐만 아니라 포드의 조립 라인은 노동자의 안전 수준을 한 단계 높여 놓았다. 노동자들을 지정된 위치에 있게 만든 이 새로운 방식으로 인해 사고율이 감소했다. 또한 포드는 하루에 5달러라는 전례 없는 급여 체계로 미국을 놀라게 했다. 우수한 노동자를 끌어 모으려는 포드의 이러한 노력 때문에 최저 임금이 두 배로 인상되었다.

1908년 모델 T의 가격은 825달러였으나 이후 해마다 가격이 떨어졌다. 1916년이 되자 모델 T의 가격은 360달러로 떨어졌다. 도로 위를 달리는 차 중에서 어떤 차보다 모델 T가 많았다. 이 모델은 색깔이 검정뿐이었다. 그 이유는 검정색 페인트가 싸고 건조도 빨리 되어서 생산비를 낮출 수 있었기 때문이었다. 헨리 포드는 "고객 누구라도 자신이 원하는 색이 검정색이기만 하면 자신이 원하는 색의 차를 살 수가 있습니다."라는 농담을 했다고 한다.

1920년대에 1천 5백만 대의 모델 T가 생산되었다. 이는 30년 동안 깨지지 않았던 기록이었다. 많은 사람들이 모델 T로 운전하는 법을 배웠고, 이 차에 대해 좋은 기억을 갖게 되었다. 모델 T 혁명은 전 세계 사람들이 일하고 이동하는 방식을 변화시켰다. 오늘날 모든 산업 국가에서는 사람들이 조립 라인에서 일을 한다. 또한 사람들은 일상 생활에서 차를 사용하고 있다.

📝 Summary Note

❶ assembly lines

❷ ninety-three minutes

❸ 15 million

Exercise 3 1 Ⓑ 2 Ⓑ 3 Ⓐ 4 Ⓓ p.102

해석

신경학의 선구자들

신경학의 역사는 고대 이집트까지 거슬러 올라간다. 두루마리 족자에 뇌질환이 설명되어 있다. 이집트인들은 신경계를 기본적으로 이해하고 있었고, 심지어 간단한 뇌수술도 진행했다. 고대 그리스에서는 히포크라테스라는 유명한 의사가 간질은 신체적인 원인에 의한 것이라는 점을 확신했다. 그 전에는 간질이 신의 형벌이라고 생각되었다. 또 다른 그리스 의사인 갈렌은 표본 상태의 신경계를 관찰했다. 그는 원숭이의 뇌에서 신경을 잘라냈다. 그런 다음 원숭이가 소리를 내지 못한다는 점에 주목했다.

1664년 토머스 윌리스가 *뇌의 해부학*이라는 책을 발표했다. 이 책에서 그는 뇌의 혈액 흐름을 가능하게 만드는 윌리스 환에 대해 설명했다. 그는 또한 *신경학*이라는 단어를 최초로 사용했다. 1700년대에는 베일리와 크루빌러가 최초로 뇌 그림을 발표하여 의사와 학자들에게 도움을 주었다. 뇌졸중의 뇌 손상과 같은 증상들이 이해되기 시작했다.

1837년에는 J.E. 푸르키네가 현미경을 통해 최초로 뉴런을 관찰했다. 이로써 과거 조잡했던 그림들을 뛰어넘는 이해가 가능해졌다. 유명한 철학자인 르네 데카르트는 뇌에 관해 생각했다. 그는 행동에 관한 이론을 세웠다. 그는 동물의 모든 행동이 외부 자극에 따른 필수적인 반응이라고 믿었다. 몇몇 의사들은 환자를 대상으로 실험을 실시했다. 그들은 신경계에 대해 더 많은 것을 알 수 있었다. 러시아 생리학자인 파블로프에 의해서는 신경학적 행동이 새롭게 이해되었다. 그는 벨이 울리면 침을 흘리도록 개를 훈련시켰다. 이는 고도의 뇌 기능에 의해 단순한 반사 작용이 바뀔 수 있다는 점을 밝혀냈다.

1878년에 윌리엄 맥퀸이 한 환자로부터 뇌종양을 제거해냈다. 이 환자는 그 후로 몇 년을 더 살았다. 그는 수술 시 텐던 해머와 같은 도구를 사용했다. X레이와 CT 스캔도 곧 등장했다. 이러한 발전으로, 오늘날 사람들에게 도움을 주는 신경학이라는 분야가 나타날 수 있었다.

📝 Summary Note

❶ Ancient Greece

❷ *Anatomy of the Brain*

❸ a brain tumor

Exercise 4 1 Ⓒ 2 Ⓒ 3 Ⓑ 4 Ⓒ p.104

해석

사막 기후의 영향

사막은 강수량이 매우 적은 지형이다. 일반적으로 사막은 연간 강수량이 250mm 이하인 곳으로 정의된다. 하지만 애리조나의 투산 같은 지역은 강수량이 그보다 많지만 사막으로 간주되는데, 그 이유는 높은 증발률 때문이다.

많은 환경 보호론자들은 사막화라는 과정을 통해 사막이 점점 늘어나고 있다고 주장한다. 사막화는 유용한 토양이 바람에 의해 쓸려갈 때 발생한다. 그 후 온도가 상승하면 한때 비옥했던 땅이 사막이 된다. 그 원인은 지구 온난화 및 과도한 개발일 수 있는데, 이 둘 모두는 인류에게 주요한 위험 요소이다.

진정한 사막에는 초목이 거의 없다. 이러한 사막은 지구상 가장 건조한 지역에 존재한다. 이러한 지역에서는 비가 많이 내리지 않고 자주 오지도 않는다. 사막에는 생물이 거의 살지 않는 것으로 알려져 있지만 이는 사실이 아니다. 사막에는 낮 동안 숨어 지내는 많은 동물들이 있다. 지구 육지의 약 5분의 1이 사막으로 덮여 있다.

사막 지형은 주로 모래와 바위로 이루어져 있다. 사구 및 레그라고 불리는 암석면이 사막에서 종종 발견된다. 한랭 사막도 비슷한 특징을 가지고 있지만, 이곳에서는 비 대신 눈이 내린다. 남극이 가장 큰 한랭 사막이고 가장 큰 열대 사막은 사하라 사막이다. 대부분의 사막에서는 기온 변화가 극심하다. 공기가 매우 건조해서 열기를 붙잡아 둘 수 없으므로 밤에는 기온이 크게 낮아질 수 있다. 해가 지자마자 사막은 차가워진다. 또한 구름 한 점 없는 하늘 때문에 밤 동안 열 방출이 증가한다.

지구상 사막의 약 20%만이 모래로 덮여 있다. 여섯 가지 종류의 사막이 존재한다. 그중 한 가지 형태는 고산 또는 분지 사막이다. 암석 사막은 고원 지대로 이루어져 있고, 자갈 사막은 암석으로 덮여 있으며, 모래 사막은 사해에 의해 형성된다. 소산간 분지는 고도가 높은 곳에서 생기며, 황무지는 점토가 풍부한 토양으로 이루어진 건조한 지역에 존재한다.

📝 Summary Note

❶ 250 mm

❷ desertification

❸ rocky surfaces

Exercise 5 1 Ⓐ 2 Ⓒ 3 Ⓑ 4 Ⓑ p.106

해석

제왕나비의 이동

제왕나비는 북아메리카에서 찾아볼 수 있다. 19세기 이후에는 뉴질랜드, 호주, 카나리아 제도에서도 발견되었다. 또한 이주 곤충으로서 아조레스 군도, 포르투갈, 그리고 스페인에서도 발견될 수 있다. 일부 지역에서는 제왕나비가 유랑 나비로도 알려져 있다.

제왕나비는 매년 장거리를 이동하는 것으로 유명하다. 이들은 8월부터 10월에 걸쳐 엄청난 수를 이루어 남쪽으로 날아간다. 그런 다음 봄이 되면 북쪽으로 이동한다. 이동을 하는 동안 암컷은 다음 세대를 위해 알을 낳는다. 북아메리카 지역의 제왕나비는 두 개의 개체군으로 나뉜다. 한 무리는 로키 산맥의 동쪽에 서식하며 멕시코의 미초아칸에서 겨울을 보낸다. 서쪽에 사는 다른 무리는 캘리포니아 중부, 즉 주로 퍼시픽 그로브와 산타 크루즈에서 겨울을 보낸다.

제왕나비의 이동 기간은 나비 한 마리의 일생보다도 길다. 나비는 초여름에 태어나 두 달을 채 살지 못한다. 여름의 마지막 세대는 약 일곱 달을 산다. 이 시기 동안 제왕나비는 겨울의 보금자리로 날아간다. 이 세대는 봄이 되어 겨울 서식지를 떠날 때까지 번식을 하지 않는다.

과학자들은 어떻게 제왕나비가 세대 간 간격이 존재함에도 불구하고 동일한 겨울 보금자리로 되돌아가는지 이해하지 못한다. 이 주제에 대해 많은 연구가 진행 중이다. 비행 패턴에 관한 지식은 유전되는 것으로 추측된다. 연구에 따르면 이는 일주기 생체 리듬과 하늘에 뜬 태양의 위치에 기반해 있다고 생각된다. 새로운 한 연구에서는 제왕나비에게 방향 감각을 가져다 주는 특별한 자외선 광수용기가 존재하는 것으로 추정되었다.

알맞은 조건을 갖춘 영국에서도 몇 년 동안 소수의 제왕나비가 관찰되었다. 또한 하와이의 섬에서도 몇몇 제왕나비들이 살고 있다. 이 제왕나비들은 이동을 하지 않는다. 자신들이 사는 뜰에 먹고 살기 충분할 정도의 꿀을 지닌 꽃이 있으면 이들은 6주에서 8주 정도 산다.

📝 Summary Note

❶ Migrate
❷ Two populations
❸ Hawaii

Exercise 6 1 Ⓐ   2 Ⓑ   3 Ⓐ   4 Ⓒ   p.108

해석

타자기의 발전

한 사람이 단독으로 타자기를 발명한 것이 아니라 많은 사람들이 타자기의 발명에 기여했다. 1714년 헨리 밀이 타자기와 비슷한 기계에 대해서 특허권을 얻었다. 하지만 그에 대해서는 그 밖에 알려진 것이 없다. 또 다른 초기 발명가는 투리라는 사람이었다. 그가 만든 기계는 시각 장애를 가진 사람들로 하여금 글을 쓸 수 있게 해 주었다. 그는 또한 먹지도 발명했다.

1829년 윌리엄 오스틴 버트가 타이포그래퍼라는 기계에 대한 특허를 획득했는데, 일부 사람들은 이를 최초의 타자기로 생각한다. 하지만 이 기계는 손으로 쓰는 것보다 그 속도가 느렸다. 1865년에는 한센이 라이팅 볼이라는 기계를 발명했는데, 이것이 생산에 들어간 최초의 타자기였다. 하지만 이 역시 여전히 속도가 느렸다. 인간의 손보다 빠르게 타자를 칠 수 있는 최초의 타자기는 1867년 숄즈와 글리든에 의해 만들어졌다. 이들은 특허를 레밍턴에게 팔았다. 그는 1873년에 이 기계를 생산하기 시작했다.

초기 타자기에 공통된 한 가지 문제는 가시성이었다. 타이프바의 위치가 페이지를 가렸다. 그래서 타이피스트들은 자신이 쓴 글자를 읽을 수가 없었다. 1895년에 "가시" 타자기가 생산됨으로써 이러한 문제는 해결되었다. 하지만 구형 모델들도 1915년까지 시판되었다.

IBM이 20세기에 셀렉트릭 전동 타자기를 생산하기 시작했다. 이 타자기의 특징은 구형 타입 볼에 있었다. 이 타자기는 곧 시장을 지배했다. 구형 타입 볼은 중요한 발전이었다. 덕분에 두 개의 키를 한 번에 쳤을 때 발생하는 고장이 사라졌다. 이 기계는 오늘날에도 여전히 이용되고 있다. 마지막 주요한 발전은 1980년대에 이루어졌다. 타입 볼이 데이지 휠로 대체되었다. 데이지 휠은 타이프 볼보다 단순하고 저렴하지만 더 빨리 마모된다.

오늘날에도 타자기는 여전히 사용되고 있다. 컴퓨터 사용이 불가능하거나 불편할 때 유용하다. 스미스 코로나, 올리베티, 브라더 같은 기업들이 아직도 타자기를 생산한다. 하지만 일반적으로 타자기는 컴퓨터에 의해 대체되고 있다.

📝 Summary Note

❶ Writing ball
❷ IBM Selectric typewriter
❸ daisy wheel

Building Summary Skills   p.110

Exercise 1 **Coral Reefs**

Coral reefs grow best in photic tropical zones with mild wave action. Reefs are made of the skeletons of millions of tiny polyps that have been turned into limestone by algae. Reefs are the most common in the tropical Indian and Pacific oceans. Reefs are important because they support a wide range of species that would otherwise become extinct. There are many threats to reefs, such as pollution, overfishing, and destructive fishing that conservation groups are fighting against.

Exercise 2 **Mass Production and the Ford Model-T**

Henry Ford changed the way people worked and lived in the twentieth century with his Ford Model-T and the assembly line it was produced on. After beginning the Ford Motor Company and inventing the Model-T car, Ford introduced moving assembly lines in his production plants. These were so effective that the Model-T became common around the world, and the price became lower every year. By the 1920s, there were more Model-T's on the road than any other car, and people around the world worked on assembly lines and drove cars.

Exercise 3 **Pioneers in Neurology**

The ancient Egyptians and Greeks were the first to experiment on and to begin to understand the brain. Scientists such as Thomas Willis created the study of neurology and furthered knowledge of the brain by describing its anatomy. By the 1800s, scientists and doctors, such as J.E. Purkinje began using microscopes to expand their knowledge of the human nervous system. By 1878, successful brain surgery was performed, leading the way to a modern age of neurological understanding and treatment.

Exercise 4 **The Effects of Desert Weather**

Deserts are regions that receive little precipitation. Desertification is the process by which fertile land becomes desert. Many environmentalists argue that temperature increases due to global warming are accelerating the rate of desertification around the world. Deserts are capable of supporting life forms that have adapted to their harsh environments. There are six kinds of deserts, including mountain or basin deserts, hamada deserts, regs, ergs, intermontane basins, and badlands.

Exercise 5 The Migration of the Monarch Butterfly

The monarch butterfly is found in some parts of the world, including North America. Scientists wonder how the monarch is able to migrate so far every year. New generations of monarchs return to the same winter location every year even though they were not alive at the time of the last migration. Scientists are curious about the fact that monarchs have very different life spans based on their place in the seasonal migration cycle.

Exercise 6 The Development of the Typewriter

No single person invented the typewriter, but many people contributed to its creation over the years. The history of the typewriter is full of small improvements made over the years. When problems such as the type bar blocking the typist's view arose, new improvements corrected them. These days, the typewriter has been replaced by the computer. But some people still use typewriters, and some companies still make them.

Mini TOEFL iBT Practice Test p.112

1 Ⓐ	2 Ⓓ	3 Ⓒ	4 Ⓒ	5 Ⓑ
6 Ⓑ				
7 Ⓓ	8 Ⓐ	9 Ⓑ	10 Ⓓ	11 Ⓑ
12 Ⓐ				

해석

[1-6]

침팬지

침팬지는 두 종류가 있다. 일반적인 침팬지는 서아프리카와 중앙아프리카에 서식하는 반면, 이들의 사촌격인 보노보 또는 피그미 침팬지는 콩고 공화국의 산림에서 산다. 콩고강이 이 두 종 간의 경계가 된다. 다 자란 수컷 침팬지의 몸무게는 35kg에서 70kg 정도 나간다. 키는 보통 0.9m에서 1.2m 사이이다. 암컷은 몸무게가 보통 26kg에서 50kg 사이이며, 키는 0.66m에서 1m 사이이다. 야생에서 침팬지는 40년 이상 살기가 힘들지만 포획 상태에 있는 경우에는 60년까지 사는 것으로 알려져 있다.

아프리카 사람들은 수천 년 동안 침팬지와 접촉해 왔다. 기록상 유럽인과 침팬지의 첫 만남은 1600년대에 이루어졌다. 포르투갈인 탐험가 두아르뜨 빠세꾸 페레이라의 일기에 침팬지의 기록이 있고, 침팬지가 간단한 도구를 사용한다는 점이 언급되어 있었다. 침팬지는 1600년대에 앙골라에서 유럽으로 들어 왔다. 최초의 침팬지는 1640년에 오란주 공에게 선물로 주어졌다. 과학자들은 침팬지와 인간 사이의 유사성에 매료되었다. 그 후 20년간 많은 침팬지들이 유럽으로 유입되었다.

1859년에 찰스 다윈이 자신의 진화론을 발표했는데, 이로써 인간에 대한 연결 고리로서의 침팬지에 대한 관심이 급증했다. 그 당시 관찰자들은 침팬지의 행동에 관심을 기울였고, 따라서 인간 행동과의 유사성을 찾으려 했다. 주된 목표는 침팬지가 유전적으로 "훌륭한가"를 밝혀내는 것이었다. 하지만 그들의 관심은 실제 과학에 기반한 것이 아니었다. 당시의 경향은 침팬지의 지능을 크게 과대 평가하는 것이었다. 침팬지로 구성된 일터를 만들기 위한 계획까지 수립되었다. 이러한 아이디어는 침팬지에게 공장 노동과 같은 단순한 육체 노동을 시키기 위한 것이었다.

20세기가 되면서 침팬지는 보다 진지한 과학적 관심의 대상이 되었다. 1960년대 이전에는 자연 서식지에서의 이들의 행동에 대해 거의 알려진 바가 없었다. 이후 제인 구달이 탄자니아의 콤베 숲에 들어가 살면서 그곳 침팬지들과 생활하며 그들의 습성을 관찰했다. 그녀가 도구를 사용하는 침팬지를 발견한 것은 획기적인 일이었는데, 그 전에는 인간만이 도구를 사용한다고 생각되었다.

보통의 침팬지들은 때때로 사람을 공격한다. 우간다에서는 많은 어린이들이 침팬지의 공격을 받고 있다. 이러한 공격은 아이들에게 보통 치명적이다. 이러한 공격의 원인 중 하나는 침팬지들이 아이들을 원숭이의 한 종인 콜로부스 원숭이라고 오인하기 때문이다. 이는 보통의 침팬지들이 가장 좋아하는 먹이 중 하나이다.

인간은 침팬지를 다룰 때 매우 주의해야 하는데, 그 이유는 이들이 인간을 경쟁자로 여기기 때문이다. 또한 평균적인 침팬지는 상체의 힘이 성인 남자보다 다섯 배나 더 강하다. 이러한 점은 전 전미 스톡 자동차 경주협회(NASCAR) 선수인 세인트 제임스 데이비드가 침팬지의 공격을 받아 거의 죽을 뻔한 사건을 통해 입증되었다.

[7-12]

유리 제조술

유리는 주로 모래의 주요 성분인 이산화규소로 이루어진 균질한 비결정질 고체이다. 유리를 만드는데 사용된 원료에 철이 1% 정도 포함된 경우 유리는 색깔을 띤다. 따라서 파인글라스 공장에서는 규소의 비중을 늘려서 유리의 순도를 높인다.

유리가 자연적으로 만들어지는 경우 철 성분 때문에 유리가 초록색을 띠는 경향이 있다. 유리를 부는 직공은 유리의 색깔을 바꾸기 위해 금속 가루를 첨가할 수도 있다. 황이나 탄소를 첨가하면 유리가 노란색에서 검정색까지의 색을 나타낸다. 산화주석을 사용하여 하얀색 유리를 만들 수도 있고, 약간의 코발트를 첨가함으로써 유리가 진한 파란색을 띠도록 만들 수도 있다. 또한 소량의 셀레늄으로 셀렌적색이라고 알려진 밝은 색깔을 낼 수도 있다.

흑요석은 뜨거운 마그마가 흘러나올 때 자연적으로 생성되는 유리이다. 이 유리는 석기 시대 이후로 날카로운 칼, 화살촉, 그리고 도구들을 만드는데 사용되었다. 역사적으로 볼 때 최초로 유리를 만든 사람은 페니키아인들로, 이들은 기원전 3000년 전에 유리를 이용하여 도기를 코팅했다. 기원전 1500년경에는 고대 이집트인들이 유리병과 목걸이를 만들었다. 이들이 만든 목걸이는 녹인 유리로 감싸인 금속 막대로 이루어져 있었다. 목걸이는 소중한 재산이었고, 신비한 힘을 갖고 있는 것으로 생각되었다.

로마인들은 새로운 유리 제조 기법을 다수 개발했으며, 중국과 영국 제도까지 유리가 사용되도록 만들었다. 북유럽에서는 1000년경에 새로운 유리 제조법이 발견되었다. 탄산칼륨이 포함된 유리가 소다를 사용해 만든 유리를 대체했다. 이러한 점은 중요한 것이었는데, 그 이유는 탄산칼륨이 매우 풍부했기 때문이었다. 탄산칼륨은 나무의 재로부터 나온다. 이때부터 북유럽과 지중해 지역의 유리 제조술은 서로 차이를 나타냈다.

11세기 독일에서는 판유리를 만드는 기술이 등장했다. 이로 인해 주택과 건물에 사용되는 현대적인 창문이 생산될 수 있었다. 14세기에는 베니스가 파인글라스 생산의 중심지가 되어 거울, 식기, 그리고 꽃병과 같은 온갖 종류의 사치품들이 이곳에서 만들어졌다.

핸드 블로우 방식으로 만든 유리는 오늘날에도 여전히 상품으로 간주된다. 가장 유명한 파인글라스 공예가로는 데일 치훌리, 르네 라리끄, 그리고 루이스 컴포트 티파니를 들 수 있다. 이들의 작품은 스미소니언 박물관 같은 박물관에 전시되어 있다. 그중 일부 작품들은 수천 달러에 판매되고 있다. 냉각 가공법은 유리를 고품질의 크리스탈로 바꿀 때 사용된다. 에딘버러 크리스탈 및 워터포드 크리스탈과 같은 크리스탈 제조업체들은 다이아몬드 톱을 이용하여 유리를 절단하고 연마해서 아름다운 디자인을 만들어 낸다.

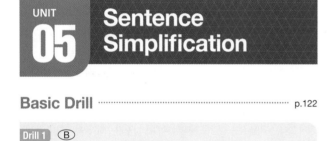

Vocabulary Check-Up
p.118

A 1 ⓑ 2 ⓒ 3 ⓓ 4 ⓐ 5 ⓐ
 6 ⓑ 7 ⓒ 8 ⓐ

B 1 ⓔ 2 ⓕ 3 ⓖ 4 ⓐ 5 ⓙ
 6 ⓘ 7 ⓑ 8 ⓒ 9 ⓓ 10 ⓗ

UNIT 05 Sentence Simplification

Basic Drill
p.122

Drill 1 ⓑ

해석

민간요법

민간요법이란 전통적인 치료법을 말한다. 민간요법은 질병이나 상처를 치료하는데 사용된다. 또한 출산이나 건강 유지에 도움을 주기 위해 사용되기도 한다. 민간요법은 과학적인 의학과는 구별되는 지식 체계이지만, 두 의학 모두 동일한 문화권에서 공존할 수 있다. 민간요법은 보통 문자로 기록되지 않으며 구두로 전달되다가 누군가에 의해 수집된다. 한 문화권 내에서는 많은 성인들이 민간요법을 알고 있을 수도 있다. 치료사나 무속인이 민간요법을 수집해서 사용하기도 한다. 산파, 무녀, 그리고 약초상들도 민간요법을 사용한다. 이 의학이 항상 체계적으로 정리되어 있는 것은 아니다. 많은 치료법들이 서로 상충되는 것처럼 보일 수도 있다.

Drill 2 ⓐ

해석

배심원 선정

미국에서는 형사 재판과 일부 민사 소송에서 배심원단이 필요하다. 이들은 해당 법정이 관할하는 지역의 성인 가운데서 무작위로 선정된다. 배심원단을 구성하는 사람을 배심원이라고 한다. 배심원의 수는 보통 6명이나 12명이다. 이들은 재판을 공정히 대할 수 있는 능력을 기준으로 선정된다. 배심원이 건강이나 기타 이유들로 재판을 마무리하지 못할 가능성이 항상 존재하기 때문에 예비 배심원이 지명될 수 있다. 이들은 재판 과정에 참여하지만, 평결을 내릴 때에는 참여하지 못한다.

Drill 3 ⓒ

해석

오크 나무

오크라는 단어는 수백 종의 나무와 관목을 지칭할 때 사용될 수 있다. 오크는 북반구가 원산지이다. 낙엽성 및 상록수의 종들이 여기에 포함되며, 이들은 한대 지방부터 열대 아시아 및 아메리카 대륙까지 분포해 있다.

많은 종의 경우 오크의 잎은 나선형으로 배열되어 있고 끝이 여러 갈래로 갈라져 있는 반면, 잎의 끝이 톱니 모양이거나 매끄러운 형태인 것들도 있다. 꽃은 꽃차례 형태로서 봄에 핀다. 열매는 도토리라고 불리는 견과류로, 컵 모양으로 생긴 구조 안에 생긴다. 각 도토리 안에는 한 개의 씨가 들어 있는데, 이들은 6개월에서 18개월이 지나면 익는다. 기간은 종에 따라 다르다. 상록수 잎을 지니는 오크는 "라이브 오크"라고 불리지만, 이들이 별개의 그룹은 아니다. 이 종에 속하는 오크들은 보통 다른 종들 사이에 섞여 있다.

Drill 4 ⓐ

해석

목재 산업

재목으로 사용하기 위해 베어낸 나무를 제재목이라고 하고, 목재를 판으로 만든 것을 목재라고 한다. 목재는 미가공 상태로도 혹은 가공된 상태로도 공급된다. 미가공 목재는 가구 제작의 원재료가 된다. 이는 여러 종에서 얻을 수 있지만 대개는 단단한 나무가 사용된다. 가공된 목재는 규격 사이즈로 공급되며 주로 건설업계에서 사용된다. 미국에서 목재 산업은 최초의 산업 중 하나였다. 초기에는 메인과 뉴욕이 생산의 중심지였다. 이후 목재 산업은 미시간, 오리곤, 워싱턴, 그리고 캘리포니아로 뻗어 나갔다. 목재를 만들기 위해 나무를 베는 사람은 벌목공이다. 이들은 초기 미국의 전례 동화에서 자주 등장하는 캐릭터이다.

Exercises with Mid-Length Passages

Exercise 1 1 ⓑ, ⓒ 2 ⓓ 3 ⓑ 4 ⓐ p.124

해석

밀 생산

밀은 전 세계에서 생산되며 인간에게 가장 중요한 곡식이다. 밀의 총 생산량은 곡류 가운데 옥수수 다음으로 많으며 쌀이 세 번째이다. 밀은 발효된 빵, 납작한 빵, 그리고 찐빵을 만드는데 필요한 밀가루의 주성분이다. 밀은 쿠키, 케이크, 파스타, 면, 그리고 쿠스쿠스에도 사용된다. 뿐만 아니라 맥주나 보드카와 같은 주류를 만들 때에도 사용된다. 요즘에는 바이오 연료를 만들 때에도 사용된다. 하얀 밀가루를 만들 때 떨어져 나오는 껍질을 밀기울이라고 한다. 밀은 가축용 사료를 얻기 위해 일정량 재배되기도 한다. 짚은 가축의 사료나 지붕을 이는 건축 자재로 사용될 수 있다.

수확된 밀은 상품 시장의 목적에 따라 낱알의 특성을 기준으로 분류된다. 밀 구매자는 이러한 분류법을 이용하여 어떤 밀을 구입해야 하는지 결정할 수 있다.

각각의 부류는 특별한 용도를 나타내며, 밀 생산자들은 이 시스템으로 어떤 밀을 경작해야 가장 높은 수익을 얻을 수 있는지 알 수 있다.

밀은 단위 면적당 수확량이 많기 때문에 현금 작물로서 널리 경작되고 있다. 또한 온대 기후에서 잘 자라고 재배 기간이 약간 짧은 지역에서도 잘 자란다. 밀은 빵을 만들 때 널리 사용되는, 품질이 우수한 밀가루를 만든다. 대부분의 빵은, 호밀빵과 오트밀빵과 같이 추가적으로 포함된 곡물에 따라 이름 붙여진 빵을 포함하여, 밀가루로 만들어진다. 기타 다수의 인기 있는 식품들도 밀가루로 만들어진다. 그 결과 주요 식량이 꽤 남아 도는 국가에서도 밀에 대한 수요는 높다.

미국에서는 여섯 종의 밀이 재배된다. 듀럼밀은 밝은 색깔을 띤 곡물로 매우 단단하며, 경질 적색 봄밀은 갈색을 띠고 단백질이 풍부하다. 경질 적색 겨울밀도 비슷한데, 이는 주로 캔자스에서 재배되고, 연질 적색 겨울밀은 부드러우며 단백질 함량이 낮다. 경질 백색밀은 밝은 색을 나타내면서 입자가 고운 편이고, 연질 백색밀은 단백질을 거의 포함하고 있지 않으며 습한 온대 지역에서 재배된다.

📝 Summary Note
❶ Six
❷ human food
❸ cash crop

Exercise 2 1 ⓓ 2 ⓑ 3 ⓑ 4 ⓓ   p.126

해석

동굴 생태계

동굴은 지면이나 산 또는 언덕의 측면에 존재하는 천연 굴이다. 크기가 매우 작은 동굴도 있을 수 있고, 길이가 수천 킬로미터에 이르는 동굴도 있을 수 있다. 입구 근처를 제외하면 동물은 완전히 어둡다. 이처럼 햇빛이 존재하지 않기 때문에 입구를 제외한 모든 곳에서 광합성으로 생존하는 식물들은 거의 존재하지 않는다. 하지만 많은 동굴에 번성 중인 생태계가 있으며, 이곳에는 다양한 생명체들이 가득하다.

동굴에서 서식하는 동물들은 각기 다른 두 개의 카테고리, 즉 외래동굴성 생물과 진동굴성 생물로 구분할 수 있다. 전자는 동굴을 이용하지만 대부분의 시간을 동굴에서 보내지는 않는다. 예를 들어 얼룩 다람쥐, 쥐, 그리고 곰은 동굴에서 종종 잠을 잔다. 하지만 먹이는 동굴 밖에서 찾는다. 박쥐 또한 외래동굴성 생물이다. 대부분의 박쥐는 곤충을 사냥해서 잡아먹는다. 따라서 낮에는 동굴에서 잠을 잘 수도 있지만 밤에는 먹이를 사냥하러 동굴을 떠난다. 반면에 진동굴성 생물은 동굴에서 모든 시간을 보내는 동물이다. 전형적으로 여기에는 거미, 흰개미, 그리고 전갈과 같은 작은 동물들이 포함된다. 하지만 다양한 물고기들도 동굴 내의 호수에 서식하는 것으로 알려져 있다. 진동굴성 생물은 보통 어둠 속 생활에 보다 잘 적응할 수 있도록 변화해 왔다. 눈은 없을지라도 다른 감각들이 발달해 있을 수 있다.

동굴에 거주하는 동물들은 다양한 방법으로 영양분을 얻는다. 실제로 박쥐와 같은 외래동굴성 생물은 구아노의 형태로 다수의 진동굴성 생물들에게 양분을 제공한다. 사실 동굴 내 모든 생물들이 박쥐의 배설물을 먹고 산다. 동굴에 있는 알이나 동물의 사체를 먹을 수도 있다. 많은 경우, 동굴 안으로 스며들거나 흘러 들어오는 물이 진동굴성 생물에게 양분을 제공하기도 한다. 또한 흘러 들어오는 물 때문에, 과일, 베리, 그리고 견과류를 포함하여, 다양한 먹이가 동굴 안으로 들어올 수도 있다. 그러면 동물들이 이러한 먹이를 먹어 치운다.

전체적으로 동물들은 어두운 환경에 적응하는 법을 배워 왔다. 따라서 몇몇 동굴에는 다양한 생물들로 이루어진 커뮤니티가 번성하고 있을 수도 있다.

📝 Summary Note
❶ Trogloxenes
❷ Troglobites
❸ water in caves

Exercise 3 1 ⓒ 2 ⓓ 3 ⓓ 4 ⓑ   p.128

해석

로마의 도로법

도로는 로마 공화국 및 이후 로마 제국의 성장에 필수적인 것이었는데, 그 이유는 도로로 인해 군대가 빠르고 효율적으로 이동할 수 있었기 때문이었다. "모든 길은 로마로 통한다."라는 속담이 있을 정도이다. 전성기 때 로마의 도로 시스템은 53,000마일에 걸쳐 있었고 약 372개의 간선 도로를 포함하고 있었다. 로마인들은 가도라고 불렸던 이러한 도로를 건설하는데 뛰어난 솜씨를 보였다.

계획된 *가도*는 로마의 거리에서 시작되었다. 기원전 약 450년에 만들어진 12표법에는 직선 도로의 폭이 8피트이어야 하고 곡선 도로의 폭은 16피트이어야 한다고 명시되어 있다. 이는 로마인들에게 도로 건설을 명하고, 도로가 파손된 경우 통행인들에게 사유지를 지나갈 수 있는 권리를 부여했다. 따라서 빈번한 보수가 필요하지 않은 도로를 건설하는 것이 이념적인 목표가 되었다.

로마인들은 도로를 사용할 수 있는 권리를 *세르위투스*, 즉 도로 사용권으로 정의했다. 갈 수 있는 권리로 인해 사유지의 땅을 가로지를 수 있는 도로 사용권이 생겼다. 수레에게는 몰 수 있는 권리가 허용되었다. 조정인이 정한 적정 너비를 갖춘 도로에서는 두 가지 권리가 모두 보장되었다. 기본 너비는 8피트였다. 다소 단순했던 이 법을 통해 공공의 영역이 개인의 영역보다 우선시되었다는 점을 알 수 있는데, 이러한 점은 로마 공화국의 특징이었다.

로마인들은 가능한 경우 표준화를 선호했다. 기원전 20년 아우구스투스는 도로 위원회의 상임 이사가 된 후 새턴 사원 근처에 금으로 된 이정표를 세웠다. 여기에는 제국의 모든 도시와 도시 간의 거리가 표시되어 있었다. 이것은 후에 로마의 중심이라고 불렸다.

로마의 도로는 로마 제국의 안정과 확대에 매우 중요한 역할을 했다. 로마 군대는 도로 위를 빠르게 이동할 수 있었고, 일부 로마의 도로들은 수천 년이 지난 후에도 여전히 사용되고 있다. 로마 제국이 몰락하던 시기에는 똑같은 도로가 야만인들의 침략 통로로서 사용되었는데, 이는 로마 군대가 패배하게 된 한 가지 이유가 되었다.

📝 Summary Note
❶ the right to use the roads
❷ according to law

Exercise 4 1 ⓓ 2 ⓓ 3 ⓒ 4 ⓐ   p.130

해석

동물의 세력권

*영역*이라는 용어는 어떤 동물이 지키고 있는 지역을 가리킨다. 영역을 지키는 동물은 세력권을 지닌다고 말한다. 동물의 세력권이라는 개념을 처음 소개한 사람은 엘리엇 하워드였다. 그는 1920년에 출판된 자신의 책에서 이러한 개념에 대한 글을 썼다. 1930년대에 이 개념은 마가렛 모스 니스에 의해 한 단계 더 진보했는데, 그녀는 멧종다리에 관한 자신의 연구에서 이를 상세히 설명했다. 이후

이 개념은 로버트 아드리에 의해 *영토적 본능*이라는 그의 책을 통해 널리 알려졌다. 책이 인기를 얻으면서 영역의 중요성이라는 개념이 과장되었다. 이 개념은 사회 생태학의 일부인 것으로 생각되었다. 하지만 소수의 종만이 경계가 명확한 영역을 가지고 있다. 그들은 이러한 경계 안에서 생활하며 필요한 모든 자원을 이곳에서 찾는다.

영역에 대한 가장 분명한 예는 조류와 어류에서 찾을 수 있다. 이들 동물은 종종 밝은 색깔을 내보임으로써 다른 동물들을 자기의 영역에서 내쫓는다. 유럽 울새와 샴 투어가 이러한 색깔을 이용해 자신의 영역을 지킨다. 보통 이러한 영역 안에는 이들의 보금자리와 자신 및 새끼를 위한 충분한 먹이가 존재한다.

방어가 격렬한 싸움 형태를 띠는 경우는 드물다. 눈에 확 띄는 모습을 보이는 경우가 더 많다. 이는 시각적인 것일 수 있다. 이에 대한 한 예가 울새의 붉은색 가슴이다. 또한 청각적인 것일 수도 있다. 많은 새들이 지저귀고 긴팔원숭이가 소리를 지르는 이유가 바로 이 때문이다. 또는 후각적인 것일 수도 있다. 냄새가 나는 표시를 함으로써 그렇게 할 수 있다. 이러한 표시는 소변이나 대변으로 이루어질 수 있다. 개들이 이러한 방식으로 냄새 표시를 한다. 또는 특별한 향선이 들어 있는 신체 부위를 영토 내에 있는 물체에 문질러서 냄새를 표시할 수도 있다. 고양이들은 사물에 얼굴과 옆구리를 문질러 냄새를 표시한다.

Summary Note
❶ Visual
❷ Olfactory
❸ Auditory

Exercise 5   1 Ⓑ   2 Ⓓ   3 Ⓑ   4 Ⓒ   p.132

해석

경기 순환

지역 경제 및 국가 경제는 항상 변화를 겪는다. 경제학자들이 이러한 변화를 분석해 왔다. 그들은 경기 순환에 네 가지 국면이 존재한다는 점을 밝혀냈다. 확장기, 호황기, 수축기, 그리고 회복기가 그것이다. 각각의 국면에는 고유한 특성이 존재한다.

경제가 확장기를 겪을 때에는 경기가 좋다. 기업들에 의해 투자와 고용이 이루어진다. 또한 전형적으로는 가장 뛰어난 직원들을 확보하기 위해 기업들이 높은 임금을 제시해야 한다. 대부분의 소비자들이 취업한 상태로 많은 돈을 가지고 있기 때문에 이들의 구매력은 높다. 따라서 소비재에 대한 수요가 높은데, 이는 기업들로 하여금 더 많은 제품을 생산하도록 만든다. 금리 또한 낮아서 기업 및 소비자들이 은행에서 융자를 받는 일이 수월하다.

호황기 단계에서는 경제가 정점을 찍는다. 대부분의 기업들이 더 이상 사업을 확장할 필요가 없고, 더 많은 직원을 고용할 필요도 없으며, 혹은 더 많은 제품을 생산할 필요도 없다. 일부 기업들의 이윤은 정체기를 맞게 되며 이윤 하락을 목격하는 기업들도 있을 수 있다. 물가 상승을 가장한 인플레이션이 나타나기 시작한다. 이때 정부는 경기가 과열되는 것을 막기 위해 금리를 높이는 경우가 많다.

수축기가 시작되면 소비 지출과 기업 이윤 모두 하락한다. 생산이 둔화되거나 감소한다. 또한 일부 기업들이 노동자를 해고하기 시작하면서 실업률이 상승한다. 생산이 줄어들며, 파산을 하는 기업들도 나타날 수 있다. 일부 경우, 경기가 최소 2분기 이상 하락할 때 나타나는, 경기 침체가 발생하기도 한다. 극심한 상황에서는 공황이 발생할 수도 있다. 이는 2년 혹은 그 이상으로 경제 상황이 악화되는 것이다.

어느 순간 경제는 최저점을 찍는다. 그런 다음에는 마지막 단계, 즉 회복기가 시작될 수 있다. 기업들이 다시 고용을 늘리기 시작하고 생산을 증가시킨다. 또

한 사람들은 일자리를 찾을 수 있다. 사람들의 지출액이 커지면서 소비 수요가 증가하기 시작한다. 인플레이션 압력이 더 이상 존재하지 않기 때문에 금리는 낮아진다.

모든 경제는 네 가지 국면을 겪는다. 하지만 일부 국면들은 길 수도 있고, 일부 국면들은 단기간 동안만 지속될 수도 있다.

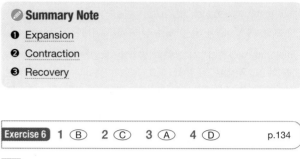

Summary Note
❶ Expansion
❷ Contraction
❸ Recovery

Exercise 6   1 Ⓑ   2 Ⓒ   3 Ⓐ   4 Ⓓ   p.134

해석

코끼리의 진화

코끼리 목에서 살아남은 유일한 과가 코끼리이다. 현존하는 코끼리종은 세 개로, 아프리카 덤불코끼리와 밀림코끼리, 그리고 아시아 코끼리가 그것이다. 다른 종들은 마지막 빙하기 이후 멸종되었다. 코끼리는 현재 살아 있는 육상 포유류 중 가장 크기가 크다. 임신 기간은 22개월로, 육상 동물 중에서 가장 기간이 길다. 새끼 코끼리는 태어났을 때 보통 120kg까지 무게가 나간다. 많은 코끼리들이 70년 정도 사는데, 그보다 더 오래 사는 코끼리들도 있다. 지금까지 기록된 코끼리 중 가장 큰 코끼리는 1956년 앙골라에서 총에 맞았다. 수컷이었고 몸무게는 약 12,000kg에 달했다. 가장 몸집이 작은 코끼리는 송아지 또는 큰 돼지 정도의 크기였는데, 이들은 선사 시대의 변종으로서 크레타 섬에서 서식했다. 이들은 기원전 5000년 전에서 기원전 3000년 사이에 멸종했다.

코끼리는 인간으로부터 점점 더 많은 위협을 받고 있으며 인간과 코끼리 간의 충돌은 종종 치명적인 것이 된다. 매년 아시아에서 150마리의 코끼리와 최대 100명의 사람들이 목숨을 잃고 있다. 아프리카 코끼리의 개체수는 1970년에 3백만이었지만, 1989년에 600,000으로 줄어들었다. 2,000년에는 그 수치가 272,000으로 줄어들었다. 최근 몇 년 동안 이 동물들을 구하려는 시도로 인해 그 수치가 증가했다. 코끼리는 현재 전 세계에서 보호를 받고 있다. 코끼리를 돕기 위한 많은 규제들이 법으로 제정되면서 코끼리의 포획과 사육이 법으로 엄격히 금지되고 있다. 상아와 같은 제품의 거래도 규제 대상이다.

일부 과학자들은 코끼리가 바다소와 먼 친척 관계에 있으며, 코끼리와 바위너구리 사이에 연관성이 존재한다고 믿는다. 많은 사람들이 이러한 점을 보여 주는 유전학적인 증거를 믿고 있지만, 화석 증거에 따르면 이에 대한 확실한 증거는 존재하지 않는다. 한 가지 이론에 의하면 이 동물들은 대부분의 시간을 물속에서 보냈을 것이다. 숨을 쉬기 위해 코를 스노클처럼 사용했을 수도 있다. 현대의 코끼리들도 여전히 이러한 능력을 가지고 있으며, 그렇게 수영을 한다고 알려져 있다. 코끼리는 대략 6시간 동안 50km 정도의 거리를 헤엄쳐 갈 수 있다.

Summary Note
❶ 2 African types
❷ 120 kg
❸ 6 hours

Building Summary Skills

p.136

Exercise 1 Wheat Production

Wheat is one of the most widely grown and important crops in the world. It has many important uses by humans. Wheat grain is harvested according to a classification system that determines the quality and the price. Wheat is a very profitable crop because it is used so widely in products that are consumed daily. There are six classes of wheat grown in the United States.

Exercise 2 Cave Ecosystems

Even though caves are dark, they have ecosystems with animals living in them. Trogloxenes use caves but get food in other places. They can be chipmunks, mice, and bears. Troglobites live their entire lives in caves. Many cave dwellers eat bat guano. They may eat other food, too, such as food brought in by water. Many cave animals have adapted to live life in dark places.

Exercise 3 Road Law in Rome

Roads were a very important part of the Roman Republic and Empire, and the Romans were very advanced at building and administering laws to control them. Roman roads were built to very strict measurements, and laws protected travelers when roads were not available or in disrepair. There was even a point from which all roads to Rome led, called the golden milestone. Roman roads eventually enabled barbarians to invade and conquer Rome, and some Roman roads still exist today.

Exercise 4 Animal Territoriality

Animals defend areas called territories, that are important to them. This concept was introduced in the early twentieth century although it was greatly exaggerated. Many animals develop bright colors or strong smells to protect their territories. Few animals fight over territory. Many common animals mark their territory with their own smell.

Exercise 5 The Economic Cycle

The economic cycle has four parts: expansion, peak, contraction, and recovery. Expansion happens during good economic times when people have jobs and production is high. The peak stage sees profits plateauing and interest rates rising. Contractions happens when an economy declines and people lose jobs. Recovery is when the economy starts to get better.

Exercise 6 The Evolution of the Elephant

There are only three species of elephants still living today. They are the largest of all land mammals and have the longest pregnancy period. These days, elephants are endangered by humans, but efforts are being made to increase their numbers. Scientists think elephants are genetically related to sea cows and possibly hyraxes although there is not enough evidence to prove this.

Mini TOEFL iBT Practice Test

p.138

1 ⓑ   2 ⓓ   3 ⓒ   4 ⓐ   5 ⓑ
6 ⓑ
7 ⓒ   8 ⓐ   9 ⓑ   10 ⓒ
11 ⓑ, ⓓ   12 ⓓ

해석

[1-6]

미국의 산업 발달

미국 혁명 후 미국 내 산업은 유럽에 비해 뒤쳐져 있었지만 그다지 많이 뒤쳐져 있던 것은 아니었다. 곧 새로운 발명과 성장의 물결이 150년이라는 기간 동안 몇 차례 밀려왔다. 이러한 발전으로 인해 미국 경제는 세계에서 가장 규모가 크고 가장 현대적인 경제가 되었다.

미국 혁명 당시 미국은 산업 시대에 들어와 있지 못했고, 대부분의 제조업은 가정에서 이루어졌다. 영국은 산업화되어 있었지만 미국은 아직 그렇지 못했다. 이후 프랜시스 캐봇 로웰이 1811년에 영국으로 건너가서 역직기를 만드는 비법을 암기했다. 그와 그의 일행은 미국으로 돌아온 후 보스턴에 여러 개의 직물 공장을 세웠다. 가장 유명한 것은 매사추세츠의 로웰에 있었던 것으로, 이 공장은 1822년에 건설되었다. 로웰 공장은 많은 "직공"들을 고용했는데, 이들은 공장을 가동시키기 위해 기숙사 생활을 했다. 뉴잉글랜드는 성장하는 직물 산업의 요람이었다. 미국에서 그처럼 빠른 성장을 경험한 지역은 그곳이 처음이었다. 이러한 성장은 또한 펜실베이니아에서도 이루어졌다. 철 산업이 주의 성장을 견인했고, 덕분에 보다 빠른 성장이 가능했다.

그리고 나서 발전의 방향이 바뀌기 시작했다. 이 새로운 시기는 1810년과 1860년대 사이에 있었다. 공장들이 확대되기 시작했다. 하지만 보다 큰 진전은 발명 분야에서 이루어졌다. 미국 제조업과 농업도 크게 발전했다. 이러한 발전은 실용적인 발명품에서 비롯되었다. 리처드 체너워스가 주철 쟁기를 발명했다. 부품을 갈아 끼울 수 있었기 때문에 이는 유용했다. 존 디어는 강철 쟁기를 만들었는데, 이 쟁기에는 흙이 달라 붙지 않았기 때문에 작업 속도가 훨씬 빨라졌다. 엘리 휘트니가 발명한 조면기와 지그는 남부에서 대규모 면화 산업이 들어서도록 만들었다. 사무엘 모스는 전보를 발명해 장거리 통신 시대를 열었다. 엘리샤 오티스는 승객용 엘리베이터를 발명함으로써 오늘날의 고층 건물들이 만들어질 수 있었다. 마지막으로 조지 풀먼은 기차의 침대차를 발명했는데, 이로써 장거리 여행이 가능해졌다.

1850년대부터 미국의 산업은 호황을 누렸다. 1860년대 남북 전쟁에서 북부가 승리한 후 북부의 사업가들은 크게 성공했다. 정부는 사업이 확장되는 것을 보고 싶어했다. 여러 가지 혁신들로 인해 신속하면서도 극적인 변화가 이루어졌다. 이제 미국 전역으로 제품을 운송하기 위한 철도가 필요해졌다. 남부의 사람들은 면화를 거래했다. 그들은 자신의 제품을 북부와 영국에 판매했다. 1900년대 초반이 되자 많은 사람들이 차를 필요로 했다. 자동차 산업은 미국에 새로운 차원의 성장을 가져다 주기 시작했다. 1920년대에 헨리 포드가 모델 T를 선보였다. 이와 함께 현대적인 조립 라인도 등장했다.

미생물

미생물이 발견되기 전에는 음식이 오래 되면 왜 변하는지 알 수 없었다. 왜 포도가 포도주가 되고 왜 우유가 치즈로 변하는지 아무도 알지 못했다. 너무 작아서 육안으로는 보이지 않는 작은 생물체가 음식에 있을 것이라고 생각한 사람조차 없었다. 그 후 1676년에 네덜란드의 한 과학자가 이 미생물들을 발견했다.

우리는 현재 미생물에 대해서 훨씬 많이 알고 있다. 미생물을 전문적으로 연구하는 과학자들이 다양한 형태의 이 작은 생물들을 관찰하고 있다. 이러한 미생물들은 박테리아, 균류, 고세균, 혹은 진핵 생물의 형태를 가지고 있을 수 있다. 바이러스는 살아 있지 않기 때문에 미생물로 간주되지 않는다. 미생물은 단세포 혹은 다세포 생물이다. 원생 생물이라고 알려진 몇몇 단세포 미생물들은 육안으로도 관찰이 가능하다.

보통 미생물은 끓는점 이하의 물이나 기타 액체에서 발견된다. 과학자들은 온천, 해저, 그리고 지각 깊은 곳에서도 미생물 표본을 채취해 왔다. 이러한 미생물들은 지구의 여러 생태계에서 중요한 부분이다. 이들은 양분의 재활용을 가능하게 만들고 질소 순환에서도 중요한 역할을 맡는다.

과학자들은 약 40억년 전에 최초의 단세포 미생물이 탄생했을 것으로 생각한다. 이들은 지구상 최초의 생물이자 30억 년 동안 유일한 생물이기도 했다. 미생물은 빠르게 엄청난 규모로 번식하며, 서로 다른 종들과 자유롭게 유전자를 교환할 수 있다. 또한 점점 빠른 속도로 변이를 하는데, 이로써 새로운 환경에 적응하기 위해 빠르게 진화할 수 있다. 이처럼 빠르게 진화하는 미생물의 능력과 관련된 한 가지 문제는 현재의 항생제에 내성을 지닌 슈퍼 버그의 출현이다.

가장 단순한 형태의 미생물은 박테리아이다. 이들은 또한 지구상의 생명체 중에서 가장 흔한 생물이다. 섭씨 140도 이하의 모든 환경에서 이들을 찾아볼 수 있다. 박테리아는 해수, 토양, 그리고 심지어는 인간의 위나 장에도 존재한다. 박테리아의 게놈은 한 가닥의 DNA로 되어 있다. 박테리아는 세포벽으로 둘러싸여 있다. 이들은 2분열이라는 과정에 의해 번식하는 것으로 알려져 있다. 이 과정을 통해 계속해서 분열을 한다. 일부 박테리아는 최적의 조건 하에서 10분마다 두 배로 늘어날 수 있다.

미생물의 또 다른 종으로 고세균이 있다. 이들은 단세포 생물로서 핵을 가지고 있지 않다. 이 미생물들은 극한의 환경을 포함해 모든 서식지에서 발견된다. 진핵 생물은 박테리아 및 고세균과 다르다. 이들은 체내에 세포 기관이라고 불리는 다세포 구조를 가지고 있다. 진핵 생물의 DNA는 핵 안에 들어 있다.

가장 흥미로운 종류의 미생물은 극한미생물이다. 이들은 매우 가혹한 환경에 적응해 온 미생물이다. 이 강인한 생물은 남극과 북극, 사막, 그리고 심해에서 찾아볼 수 있다. 이 미생물들은 심지어 지표면 아래 7km나 되는 깊은 곳에서도 발견된 적이 있다. 일부 극한미생물들은 진공 상태에서도 살아남으며 방사선에 대한 내성을 갖기도 한다. 이러한 점 때문에 과학자들은 극한미생물이 우주에서도 살아남을 수 있을 것으로 생각한다.

Vocabulary Check-Up
p.144

A
1	D	2	C	3	B	4	D	5	B
6	A	7	C	8	D				

B
1	I	2	F	3	H	4	J	5	A
6	D	7	C	8	G	9	E	10	B

PART II Making Inferences

UNIT 06 Rhetorical Purpose

Basic Drill
p.150

Drill 1 ⓒ

해석

빗해파리

빗해파리는 해양 생물이지만 진짜 해파리는 아니다. 그 이유는 독침이 없기 때문이다. 전 세계 해양에서 살고 있는 빗해파리는 100여종이 넘는다. 이들은 플랑크톤 생물량 중 상당 부분을 차지한다. 그중 한 종이 북해에서 자생하는 바다 구즈베리이다. 이들은 개체수가 너무 많이 증가해서 종종 어부의 그물을 막히게 만들기도 하는데, 다른 종에 의해서는 이런 일이 발생한 적이 없다고 알려져 있다. 빗해파리의 조직은 매우 약해서 연구하기가 상당히 어렵기 때문에 이들의 수명에 대한 데이터도 없다. 하지만 빗해파리는 다 자라기도 전이라도 번식을 한다고 알려져 있으며, 따라서 세대 주기가 짧을 것으로 예상된다.

Drill 2 Ⓑ

해석

백색 왜성과 갈색 왜성

질량이 작거나 중간 정도인 항성은 소멸할 때 백색 왜성의 단계로 들어간다. 항성이 적색 거성 단계에 진입하여 바깥 층 물질이 떨어져 나간 후에 이러한 단계에 도달한다. 백색 왜성은 지구 정도의 크기를 나타내지만 밀도는 태양과 같다. 이로써 백색 왜성은 블랙홀, 중성자별, 그리고 쿼크별을 제외하고는 우주에서 가장 밀도가 높다. 반면에 갈색 왜성은 밀도가 매우 낮다는 점에서 백색 왜성과는 차이를 보인다. 이들은 대부분 가스로 이루어져 있으며, 종종 크기가 큰 행성과 구별하기가 힘들다.

Drill 3 Ⓓ

해석

거미의 사회성

거미는 포식 동물이다. 많은 경우, 암컷은 짝짓기가 끝나면 수컷을 잡아먹는다. 어떤 종류의 거미는 자기 새끼도 잡아먹는 것으로 알려져 있다. 대부분의 거미는 혼자서 생활하지만, 거미집을 짓는 일부 종은 거대한 군락을 이루고 함께 살아간다. 거미가 사회성을 보이기는 하나 벌이나 개미 같은 사회적 곤충만큼 진화한 것은 아니다. 가장 사회성이 강한 거미는 꼬마거미과의 *아넬로시무스 엑시미우스*일 것이다. 이들은 최대 50,000마리로 구성되는 군락을 형성할 수도 있다. 많은 거미들이 불과 1년이나 2년 동안만 산다. 하지만 타란툴라는 보통 20년 정도 살 수 있다.

Drill 4 Ⓐ

해석

수제품

수제품은 유용하면서도 매력적인 물건이다. 이들은 보통 손으로 만들어지지만 때때로 간단한 도구가 사용되기도 한다. 이 용어는 보통 전통적인 방식으로 만들어진 제품에 쓰인다. 제품의 독특한 스타일이 중요하다. 그러한 제품들은 종종 문화적이고 종교적인 의미를 지닌다. 대량 생산에 의해 혹은 기계로 만들어진 제품은 수제품이 아니다. 수제품은 사용이나 착용을 목적으로 만들어진다. 이것이 장식품 및 공예품과 다른 점이다. 이들의 목적은 단지 장식을 위한 것이 아니다. 일반적으로 수제품은 보다 전통적인 제품으로 생각된다. 이들은 일상 생활의 일부로서 제작된다.

Exercises with Mid-Length Passages

Exercise 1 1 ⓓ 2 ⓑ 3 ⓓ 4 ⓒ   p.152

해석

해왕성

해왕성은 태양계의 여덟 번째 행성으로 가장 바깥쪽에 위치해 있다. 행성들 중에서 직경은 네 번째로 크고 질량은 세 번째로 크다. 실제로 해왕성의 질량은 지구의 17배이다. 천왕성은 해왕성과 쌍둥이별에 가깝지만 해왕성이 약간 더 크다. 해왕성은 로마의 바다의 신 이름을 따서 그 이름이 지어졌다. 해왕성의 대기는 주로 수소와 헬륨으로 이루어져 있으며, 메탄도 소량 존재한다. 그래서 해왕성은 푸른 빛을 띤다. 비슷한 양의 메탄을 가진 천왕성보다 색이 선명하다. 따라서 알려지지 않은 성분 때문에 해왕성의 색이 강렬한 것으로 추측된다.

해왕성의 여러 측면들이 과학자들의 흥미를 끌고 있다. 그러한 측면 중 하나는 태양계의 어떤 행성보다도 해왕성의 바람이 가장 강하다는 것이다. 시속 2,500km 정도의 강풍이 불 수 있다. 또한 16개의 달들이 해왕성 주위를 도는 것으로 확인되었다. 트리톤은 역행 궤도로 유명하다. 이 달의 대기는 질소 및 메탄으로 이루어져 있으며, 이 달은 대단히 춥다.

해왕성의 구름 가장 위쪽의 온도는 섭씨 −210도 정도로, 해왕성은 태양계에서 가장 추운 행성에 속한다. 이처럼 추운 이유는 해왕성이 태양으로부터 멀리 떨어져 있기 때문이다. 해왕성 중심부의 온도는, 핵 안의 극도로 뜨거운 기체와 암석 때문에, 섭씨 7,000도에 이른다. 이는 태양의 표면 온도보다 뜨거운 온도이다. 하지만 해왕성의 가장 바깥 층은 극도로 차갑다.

1989년 보이저 2호가 해왕성을 지나치다가 대암반이라는 지역을 발견했다. 이곳은 해왕성의 남반구에서 보이며 목성의 대적점에 맞먹는 곳이다. 또한 해왕성 주변에서는 희미한 고리가 보인다. 이들은 토성의 고리보다 훨씬 더 작다. 이 고리들은 에드워드 귀넌의 연구팀에 의해 발견되었다. 고리가 희미해서 해왕성의 주위를 다 감지하지 못하는 것으로 보였기 때문에 처음에는 고리가 불완전한 것으로 생각되었다. 하지만 보이저 2호가 찍은 사진에 의해 이러한 생각은 잘못된 것으로 판명되었다.

Summary Note
❶ 7,000°C
❷ hydrogen, helium, and methane
❸ 16 moons

Exercise 2 1 ⓒ 2 ⓓ 3 ⓑ 4 ⓓ   p.154

해석

아리스토텔레스의 형이상학

아리스토텔레스는 전 시대를 통틀어 가장 영향력이 큰 사상가 중 한 명이었다. 과학이나 기술이 존재하지 않던 시대에 그는 많은 학문 분야를 탄생시켰는데, 그중 하나가 형이상학이었다. 그는 모든 것의 원인은 그 시작을 살펴봄으로써 알아낼 수 있다고 주장했다. 또한 사람들이 무언가의 원인을 알게 되면 과학적인 지식을 갖게 된다고 말했다. 무언가의 존재를 안다는 것은 그것의 존재 이유를 아는 것이다. 그는 이후의 모든 인과론에 대한 가이드라인을 마련한 최초의 사람이었다. 아리스토텔레스의 이론에 따르면 모든 원인은 몇 가지 부류로 나눌 수 있다.

그는 원인을 네 개의 대분류로 구분함으로써 원인을 규정했다. 질료인은 부분들이 결합해서 어떤 것이 존재하게 되는 방식이다. 이에 대한 한 가지 예는 치즈버거이다. 치즈버거는 고기, 빵, 그리고 치즈가 모여 만들어진다. 이들이 단독으로는 치즈버거를 만들지 못하지만, 서로 합쳐지는 경우, 치즈버거의 존재의 원인이 된다. 형상인은 어떤 것이 무엇인지를 말해 준다. 예컨대 홍수의 형상인은 넘쳐나는 물이다. 시동인은 변화의 이유를 설명해 준다. 이에 대한 한 가지 예는 불이 타고 있는데 비에 의해 불이 꺼지는 것으로, 비 때문에 불은 소멸한다. 목적인은 무엇인가가 이루어지는 이유이다. 예를 들어 한 나라가 국경을 지키기 위해 전쟁을 할 수 있는데, 이것이 전쟁의 원인이 된다.

실체라는 개념도 아리스토텔레스의 형이상학에서 다루어진다. 그는 특정한 실체는 질료와 형상이 결합된 것이라고 결론지었다. 그는 나아가 다섯 가지 주요 원소를 규정한다. 뜨겁고 건조한 것을 불로, 그리고 차갑고 건조한 것을 흙이라고 명명했다. 공기는 뜨겁고 습한 것이고 물은 차갑고 습한 것이다. 마지막으로 천구와 천체를 구성하는 신성한 물질을 영기라고 명명했다. 아리스토텔레스에 의해 기록된 이러한 분류법은 현대 물리학의 토대를 닦아 주었다. 그의 업적은 콘크리트 기초 공사에 비유될 수 있는데, 이를 기반으로 현대 물리학이라는 건물이 세워질 수 있었다.

Summary Note
❶ Material cause
❷ Formal cause
❸ Efficient cause
❹ Final cause

Exercise 3 1 ⓒ 2 ⓐ 3 ⓑ 4 ⓐ   p.156

해석

시쿼야

시쿼야는 체로키족 인디언으로, 조지 지스트로도 알려져 있었다. 그의 장기는 은세공이었다. 하지만 그는 체로키 문자를 만든 것으로 유명하다. 이로 인해 그는 문자를 만든 사람의 명단에 오르는 명예를 얻었다.

시쿼야의 정확한 출생지와 출생일은 알려져 있지 않다. 그 당시의 문자 기록이 존재하지 않기 때문이다. 역사가들의 추정에 의하면 출생연도는 1760년과 1776년 사이일 것이다. 출생지로는 테네시, 조지아, 노스 캐롤라이나, 앨라배마, 그리고 사우스 캐롤라이나 내의 지역이 추정되고 있다. 체로키족을 연구하는 저명한 역사학자인 제임스 무니는 한 사촌의 말을 인용하여 시쿼야와 그의 어머니가 테네시의 터스키기 마을에서 어린 시절을 보냈다고 말한다.

시쿼야라는 이름은 체로키어로 "돼지"라는 뜻이다. 이러한 별명은 아동기 때의 장애를 가리키는 것일 수도 있고, 나중에 그를 장애인으로 만든 부상을 지칭하는 것일 수도 있다. 시쿼야의 아버지는 백인이거나, 백인과 인디언 사이의 혼혈이었을 것이다. 하지만 시쿼야는 영어를 하지 못했다. 이를 통해 그의 아버지가 그와 그의 어머니를 버렸을 것이라고 생각할 수도 있다. 시쿼야는 1809년의 어느 시점에 앨라배마의 윌스타운으로 이사했다. 그는 그곳에서 은세공사로 일을 시작했다.

백인 주민들의 문자는 종종 시쿼야에게 큰 인상을 남겼다. 그는 영어가 적힌 종이를 "말하는 나뭇잎"이라고 불렀다. 시쿼야는 1809년경 체로키어의 문자를 만들기 시작했다. 그는 다양한 음절을 나타내기 위해 85개의 기호를 만들었다. 시쿼야가 이 일을 완성하기까지 12년이 걸렸다. 이후 시쿼야는 자신의 딸에게 자기가 만든 문자를 읽고 쓰는 법을 가르쳤다. 부족 사람들은 이를 보고 놀라워했다. 하지만 체로키족의 주술사들은 그가 악령의 지배를 받고 있다고 말했다. 그래서 시쿼야는 자신의 문자를 전사들에게 가르쳤다. 그러자 부족의 다른 사람들도 이를 받아들였다. 1823년에 체로키족은 이 새로운 문자 시스템을 완전히 받아들였다. 이로써 그들에게는 후대를 위해 자신들의 역사를 기록할 수 있는 길이 열렸다.

Summary Note
❶ 1821
❷ daughter
❸ warriors

Exercise 4 1 ⒟ 2 ⒞ 3 ⒟ 4 ⒞   p.158

해석

최초의 대륙 횡단 철도

최초의 대륙 횡단 철도는 미국에서 건설되어 북아메리카를 가로질렀다. 1860년대에 공사가 시작되고 완공되었다. 이로써 미국 동부와 캘리포니아 간의 철도망이 연결되었다. 1869년 5월 9일에 그 유명한 골든 스파이크 행사가, 즉 철도 개통식이 열렸다. 이 철도로 인해 전국 여행이 가능해졌고, 미 서부의 인구와 경제가 변화했다. 또한 마차가 자취를 감추게 되었다.

이 철도는 1862년 태평양 철도법에 의해 건설이 승인되었고 연방 정부의 막대한 지원을 받았다. 그와 같은 철도가 건설된 것은 10년 동안 지속된 노력의 결실이었다. 이는 아브라함 링컨의 중요한 업적 가운데 하나였는데, 그가 사망한지 4년 후에야 철도가 완공되었다. 철도 건설에는 엄청난 기술과 노동이 요구되었다. 철로는 평원과 고산 지대를 통과했다. 선로는 유니언 퍼시픽 철도와 센트럴 퍼시픽 철도로 구성되었다. 이 둘은 민간 회사에 의해 건설되었지만, 모두 연방 정부의 지원을 받았다. 이들은 동쪽과 서쪽으로 이어졌다.

철도 건설은 남북 전쟁이라는 갈등의 시기에 미국을 하나로 묶기 위해 추진되었다. 이로써 서부는 백인들로 가득하게 되었다. 이러한 사실은 이 지역에서 미 원주민들이 줄어드는 원인이 되었다. 유니언 퍼시픽 철도의 철로는 대부분 아일랜드 노동자들에 의해 건설되었다. 남부와 북부의 퇴역 군인 및 몰몬교인들 또한 철로 건설에 도움을 주었다. 센트럴 퍼시픽 철도의 철로는 대부분 중국 노동자들에 의해 건설되었다. 처음에는 이런 종류의 일을 하기에 중국인들이 너무 약하다고 생각되었다. 하지만 이후에 중국에서 보다 많은 사람들이 들어왔다. 대부분의 인부들이 하루에 1달러에서 3달러 사이의 금액을 받았지만, 중국인 노동자들은 그보다 훨씬 적은 돈을 받았다. 마침내 중국인들은 파업에 들어갔는데, 이로써 그들의 급여가 소폭 인상될 수 있었다.

Summary Note
❶ Union Pacific Line
❷ Irish immigrants
❸ Central Pacific Line

Exercise 5 1 ⒞ 2 ⒟ 3 ⒞ 4 ⒞   p.160

해석

기계화

인간의 노동이 기계로 바뀌는 것을 기계화라고 한다. 기계화는 인간의 역사를 완전히 바꾸어 놓았다. 기계로 인해 사람들은 훨씬 더 적은 힘으로 훨씬 더 많은 일을 할 수 있다. 인간은 선사 시대 이래로 간단한, 그리고 복잡한 형태의 기계를 만들어왔다.

가장 간단한 기계는 지렛대로, 지렛대는 어떤 물체의 아래에, 그리고 돌이나 또 다른 물체 위에 놓이는 막대이다. 막대 밑의 물체는 받침점 역할을 하는데, 이렇게 하면 막대에 지레의 힘이 생긴다. 강하게 막대를 밑으로 누르면 막대가 받침점을 밀어내면서 막대 끝에 있는 물체가 올라간다. 이러한 동작에서 사람의 힘은 지레에 의해 증폭되는데, 이때 사람은 보다 적은 힘으로 보다 무거운 무게를 들어 올릴 수 있다. 이는 모든 기계 개발의 기본 원칙 중 하나이다. 기계는 최소한의 힘을 사용하는 사람을 대신해서 일을 한다.

한 가지 중요한 기계는 증기로 작동하는 선반이었다. 이 장치는 금속 및 목재 가공의 속도와 정확도를 높여 주었다. 또 다른 유용한 기계는 증기 기관이었는데, 이로써 증기선과 증기 기관차가 만들어질 수 있었다. 이는 운송 수단의 혁명으로 이어졌다. 콜트 권총은 연속 발사가 가능한 최초의 자동 권총이었다. 이 총 때문에 전쟁은 보다 치명적인 것이 되었다. 20세기 초에는 포드의 시스템과 함께 기계화된 자동차 조립 라인이 등장했는데, 이는 사람들의 작업 방식과 이동 방식을 변화시켰다.

*기계화*라는 용어는 군대에서도 사용된다. 이 용어는 궤도형 장갑차를 사용하는 것을 지칭한다. 병력 수송 장갑차도 이러한 차량 중 하나이다. 이 차량은 많은 수의 군인을 전쟁터로 빠르게 이동시키기 위해 사용되며, 전쟁터로 가는 도중에도 군인들의 피해가 최소화될 수 있도록 군인들을 보호한다. 과거에는 전투를 치루기도 전에 많은 군인들이 사망했다. 기계화로 인해 이동성과 전투력이 크게 향상되었다. 현대 국가에서 모든 군대는 기계화 보병들의 지원을 받는다.

Summary Note
❶ A lover
❷ The Colt revolver
❸ Assembly lines

Exercise 6 1 ⒝ 2 ⒟ 3 ⒞ 4 ⒝   p.162

해석

매머드

가장 흔히 발견되는 선사 시대 화석은 매머드 화석인데, 매머드는 코끼리의 변종으로 지금은 멸종했다. 매머드는 엄니라고 불리는 길고 구부러진 이빨을 가지고 있었다. 북부 종은 두꺼운 털로 덮여 있었다. 이들은 최신세 때 지구를 돌아다녔다. 이때는 대략 1백 6십만 년 전부터 1만 년 전까지의 시대였다.

매머드의 혈통은 현대의 아시아 코끼리와 가장 비슷하다. 두 종의 아프리카 코끼리의 유전자는 매머드의 유전자와 그 정도로 비슷하지는 않다. 아시아 코끼리와 매머드의 공통 조상은 아프리카 코끼리의 혈통에서 떨어져 나왔다. 이러한 분기는 약 6백만 년 전부터 7백 3십만 년 전 사이에 이루어졌다. 아시아 코끼리와 매머드는 그로부터 5십만 년 후에 분기되었다.

과학자들은 매머드가 처음에 북아프리카에서 진화했다고 믿는다. 매머드의 기원은 약 480만 년 전으로 거슬러 올라간다. 그만큼 오래된 것으로 추정되는 뼈가 차드, 리비아, 모로코, 그리고 튀니지에서 발견되었다. 남아프리카와 케냐에 있는 지역에서는 가장 오래된 매머드 종으로 생각되는 고대 화석이 발견된 바 있다.

이후 아프리카 매머드는 이동을 했다. 화석 기록에 의하면 아프리카 매머드는 마침내 북쪽의 유럽에 도착했다. 얼마 지나지 않아 남부 매머드라는 이름의 새로운 종이 나타났다. 이 종은 아시아와 유럽 전역에 서식했다. 연구에 따르면 이들은, 지금은 물속에 가라앉은, 베링 해협 육교를 건넜을 것으로 생각된다. 이는 현재의 시베리아와 알래스카에 걸쳐 있으면서 아시아와 북아메리카를 연결시켰던 얼어붙은 땅덩어리였다. 이를 통해 매머드가 북아메리카에 도달할 수 있었다.

그 후 70만년 전 무렵에 따뜻했던 기후가 변하기 시작했다. 유럽, 아시아, 그리고 북아메리카의 사바나 평원이 보다 춥고 덜 비옥한 스텝 지역이 되었다. 남부 매머드 종이 가장 먼저 멸종되었다. 새로운 종인 털매머드가 30만년 전에 진화했다. 이 매머드는 두꺼운 털로 덮여 있어서 빙하기의 극심한 추위를 견디어 낼 수 있었다.

Summary Note

❶ 4.8 million years ago

❷ 700,000 years ago

❸ 10,000 years ago

Building Summary Skills

p.164

Exercise 1 Neptune

Neptune is the outermost planet of the solar system and is the fourth largest in diameter and the third largest in mass. Its atmosphere is composed mostly of gas, and it has a vivid blue appearance. There are many interesting facts about the planet, such as its high winds, sixteen moons, and hot core temperature that make it interesting to scientists. The only human probe ever to visit and collect information of Neptune was *Voyager 2*.

Exercise 2 The Metaphysics of Aristotle

Aristotle was one of the most important thinkers of all time because he created many fields of study, one of which is metaphysics. He created the guidelines for understanding the causes of things, of which there are four major categories. He made many conclusions about the substance of matter and form and also defined five major elements. His classifications laid important foundations for modern science that are used today.

Exercise 3 Sequoyah

Sequoyah was a Cherokee Native American who is famous for creating the first system of writing for the Cherokee people. His exact place and date of birth are unknown because his people lacked a system of writing for recording historical data. After twelve years of work, Sequoyah created a writing system for the Cherokee language that used eighty-five characters to represent the sounds of the language. This system was at first rejected by the Cherokee people, but they later accepted it after Sequoyah taught it to a group of warriors. This system gave the Cherokee people a way to record their history for future generations.

Exercise 4 The First Transcontinental Railroad

The first transcontinental railroad to run across North America was completed in 1869 and was commemorated with the famous Golden Spike event. The railroad was heavily backed by the federal government and stands as one of the great achievements of President Abraham Lincoln. The building had many effects, such as bringing the Union states together during the Civil War as well as leading to the decline of Native Americans in the west by populating it with white settlers. Much of the railroad was built by immigrant laborers from Ireland and China as well as by veterans of the Union and Confederate armies and Mormons.

Exercise 5 Mechanization

Human history has been changed by the shift from human labor to mechanization. A good example of a simple machine that relieves a human of labor is the lever. Some very important machines were the steam-powered lathe, steam-powered trains, the Colt revolver, and the mechanization of car assembly lines. Military forces have also mechanized their forces, which results in many advantages in warfare.

Exercise 6 The Mammoth

The mammoth was a prehistoric animal that is now extinct and whose fossil remains are the most commonly found. Mammoths are the most closely related to the Asian variety of elephant, having genetically split off from the African varieties of elephant over seven million years ago. Due to fossil evidence, scientists believe the mammoth originally evolved in North Africa and then migrated around the world, ending up in North America. Mammoths began to die off due to climate changes that began 700,000 years ago.

Mini TOEFL iBT Practice Test　　p.166

1 Ⓓ　2 Ⓑ　3 Ⓓ　4 Ⓐ　5 Ⓒ
6 Ⓑ

7 Ⓓ　8 Ⓓ　9 Ⓒ　10 Ⓐ　11 Ⓑ
12 Ⓑ

해석

[1-6]

흑점

흑점은 태양 표면에 있는 검은 부분으로, 수천 년 동안 천문학자들에게 미스터리한 존재였다. 중국 천문학자들은 기원전 28년에 이에 대한 기록을 남겼다. 그들은 가장 큰 점들을 볼 수 있었는데, 중앙아시아의 사막에서 불어오는 먼지바람이 태양의 섬광에 대한 필터 역할을 해서 그들이 흑점을 볼 수 있었다. 서양에서는 중세 시대에 커다란 흑점이 관측되었다. 하지만 이러한 관찰의 미스터리는 1612년에 갈릴레오가 이를 설명하기 전까지 완벽하게 이해되지 못했다.

흑점은 기원후 1700년 이래로 천문학자들에 의해 기록되어 왔다. 현재의 과학자들은 이러한 흑점의 출현 주기를 기원전 11,000년까지 추정할 수 있다. 가장 최근의 흑점의 출현 빈도는 1900년에서 1960년대까지 증가했다. 8,000년 전에도 태양은 비슷하게 활동했다.

흑점 지역은 주변보다 기온이 낮으며, 또한 활발한 자기 활동을 나타낸다. 이와 같은 높은 자성 때문에 태양의 정상적인 대류가 일어나지 않는다. 그 결과 표면 온도가 낮은 지역이 생긴다. 하지만 이러한 지역은 여전히 너무 밝아서 직접 볼 수는 없다. 흑점의 온도는 낮은 편으로 절대온도 4,000도 정도이다. 반면에 태양의 나머지 부분의 온도는 절대온도 5,700도이다. 이러한 차이로 인해 뚜렷하게 보이는 어두운 부분이 나타난다. 이와 비슷하게 태양 외의 다른 항성에서 관측되는 부분은 항성 흑점이라고 불린다.

왜 흑점이 생기는지는 확실히 밝혀지지 않았지만, 흑점이 자속관의 일부로서 태양의 대류권에서 보이는 부분이라는 점은 분명하다. 자속관은 차동 회전에 의해 "감기게" 된다. 자속관에 가해지는 힘이 일정 수준의 한계에 이르면 자속관은 고무밴드처럼 꼬여서 태양의 표면을 뚫고 나오게 된다. 뚫리는 곳에서는 대류가 일어나지 않는다. 그러면 태양 내부에서 나오는 에너지 흐름이 감소해서 표면 온도가 낮아진다.

흑점의 수는 태양 복사열의 강도와 관련이 있다. 위성에 의한 복사열 측정이 가능해진 1979년 이후로 이러한 관련성이 기록되어 왔다. 흑점이 어둡기 때문에 당연히 흑점이 많을수록 태양 복사열은 줄어들 것이라고 생각할 수 있다. 하지만 흑점의 주위는 더 밝다. 따라서 전체적으로는 흑점이 많을 수록 태양이 더 밝아진다. 하지만 이러한 차이는 너무 미미해서 육안으로는 알아차릴 수가 없다. 마운더 극소기라고 하는 시기는 태양에 흑점이 거의 없었던 때를 가리킨다. 이 당시 지구 온도는 1℃ 정도 낮아졌을 것으로 생각된다.

[7-12]

뇌우의 빈도

뇌우는 번개와 천둥을 동반하기 때문에 전기 폭풍이라고 불린다. 이처럼 격렬한 폭풍은 폭우나 우박을 발생시킬 수 있는 적란운에 의해 만들어진다. 드물기는 하지만 이러한 구름 때문에 눈이 내릴 수도 있다. 이러한 눈은 보통 겨울에 내리며 뇌설이라고 불린다.

불안정한 대기에서 응결 현상이 심하게 일어날 경우 뇌우가 만들어진다. 이러한 현상을 통해 다양한 물방울과 얼음 결정이 생긴다. 아래쪽에 있는 상승 기류가 이를 떠받친다. 이는 종종 세 가지 조건의 유무로 판단할 수 있다. 첫 번째는 온도가 낮은 대기 속에 충분한 수분이 있어야 한다. 이는 높은 이슬점에 의해 반사된다. 두 번째는 큰 폭의 기온 하락과 고도의 증가이다. 이는 단열감률이라고 불린다. 세 번째는 역학적 난류와 같은 힘이다. 이러한 힘은 한랭 전선을 따라 발생하며 양력을 집중시킨다.

뇌우는 전 세계 각지에서 발생하며 극지방에서도 뇌우가 발생한다. 가장 뇌우가 많이 발생하는 지역은 열대 우림 지대이다. 이곳에서는 거의 매일 발생한다. 우간다의 캄팔라와 토로로는 지구에서 그 어떤 곳보다 뇌우가 많이 발생하는 곳으로 알려져 있다. 인도네시아의 보고르 역시 뇌우가 빈번하게 발생하는 곳으로 알려져 있다. 온대 지역에서는 뇌우가 대부분 봄에 발생한다. 하지만 연중 어느 때나 한랭 전선을 따라 일어날 수 있다. 플로리다는 열대 지방을 제외하고 뇌우가 가장 빈번하게 발생하는 곳이다. 플로리다의 남부와 중부에서 강력한 뇌우가 발생하며, 여름에는 종종 매일 발생하기도 한다.

미국에서 가장 강력하면서도 위험한 뇌우가 발생한다. 가장 강력한 뇌우는 중서부 및 남부의 주에서 나타난다. 이러한 뇌우로 인해 매우 커다란 우박이 내리기도 하고 강력한 토네이도가 만들어지기도 한다. 미국의 서부 해안에서는 뇌우가 잘 치지 않는다. 하지만 내륙 지역에서는 뇌우가 친다. 새크라멘토와 캘리포니아의 샌호아퀸 밸리에서 뇌우가 친다. 북서부의 뇌우는 중서부 뇌우와 비슷한 패턴을 나타낸다. 하지만 이들의 빈도와 강도는 훨씬 낮다.

초기 인류 문명은 뇌우의 빈도에 막대한 영향을 받았다. 로마인들이 생각하기에 뇌우는 불칸이 만든 번개를 주피터가 던져서 생긴 전투라고 생각했다. 뇌우가 자주 발생하면 로마인들은 화난 신을 달래기 위해 많은 동물을 제물로 바쳐야 한다고 생각할 정도로 걱정을 했다. 미 원주민들은 이러한 뇌우가 주신의 하인들과 관련이 있다고 믿었다. 또한 그 빈도는 주신의 분노와 관련이 있다고 생각했다. 오늘날에는 봄마다 뇌우를 쫓는 사람들이 미국의 대평원과 캐나다의 평원으로 향한다. 여름에는 눈으로 보면서 과학적으로 뇌우와 토네이도를 연구한다. 이처럼 스릴을 즐기는 사람들에게는 뇌우가 잦을수록 모험에 대한 욕구가 충족된다.

Vocabulary Check-Up　　p.172

Ⓐ 1 Ⓐ　2 Ⓒ　3 Ⓑ　4 Ⓐ　5 Ⓐ
　 6 Ⓒ　7 Ⓑ　8 Ⓑ

Ⓑ 1 Ⓓ　2 Ⓗ　3 Ⓙ　4 Ⓒ　5 Ⓑ
　 6 Ⓖ　7 Ⓕ　8 Ⓘ　9 Ⓔ　10 Ⓐ

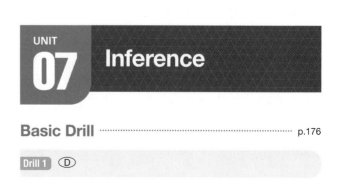

UNIT 07 Inference

Basic Drill　　p.176

Drill 1　Ⓓ

28

해면동물

해면동물은 해면동물문에 속하는 동물이다. 이들은 물속에 사는 원시적인 여과 섭식 동물이다. 해면동물은 몸에 물을 통과시켜 먹이 입자를 걸러낸다. 해면동물은 가장 단순한 동물에 속한다. 진정한 의미의 조직도 없고, 근육, 신경, 그리고 내부 기관도 없다. 알려진 종은 5천 종이 넘는다. 이들은 바위 표면에 붙어 있을 수 있는 모습을 보일 수 있고 조간대에 서식한다. 8,500m 이상의 깊이에서도 발견될 수 있다. 해면동물의 화석 기록은 선캄브리아대까지 거슬러 올라가지만, 지금까지도 새로운 종이 발견되는 일이 흔하다.

Drill 2 Ⓐ

해석

테노치티틀란

테노치티틀란은 고대 아즈텍 왕국의 수도로, 현재 멕시코 시티에 해당되는 곳이다. 이 고대 도시는 텍스코코 호수의 작은 섬들 위에 건설되었다. 도시 내부는 좌우 대칭적인 배치에 기반해 있었다. 도시는 *캄판*이라고 불리는 네 개의 구역으로 나뉘었다. 도시는 수로로 연결되어 수송이 용이했다. 이 도시는 계획에 따라 건설되었고 그 중심에는 제사를 지내는 곳이 있었다. 이곳에 지상 60m 높이의 테노치티틀란 대피라미드가 솟아 있었다. 주택은 나무와 양토로 지어졌고 지붕은 갈대로 만들어졌다. 하지만 피라미드, 사원, 그리고 왕궁은 대개 돌로 지어졌다.

Drill 3 Ⓑ

해석

전자 음악

전자 음악은, 모두 전기로 작동하는, 장비를 이용해서 만들어진다. 이들은 소량의 전력을 사용하는 시스템이다. 전자 음악이 나오기 전, 많은 작곡가들은 새로운 기술을 사용하고 싶어했다. 그들은 이러한 기술을 이용해서 음악을 만들고자 했다. 새로운 전자 및 기계 디자인을 이용한 몇 가지 악기가 만들어졌다. 무그 키보드도 그러한 악기 중의 하나였다. 이 키보드는 1970년대 영화 *시계 태엽 오렌지*에 들어간 베토벤 곡을 녹음하는데 사용되었다. 이것이 최초로 전자 음악이 녹음된 사례 중 하나였다. 1990년대 말에 전자 음악은 여러 장르로 갈라졌다. 스타일 및 하위 스타일이 너무나 많아서 열거하기가 힘들 정도이다. 이러한 종류의 음악에는 엄격한 규칙이 존재하지 않는다.

Drill 4 Ⓓ

해석

해류

지구의 대양으로 흘러 들어가는 끊임없는 물의 운동으로 인해 해류가 발생한다. 해류는 수천 킬로미터를 이동할 수도 있다. 이러한 해류는 바다와 경계를 이루는 지역에서 보다 빈번하게 발생한다. 멕시코 만류가 한가지 예이다. 이 해류 때문에 유럽의 북서쪽은 같은 위도에 위치한 다른 지역보다 기후가 훨씬 온화하다. 하와이 제도도 또 다른 예이다. 이곳 기후는 동일한 열대 위도에 위치한 섬들에 비해 상당히 시원하다. 이는 캘리포니아 해류 때문이다. 표층 해류를 이해하는 것이 중요하다. 그러한 지식이 있으면 선박 운송 비용이 크게 줄어든다. 그 이유는 해류의 움직임이 선박의 이동에 도움을 주기 때문인데, 이로 인해 연료비가 크게 절감될 수 있다.

Exercises with Mid-Length Passages

Exercise 1 1 Ⓒ 2 Ⓑ 3 Ⓓ 4 Ⓐ   p.178

해석

박쥐와 반향 정위

박쥐는 앞다리가 날개로 진화한 포유 동물이다. 이러한 점 때문에 박쥐는 전 세계 포유 동물 중에서 유일하게 비행이 가능하다. 전 세계적으로 약 1,100종의 박쥐가 존재한다.

박쥐는 두 가지 아목, 즉 큰박쥐와 작은박쥐로 나뉜다. 모든 큰박쥐들이 작은박쥐보다 큰 것은 아니다. 이들 두 종류의 박쥐 사이에는 두 가지 중요한 차이점이 있다. 작은박쥐는 반향 정위를 이용해서 방향을 찾는다. 또한 이러한 능력을 이용해 먹이를 찾는다. 하지만 큰박쥐에게는 이러한 능력이 없다. 대신 이들은 두 번째 발가락에 발톱을 지니고 있고 앞다리를 가지고 있다. 작은박쥐에게는 이러한 발톱이 없다. 큰박쥐들은 과일, 꿀, 그리고 꽃가루를 먹는 것으로 알려져 있다. 작은박쥐는 곤충, 커다란 동물의 피, 작은 포유 동물, 그리고 어류를 먹는다. 작은박쥐가 사용하는 반향 정위는 일종의 생물학적 음파 탐지 장치로, 돌고래와 고래도 이를 이용한다.

반향 정위는 동물이 자신의 주변에 소리를 방출하는 방법이다. 그들은 해당 지역에 있는 여러 물체로부터 되돌아오는 소리를 듣게 된다. 그런 다음에 이러한 메아리를 이용해 물체들의 위치, 거리, 그리고 정체를 확인한다. 자기가 낸 소리와 돌아온 메아리 간의 시간차를 측정함으로써 거리를 알아낸다. 작은박쥐는 귀를 사용해서 그렇게 한다.

1794년에 한 과학자가 박쥐에 관한 일련의 실험을 진행했다. 그는 박쥐가 청각을 이용하여 길을 찾는다고 결론지었다. 하지만 과학계는 그의 실험 결과를 받아들이지 않았다. 1938년, 또 다른 과학자가 박쥐가 사용하는 초음파 반향 정위에 대해 설명했다. 작은박쥐는 완전히 어두운 곳에서도 반향 정위를 이용해 길을 찾고 먹이를 사냥한다. 이들은 해가 지면 동굴이나 보금자리로부터 나와서 밤에 곤충들을 사냥하러 돌아다닌다. 이들의 능력 덕분에 박쥐는 특별한 장소를 선점할 수 있다. 이때는 곤충들이 많은 때이다. 활동 중인 포식자가 적기 때문에 이들은 밤에 나온다. 이 시간에는 먹이를 차지하기 위한 경쟁도 훨씬 덜 심할 뿐만 아니라 박쥐를 잡아먹는 종들도 더 적다.

📝 Summary Note
❶ claw
❷ echolocation
❸ night

Exercise 2 1 Ⓑ 2 Ⓓ 3 Ⓒ 4 Ⓑ   p.180

해석

모더니즘

모더니즘은 진보를 추구한 운동이었다. 이는 20세기 문화의 모든 영역을 휩쓸었다. 모더니즘은 인간의 힘을 강조했다. 또한 전통 방식의 타파를 장려했다. 모더니스트들은 자신들이 자기 자신의 삶과 세계를 만들고, 개선시키고, 그리고 재정립할 수 있다고 믿었다. 과학과 기술을 이용함으로써 그럴 수 있다고 생각했다. 모더니즘은 사고의 변화를 의미했기 때문에 매우 중요했다. 모더니즘은 산업 혁명이 인간의 생각에 끼친 영향을 표현했다. 또한 예술, 철학, 그리고 기술 간의 합류점으로도 기능했다.

모더니즘의 역사는 일련의 운동으로 구성된다. 이러한 그룹의 사람들은 진보를 이루고 싶어했다. 이는 1800년대 중반 프랑스의 화가들로부터 시작되었다. 초창기에 활동했던 사람들은 에두아르 마네와 끌로드 모네 같은 인상파 화가들이었다. 이러한 화가들은 인간이 회화 속 대상을 보는 것이 아니라 이미지를 눈에 가져다 주는 빛과 그림자를 본다는 점을 알려 주었다. 또 다른 초기 모더니스트로 귀스타브 에펠이 있었다. 그가 만든 에펠탑은 건축과 건축의 가능성에 대한 사람들의 생각을 바꾸어 놓았다.

하지만 모더니스트들의 한 가지 문제는 그들이 종종 다른 모더니스트들의 진실성을 부인했다는 점이다. 이러한 갈등은 보통 상대적인 이슈에서 일어났다. 그들은 누가 어떤 스타일을 처음 사용했는가에 대해, 또는 누구의 스타일이 다른 인기 모더니스트를 더 따라한 것인지에 대해 논쟁을 하곤 했다. 이러한 논쟁에는 답이 없는 경우가 많았다. 시간과 노력만 낭비될 뿐이었다.

일부 역사가들은 20세기를 근대 시대와 근대 이후의 시대로 나눈다. 그들은 포스트모더니스트들이 소비재에 모더니즘 스타일과 원칙을 적용했다고 주장한다. 이러한 스타일은 여러 상품에서 나타났다. 포스트모더니즘 스타일은 레코드 앨범 재킷, 엽서, 그리고 런던 지하철의 간판 디자인에 적용되었다. 하지만 모더니스트들과 포스트모더니스트들을 같은 부류로 보는 사람들도 있다. 목표는 항상 진보를 방해하는 것을 찾아내는 것이다. 그 원인으로 밝혀진 것은 그것이 무엇이던 대체되었다. 동일한 목적을 이루기 위한 새로운 방식으로 대체되었다. 이러한 방법은 새로운 것이었기 때문에 더 낫다고 생각되었다.

Summary Note
❶ the new
❷ skeptically
❸ Gustave Eiffel

Exercise 3   1 Ⓑ   2 Ⓐ   3 Ⓒ   4 Ⓑ   p.182

해석

음악극

음악극은 노래, 대사, 그리고 춤을 통해 이야기를 들려 주는 공연의 한 형태이다. 이러한 공연의 역사는 수천 년 전에 시작되었다. 최초의 음악극 중 일부는 고대 인도와 그리스에서 발전했다. 그리스인들은 인기 있는 무언극에 음악과 춤을 가미했고, 몇몇 위대한 그리스 극작가들은 자신들의 희곡에 들어가는 음악을 직접 작곡한 것으로 알려졌다.

수백 년이 지난 기원전 3년에 이러한 공연이 부활했다. 로마의 희극 작가인 플라우투스가 자신의 극에 노래, 춤, 그리고 관현악법을 가미했다. 배우들은 넓고 개방된 극장에서 관객들이 충분히 들을 수 있을 정도로 댄스 스텝의 소리를 크게 만들기 위해 신발에 급속 조각을 부착했다. 이것이 최초의 탭 슈즈였다. 중세 시대에는 희곡이 교회의 가르침을 전파하는 수단이 되었는데, 찬송가에 맞춰 만들어진 종교극을 통해서 예배식이 가르쳐졌다. 이러한 희곡은 너무나 인기가 있었기 때문에 교회와는 상관 없는 일종의 공연이 되었다. 이러한 극에서는 산문체의 대화와 전례 성가가 번갈아 나옴으로써 관객의 흥미를 끌었다.

이러한 공연은 르네상스 시대에도 계속 발전해서 이탈리아의 전통이 되었다. 우스꽝스러운 광대들이 공연을 통해 백성들이 알고 있는 이야기를 들려 주었다. 이러한 희극 공연 형태는 오페라 부파라고 알려졌다. 이 새로운 전통은 1600년대에 프랑스로 넘어갔다. 프랑스의 위대한 작가인 몰리에르는 자신의 희곡을 뮤지컬로 개작할 수 있었는데, 여기에는 장 밥티스트 륄리가 쓴 음악이 들어갔다.

이러한 형태의 공연은 유럽의 여러 나라로 퍼져 나갔고 계속해서 변화했다. 독일과 영국에서는 1700년대에 두 개의 서로 다른 뮤지컬 공연이 등장했다. 첫

번째는 발라드 오페라였다. 이 극적인 형태의 음악극을 만든 작가들은 당시 인기 있던 노래들을 차용해서 필요에 따라 개사를 했다. 하지만 희극 오페라는, 원래 악보와 낭만이 가득한 줄거리를 가지고 있었다는 점에서, 차이가 있었다.

Summary Note
❶ ancient India and Greece
❷ the Church in the Middle Ages
❸ Germany and Britain

Exercise 4   1 Ⓓ   2 Ⓓ   3 Ⓒ   4 Ⓐ   p.184

해석

물고기의 지느러미

물고기는 유선형의 몸을 가지고 있기 때문에 물에서 쉽게 헤엄을 칠 수 있다. 진화된 부분은 지느러미로, 지느러미는 연골 조직으로 이루어진 부속 기관으로서 비늘로 덮여 있다. 물고기의 몸에는 여러 종류의 지느러미들이 붙어 있어서 헤엄을 칠 때 제어가 가능하다. 지느러미로 인해 물고기는 방향을 전환하고, 속도를 조절하고, 그리고 정지해서 물속의 한 지점에 머물러 있을 수 있다.

등지느러미는 등의 중앙에 위치해 있으며 뾰족하거나 뭉툭한 형태를 띨 수 있다. 뾰족한 등지느러미는 물고기의 속도를 증가시키는 반면 뭉툭한 지느러미는 물살이 센 곳에서 작은 물고기가 제어를 더 잘 할 수 있도록 만든다. 이러한 지느러미는 등에 최대 3개까지 있을 수 있다. 이들은 두 종류의 지느러미 가시, 즉 뾰족한 가시와 부드러운 가시에 의해 지지된다. 지느러미에는 이 둘 모두 들어 있을 수도 있고, 둘 중 하나만 들어 있을 수도 있다. 뾰족한 가시는 그 끝이 날카롭거나 심지어 독성을 지니고 있어서 방어 수단으로서도 기능한다.

뒷지느러미, 가슴지느러미, 그리고 배지느러미도 뾰족한 가시에 의해 지지된다. 이 작은 지느러미들로 인해 물고기는 자신의 움직임을 미세하게 제어할 수 있는데, 이로써 물고기들은 순식간에 몸을 움직일 수 있다. 이를 이용해서 물고기들은 자리를 잡고 먹이를 먹거나 다른 물고기들과 대형을 이룰 수 있다. 배지느러미는 물고기의 항문 뒤쪽 가장 아랫부분에 위치해 있다.

가슴지느러미는 새의 날개처럼 물고기의 측면에 위치해 있다. 이들의 연골 구조는 형태상 육상 동물의 앞다리에 대응된다. 짝을 이루고 있는 배지느러미는 가슴지느러미의 아래쪽 뒤에 있으며, 이들은 육상 생물의 뒷다리에 대응된다. 이 지느러미들을 펄럭임으로써 물고기는 물에서 나아갈 수 있는 힘을 얻는다.

꼬리지느러미는 미기라고도 불리며 방향을 전환하고 물속에서 급히 나아갈 때 사용된다. 헤엄치는 속도가 매우 빠른 일부 물고기들의 경우 꼬리지느러미 앞에 수평의 꼬리용골지느러미가 있다. 이로써 꼬리에 일종의 융기 형태가 나타나는데, 이는 속도와 안정성을 높여 준다.

Summary Note
❶ speed and control
❷ small movements
❸ momentum
❹ turning

Exercise 5   1 Ⓐ   2 Ⓐ   3 Ⓐ   4 Ⓒ   p.186

인간의 뇌의 기능

인간의 뇌는 열구에 의해 명확히 두 개의 부분으로 나뉜다. 뇌의 각 측면에 있는 모든 구조는 반대쪽에서도 그대로 찾아볼 수 있다. 하지만 각 측면은 서로 다른 기능을 담당한다. 이로 인해 사람들이 좌뇌 또는 우뇌만 사용한다는 잘못된 믿음이 생겨났다. 하지만 이는 사실이 아닌데, 그 이유는 모든 기능이 정상적인 사람이라면 뇌의 양쪽을 모두 사용해야 모든 기술과 기능을 실행할 수 있기 때문이다. 인간의 뇌는 다섯 개의 영역, 즉 두정엽, 전두엽, 후두엽, 측두엽, 그리고 소뇌로 이루어져 있다.

두정엽은 신체의 모든 부분에서 온 감각 정보가 합쳐지는 뇌의 부분이다. 또한 시각을 통해 공간을 판단하는 경우에도 사용된다. 이는 뇌 중에서 가장 잘 알려지지 않은 영역이다. 전두엽에는 뇌회와 운동 피질 조직이 포함되어 있다. 이 부분을 통해 뇌가 신체의 수의적 운동을 통제할 수 있다. 전두엽은 또한 충동 억제, 판단, 기억, 언어, 운동 기능, 문제 해결, 성적 행동, 사회화, 그리고 자발성을 담당하는 것으로 알려져 있다. 신체의 여러 활동들도 전두엽에 의해 통제된다. 후두엽은 시각 정보를 처리하는 부분이다. 네 개의 엽 가운데 크기가 가장 작으며 뇌의 뒷부분에 위치해 있다. 후두엽 부위는 색깔, 공간, 그리고 동작 인식과 관련된 정보를 처리한다. 이곳에 손상을 입으면 시력이 약화되거나 시력을 잃을 수도 있다.

측두엽은 뇌의 양쪽 아랫부분에 있다. 이곳에는 청각 피질이 포함되어 있다. 이곳은 신체의 청각 능력을 제어하고 청각 정보를 처리한다. 또한 말하기와 같은 고도의 처리 작업을 제어하며, 이해, 언어적 기억, 명명, 그리고 언어를 담당한다. 소뇌는 뇌의 아래쪽에 있으며 척수와 연결되어 있다. 이 부위는 감각 인지 후 신경계를 통해 근육을 조절하는 기능을 한다.

> ✏️ **Summary Note**
> ❶ Parietal lobe
> ❷ Occipital lobe
> ❸ Cerebellum

Exercise 6   1 ⓓ   2 ⓒ   3 ⓐ   4 ⓑ   p.188

미국의 농업

미국은 미국 내 모든 사람을 먹여 살리고 전 세계의 다른 나라로 식량을 수출할 수 있게 해 주는 농업에 기반해 있다. 하지만 농업이 단기간에 발전한 것은 아니었다. 인구 전체를 부양할 수 있을 정도로 농업의 기반을 다지기 위해 수 세기 동안의 노력이 필요했다.

식민지의 서부 진출로 농장은 미국 전역에 퍼지게 되었다. 정착민들이 새로운 지역으로 이주하여 농장을 세웠다. 이들의 노력으로 새로운 마을과 도시가 탄생했다. 이렇게 새로 생긴 지역으로 이어지는 공급망들은 현재 미국 전역을 가로지르는 여러 도로가 되었다. 북부 지역에서는 밀을 경작하는 경우가 많았는데, 그 이유는 밀이 추운 지방에서도 잘 자라기 때문이다. 보통 새로 생긴 정착지에는 밀이 심어졌다. 이러한 새로운 지역은 "밀 전선"으로 알려졌다. 이처럼 새로 생긴 밀 농장 지대는 여러 해에 걸쳐 서쪽으로 이동했다. 이러한 밀 농장들이 이동한 후, 그 자리에는 보다 다양한 작물들을 재배하는 농장들이 들어섰다.

중서부 지역에서는 옥수수와 돼지를 함께 기르는 것이 일반적인 농사 방식이었다. 돼지와 옥수수는 상호 보완 관계이다. 그 이유는 운하와 철도가 없던 시대에는 곡물을 시장으로 가져가는 것이 힘들었기 때문이었다. 그래서 곡물을 돼지에게 먹일 수 있었는데, 돼지는 운송하기가 훨씬 더 쉬웠다. 따뜻한 남부 지방에

서는, 더위에도 잘 자란다는 이유에서, 면화와 육우가 가장 인기 있는 생산품이었다. 담배 농사 또한 남부 지역에서 일반적이었다. 남북 전쟁 때까지 담배 농사는 노예 노동을 통해 이루어졌다. 1800년대 초까지는 북동부에서도 농사에 노예들이 이용되었다. 하지만 노예제는 1787년 자유의 조례에 의해 중서부 지역에서 폐지되었다.

대공황 시기에는 중서부의 많은 지역들이 황폐화되었다. 이는 더스트 볼 폭풍이 이 지역을 휩쓸고 지나가 토양을 농사에 쓸 수 없는 상태로 만들어 버렸기 때문이었다. 이후 이러한 지역 중 다수는 국유림이 되었다. 하지만 1940년대에는 2차 대전의 전쟁 물자를 지원하기 위해 이들 지역을 농장으로 바꾸려는 시도가 재개되었다.

> ✏️ **Summary Note**
> ❶ Cotton and cattle
> ❷ Northern areas
> ❸ Hogs and corn

Building Summary Skills   p.190

Exercise 1   **Bats and Echolocation**

Bats are the only mammals that can fly. There are two suborders of bats: megabats and microbats. These bats are different from each other. Megabats have a claw on their legs and are typically herbivorous. Microbats use ultrasound echolocation to get around and hunt insects, small animals, and fish. They usually hunt at night when there are a lot of insects, much less competition for food, and fewer enemies.

Exercise 2   **Modernism**

Modernism was an important movement in the twentieth century. It encouraged people to forget about traditional ways and to try to improve their lives. Its members, like Eduard Manet and Gustave Eiffel, wanted to create progress. But sometimes they got into useless arguments. Still, the effects of modernism can be seen everywhere today.

Exercise 3   **Musical Theater**

The musical theater is a kind of entertainment that is very old. It goes back to ancient India and Greece. Over the years, it has undergone a number of different changes. The Church in the Middle Ages used it to tell religious stories. Other cultures created musical theater productions that were comedies or dramas.

Exercise 4   **Fish Fins**

An important evolutionary development in fish is their fins. Dorsal fins are located on the back and help a fish control its speed. The anal, pectoral, and pelvic fins let a fish dart quickly through the water. The pectoral fins on the sides of a fish help give it momentum. And the tailfins let a fish turn in the water.

Exercise 5 The Functions of the Human Brain

The human brain is divided into two separate halves: the left and the right. There are five different sections: the parietal, frontal, occipital, and temporal lobes and the cerebellum. The parietal lobe controls sensory information while the frontal lobe controls the body's movements. The occipital lobe controls vision, and the temporal lobe controls hearing. The cerebellum controls the senses and the muscles.

Exercise 6 Agriculture in America

Agriculture has long been important in America for a number of reasons. As people moved west across the country, they lived by farming the land. Various regions in the country raised different crops and animals, including cotton, wheat, corn, hogs, and cattle. Some parts of the country have gone back and forth between being farmed and unfarmed.

Mini TOEFL iBT Practice Test   p.192

| 1 ⒷB | 2 Ⓐ | 3 Ⓐ | 4 Ⓑ | 5 Ⓓ |

6 Endoparasites: ②, ④, ⑥ Ectoparasites: ①, ⑤

| 7 Ⓐ | 8 Ⓒ | 9 Ⓓ | 10 Ⓐ | 11 Ⓓ |

12 ②, ③, ⑤

해석

[1-6]

기생

기생은 서로 다른 두 생물 간의 관계 중 하나이다. 이는 한 생물이 다른 생물에게 피해를 입히는 경우에 성립한다. 기생으로 규정되기 위해서는 두 생물이 오랫동안 함께 살아야 한다. 먹이를 사냥해서 잡아먹는 동물이나 숙주로부터 피를 빨아먹는 모기의 경우는 여기에 해당되지 않는다.

기생 생물에는 두 가지 종류, 즉 체내 기생체와 체외 기생체가 있다. 체내 기생체는 숙주의 몸속에서 산다. 그 예로 십이지장충을 들 수 있는데, 이들은 사람이나 동물의 위 안에서 산다. 이러한 기생체 중 다수는 수동적인 방법으로 숙주를 찾는다. 이들은 장에서 산다. 장에서 알을 낳으면 알이 배설물을 통해 외부 환경으로 나간다. 일단 숙주의 몸 밖으로 나간 후에는 비위생적인 곳에서 다른 사람이나 동물의 몸에 묻게 된다. 체외 기생체는 복잡한 방법을 이용해서 새로운 숙주를 찾는다. 일부 바다거머리는 동작 센서로 숙주를 찾는다. 피부 온도와 화학적 단서를 통해 숙주의 정체를 파악한다. 그것이 마음에 드는 숙주라고 확신을 하면 고리처럼 생긴 이빨을 이용해서 몸을 붙인다. 몸을 붙인 후에는 피부에 구멍을 뚫고 피를 빨아먹기 시작한다.

또한 기생 생물이 숙주로부터 양분을 얻는 방식은 두 가지 종류, 즉 사물영양체 방식과 활물영양체 방식으로 구분된다. 사물영양체란 숙주가 죽을 때까지 숙주의 조직을 먹는 기생체이다. 이 관계에서는 숙주가 보통 조직이나 영양분의 손실로 죽게 된다. 활물영양체는 숙주가 죽으면 숙주에 기생해 살 수가 없다. 자신이 살아남기 위해서는 숙주가 살아 있어야 한다. 많은 바이러스들이 활물영양체이다. 이들은 숙주의 유전적 프로세스 및 세포 과정을 이용해서 번식을 한다. 활

물영양체 방식의 기생은 생물이 생존하기 위해 사용하는 매우 흔한 방법이다. 모든 동물 중 적어도 절반 이상이 생의 어느 시점에서는 기생 생활을 한다. 여기에는 인간의 태아가 어머니의 자궁 속에서 사는 시기도 포함된다. 이런 행태는 식물과 균류에서도 흔한 것이다. 독립 생활을 하는 모든 동물들은 한 종류 이상의 기생체들의 숙주이다.

일부 기생 생물들은 사회성이 있는 숙주의 행태를 어떻게 이용할 수 있는지 알고 있다. 선충과 같은 일부 기생 곤충은 개미나 흰개미 군락으로 들어간다. 그들은 무리가 너무 약해져서 더 이상 존재할 수 없을 때까지 군락의 구성원들을 잡아먹을 수 있다. 한편 많은 종의 뻐꾸기들은 숙주가 잡은 먹이를 훔친다. 심지어 자신의 알을 다른 새의 둥지에 넣음으로써 다른 새를 유모로 이용하기도 한다. 어미 뻐꾸기는 스스로 살아가는 반면, 새끼 뻐꾸기는 다른 종의 어미새에 의해 키워진다.

[7-12]

판게아

1900년대 초반에 과학자들이 대륙 이동설을 생각해 냈다. 그들은 현재 존재하는 일곱 개의 대륙이 아주 오래 전에는 하나의 거대한 대륙이었다고 생각했다. 알프레드 베게너라는 과학자가 이를 판게아라고 불렀다. 판게아라는 이름은 "전 지구"를 뜻하는 그리스어에서 나왔다. 이 이론은 엄청난 논쟁을 불러 일으켰다. 이 이론의 시간표는 지구의 나이가 수천 살에 불과하다는 일반적인 믿음과 상충되었다. 사람들은, 자연의 힘이 아니라, 신이 지구를 만들었다고 믿고 싶어했다. 1920년에 베게너는 대륙 이동설을 지지하는 주장을 했다.

판게아는 적도를 가로질러 있었던 C자 형태의 땅덩어리였다. 초승달 안쪽에 있는 커다란 수역은 바다는 테티스해라고 불렸다. 대륙 주위를 흘렀던 거대한 해양은 판탈라사라고 불렸다. 판게아는 거대한 지역이었을 것이다. 내륙은 물이 없는, 극도로 건조한 지역이었을 것이다. 동물들은 자유롭게 북극에서 남극까지 이동할 수 있었다. 판게아는 세 개의 주요 단계를 통해 분열했다. 약 1억 8천만년 전에 분열이 시작되었을 것으로 생각된다. 이때는 쥐라기 시대였다. 수백만 년에 걸쳐 판게아는 현재 존재하는 7개의 대륙으로 분열되었다.

분열의 첫 단계는 약 1억 8천만 년 전에 시작되었다. 이러한 변화는 커다란 단층선이 끊어지면서 시작되었다. 지진이나 화산 폭발로 활동이 시작되었을 것이다. 테티스해에서 동쪽까지 판게아를 가로지르는 균열이 발생했다. 지금의 북아메리카와 아프리카 사이에 해당되는 지역에 생겼다. 첫 번째 분열로 보다 작은 두 개의 대륙이 만들어졌다. 남쪽 대륙은 곤드와나로 알려져 있고, 북쪽 대륙은 로라시아라고 불린다. 분열의 두 번째 단계는 약 1억 5천만 년과 1억 4천만 년 사이에 시작되었다. 이때에 작은 쪽이었던 곤드와나 대륙이 네 개의 땅덩어리로 분열했다. 이들은 아프리카, 남아메리카, 인도, 그리고 오스트레일리아가 되었다. 분열의 세 번째이자 마지막 단계는 약 6천만 년에서 5천 5백만 년 전에 일어났다. 북아메리카가 유라시아에서 떨어져 나왔다. 이로 인해 노르웨이해가 생겼다.

하지만 이 이론을 지지하는 사람들은 판게아가 최초의 초대륙이 아니었다고 주장한다. 그들은 지구의 지질학적 역사를 조사함으로써 몇몇 대륙의 단계를 재구성했다. 판게아 이전의 가장 최근의 대륙은 판노티아이다. 과학자들은 이것이 약 6억 년 전에 생겼을 것으로 생각한다. 판노티아는 약 5천만 년 후에 갈라졌을 것으로 추측된다. 이보다 더 오래된 대륙은 로디니아이다. 과학자들은 이것이 11억 년 전에 형성되었고, 이후 7억 5천만 년 후에 갈라졌을 것이라고 생각한다. 가장 먼저 생긴 것으로 생각되는 초대륙은 콜롬비아이다. 과학자들은 이것이 18억 년에서 15억 년 전 사이에 존재했을 것으로 생각한다.

A

1 Ⓐ		2 Ⓒ		3 Ⓑ		4 Ⓑ		5 Ⓐ	
6 Ⓓ		7 Ⓑ		8 Ⓓ					

B

1 Ⓓ		2 Ⓕ		3 Ⓘ		4 Ⓒ		5 Ⓙ	
6 Ⓗ		7 Ⓔ		8 Ⓑ		9 Ⓐ		10 Ⓖ	

UNIT 08 Insert Text

Basic Drill p.202

Drill 1 ❸

해석

분자

분자란 두 개 이상의 원자가 결합되어 있는 것이다. 이러한 물질은 동일한 물질의 더 작은 형태로 쪼개질 수 없다. 분자는 어떤 물질의 가장 작은 입자라고 생각된다. 이러한 상태에서는 구성 및 화학적 특징이 유지된다. 많은 물질들이 원자나 이온으로 이루어져 있다는 점을 고려하면 더 좋다. [그렇게 하면 개념을 이해하기가 더 쉬워진다.] 과학자들은 분자 단위 대신 이러한 방식으로 물질을 생각한다. 분자의 개념은 1811년에 처음으로 제시되었다. 아보가드로라는 과학자가 이를 생각해 냈다.

Drill 2 ❸

해석

식

식이라는 단어는 "사라지다"라는 뜻의 그리스 단어로부터 유래되었다. 식은 천문학적 현상으로, 하나의 천체가 다른 천체의 그림자 안으로 들어갈 때 식이 발생한다. 이 용어는 일식을 설명할 때 가장 많이 사용되는데, 일식은 달의 그림자가 지구 표면 위에 드리워질 때 나타난다. 또한 월식도 있는데, 월식은 달이 지구의 그림자 안에 들어올 때 나타난다. [하지만 식은 태양계 전체에서도 나타난다.] 식은 지구와 달 시스템 이외의 영역에서 일어나는 현상도 가리킬 수 있고, 어느 행성이 자신의 위성 중 하나가 드리운 그림자를 통과하는 경우를 설명할 때에도 사용될 수 있다. 한 위성이, 자기가 돌고 있는 행성이 드리운 그림자 안으로 들어가는 경우도 그렇고, 혹은 한 위성이 또 다른 위성의 그림자 속으로 들어가는 경우도 마찬가지이다.

Drill 3 ❶

해석

재즈

재즈는 미국에서 시작된 음악 예술이다. 재즈는 대략 20세기 초에 뉴올리언즈에서 처음 연주되었다. 재즈는 뿌리는 흑인 음악에 있다. [하지만 다른 영향들도 많이 받았다.] 이후에는 서양의 음악 기법 및 이론과 결합되었다. 재즈에서는 블루노트, 스윙, 콜 앤 리스폰스, 그리고 즉흥곡이 연주된다. 흑인 사회에서 시작된 이 스타일은 1920년대에 미국 전역으로 퍼져 나갔다. 이는 다른 여러 음악 스타일에도 영향을 끼쳤다. 세기가 바뀌는 시기에 행진 악대나 댄스 밴드에서 사용되던 악기가 재즈의 기본 악기가 되었다. 베이스, 리드, 그리고 드럼이 서양 12음계와 함께 사용되었다. *재즈*라는 단어가 어디에서 혹은 누구에 의해 처음 사용되었는지는 확실하지 않다.

Drill 4 ❷

해석

소포클레스

소포클레스는 고대 그리스의 3인의 위대한 비극 작가 중 한 명이었다. 한 문서에서는 그가 123편의 희곡을 썼으며, 희곡 경연 대회에서 다른 어떤 희곡 작가보다 우승을 많이 차지했다고 기록되어 있었다. 희곡 경연 대회에는 네 편의 희곡이 제출되었다. 세 편은 비극이었고, 마지막 하나는 사튀로스극이라는 것이었다. [이는 드라마보다 희극에 가까운 작품이었다.] 그는 또한 자신이 참가했던 기타 모든 경연 대회에서 2위를 차지했다. 그는 기원전 468년에 처음으로 우승을 했지만, 오늘날 학자들 이것이 그가 참여한 첫 번째 대회는 아닐 수도 있다고 생각한다. 소포클레스의 비극 가운데 7편만이 완전한 형태로 전해진다. 이들 중 가장 유명한 것은 오이디푸스와 안티고네에 관한 세 편의 희곡으로, 이는 오*이디푸스 신화*로 알려져 있다.

Exercises with Mid-Length Passages

Exercise 1   1 Ⓓ   2 Ⓒ   3 **A1**   4 **B3**   p.204

해석

마누아 케아의 천문대

마누아 케아에는 11개의 연구 기지가 있는데, 이곳은 전 세계에서 별을 관찰하기 가장 좋은 곳이다. *마누아 케아*는 하와이말로 "하얀 산"이라는 뜻이다. 이 산은 하와이섬에 있는 휴화산으로, 태평양 해역에서 가장 높은 곳이다. 또한 전 세계 섬에 있는 산 중에서 가장 높은 산이기도 하다. 마누아 케아는 해저로부터 9,750m의 높이까지 솟아 있다. 해발 고도는 4,205m에 이른다. 정상은 지구 대기의 40% 이상 높이에 위치해 있다.

마누아 케아 위쪽의 대기는 대단히 건조하고 깨끗하다. 이러한 상태는 정상 위에 떠 있는 구름층 때문이다. 이 구름이 위쪽의 대기를 아래쪽의 습한 해양 대기와 분리시켜 놓는다. 이로써 정상의 하늘은 맑고 건조하다. 구름 때문에 정상 주위의 대기에는 오염 물질이 없다. 이러한 청명함 때문에 마누아 케아는 별을 연구하기에 이상적인 장소이다. 맑은 밤하늘이 나타나는 빈도가 전 세계에서 가장 높다. 이곳의 시상 또한 매우 높다. 별을 그처럼 명확하게 보이도록 만드는 또 다른 요인은 산과 도시 불빛과의 거리에 있다. 섬 전체에 적용되는 엄격한 조명법 덕분에 새까만 하늘을 볼 수 있다.

마누아 케아의 천문학 특구는 1967년에 지정되었다. [이는 50년 넘게 존재해 왔다.] 천문학 특구는 보호 지역에 위치해 있다. 이 지역은 하와이에서 신성한 장소로 여겨지기 때문에 보호를 받는다. 이 특구는 천문학자들이 별을 연구하기 위해 찾을 수 있는 국제 센터로 지어졌다. 과학자들의 숙소는 정상 아래에 위치해 있다. 해발 약 3,000m 높이에 있다. 방문객 안내소는 그보다 100m 더 먼 곳에 위치해 있다. 과학자들과 다른 방문객들은 30분 동안 더 낮은 곳에 있어야 한다는 말을 듣는다. 이렇게 하는 이유는 정상에 오르기 전에 적응 과정을 거치기 위함이다. 그러면 고산병을 예방할 수 있다.

정상에는 12개의 망원경이 있다. 이들은 여러 국가의 기업 및 기관의 후원을 받는다. 하와이 대학이 2개의 망원경을 관리한다. 2개의 쌍둥이 망원경은 켁 천문대가 관리한다. 스바루가 또 다른 한 개의 망원경을 소유하고 관리하고 있다. 영국은 적외선 망원경을 소유하고 있고, 캐나다와 프랑스는 공동으로 한 개의 망원경을 소유하고 있다. 또 다른 망원경은 캘리포니아 공과 대학이 소유 및 운용하고 있다. [나머지 망원경들은 기타 다양한 단체들이 운용 중이다.] 이러한 노력을 기울이는 단체들은 인류가 우주를 보다 잘 이해할 수 있도록 도움을 주고 있다.

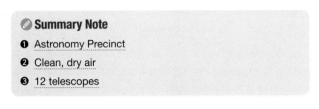

Summary Note
❶ Astronomy Precinct
❷ Clean, dry air
❸ 12 telescopes

Exercise 2   1 ⓒ   2 ⓓ   3 **A1**   4 **B3**   p.206

해석

원소 이름 논쟁

1960년대는 미국과 소련 사이에 긴장감이 컸던 시대였다. [이때는 냉전이 한창이었다.] 미국과 소련의 과학자들조차 논쟁을 벌이고 있었다. 당시 많은 과학자들이 인공 원소를 만든 최초의 과학자가 되기 위해 경쟁을 하고 있었다. 원소의 이름을 짓기 위해 최초의 과학자가 되고 싶어한 것이었다. 큰 논쟁이 일어났고, 이 논쟁은 1997년까지 해결되지 못했다. 이러한 문제는 몇몇 그룹의 학자들이 동일한 시기에 동일한 원소를 만들었다고 주장하면서 시작되었다. 이 사태와 관련된 주요 연구소는 버클리에 있는 미국 연구소와 두브나에 있는 소련 연구소였다.

소련 과학자들은 104번 원소를 만들었을 때 소련 원자 폭탄의 아버지인 이고르 쿠르차토프의 이름을 따서 원소의 이름을 지었다. 미국인들은 이를 강력히 반대했다. 자신의 나라를 파괴할 수 있는 무기를 개발한 적의 이름을 딴 원소를 입에 담고 싶어하지 않았다. 하지만 이들은 위선자라고 불렸는데, 그 이유는 이미 핵무기 개발과 관련된 아인슈타인의 이름을 따서 원소의 이름을 지은 적이 있었기 때문이었다.

이후 원소 이름과 관련이 있는 국제 순수 및 응용 화학 협회가 106번 원소에 미국이 붙인 이름, 즉 시보귬을 반대했다. 그 이유는 글렌 T. 시보그라는 과학자가 여전히 살아 있었기 때문이었다. 그는 자신의 서명이 들어 있는 주기율표를 나누어 주고 있었다. 이는 협회 규정에 어긋나는 일이었다. [그래서 협회는 그 이름이 원소명으로 쓰이는 것을 허용하지 않았다.] 1994년에 협회가 새로운 원소명들을 제안했다. 논쟁을 해결하고자 했던 것이었다. 104번 원소의 이름을 소련의 두브나 연구 센터의 이름에서 가져옴으로써 그렇게 하려고 했다. 또한 106번 원소의 경우 시보그의 이름을 따지 말 것을 제안했다.

이러한 해결 방안은 미국 화학 학회가 반대했다. 106번의 이름을 제안할 수 있는 권리는 자신들의 학회에 있다고 생각했다. 그것이 무엇이든 학회가 원하는 이름이 지어져야 했다. 국제 화학 협회는 106번 원소에 대한 공적은 버클리와 두브나가 나누어 가져야 한다고 결정했다. 하지만 두브나 측에서는 아직 이름을

제안하지 않은 상태였다. 게다가 미국의 여러 도서에서 이미 이전 이름을 사용하고 있었다.

마침내 1997년에 이름에 대한 합의가 이루어졌다. 하지만 1999년 자신이 사망하기에 앞서 시보그가 105번 원소의 이름 변경에 문제를 제기했다. 이 원소는 하늄에서 두브늄으로 이름이 변경되어 있었다. 그는 이 원소를 발견한 것으로 인정받은 두브나 측이 실제로는 이 원소를 발견하지 않았다고 주장했다. 그러나 두브나 측은 자신들의 주장을 철회하지 않았다. 버클리의 일부 과학자들은 아직도 105번 원소를 하늄이라고 부른다.

Summary Note
❶ element 104
❷ element 106
❸ element 105

Exercise 3   1 ⓒ   2 ⓓ   3 **A2**   4 **B1**   p.208

해석

플라톤

플라톤은 고대 그리스의 황금기에 태어났다. 그의 실제 이름은 아리스토클레스였지만, 역사가들은 그가 우람한 체격 때문에 플라톤이라는 별명을 얻게 되었을 것으로 생각한다. 그리스어로 *플라톤*은 "넓다"라는 뜻을 나타낸다. 또한 플라톤은 이마가 크고 넓었던 것으로 전해진다. 그의 부모는 아테네에서 영향력이 있는 시민이었다. 플라톤의 이력은 소크라테스의 제자로서 시작되었다. [그는 스승의 사상과 아이디어로부터 큰 영향을 받았다.] 스승이 죽자 플라톤은 이집트와 이탈리아에서 공부를 했다. 이후에는 아테네로 돌아가 직접 학교를 세웠다. 그곳에서 플라톤은 소크라테스식 사고를 전수하고자 했다. 그는 학생들이 진리를 발견할 수 있도록 지도했다.

플라톤은 소크라테스의 가르침을 전하려고 했다. 그는 스승의 대화를 기록함으로써 그렇게 했다. 이 대화들은 소크라테스에 관한 역사적인 정보를 얻을 수 있는 중요한 자료이다. 초기의 대화들은 한 가지 주제만을 다루고 있다. 하지만 그러한 주제들에 관해 결론이 내려지는 경우는 거의 없다. 플라톤의 대화편 중의 하나인 *에우티프론*은 윤리적인 판단을 옹호하기 위해 권력에 호소하는 일에 대한 딜레마를 지적한다. *변명*에서는 철학적인 삶이 묘사되고 있다. 이러한 묘사는 소크라테스가 아테네의 배심원단 앞에서 자신을 변호하는 상황으로 나타나 있다.

플라톤의 대화편은 허구적 인물로 소크라테스를 이용한다. 하지만 중기 대화편에서는 철학적 문제에 관한 플라톤 자신의 견해가 나타나 있다. [여기에서는 소크라테스가 주인공이 아니다.] 플라톤은 *메논*에서 아무도 알면서 잘못된 행동을 하지는 않는다는 소크라테스의 견해를 들려 준다. 그는 또한 상기설을 소개한다. 이는 덕이 가르쳐질 수 있는 것인지, 혹은 그렇지 않은지를 알아내려고 할 때 적용된다. *파이돈*은 계속해서 플라톤의 견해를 발전시킨다. 이는 형상론을 설명한다. 이러한 주장은 인간 영혼의 불멸성이 존재한다는 점을 보여 준다.

중기 대화편 가운데 걸작은 *국가론*이다. 이는 정의의 본질에 대한 대화로 시작된다. 그런 다음 바로 정의, 지혜, 용기, 그리고 절제에 관한 폭넓은 토론이 이어진다. 그는 이러한 것들이 개개의 인간과 사회 전체에 어떤 식으로 비춰지는지 살핀다. 동굴의 비유는 인간의 삶의 가능성에 대한 강력한 이미지를 담고 있다. 이 대화편은 다양한 정부 형태에 대한 논평으로 끝을 맺는다. 여기에서는 이상 국가가 명확하게 설명되어 있다. 이상 국가는 철학자들만이 통치할 수 있는 국가이다. 또한 불의보다 정의가 낫다는 점을 보여 주는 설명도 들어 있다.

Summary Note

❶ Aristocles

❷ the early dialogues

❸ The *Republic*

Exercise 4   1 Ⓑ   2 Ⓐ   3 **A3**   4 **B1**   p.210

해석

로이 풀러

로이 풀러는 현대 무용 분야를 개척했으며 또한 조명 기술 분야의 혁신가이기도 했다. 그녀는 시카고에서 태어나 야역 배우로서 경력을 시작했다. 이후에는 벌레스크, 보드빌, 그리고 서커스 공연에서 춤을 췄다. 그녀는 최초로 프리 댄스 기법을 사용했다. 스스로 만들어 낸 자연스러운 동작으로 춤을 추었다. 또한 춤 동작과 흘러내리는 듯한 실크 의상을 결합하여 즉흥적인 기술을 만들어 내기도 했다. 여기에는 그녀가 고안한 컬러 조명으로 빛이 비춰졌다.

풀러는 미국에서 유명해졌다. 그녀는 뱀의 춤과 같은 작품으로 유명했다. 하지만 그녀는 대중들이 자신을 진지하게 바라보지 않는다는 점에 불만을 느꼈다. 사람들이 아직도 자신을 배우로 생각한다고 느꼈다. [하지만 유럽에서는 다르게 느꼈다.] 파리 시민들은 그녀를 따뜻하게 맞아 주었다. 그녀는 프랑스에 머물면서 일을 계속했다. 폴리 베르제르에서 정기적으로 공연을 했다. 그곳에서 그녀는 불의 춤과 같은 작품을 공연했다. 그녀는 아르 누보 운동의 화신이 되었다.

프랑스의 많은 예술가들과 과학자들이 풀러의 혁신적인 공연에 매료되었다. 그녀의 팬 중에는 쥘 셰레, 앙리 드 툴루즈-로트렉, 그리고 퀴리 부인과 같은 유명 인사들도 있었다. [하지만 그녀에게는 평범한 팬들도 많았다.] 풀러는 또한 무대 조명과 관련된 여러 특허를 신청하기도 했다. 여기에는 컬러젤을 만들어 내는 화합물도 포함되어 있었다. 그녀는 심지어 프랑스 천문학 협회의 회원이기도 했다.

풀러는 초기의 현대 무용가로서 여러 차례 유럽에서 순회 공연을 했다. 그녀는 유럽에서 공연한 미국 최초의 현대 무용가로 알려졌다. 또한 이사도라 던컨을 파리의 관객들에게 소개하기도 했다. 던컨은 현대 무용을 진정한 예술로서 인정받게 만든 것으로 유명하다.

풀러는 가끔씩 미국으로 돌아왔다. 그녀는 풀러렛 또는 뮤즈라고 불렸던 제자들의 무대 공연에 다시 출연했다. 하지만 인생의 마지막 순간에는 파리에 있었다. 1928년에 유방암이 발병했다. 그녀는 화장되었고 유골은 파리에 묻혔다.

Summary Note

❶ modern dance

❷ new dance movements

❸ French fans

Exercise 5   1 Ⓓ   2 Ⓒ   3 **A4**   4 **B1**   p.212

해석

고대의 천문학

많은 고대 사회에서 별을 연구했다. 현재에는 많은 과학자들이 고대 사회의 별 관측 방식을 연구하고 있으며, 이러한 방식의 초기 사회에서 별을 관찰하기 위해 만들어졌던 도구들을 살펴보고 있다. 이러한 유형의 고고학 및 천문학은 현재 진지한 학문 분야로서 연구되고 있다. 하지만 처음에는 심한 논쟁이 있었는데, 그 이유는 원시인들이 천문학을 이해했을 것이라는 점을 사람들이 믿으려 하지 않았기 때문이었다.

19세기 말에 천문학자인 노먼 로키어가 이 분야에서 활발한 활동을 했다. 스톤헨지와 이집트의 피라미드가 그의 연구 대상이었다. 그는 이 분야가 진지한 학문으로서 널리 인정받을 수 있도록 노력했다. 하지만 영국 제도에서는 이 분야에 대한 관심이 점점 줄어들었다. [사람들은 그에 대한 연구에 관심이 없었다.] 이후 1960년대가 되자 천문학자인 제럴드 호킨스에 의해 새로운 관심이 생겨났다. 그는 스톤헨지가 석기 시대의 컴퓨터라고 주장했다. 이 독특한 개념은 사람들의 관심을 다시 이끌어 냈다.

비슷한 시기에 알렉산더 톰이라는 공학자가 연구 결과를 발표했다. 그의 논문에는 고대 문명에서 정확한 천문학이 널리 통용되었다고 적혀 있었다. 그는 스톤헨지가 고대 영국 제도에서 사용되었다고 주장했다. [그의 결론은 많은 사람들을 크게 놀라게 만들었다.] 호킨스의 주장은 대체로 무시되었다. 하지만 톰의 분석은 문제를 불러 일으켰다. 이는 역사에 대한 당시의 학문적 믿음을 흔들어 놓았다. 클리브 러글스는 톰의 주장에 근거가 없다는 점을 입증하기 위해 그의 현지 조사를 재평가했다. 하지만 이들 석기 시대 유적지에서 천문학에 관한 관심이 광범위했다는 점을 보여 주는 증거들이 나왔다.

유안 맥키라는 단 한 명의 과학자만이 톰의 이론을 검증해야 한다는 점에 동의했다. 그는 1970년과 1971년에 아길셔에 있는 킨트로 석상 유적지를 찾았다. 그곳에서 그는 석상 위에 있는 관측대의 정확성에 관한 톰의 예측이 맞는지 확인했다. 그는 관측대와 석상의 일렬 배치를 확인해서 그가 옳았다는 점을 알아냈다. 톰의 결론은 인정을 받았고 영국 선사 시대에 대한 새로운 설명으로 발표되었다. 이러한 집요한 과학자들 덕분에 오래 전 사람들도 정확한 자료를 가지고 별을 연구했다는 점이 밝혀졌다. 이후 역사는 완전히 바뀌었다.

Summary Note

❶ Norman Lockyer

❷ Gerald Hawkins

❸ Alexander Thom

❹ Euan Mackie

Exercise 6   1 Ⓐ   2 Ⓒ   3 **A1**   4 **B4**   p.214

해석

멜빈 캘빈

멜빈 캘빈은 위대한 화학자로서 영원히 기억될 것이다. 그는 평생 발견을 위해 노력했다. 그와 그의 팀은 캘빈 회로를 발견했다. 이 회로는 탄소가 식물 안에서 이동하는 경로이다. 이 발견은 식물 광합성의 비밀을 풀었다는 점에서 전 세계적으로 유명하다. 이에 대해 그는 1961년에 노벨 화학상을 받았다.

캘빈은 1937년 버클리에 있는 캘리포니아 주립 대학의 교수가 되었다. [그는 그곳에서 곧 중요한 교수가 되었다.] 1963년에는 분자 생물학 교수로 임명되었다. 그는 화학 생물 역학 연구소의 창설자이자 연구소장이었다. 또한 동시에 버클리 방사선 연구소의 부소장이기도 했다.

전해 오는 이야기에 따르면 2차 세계 대전에서 일본이 항복한 날 연구소 소장이 캘빈을 찾아왔다. 그는 "이제야말로 방사성 탄소로 뭔가 유용한 것을 해 볼 때입니다."라고 말했다. 그는 1940년에 발견된 탄소의 동위 원소를 말하고 있었다. 이 동위 원소는 일본에 떨어뜨린 원자 폭탄에 사용된 것이었다. 캘빈은 그에 대한 응답으로 방사선 연구팀을 조직했다. 그들은 광합성 과정을 연구하기 시작했다. 광합성은 녹색 식물이 태양 에너지를 화학 에너지로 전환시키는 과정이다.

캘빈과 그의 팀은 탄소14 동위 원소를 추적 물질로 사용했다. 그들은 탄소가 식물 내에서 이동하는 완전한 경로를 밝혀냈다. 이 경로는 공기 중에서 이산화탄소를 흡수하는 것으로부터 시작해서 그것이 탄수화물로 바뀌는 곳까지 이어진다. 그러한 과정에서 캘빈의 팀은 햇빛이 식물의 엽록소에 영향을 끼친다는 점을 보여 주었다. 햇빛이 유기 화합물을 만드는 연료 역할을 하는 것이다. 이러한 발견이 있기 전까지 햇빛은 식물 내의 이산화탄소에만 영향을 미치는 것으로 생각되었다. [하지만 현재 과학자들은 이 과정을 훨씬 더 잘 알고 있다.]

캘빈의 연구는 에너지 생산에 대한 평생의 관심으로 이어졌다. 그는 또한 생명의 화학적 진화를 연구하는데 많은 세월을 바쳤다. 그는 이 주제에 대한 책을 집필해서 1969년에 책이 출간되었다. 캘빈은 노년까지 과학 연구에 매진했다. 그는 기름을 만들어 내는 식물의 용도에 대해 연구했다. 그는 이 식물들을 재생 가능한 에너지원으로 보았다. 캘빈은 달의 암석을 연구하기도 했다. 그는 과학을 사랑한 사람이었다. 과학은 자신이 받았던 많은 상보다 더욱 중요한 것이었다.

> ✎ **Summary Note**
> ❶ the Calvin cycle
> ❷ photosynthesis
> ❸ carbon-14

Building Summary Skills
p.216

Exercise 1 The Observatories at Mauna Kea

There are many research stations located on Mauna Kea in Hawaii. These observatories are located there because of the air quality and the fact that the night skies are very dark and clear. The Astronomy Precinct there was established in 1967. There are twelve telescopes located there that are run by different countries or corporations.

Exercise 2 The Element Naming Controversy

In the 1960s, tensions between the United States and the Soviet Union even caused problems between scientists. There were naming controversies over various elements that different laboratories created. The Americans objected to the Soviet name, and the Soviets objected to the American name. Finally, an agreement on the name was arrived at, but some American scientists still use the old name.

Exercise 3 Plato

Plato was a great Greek philosopher who lived in Athens and studied with Socrates. After Socrates died, Plato opened his own school and tried to imitate the Socratic method of philosophy. Many of his early dialogues looked at single issues but never came up with answers. His middle dialogues stopped using Socrates as a character and expressed Plato's own thoughts. The *Republic* was one of Plato's greatest works.

Exercise 4 Loie Fuller

Loie Fuller was a pioneer in the field of modern dance. She created many new dance movements through improvisation.

She became famous in America, but she felt unappreciated, so she moved to France, where she had many fans. She had many important French fans, including Jules Cheret, Henri de Toulouse-Lautrec, and Marie Curie. She toured Europe and also helped other artists do so.

Exercise 5 Ancient Astronomy

Nowadays, many scientists study the stargazing practices of ancient societies. Norman Lockyer was an early scholar who looked into these practices. Gerald Hawkins also looked at Stonehenge and noticed how it was connected to astronomy. Most people discounted Hawkins's work, but Alexander Thom produced new evidence to support it. Euan Mackie went to Stonehenge and proved that Thom's conclusions were correct.

Exercise 6 Melvin Calvin

Melvin Calvin was a great chemist who won a Nobel Prize. He discovered the Calvin cycle, which helped unlock the secrets of photosynthesis. He worked at U.C. Berkeley, where he was a professor. He used the carbon-14 isotope to trace the route of carbon through the plant. He studied many different things through the course of his life.

Mini TOEFL iBT Practice Test
p.218

1 Ⓑ   2 Ⓐ   3 Ⓓ   4 Ⓐ   5 Ⓒ
6 **2**
7 Ⓐ   8 Ⓑ   9 Ⓒ   10 Ⓓ   11 Ⓓ
12 **3**

해석

[1-6]

포틀래치 의식

포틀래치는 일부 아메리카 인디언들이 진행했던 종교 의식이었다. 이 의식은 그들의 사회 구조에 대단히 중요한 것이었다. 이 부족들은 태평양의 북서 해안 지역 출신이었다. 이 지역은 미국에서부터 캐나다의 브리티시 콜롬비아까지 걸쳐 있었다. 부족들 중에는 하이다족, 누트카족, 살리시족, 그리고 틀린깃족이 있었다.

*포틀래치*라는 명칭은 치누크어에서 유래된 것이다. 이 의식에 참여했던 모든 그룹들이 이 의식을 서로 다르게 말한다. 치누크 단어는 영단어인 "포트(pot)"와 "래치(latch)"를 합친 것처럼 들린다. 하지만 이들과는 아무 상관이 없다. 원래 포틀래치는 중요한 사건을 기념하기 위해 진행되었다. 많은 존경을 받던 인물이 사망하거나 아이가 출생하는 일이 해당될 수 있다. 아메리카 인디언 사회에서 사회적 계급은 제한되어 있었다. 따라서 어떤 사람이 더 높은 계급으로 올라가는 경우, 사람들이 이를 받아들이기 위해서는 증인이 있어야 했다.

포틀래치는 축제의 형태를 띠었다. 전통적으로 물개 고기나 연어가 제공되었다. [하지만 다른 특별한 음식도 많았다.] 축제에서는 그룹 간의 서열 관계가 정해졌고, 이는 선물 교환, 춤 공연, 그리고 다른 의식들을 통해 강화되었다. 주최측 가족은 재산을 나누어 줌으로써 자신들의 부를 과시하려고 크게 노력했다. 그러면 저명한 손님들은 자신들의 포틀래치 의식을 열어 호의에 보답을 했다.

유럽인들이 도착하기 전 포틀래치 선물은 보존 식품, 배, 혹은 노예 등이었다. 18세기 후반 및 19세기에 담요 및 구리와 같은 새로운 종류의 선물이 들어오면서 포틀래치는 부정적인 변화를 겪었다. 일부 그룹들은 포틀래치를 싸움터로 사용했다. 여기에서는 매우 치열한 신분 과시 경쟁이 벌어졌다. 몇몇 경우, 받은 선물을 부숴 버리기도 했다.

선교사들 및 정부 기관들의 요구로 인해 캐나다에서는 1885년에, 그리고 미국에서는 19세기 후반에 포틀래치가 불법화되었다. 그들은 이것이 어리석은 전통이라고 생각했다. 그들의 눈에는 이 의식이 낭비적이고, 비생산적이며, 의식을 행하는 사람들에게 악영향을 미친다고 생각했다. 금지되었음에도 불구하고, 포틀래치는 수년 간 비밀리에 계속되었다. 여러 해가 지난 후 수많은 부족들이 정부에게 금지 조치를 철회해 달라고 요청했다. 그들은 포틀래치를 크리스마스에 비유했다. 포틀래치는 크리스마스와 마찬가지로 친구들이 선물을 교환하는 축제라고 주장했다. 20세기에 포틀래치는 큰 문제가 되지 않았고, 이로써 금지 조치는 해제되었다.

오늘날 많은 민속학자들이 포틀래치를 연구하고 있다. 그들은 이 축제에 매료되어 있다. 포틀래치의 후원자들은 많은 귀중품들을 나누어 주고 그 대가로서 명예를 얻는다. 이러한 명예는 포틀래치가 풍요로울 수록 커진다.

[7-12]
문학 비평

전 세계의 학생들이 학교에서 위대한 문학을 배운다. 하지만 자신들이 읽는 내용을 더 잘 이해하기 위해서는 때때로 전문가의 도움이 필요하다. 작가의 작품을 연구하고 그에 대해 토론하는 것이 문학 비평가가 하는 일이다. 그들은 작가의 의도에 대해 생각하고 이를 밝혀낸다. 이러한 일은 문학 이론에 기초를 두고 있다. 하지만 모든 비평가들이 이론가는 아니라는 점을 아는 것이 중요하다.

요즘에는 문학 비평이 에세이나 책 형태를 띠는 경우가 많다. 평론가들은 이러한 주제에 대해 강의를 하며, 결과를 학술지에 발표하기도 한다. 아이러니컬하게도 때때로 비평문이 원래 책보다 더 긴 경우도 있다. 보다 인기있는 비평가들은 잡지에 비평문을 발표한다. 문학 비평을 싣는 유명한 잡지로 뉴욕 *타임즈 북 리뷰*, *네이션*, 그리고 *뉴요커*를 들 수 있다.

문학이 존재했을 때부터 그에 대해 토론하는 비평가들이 존재했다. 아리스토텔레스와 플라톤은 그리스 시가에 대한 매우 비판적인 글을 썼다. 중세 시대의 고전 비평가들은 종교적인 글에 집중했다. 하지만 당시에 성경을 비판하는 것은 위험한 일이었다. [그래서 사람들이 비평을 할 때에는 위험을 감수해야 했다.] 성경과 같은 성스러운 책에 대한 비판은 교회 지도자의 공식적인 의견을 염두에 두고 이루어졌다. 르네상스 때에는 글에 대한 많은 새로운 아이디어들이 나타났다. 형태 및 내용에 관한 이러한 아이디어들로 인해 새로운 무리의 비평가들이 등장했다. 그들은 글이 모든 문화의 중심이라고 주장했다. 시인과 작가들은 오랜 문학적 전통의 수호자라고 주장했다. 이러한 고귀한 시인 중 일부가 과거의 위대한 작품을 복원하기 시작했다. 되살아난 고전 작품 중 하나는 아리스토텔레스의 *시학*이었다.

영국의 낭만주의 운동으로 인해서 문학 비평 분야에 새로운 아이디어들이 더 많이 등장했다. 19세기 초의 이러한 비평가들은 글의 대상이 반드시 아름다울 필요는 없다고 생각했다. 평범하거나, 껄끄럽거나, 혹은 추해도 문제가 될 것이 없었다. 그들은 문학을 창조하는 행위 자체가 평범한 대상을 고귀하게 만들 수 있다고 생각했다. 문학 작품이 얻을 수 있는 가장 높은 수준은 "숭고함"이었다. 이후 20세기 초에 새로운 그룹의 비평가들이 비평을 발표하기 시작했다. 영국과 미국 출신의 이 비평가들은 자신들의 비평을 신비평이라고 불렀다. 이 비평가들은 작품을 분석하기 위한 가장 중요한 방법은 작품을 아주 자세하게 읽는 것이라

고 생각했다. 그들은 사람들에게 단어 자체에 집중할 것을 장려했다. 이 방법은 지금도 많이 사용되는 독서 방법이다.

신비평은 1960년대 후반까지 가장 일반적인 작품 분석법이었다. 이 시기에 대학 교수들은 대륙 철학의 영향을 많이 받았다. 이 새로운 사고 방식은 새로운 스타일의 비평으로 이어졌다. 이러한 철학과 비평 방식 두 가지 모두 정보의 형태에 초점을 맞추었다. 그들은 정보가 어떻게 제시되는지를 면밀히 살펴보았다. 비평가는 작품을 분해하는 과정을 거쳐야 했다. 이러한 과정은 해체라고 불린다.

Vocabulary Check-Up

A
1 (B) 2 (C) 3 (D) 4 (C) 5 (A)
6 (A) 7 (C) 8 (D)

B
1 (D) 2 (F) 3 (A) 4 (I) 5 (B)
6 (J) 7 (G) 8 (C) 9 (H) 10 (E)

Answers and Translations **37**

UNIT 09 Prose Summary

Basic Drill p.230

Drill 1 2, 4

해석

초상화

초상화는 대상의 시각적 이미지를 나타내기 위한 의도를 지닌 미술 작품으로, 보통은 인물이 그 대상이다. 초상화는 대상의 실제 모습을 나타낼 것으로 기대된다. 초상화가들은 자신을 고용해서 비용을 지불하는 사람들의 초상화를 그린다. 때로는 대상에 대한 자신들의 강력한 감정에 의해서 영감을 얻기도 한다. 자화상은 화가가 직접 자기 자신을 그린 그림이다. 초상화는 대상의 전신, 반신, 혹은 어깨부터 머리까지의 모습인 흉상을 나타낼 수도 있다. 때때로 동물이나 애완 동물, 심지어는 주택이 초상화의 주제로 선택되기도 한다.

Drill 2 2, 3

해석

편형동물

편형동물은 몸이 매우 부드럽고 척추가 없는 단순한 생물이다. 이들은 바닷물과 민물, 그리고 습한 곳에서 찾아볼 수 있다. 대부분은 독립 생활을 하지만, 일부 종들은 기생 생물로서 다른 동물에 붙어서 산다. 편형동물에는 네 가지 종류, 즉 흡충강, 촌충강, 단생흡충아강, 그리고 와충강이 있다. 편형동물의 부드러운 몸은 리본 모양이다. 편형동물은 가장 단순한 동물로서, 세 개의 배엽에서 기관이 만들어진다. 외배엽과 내배엽이 있고 그 사이에 중배엽이 있다. 이 동물에는 장을 제외하면 진정한 체강이 없다. 신체 내부는 드문드문 떨어져 있는 조직으로 채워져 있다.

Drill 3 1, 4

해석

삼각주

삼각주는 강이 해양, 바다, 사막, 혹은 호수로 흘러 들어가는 곳에 생기는 지형이다. 이러한 흐름 때문에 물이 빠져나가는 쪽에 삼각형 모양의 퇴적물이 생긴다. 삼각주는 강이 운반한 침전물에 의해 형성된다. 이러한 침전물은 물살이 빠져나가면서 퇴적된다. 다량의 침전물을 지닌 보다 큰 강의 삼각주 퇴적물은 강의 물골을 여러 개의 지류로 나눈다. 이들 지류는 나누어지고 또 다시 합쳐져서 활동성 및 비활동성 물골을 형성한다. 강어귀에 생기는 퇴적물은 거의 삼각형 형태를 띤다. 강어귀가 침니에 막히면 그러한 모양이 생기며, 이때 삼각주 아랫부분의 폭이 증가한다.

Drill 4 2, 3

해석

사회 심리학

사회 심리학이라는 분야는 사람들이 무리 속에서 어떻게 행동하는지를 지속적으로 연구한다. 사람들이 어떻게 타인들을 인식하고, 타인들에게 영향을 미치며, 그리고 타인들과 관계를 맺는지에 초점을 맞춘다. 고든 올포트는 이 학문의 고전적 정의를 내린 사람으로 알려져 있다. 그는 사회 심리학이란 사람들이 어떻게 타인의 영향을 받는지를 이해하고 설명하기 위한 시도라고 말했다. 여기에는 다른 사람들의 존재를 상상하거나 가정하는 상황에 대한 대처 방식도 포함될 수 있다. 이 분야의 연구는 대부분 소규모 그룹의 관찰을 통해 이루어진다. 이 그룹들은 모여서 수행해야 할 과제를 부여받는다. 연구자들은 이들이 주어진 과제를 완수하려고 시도할 때 집단 상호 작용을 관찰한다.

Exercises with Mid-Length Passages

Exercise 1   1 Ⓑ   2 Ⓐ   3 1, 3, 6   p.234

해석

하구

하구는 조수의 영향을 받는 강어귀에 형성된다. 하구는 반폐쇄 형태의 연안 수역으로, 이곳의 물은 넓은 바다로 자유롭게 흘러간다. 하구의 주된 특성은 바닷물과 민물이 만나는 연결 지점에서 드러난다. 바닷물과 강이나 시내에서 온 민물이 섞이면서 약간 짠맛이 나는 물이 만들어진다. 이 두 가지 물이 만나는 지점에서 움직임이 생기기 위해서는 반드시 조수가 필요하다. 조수가 없는 바다의 경우, 강에 의해 자연적으로 삼각주가 형성된다.

일반적으로 조수의 영향을 받는 강어귀에 하구가 존재한다. 하구에는 보통 여러 퇴적물들이 포함되어 있는데, 이들은 내륙에서 유입된 물속에 들어 있는 침니로 이루어져 있다. 하구는 해수면이 상승해서 땅이 더 낮은 곳에 위치해 있는 침하 해안에 더 자주 생긴다. 이러한 과정에서 계곡이 범람을 하면 리아스식 해안이나 피요르드와 같은 지형이 만들어진다. 만약 시냇물이나 강물이 여기로 흘러들어올 경우 하구가 형성된다.

하구에서 만들어지는 짠맛의 물이 바닷물만큼 짠 것은 아니다. 하지만 민물보다는 짜다. 이러한 물 덕분에 하구에서는 생태계가 번성한다. 가장 잘 알려진 하구 중 하나는 런던을 관통하는 템즈강이다. 템즈강은 런던에서 서쪽으로 몇 마일 떨어져 있는 테딩턴까지 이어진다. 이 지역은 템즈강에서 조수의 영향이 미치는 마지막 부분이다. 하지만 서쪽 배터시까지도 민물인 강물이 흐른다.

이 부분의 템즈강에서는 동물군이 주로 민물 어종으로 이루어져 있다. 잉어, 황어, 농어, 그리고 강꼬치고기 등 많은 어종들이 이곳에서 발견된다. 배터시와 그레이브샌드 사이에서 템즈강의 물은 짠물로 바뀐다. 이 지역에는 제한된 수의 민물 어종 및 해양 어종이 서식한다. 동쪽으로 가면 염분이 조금 더 증가해서 해양 어종이 민물 어종을 완전히 대체하게 된다.

📝 Summary Note

❶ the mouths of rivers

❷ fresh water and sea water

❸ marine species

Exercise 2   1 Ⓑ   2 Ⓓ   3 2, 4, 6   p.236

배아

배아는 다세포 생물의 발단 단계 중 가장 초기 단계를 뜻한다. 배아의 발달은 유성 생식과 함께 시작된다. 일단 유성 생식이 이루어지면 정자가 난자를 수정시킨다. 이 과정에서 만들어지는 세포가 수정란이다. 두 부모의 모든 DNA가 그 안에 들어 있다. 이러한 초기 단계에서 인간의 배아는 의식을 갖지 않는다. 이는 낙태할 권리를 찬성하거나 반대하는 사람들 간에 격렬하게 논쟁이 이루어지는 부분이다.

인간 배아의 경우, 세 가지 주요 발달 단계가 존재한다. 1주에서 4주까지는 배아가 자궁벽에 달라붙을 수 있는 장소를 찾기 시작한다. 만약 적당한 장소를 찾으면 거기에서 착상을 한다. 이때 엄마와 배아 사이에 연결 고리가 만들어진다. 이 시기에 탯줄이 생긴다. 5주에서 6주 사이에는 배아가 화학 물질을 내보내서 엄마의 생리를 멈추게 만든다. 뇌가 발달하기 시작해서 6주 정도가 되면 뇌파 활동이 시작된다. 또한 이 시기에 심장이 뛰기 시작한다. 팔다리가 자라 나오게 될 뭉툭한 부분이 보이고, 모든 주요 기관들이 발달하기 시작한다. 7주에서 8주 사이에는 태아의 혈액형이 결정되며, 배아가 움직일 수 있고, 눈이 나타난다. 대부분의 기관은 완전히 발달하거나 발달 단계에 있게 된다. 8주가 끝날 무렵에는 배아기가 끝나고 태아기가 시작된다.

인간 배아라는 주제를 둘러싸고 많은 논쟁과 논란이 제기되어 왔다. 문제는 어느 시점에 배아가 의식과 정신을 지닌 인간이 되는지에 있다. 이 문제는 미국에서 낙태 문제의 핵심이 되고 있다. 많은 사람들이 배아도 인간이며 보호를 받아야 한다고 믿는다. 배아에 대한 실험과 낙태가 일종의 살인 행위로서 불법화되기를 바란다. 하지만 반대편 사람들은 배아가 단지 미발달된 조직에 지나지 않는다고 믿으며, 배아가 태아기에 들어가기 전까지는 배아의 낙태 여부를 여성들이 스스로 결정할 수 있어야 한다고 주장한다.

📝 Summary Note
❶ Weeks 1-4
❷ Weeks 5-6
❸ Week 8

Exercise 3 1 Ⓑ 2 Ⓒ 3 ②, ⑤, ⑥ p.238

요하네스 구텐베르크와 금속 활자

요하네스 구텐베르크는 발명가였다. 그는 활자가 들어 있는 인쇄기를 발명한 것으로 명성을 얻었다. 그의 인쇄기에는 활자 합금, 유성 잉크, 그리고 활자 주형이 들어 있었다. 이러한 발명으로 인해 서적은 일반인들도 쉽게 구할 수 있는 상품이 되었다.

구텐베르크의 첫 번째 인쇄기의 기원에 대해서는 알려진 바가 없다. 그는 유럽에서 활자를 발명했다고 전해진다. 이미 그곳에서 사용되던 목판 인쇄에 개량이 이루어진 것이었다. 그는 이러한 요소들을 생산 시스템으로 결합시킴으로써 문서의 빠른 인쇄를 가능하게 만들었고, 이로써 르네상스 시대의 유럽 전역에서 정보가 폭발적으로 증가하게 되었다. 구텐베르크는 1430년경에 고향인 마인츠에서 스트라스부르로 이사했다. 그는 이사 후 금속 활자로 실험을 하기 시작했다. 그는 목판 활자의 경우 모든 것을 손으로 새겨야 했기 때문에 이를 생산하기 위해서는 많은 시간과 비용이 든다는 점을 알고 있었다. 구텐베르크는 일단 주형을 하나만 만들면 금속 활자는 훨씬 더 빠르게 복제를 할 수 있다고 결론지었다.

1455년에 구텐베르크는 2권짜리 성경책을 각각 300독일플로린에 판매하면서 인쇄기를 시연했다. 이는 평균 노동자의 3년치 임금에 해당되는 액수였지만, 손으로 쓴 성경보다는 훨씬 저렴한 것이었다. 보통은 수사 한 명이 손으로 책 한 권을 쓰는데 20년이 걸렸다. 구텐베르크에게는 요한 푸스트라는 동업자가 있었다. 구텐베르크가 인쇄로 번 돈은 푸스트가 투자한 돈을 갚기에 충분하지 않았다. 푸스트는 구텐베르크를 고소해서 승소를 했다. 법원의 판결로 구텐베르크는 파산했고, 금속 활자 및 인쇄 장비에 대한 관할권은 푸스트에게 넘어갔다. 구텐베르크는 죽기 직전까지 작은 인쇄소를 운영했다. 하지만 자기 이름이 찍힌 책을 발간한 최초의 인쇄업자는 푸스트였다.

📝 Summary Note
❶ an information explosion
❷ own books
❸ sued

Exercise 4 1 Ⓓ 2 Ⓒ 3 ①, ④, ⑤ p.240

유전자 형질 변환 식물

유전자 형질 변환 식물은 다른 종의 유전자를 공유한다. 1800년대 후반에 최초의 유전자 형질 변환 식물, 즉 밀과 호밀의 교배종이 기록되었다. 이러한 두 식물종의 이종 교배로 새로운 농업의 시대가 열렸다. 한 식물에서 다른 식물로 유전자를 이동시킴으로써 농부는 질병에 훨씬 더 강한 농작물을 기를 수 있다. 이러한 식물들은 식량과 수익을 가져다 주는 많은 농장을 황폐화시키는 전염병으로부터 안전하다.

1930년대에 E.S. 맥패든은 품종 개량을 통해 잡초의 형질 전환 유전자가 들어 있는 밀 품종을 만들었다. 이 품종은 호프라고 불렸고, 미국 전체의 밀 농사를 위협했던 줄기녹병에 대한 내성을 가지고 있었다. 이 새로운 품종의 밀은 농부들을 흉작에서 구해냈다. 또한 많은 사람들이 기근을 면할 수 있었다. 유전자 형질 변환 식물의 성장은 정상적인 이종 교배 방식으로 시작되었다. 하지만 1970년대에 과학자들은 식물과 동물종 간의 DNA 이식까지 시도하고 있었다. 1985년 벨기에의 한 연구소는, 곤충을 죽일 수 있는 단백질로 코드화된 유전자를 주입함으로써, 곤충에 대한 내성을 지닌 담배를 유전 공학적으로 만들었다.

이러한 발전으로 유전자 형질 변환 재조합 식물이라는 분야가 등장했다. 이 분야는 여러 국제 단체에서 논쟁의 대상이 되고 있다. 논쟁 중인 이들 단체들은 유전자 변형 농작물이나 식품에 대해 찬반 입장을 보이고 있다. 식물 DNA의 사용에 관한 이러한 논쟁으로 인해 새로운 생물학적 분류가 만들어졌다. 이 부류에 속하는 대상은 유전자 변형 농산물(GMOs)로 알려져 있다.

유용한 유전자 형질 변환 식물의 한 가지 예는 황금쌀이다. 이 품종의 쌀은 실험실에서 만들어졌다. 여기에는 일반 백미에 비해 23배나 많은 비타민A가 함유되어 있다. 비타민A는 전 세계 여러 지역에서 부족한 중요 영양소이다. 이 품종의 쌀은 이러한 지역의 사람들을 돕기 위한 인도주의적인 도구로서 개발되었다. 하지만 유전자 형질 변환 식품을 반대하는 여러 단체들의 반대 때문에, 일부 지역에서는 이 쌀을 구할 수가 없다.

📝 Summary Note
❶ diseases and insects
❷ A wheat variety
❸ International controversy

해석

지그문트 프로이드

지그문트 프로이드는 오스트리아의 신경학자로, 새로운 종류의 심리학을 창시한 인물이었다. 그는 성욕과 꿈에 대한 이론으로 가장 잘 알려져 있다. 또한 억압과 무의식에 대한 연구로도 유명하다. 많은 사람들이 그를 "심리 분석의 아버지"라고 부른다.

프로이드는 1856년 프라이브룩에서 태어났다. 그의 가족은 사람들로 가득한 아파트에서 살았다. 하지만 그의 부모는 그의 지성을 키워 주기 위해 노력했다. 그는 8년간의 학창 시절 중 6년 동안 반에서 일등을 했다. 17세의 나이로 비엔나 대학에 입학을 했다. 프로이드는 신경질환과 뇌질환을 가진 환자들을 위한 병원을 개업했다. 그는 가장 신경질적이고 신경과민인 환자들에게 최면 요법을 시도했지만, 결국 이러한 시도를 중단했다. 훨씬 더 쉬운 방법으로 환자가 말을 하도록 만들 수 있다는 점을 알게 된 것이었다. 그는 환자들을 소파에 앉히고 마음 속에 떠오르는 아무것이나 말해보라고 권유했다. 이러한 과정을 "자유 연상"이라고 한다.

프로이드는 40대에 들어서자 자신에게 많은 정신적 문제가 있다고 느꼈다. 그는 자신의 꿈을 연구하기 시작했다. 또한 자신의 기억 및 자신의 성격의 역동성에 대해서도 연구를 했다. 이러한 자기 분석 과정에서 그는 자신이 아버지에 대해 느꼈던 적대감을 깨닫게 되었다. 또한 어머니에 대한 아동기 때의 감정들도 회상했는데, 어머니는 매력적이고, 따뜻하고, 그리고 보호해 주려고 했다. 프로이드를 연구한 학자들은 감정적인 어려움을 겪었던 이 시기가 그의 일생에서 가장 창의적인 시기였다고 생각한다.

프로이드의 이론과 연구 방법은 그의 일생 동안 논란의 대상이었다. 리디아 드 H. 호튼이 쓴 논문에서는 프로이드의 꿈 해석이 "위험할 만큼 부정확한 것"이라고 언급되었다. 프로이드를 비판한 또 다른 사람은 줄리엣 미첼이었다. 그녀는 우리의 의식적 사고가 무의식적인 공포 및 욕구로부터 비롯된다는 프로이드의 기본 주장은 거부되어야 한다고 주장했다. 이는 세상에 대한 보편적이고 객관적인 주장이 가능하다는 점을 부정하는 것이기 때문에 그렇게 말을 한 것이었다. 많은 비평가들은 프로이드의 아이디어가 과다한 코카인의 복용에 따른 결과였다고 생각한다.

📝 Summary Note
❶ psychoanalysis
❷ free-association
❸ inaccurate and too subjective

해석

지도 제작의 역사

지도나 지구의를 연구하고 제작하는 것을 지도 제작법이라고 하며, 이는 기록이 남아 있는 오래전부터 인류 역사의 중요한 부분이었다. 지금까지 알려진 최초의 지도는 지구의 지도가 아니라 별자리에 관한 지도였다. 기원전 16,500년에 만들어진, 점으로 표시된 밤하늘 지도가 발견되었다. 이 점들은 프랑스의 라스코 동굴 벽에서 발견되었다. 이 벽에는 세 개의 밝은 별, 즉 직녀성, 견우성, 그리고 데네브가 포함되어 있었다. 또한 이 동굴 벽화에는 플레이아데스 성단도 표시되어 있었다.

고대 바빌론에서는 매우 정확한 조사 기법을 이용해서 지도를 만들었다. 오늘날 이란 북부의 키르쿠크 인근인 가수르에서 1930년에 발견된 점토판에는 좋은 예가 되는 지도가 들어 있다. 이는 두 언덕 사이에 있는 계곡을 나타낸다. 이 점토판에 새겨진 글씨는 그 지역이 아잘라라는 사람의 것이라는 점을 보여 준다. 학자들은 이 점토판의 연대가 기원전 2300년에서 2500년 사이일 것으로 추정한다. 고대 이집트에서는 지도가 상당히 귀한 것이었지만, 현존하는 지도들은 기하학적인 계산법과 조사 기법에 중점이 있었음을 보여 준다. 기원전 1300년 것으로 추정되는 투린 파피루스에는 금과 은이 채굴되는 중요한 지역이었던 나일강 동쪽의 산들이 표시되어 있다.

지도 제작에 있어서 초기 혁명은 클라우디우스 톨레미 시대에 일어났는데, 그는 90년과 168년까지 고대 그리스 시대의 이집트 도시인 알렉산드리아에서 살았다. 그는 지구를 구로서 나타내기 시작했고, 오늘날 사용되는 위도선과 경도 자오선의 평행 개념을 보여 주었다. 중세 시대 동안 지도 제작법은 진보했다. 르네상스 시대에는 포르투갈 출신의 지도 제작자들이 선박 항해를 위한 해도를 만들고 있었다. 가장 오래된 것으로 알려진 해도는 1485년 페드로 레이넬에 의해 제작되었다. 이 해도에는 위도가 표시되어 있다.

1569년 제라두스 메르카토르라는 플랑드르 지리학자가 메르카도르 도법에 기초한 최초의 지도를 발표했다. 이것은 둥근 구 모양의 지구의를 평면에 펼쳐 놓은 정확한 세계 지도였다. 1900년대에는 인쇄술과 사진술의 발달로 지도가 훨씬 많아졌다. 이러한 요인들 덕분에 지도 생산이 훨씬 저렴하고 용이해졌다. 또한 비행기로 인해 넓은 지역을 한 번에 촬영할 수 있게 되었고, 사람들은 과거 어느 때보다 높은 고도에서 지구를 바라볼 수 있게 되었다.

📝 Summary Note
❶ land ownership
❷ latitude and longitude
❸ Nautical charts

Building Summary Skills   p.246

Exercise 1 Estuaries

Estuaries are semi-enclosed bodies of water that form near the tidal mouth of a river. They combine both salt water and fresh water. The water formed is somewhat salty. Mostly freshwater species live in estuaries, but marine species live in them closer to the ocean. The River Thames is among the most famous estuaries in the world.

Exercise 2 The Embryo

The embryo is the earliest stage of development for multi-celled life forms. There are three major stages of development in the human embryo. These stages include the connection forming stage, the brain forming stage, and the organ forming stage. This marks the point at which the embryo becomes a fetus. After eight weeks, the fetal stage begins. There is a lot of controversy around the development of the embryo because of abortion rights.

Exercise 3 Johannes Gutenberg and Metal Type

Johannes Gutenberg invented movable type. This revolutionized Europe and led to an information explosion.

He used metal type instead of wood-block type. In 1455, he sold copies of a two-volume Bible that were much cheaper than handwritten ones. However, Gutenberg's partner Johann Fust sued him and took the rights to his invention. Gutenberg died in poverty.

Exercise 4 Transgenic Plants

Transgenic plants share the genes of other species. Scientists transfer genes from one plant to another to give the plants better resistance to diseases or insects or to make them more nutritious. Wheat, tobacco, rice, and even animals have had their genes modified. Some people are opposed to transgenic plants, which they call genetically modified organisms.

Exercise 5 Sigmund Freud

Sigmund Freud was a neurologist who founded a new kind of psychology. He is often referred to as the father of psychoanalysis. He had his own practice and soon began to use free-association methods with his patients. He also interpreted his dreams and his relationships with his parents. He did, however, have many critics during his life and afterward.

Exercise 6 The History of Cartography

Making maps or globes is called cartography, and people have been making them for thousands of years. Early maps just showed stars and constellations as in the wall paintings in Lascaux Cave. There were also early maps in Babylon and Egypt. Mapmaking improved in the Middle Ages and the Renaissance. Later mapmakers showed lines of latitude and longitude and made maps for sailors. By the 1900s, advancements in photography as well as the advent of airplanes and later, satellites, led to giant leaps forward in the accuracy and efficiency of mapmaking.

Mini TOEFL iBT Practice Test p.248

1 ⓑ   2 ⓐ   3 ⓒ   4 ⓐ   5 ⓓ
6 ①, ④, ⑤

7 ⓐ   8 ⓒ   9 ⓒ   10 ⓑ   11 ⓓ
12 ②, ③, ⑤

해석

[1-6]
고대 그리스의 도자기

학자들은 현존하는 고대 그리스의 도자기를 통해 고대 그리스의 예술에 대해 알고 있다. 그리스 회화와 공예품은 거의 남아 있지 않은 반면, 그리스 도기는 100,000점 이상 존재한다. 다수의 도기는 그리스의 인물이나 풍경으로 장식되어 있다. 이러한 도기는 그리스 사회의 모든 계층에서 일반적인 것이었는데, 그

이유는 그리스인들이 물을 마시거나 음식을 담는 등의 일상적인 용도를 위해 도기를 만들었기 때문이었다.

그리스 문명의 초기에는 작은 도시 국가들이 각자 도자기를 만들었다. 하지만 나중에는 코린트와 아테네에서 이러한 도기들이 거의 다 만들어졌다. 이들 도시에서 생산된 도자기는 그리스 전역에서 표준이 되었고 널리 수출되는 바람에 다른 지역의 도자기들은 더 이상 생산되지 않았다.

고대 그리스에서 도자기 생산의 주요 두 시기는 흑색 인물 기법 시기와 적색 인물 기법 시기였다. 흑색 인물 기법 시기는 기원전 약 700년경에 시작되었고, 코린트라는 도시에 그 기원을 두고 있었다. 이 방법을 통해 철 성분이 많은 옅은 색 점토로 도기가 만들어졌다. 불에 구우면 도기의 색깔이 붉은 오렌지색으로 변했다. 도기의 표면에는 밑그림이 그려졌다. 그런 다음 정제된 점토를 이용해서 그려진 인물 형태에 색이 칠해졌다. 조각 도구를 사용해서 보다 세부적인 부분을 그려 넣었고, 그 후 항아리는 다시 불에 구워졌다. 두 번째로 구울 때에는 칠해진 부분이 광택을 내는 검정색으로 바뀌었다.

적색 인물 기법의 도자기들은 기원전 530년경에 등장했다. 이 스타일은 대단히 인기가 높아서 흑색 인물 기법보다 더 많이 사용되었다. 심지어 오늘날에도 이 스타일은 그리스 도자기 미술의 정점으로 여겨진다. 현존하는 가장 가치가 높은 그리스 도기도 이 양식으로 만들어졌다. 이 양식의 도자기를 완성시켰던 과정에서는 도공과 화공 사이의 긴밀한 협력이 요구되었다. 이 과정에서 화공은 도기를 굽기 전에 밑그림을 그렸다. 도기가 아직 구워지지 않은 상태이기 때문에 그림과 점토는 같은 색을 띠었고 화공은 그림을 보지 못하는 상태에서 그림을 그려야 했다. 도공이 도기를 굽고 나면 그림이 눈에 보였다. 이 과정에서 화공은 기억에만 의존해서 매우 빠르고 정확하게 작업을 해야 했다.

이러한 도기에 그림을 그린 화공들이 서명을 남기는 경우는 드물었다. 따라서 오늘날의 학자들이 이러한 화공들을 식별할 수 있는 유일한 방법은 그들이 반복적으로 그린 이미지를 통해서이다. 예를 들어 가장 위대한 도기 화공 중 한 명은 "아킬레스 화가"라고 불리는데, 그 이유는 그가 가장 자주 그린 그림의 대상이 아킬레스라는 그리스의 인물이었기 때문이다. 화공을 식별할 수 있는 또 다른 방법은 그들과 함께 일했던 도공의 이름을 통해서다. 도공들은 종종 도기에 서명을 남겼기 때문에 클레오프라데스와 함께 작업했던 화공은 "클레오프라데스 화공"으로 알려져 있다.

[7-12]
절벽과 침식

절벽은 급격한 수직 형태의 암석이 노출되어 있는 지형이다. 절벽은 침식 및 풍화 작용에 의해 만들어진다. 이들은 해안가나 산악 지대에서 가장 흔히 볼 수 있다. 절벽 밑의 튼튼한 기반은 보통 침식이나 풍화에 잘 견디는 암석으로 이루어져 있다. 사암, 석회암, 백악, 그리고 백운석과 같은 퇴적암에 의해 절벽이 형성되는 경우가 가장 많다. 화강암 및 현무암 같은 화성암으로 이루어진 절벽 역시 찾아볼 수 있다.

침식은 바람, 물, 혹은 얼음 등의 요인에 의해 고체 물질이 떨어져 나가는 것을 가리킨다. 이러한 고체 물질은 흙, 진흙, 바위 그리고 기타 입자들일 수 있다. 침식 과정은 중력에 의한 내리막 운동에 의해 일어난다. 또한 생물체 때문에 일어날 수도 있는데, 이는 생물 침식이라고 불린다. 침식은 풍화와 다르며, 풍화는 움직임과 관련이 없는 과정을 통해 암석이나 입자가 분해되는 것이다. 하지만 같은 장소와 같은 시간에 이 두 가지 과정이 일어날 수도 있다.

침식은 자연적으로 일어나는 과정이다. 하지만 많은 지역에서 인간의 토지 이용에 따라 증가하고 있다. 나무를 베어내고 동물들에게 과도할 정도로 풀을 뜯어 먹게 하는 일은 바람직하지 않은 토지 사용으로서 침식을 가속화시킨다. 관리가 이루어지지 않는 건설 작업 및 도로 또는 철도 건설 작업 역시 마찬가지이다. 침식은 올바른 토지 사용으로 막을 수 있다. 테라스를 만들고 나무를 심는 등의 행

위로 손상된 지역을 되살릴 수 있다.

단층의 움직임이나 산사태로 형성된 절벽은 단층 절벽이라고 한다. 대부분의 절벽 아랫부분에 애추 사면이 있다. 이는 보통 건조한 지역이나 높은 절벽 아래에서 땅에 떨어진 암석들이 드러나 있는 곳이다. 공기 중에 수분이 보다 많은 지역에서는 토양 사면에 가려 애추 사면이 잘 보이지 않을 수도 있다. 폭포나 석굴 역시 절벽에 잘 나타나는 특징이다. 때로는 절벽이 산등성이의 끝부분에서 점차 작아져서 티 테이블이나 다른 모양의 암석 기둥이 생길 수도 있다. 절벽이 절벽으로 분류되기 위해 정확히 수직으로 서 있어야 하는 것은 아니다. 그렇기 때문에 어떤 사면이 실제로 절벽인지 아닌지에 관해 애매한 경우가 있을 수 있다.

세계 각지에 독특한 절벽들이 존재한다. 가장 높은 절벽은 그레이트 트랭고의 동쪽 면으로 알려져 있다. 이곳은 파키스탄 북부의 카라코람 산맥에 있으며 높이는 1,340m 정도이다. 하와이의 카라우파파에는 높이가 1,010m에 이르는 가장 높은 해안 절벽이 있다. 캐나다 북극 지방에 있는 배핀섬의 토르산에는 전체 높이가 1,370m에 이르는 가장 높은 수직 절벽이 존재한다. 여기에는 지구에서 가장 긴 수직 절벽도 있는데, 그 높이가 1,250m에 이른다.

Vocabulary Check-Up   p.254

A 1 ⓒ   2 ⓓ   3 ⓐ   4 ⓒ   5 ⓑ
   6 ⓓ   7 ⓑ   8 ⓐ

B 1 ①   2 ⓕ   3 ⓗ   4 ⓙ   5 ⓑ
   6 ⓖ   7 ⓒ   8 ⓓ   9 ⓐ   10 ⓔ

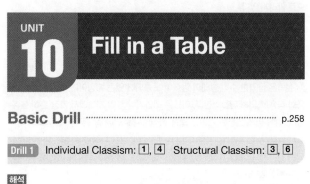

UNIT 10 Fill in a Table

Basic Drill   p.258

Drill 1 Individual Classism: ⓵, ⓸ Structural Classism: ⓷, ⓺

해석

계급 차별주의

"계급 차별주의"라는 말은 일종의 편견을 나타내는 용어로, 사회적 계급이 더 낮은 사람을 상대로 발생한다. 이것은 사회적 엘리트 의식의 한 형태이다. 개인적 계급 차별주의는 사람들에 의해 행해지며 부자들이 자신보다 돈을 덜 버는 사람을 무시할 때 나타난다. 또한 부자가 중산층 및 빈민층보다 나은 혜택을 받을 때에도 나타난다. 구조적 계급 차별주의는 계급이 낮은 사람들을 배제시키기 위한 방법으로서 행동이 취해질 때 나타난다. 많은 사람들이 미국 정치에서 이러한 종류의 계급 차별주의를 목격하고 있는데, 그 이유는 정치 후원금을 가장 많이 내는 사람들이 정부에 더 많은 영향력을 끼치는 것으로 보이기 때문이다. 이러한 관행 때문에 노동자 계급은 그와 동등한 수준을 영향력을 가질 수가 없다.

Drill 2 Causes: ⓵, ⓹ Effects: ⓶, ⓺

해석

메소포타미아

메소포타미아는 "문명의 요람"이라고 불리는데, 그 이유는 이 지역에서 인류 사회가 최초로 시작되었기 때문이다. 이 지역은, 인류의 농작물 재배를 가능하게 만든, 두 개의 강 사이의 비옥한 지대에 위치해 있다. 인류가 번성하자 도시들이 생겨났다. 도시들이 생겨나자 많은 발견들이 이루어졌다. 예를 들면 최초의 문자가 만들어졌고, 이들 도시에 사는 사람들은 금속 세공 기술을 알아냈다. 이들은 최초의 청동기 시대 사람들이었다. 구리, 청동, 그리고 금을 사용해서 궁전과 사원을 장식했다. 또한 천문학도 이용했다. 별을 연구함으로써 지구년의 길이를 계산할 수 있었다. 이로써 1시간을 60분으로, 그리고 1일을 24시간으로 계산하게 되었는데, 이러한 방식은 오늘날까지도 사용되고 있다.

Drill 3 Positive Effects: ⓶, ⓸ Negative Effects: ⓷, ⓹

해석

녹색 혁명

녹색 혁명이라는 말은 1940년대와 1960년대 사이에 많은 개발 도상국에서 일어났던 농업 분야의 급격한 변화를 가리킬 때 사용된다. 이로 인해 곡물 생산량이 크게 증가했다. 이러한 변화는 농업 연구 프로그램의 결과였다. 녹색 혁명은 사회 및 지구에 긍정적인 효과와 부정적인 효과를 미쳤다. 한 가지 긍정적 효과는 기근이 사라졌다는 것이다. 하지만 이는 일부 지역의 경우 인구 과잉이라는 부정적인 효과로 이어졌다. 또한 녹색 혁명으로 대규모 농업이 성공할 수 있었다고 생각된다. 하지만 이러한 성공으로 인해 소규모 농업이 이익을 내기가 상당히 어려워졌다. 경제에서의 이러한 변화는 사회주의 운동에 막대한 피해를 가져다주었다.

Drill 4 Physical Phenomena: ⓶, ⓹ Geological Phenomena: ⓷, ⓸

해석

자연 현상

자연 현상이란 인간에 의해서 발생하지 않고 자연에서 일어나는 현상이다. 하지만 인간에게 영향을 미칠 수 있다. 일부 자연 현상은 물리학으로 설명이 가능하기 때문에 물리학적 현상이라고 불린다. 번개가 이러한 현상의 한 가지 예이다. 중력 때문에 일어나는 행성의 궤도도 마찬가지이다. 지구 내부로부터 비롯되는 자연 재해는 지질학적 현상으로 간주된다. 흔한 예로 화산 분출을 들 수 있다. 거대하고 빠르게 움직이는 파도인 쓰나미도 이러한 현상의 예가 된다. 이러한 현상들은 제어가 불가능하다. 인간이 이러한 현상을 만들어 낼 수도 없고, 멈추게 할 수도 없다. 하지만 과학을 통해 이러한 현상들을 이해할 수는 있다.

Exercises with Mid-Length Passages

Exercise 1 1 ⓑ   2 ⓐ   3 Structural   p.262
Emergence: ⓶, ⓹, ⓻ Cultural Emergence: ⓷, ⓺

창발

창발이라는 개념은 복잡한 형태가 만들어지는 과정을 나타낸다. 이러한 형태는 기본적인 부분에서 시작된다. 창발성은 이러한 부분들 간의 관계로부터 비롯된다. 이는 끊임없이 변화하는 과정으로서 오랜 시간에 걸쳐 일어날 수도 있다. 인체의 진화가 좋은 예이다. 그 형태는 수천 세대를 지나오면서 만들어졌다. 인체는 대단히 복잡하지만, 복잡하지 않은 수백만 개의 세포들로 이루어져 있다.

창발은 크기가 서로 다른 수준에서 일어난다. 한 가지 예가 뉴런과 인간의 뇌 사이의 경우이다. 여러 뉴런 사이의 상호 작용에 의해 인간의 뇌가 만들어지는데, 뇌는 사고를 할 수 있다. 하지만 뇌를 구성하는 뉴런 중 어떤 것도 사고를 할 수 없다. 다수의 뉴런으로 만들어진 뇌 하나는 뇌를 구성하는 개개의 뉴런들 중 어떤 뉴런보다도 훨씬 더 크다.

자연 속에서 창발을 관찰할 수 있는 쉬운 방법은 구조를 살펴보는 것이다. 구조는 유기 물질 또는 무기 물질로부터 나타날 수 있다. 살아 있는 구조의 한 가지 좋은 예는 새떼이다. 새떼는 형태를 띠며 행동 특성을 보이지만, 이러한 특징들이 각각의 새에 의해 나타나지는 않는다. 또 다른 유기 물질의 창발적 구조의 예는 개미 군락이다. 개미 군락은 창발적인데, 그 이유는, 여왕 개미를 포함해서, 어떠한 개미도 그처럼 효과적인 일개미 군락을 조직화할 수 없기 때문이다. 하지만 모여 있으면 군락의 구조가 만들어진다. 무기 물질의 창발적 구조의 예는 허리케인이다. 이 폭풍은 여러 가지 요소가 작용한 결과로 만들어지는데, 이러한 요소에는 기압, 기온, 그리고 습도가 포함된다. 이들이 결합되어 격렬한 폭풍이 만들어진다. 하지만 어느 한 요소만으로는 그와 같은 폭풍이 만들어질 수 없을 것이다.

창발은 인간 문명에서도 일어난다. 이러한 창발이 대규모로 일어나는 한 장소가 주식 시장이다. 하나의 시스템으로서 주식 시장은 전 세계의 기업들의 가격을 조정한다. 하지만 시장 전체를 통제하는 한 명의 지도자는 존재하지 않는다. 중개인들은 제한된 수의 기업에 대해서만 알고 있을 뿐이고, 시장의 엄격한 규칙을 따라야 한다. 이러한 상호 작용을 통해 주식 시장 전체의 복잡성이 나타난다. 이러한 창발의 또 다른 예는 월드 와이드 웹과 관련이 있다. 이 경우 중심적인 웹사이트가 존재하지 않지만, 크고 작은 웹사이트들이 연결됨으로써 월드 와이드 웹이라고 하는 복잡한 존재가 만들어진다.

Summary Note

❶ A flock of birds

❷ An ant colony

❸ The World Wide Web

Exercise 2 1 Ⓓ 2 Ⓑ 3 Advocates: [1], [5], [6] p.264
Critics: [4], [7]

미디어 영향 이론

미국의 엔터테인먼트 산업은 많은 비평을 받아 왔다. 비평가들은 엔터테인먼트 산업이 보여 주는 가짜 폭력 연기를 못마땅하게 생각한다. 미디어 영향 이론은 이러한 문제를 설명한다. 이는 실제 폭력 사건의 발생률 증가가 오락물과 관련이 있다고 주장한다. 이 이론은 많은 폭력 행위를 고려한다. 고등학교 총격 사건이 가장 일반적인 것이다. 이 이론은 미디어에 폭력적인 장면이 많은 탓에 그러한 일이 발생한다고 주장한다. 인기 있는 오락물에서 폭력적인 장면은 다양한 형태로 나타난다.

이 이론은 많은 사람들이 폭력 수위가 높은 미디어 컨텐츠에 노출되어 있다는

가정에 기반한다. 이러한 사람들 중 적은 비율은 자신들이 보는 폭력과 관련해서 가상과 현실을 구별하는데 어려움을 겪는다. 이러한 사람들은 폭력 행위를 저질러도 괜찮다고 생각한다. 이 이론을 지지하는 사람들의 가장 빈번한 공격 목표는 비디오 게임 회사이다. 이 회사들은 1인칭 슈팅 게임을 많이 만들어 낸다. 대부분의 게임에 폭력과 선혈 장면이 난무하다. 지지자들은 이러한 게임들이 생명을 값싼 것으로 보이게끔 만든다고 주장하는데, 그 이유는 이러한 게임들이 플레이어에게 폭력 행위에 대한 보상을 해 주기 때문이다.

또한 지지자들은 증오에 찬 노래를 부르는 가수들도 목표로 삼는다. 그들은 이 예술가들이 폭력을 선동한다고 주장한다. 폭력적인 영화 또한 비난을 피할 수 없다. 사람들은 이러한 종류의 영화들이 폭력을 멋지게 보이도록 만든다고 주장한다. 이 모든 것들은 오락물이고, 사람들은 기업들이 자신의 상품에 대해 보다 많은 책임을 지기를 바란다. 사람들은 기업들이 매우 폭력적인 상품에 라벨을 붙이기를 바란다. 또한 이러한 상품에 대해서는 미성년자들의 접근을 제한하거나 금지하기를 바란다.

하지만 이 이론을 비판하는 사람들은 정부가 미디어를 규제해서는 안 된다고 말한다. 그러한 규제는 미국 시민의 언론의 자유를 손상시킬 것이라고 말한다. 그들은 미국과 다른 나라 간의 폭력에 관한 통계 자료를 비교한다. 다른 나라들 가운데 일부 국가에는 미국과 동일한 종류의 폭력적인 미디어가 존재한다. 하지만 폭력 행위는 훨씬 더 적게 일어난다. 따라서 이들 비평가들은 미국의 폭력 문제가 미디어 때문은 아니라고 주장한다. 그들은 그 원인이 총기 소지에 있다고 말한다.

Summary Note

❶ Entertainment companies

❷ control the entertainment industry

❸ availability of weapons

Exercise 3 1 Ⓑ 2 Ⓒ 3 Reported Causes: p.266
[2], [3], [7] Effects: [1], [5]

시카고 대화재

시카고 대화재는 1871년 10월 8일부터 10일 사이에 발생했다. 그 결과는 끔찍했다. 화재로 수백 명이 목숨을 잃었고, 도시의 상당 부분이 재로 변했다. 이는 19세기 미국에서 일어난 가장 규모가 컸던 재앙 중 하나였다. 하지만 시카고 사람들은 곧 도시를 재건하기 시작했고, 이로써 시카고는 미국에서 경제적으로 가장 중요한 도시 가운데 하나로 자리잡게 되었다.

화재는 10월 8일 일요일 저녁 9시경에 발생했다. 더코벤가의 골목에 있는 작은 헛간에서 시작되었다. 가장 널리 알려진 이유는 헛간 안에 있던 소가 랜턴을 발로 차서 화재가 시작되었다는 것으로, 이곳의 주인은 패트릭과 캐서린 오리리 부부였다. 지금은 오리리 부인이 희생양으로 이용당했다고 알려져 있다. 역사가들은 그녀가 여성이고, 이민자이며, 그리고 카톨릭교 신자였기 때문에 비난을 받았다고 생각한다. 이 모든 그룹은 미국 역사 상 이 시기에 박해를 받고 있었다. 화재 발생 직후 처음 발행된 *시카고 트리뷴*이 오리리 부인의 부주의가 화재 원인이라고 주장했다. 하지만 나중에 그 기사를 썼던 기자는 자신이 기사를 조작했다는 점을 시인했고, 그렇게 한 이유는 흥미진진한 기사가 될 것이라고 생각했기 때문이라고 말했다.

리처드 베일즈는 아마추어 역사가로, 그는 화재가 다니엘 설리번에 의해 시작되었다고 믿는다. 그는 첫 번째로 화재를 신고한 사람이었다. 베일즈는 이 사람이 헛간에서 건초에 불을 붙였다는 주장을 제기했다. 설리번이 우유를 훔치는 과정에서 그렇게 했다고 말한다. 하지만 안소니 드바르톨로가 최근에 *시카고 트리*

분에 몇 가지 새로운 증거를 제시했다. 그는 루이스 M. 콘이라는 도박꾼이 불을 냈을 것이라는 주장을 제기했다. 드바르톨로는 콘이 주사위 노름을 하다가 그렇게 했다고 주장한다. 앨런 와익스가 쓴 책에 따르면 사라진 콘의 유언장에 자신이 불을 질렀다는 고백이 포함되어 있다고 한다.

Summary Note
❶ Oct. 8 to 10
❷ Catherine O'Leary's cow
❸ Louis M. Cohn

Exercise 4 1 Ⓑ 2 Ⓓ 3 Matrifocal Family: p.268
④, ⑦ Consanguineal Family: ①, ⑥
Conjugal Family: ②, ⑤, ⑨

해석

가족 개념의 차이

가족은 함께 사는 사람들로 구성되며, 출생이나 결혼에 의해 연결된다. 또한 기타 법적 관계로도 연결될 수 있는데, 동거 및 입양 등이 여기에 해당된다.

많은 사람들은 가족이 혈연으로만 이루어진다고 생각한다. 하지만 여러 사회학자들은 혈연이라는 개념은 은유적으로 받아들여야 한다고 말한다. 많은 사회들이 그와 다른 개념으로 가족에 대한 정의를 내리고 있다. 세계 인권 선언 16조는 가족을 사회의 자연 집단으로 정의한다. 가족은 사회와 국가의 보호를 받아야 한다고 쓰여져 있다. 가족 구조는 부모와 자녀 간의 유대 관계에 기반하며, 또한 배우자 사이의 관계에 기반하기도 한다. 또는 두 가지 모두에 기반할 수도 있다.

가족의 주요 형태는 세 가지이다. 모계 중심 가족은 어머니와 자녀들로 구성된다. 자녀들은 보통 어머니의 생물학적 자식이다. 하지만 입양이 배제되지는 않는다. 이러한 형태는 보통 여성이 혼자서 가족을 부양할 수 있을 정도로 충분한 재산을 가지고 있는 경우에 성립한다. 혈연 가족은 여러 가지 형태를 띨 수 있다. 가장 흔한 형태는 어머니와 자녀, 그리고 그 어머니의 가족으로 구성된다. 아버지가 없는 경우가 많다. 특히 재산이 상속될 때에 그렇다. 남자가 재산을 소유한 경우에는 이러한 형태의 가족에 남편의 가족이 포함될 수도 있다. 부부 가족은 한 명 이상의 어머니와 자녀들로 구성된다. 여기에는 한 명 이상의 아버지도 포함된다. 이러한 종류의 가족은 분업이 존재하는 경우와 관련이 있다. 이러한 형태의 가족에서는 남자와 여자가 서로 다른 종류의 노동을 해야 한다. 이러한 상황에 있는 가족들은 이동성이 매우 높다.

핵가족은 부부 가족 형태의 하위 그룹이다. 이러한 형태는 한 명의 여자와 한 명의 남편으로 이루어진다. 두 사람은 함께 자녀를 키운다. 현대 산업 사회에서는 이러한 가족 형태가 가장 흔하다.

Summary Note
❶ Matrifocal Family
❷ Consanguineal Family
❸ Conjugal Family

Exercise 5 1 Ⓐ 2 Ⓓ 3 Topics: ①, ⑤, ⑥   p.270
Functions: ③, ④

해석

생명 윤리학

생명 윤리학은 응용 철학의 한 분야로, 과학과 의학을 면밀히 연구한다. 생명 윤리학의 기능은 연구와 치료의 도덕성에 대해 의문을 제기하는 것이다. 또한 과학을 규제하는 법의 윤리도 평가한다. 이 분야는 인류를 보호하기 때문에 매우 중요하다. 생명 윤리학이 없다면 과학과 의학의 진보로 인해 인간이 커다란 위험에 빠질 수 있을 것이다.

생명 윤리학의 연구는 다수의 법에 영향을 미친다. 많은 과학자들이 이러한 이유 때문에 생명 윤리학을 연구하는 사람들을 맹목적으로 반대한다. 이러한 과학자들은 자신의 연구가 본질적으로 윤리적이라고 믿는다. 생명 윤리학은 빠르게 성장하고 있는 학문 분야이다. 정식 학문으로서 인정을 받은 것은 30년 전 일이다. 현재 많은 학교에서 생명 윤리학 학위를 주고 있다. 1990년대에 사회과학자들이 담론의 장을 마련했다. 이로써 윤리적 문제에 관한, 사회와 함께 이러한 문제를 해결하고자 하는, 연구 방법이 정해졌다. 생명 윤리학자들에 의해 수집된 자료는 다른 사회과학들과 마찬가지로 동료 학자들의 검토를 거쳐야 한다.

생명 윤리학과 관련된 몇 가지 중요한 문제가 있다. 학문 분야로서의 타당성에 의문이 제기되고 있다. 왜 철학과 별도로 존재해야 하는가? 모든 사람들이 윤리주의자가 아닌가? 이러한 질문은 제도의 필요성에 의해 답해진다. 생명 윤리학자들은 막대한 양의 연구와 역사를 연구한다. 이를 생명 윤리학의 질문에 적용한다. 그들은 공정하고, 정직하며, 그리고 현명한 방식으로 그렇게 한다. 그들은 이러한 목표를 달성하기 위해 공동으로 헌신한다.

생명 윤리학자들은 여러 가지 주제를 연구한다. 사회에서 논쟁이 되는 주제에 초점을 맞추는 경우가 많다. 그들은 자료를 수집해서 여론 형성에 이용할 수 있는 보고서를 발표한다. 또한 정책도 수립한다. 생명 윤리학자들이 다루는 주제에는 낙태와 복제가 포함된다. 또한 줄기 세포 연구에서 배아를 사용하는 것도 포함된다. 이들은 어려운 윤리적 문제이다. 이 문제들은 인간의 생명에 대한 질문에서 비롯된다. 생명 윤리학자들은 입법자 및 기타 권력을 가진 사람들을 교육시키기 위해 노력한다. 이들은 경계를 정하는 사람들이다. 이들이 의학과 과학에서 무엇이 수용 가능한 것인지를 결정한다.

Summary Note
❶ morality
❷ Cloning
❸ public policy

Exercise 6 1 Ⓒ 2 Ⓓ 3 Kenya: ①, ⑥   p.272
Tanzania: ④, ⑦ Germany: ③

해석

고인류학

인류 화석과 전인류 화석을 연구하는 것을 고인류학이라고 한다. 이는 여러 시대에 걸쳐 인간의 진화를 집중적으로 추적하는 자연 인류학의 한 분야이다. 이 분야의 과학자들은 해부학적, 행태적, 그리고 유전적 연관성을 조사한다. 이러한 연관성은 인류가 어떻게 전인류로부터 발전했는지를 보여 준다. 과학자들은 이러한 연관성을 이용해서 인류 출현의 연대표를 재구성할 수 있다. 이 연대표는 선사 시대부터 현대까지 이어져 있다.

고인류학자들은 화석 잔해를 발굴함으로써 초기 원인을 연구할 수 있다. 그들은 땅을 샅샅이 뒤져서 작은 흔적들을 찾아낸다. 그들이 발견하는 이러한 작은 단서들로 고대의 삶의 모습을 파악할 수 있다. 보존된 뼈, 도구, 그리고 발자국이 그러한 화석 증거를 제공해 준다.

고인류학은 인류의 진화에 관한 연구로 이어진 몇 가지 중요한 발견이 이루어졌던 1800년대 후반에 시작되었다. 첫 번째 발견은 1856년에 이루어졌다. 독일에서 네안데르탈인이 발견되었다. 이는 중요한 사건이었다. 이로써 이 분야의 과학이 탄생하게 되었다. 주목할 만한 또 다른 사건은 이 주제에 관한 두 권의 중요한 저서가 출간된 것이었다. 첫 번째는 토머스 헉슬리의 *자연에서의 인간의 위치*였다. 두 번째 중요한 책은 찰스 다윈의 *인간의 유래*였다.

이 분야에서 가장 중요한 발견 중 일부는 리키 가족에 의해 이루어졌다. 다수의 중요 화석들이 루이스 리키에 의해 처음 발견되었다. 그는 아프리카 케냐의 올두바이 협곡에서 발굴 작업을 시작했다. 1959년에 그와 그의 아내는 초기 원인의 두개골 잔해를 발견했다.

1972년 루이스가 사망한 뒤 그의 아내 메리 리키가 그의 연구를 이어받았다. 그녀의 가장 주목할 만한 발견 중 하나는 라이톨리 발자국의 발견이었다. 그녀는 이 발자국을 1976년 탄자니아에서 발견했다. 이 발자국들은 화산재에 의해 보존되어 있었다. 3백 7십만 년 전의 것이었다. 이 발자국은 초기 전인류가 두 발로 걸었다는 점을 나타내는 가장 결정적인 증거이다. 리키의 아들인 리처드 역시 몇 가지 중요한 화석을 발견한 것으로 알려져 있다. 1972년에 그의 팀이 탄자니아에서 *호모 하빌리스*의 두개골을 발견했다. 그리고 1975년에는 케냐에서 *호모 에렉투스*의 두개골도 발견했다.

> 🖉 **Summary Note**
> ❶ early hominid skull
> ❷ the Laetoli footprints
> ❸ *Homo habilis*

Building Summary Skills
p.274

Exercise 1 Emergence

Emergence is the concept that describes how a complex pattern forms from lesser parts. It is evident in all forms of organic and inorganic structures. Scientists who study emergence look at the characteristics of organic emergent structures such as ant colonies and flocks of birds and at inorganic structures such as hurricanes. Another form of emergence is cultural, in which some form of human organization results in a highly complex structure that is more than the sum of its parts. The World Wide Web and the stock market are prime examples of the sort of phenomenon in which simple components combine to form a complex whole.

Exercise 2 The Media Influence Theory

The Media Influence Theory states that rising levels of violence in society are attributable to individuals who see violence depicted in entertainment and are unable to distinguish it apart from reality. Advocates of this theory target video games, music with hateful lyrics, and movies as being responsible for many acts of violence. They want to see these forms of entertainment heavily regulated by the government. On the other hand, critics of this theory think that the government should not control the entertainment industry and that rising levels of violence are due to the availability of weapons.

Exercise 3 The Great Chicago Fire

From October 8 to 10, 1871, the Great Chicago Fire burned down much of the city and killed hundreds of people. The fire was originally blamed on Mrs. O'Leary's cow kicking down a lantern in the barn. But the reporter who wrote this story later said he made it up because it sounded interesting, so this led people to believe that Mrs. O'Leary was made a target because she was a female Catholic immigrant. Some other possible causes of the fire were Daniel Sullivan, who may have started it while trying to steal some milk, and Louis M. Cohn, who is said to have started it during a game of craps.

Exercise 4 Differences in the Concept of Family

A family consists of people who live together and are linked by genetic or other types of bonds. Although blood relation defines many families, it is not the only thing that can link people together. There are three major types of families: matrifocal, consanguineal, and conjugal. The most common type of family in modern society is a sub-group of the conjugal family called the nuclear family.

Exercise 5 Bioethics

Bioethics is a branch of applied philosophy that looks closely at the ethics of scientific and medical practices. This field is very important because it asks questions about and examines policies and treatments that greatly affect the human race. It is also an area of academic growth, as many universities have created bioethics programs. Although bioethicists' roles are often questioned, they do many activities such as researching and compiling reports that greatly affect public opinion and the policies made by politicians.

Exercise 6 Paleoanthropology

The study of human and pre-human fossils is paleoanthropology. This field began with several important discoveries and publications in the late 1800s, including the discovery of Neanderthal man fossils. Some of the most important discoveries in this field have been made by a family named the Leakeys. Their long list of discoveries began in the 1950s when Louis and Mary Leakey found the skull of a hominid in Kenya. But Mary Leakey's most important discovery came after her husband's death, when she found the Laetoli footprints in 1976. These footprints offered conclusive evidence that early man walked upright on two legs. Their son, Richard, also found the skulls of a *Homo habilis* and a *Homo erectus*.

Mini TOEFL iBT Practice Test
p.276

1 ⓑ 2 ⓒ 3 ⓒ 4 ⓐ 5 ⓓ

6 Criteria: ③, ④, ⑧ Forms: ②, ⑤

7 ⓒ 8 ⓓ 9 ⓐ 10 ⓑ 11 ④

12 Storage Room: ①, ⑥ Kiva: ②, ④ Tower: ⑤

해석

[1-6]

동업

동업이란 둘 이상의 동업자들이 이익과 손실을 공유하는 비즈니스 형태이다. 동업자는 동일한 비즈니스에 참여하기 위해 모인 사람들을 말한다. 이러한 형태의 비즈니스는 자신이 신뢰하는 친구나 사람들과 함께 일하고 싶어하는 사람들에게 좋다. 또한 전문 분야가 다른 두 명 이상의 사람들에게도 유용하다. 동업 관계를 맺음으로써 자신들의 기술을 결합할 수 있다. 동업 관계는 기존 업체들끼리도 맺을 수 있다.

동업자는 동업 계약서를 가지고 있을 수도 있고, 동업 신고서를 작성할 수도 있다. 일부 사법권에서는 그와 같은 계약서를 등록해야 한다. 그렇게 한 뒤에는 대중들의 열람이 가능하다. 많은 국가에서 동업 기업은 법적 실체이다. 동업 기업은 종종 세금 문제 때문에 법인 회사보다 선호된다. 이러한 이유로 막대한 세금 문제에 직면한 사업체들에게는 동업이 보다 유용하다. 동업 구조에서는 배당 세액이 면제될 수도 있다. 배당세액이란 법인 회사의 소유주가 거둔 이익에 부과되는 세금이다.

합명 회사가 가장 기본적인 형태이다. 이 형태에서는 모든 동업자들이 경영에 참여하며, 회사의 부채에 대해 모두가 개별적으로 책임을 진다. 사업체로서의 동업 기업에는 두 가지 형태가 더 있다. 그중 하나는 합자 회사이다. 이 형태에서는 특정한 유한 책임 사원들이 경영에 대한 참여를 포기한다. 합자 회사의 부채에 대해 유한 책임만을 지기 위해 그러한 권리를 넘기는 것이다. 나머지 다른 종류는 유한 책임 회사이다. 이 유형에서는 모든 사원들이 일정 정도의 책임을 진다.

1958년의 파트너쉽 법에 따르면 동업이 성립하기 위해서는 네 가지 기준을 따라야 한다. 첫 번째는 당사자 간에 유효한 계약이 있어야 하고, 두 번째는 이들이 하나의 비즈니스를 해야 한다. 이는 계약서 상 특정 거래, 사업, 혹은 업종으로 규정된다. 세 번째는 공동이어야 한다. 다시 말해, 권리의 상호성이 존재해야 한다. 여기에는 이자와 의무가 포함된다. 마지막으로 목적이 이익이여야 한다. 이런 이유 때문에 자선 단체는 동업 기업이 될 수 없다.

동업 관계를 맺으려는 사업가들은 어떤 형태가 자신에게 가장 적합한지 선택해야 한다. 일부 동업자는 더 많은 권한을 가지고 싶어할 것이다. 기꺼이 더 큰 책임을 지려고 할 것이다. 반면에 책임을 덜 지려는 동업자도 있을 수 있다. 경영에 대한 참여를 기꺼이 포기하려고 할 수도 있다. 권한, 이익, 그리고 책임 사이의 균형을 새 동업자들이 찾아야 한다. 하지만 이들의 성공적인 관계 형성에 가장 중요한 요소는 신뢰이다.

[7-12]

아나사지 건축과 절벽 궁전

북아메리카에 있는 가장 큰 절벽 주거지는 절벽 궁전이라고 불리는 고대 푸에블로의 건축물이다. 이는 콜로라도의 남서쪽 코너에 있는 메사버드 국립 공원 안에 있다. 이곳은 고대 아나사지족의 보금자리였다.

절벽 궁전은 많은 이들이 경탄해 하는 거대한 유적이다. 이 궁전은 사암 절벽의 빈 공간에 지어졌다. 이 움푹 들어가 있는 공간은 깊이가 약 40m이고, 높이는 약 25m이며, 석조 건축물의 길이는 약 130m이다. 절벽 궁전에는 150개의 방이

있지만, 모든 방에 난로가 있던 것은 아니었다. 불을 피우는데 사용되는 난로가 있다는 점은 방이 사람들의 주거 공간이었다는 사실을 알려 준다. 절벽 궁전의 방들 가운데 약 25개에서 30개의 방에만 난로가 있었다. 나머지 방들은 아마 저장실로 사용되었을 것이다.

절벽 궁전에는 아직까지 기능이 밝혀지지 않은 개방된 공간과 방들이 많다. 9개의 저장실은 위층 높은 곳에 지어졌는데, 이곳은 수분과 해충으로부터 안전했다. 추수한 곡식의 잉여분이 여기에 저장되었을 가능성이 매우 크다. 사람들은 이동식 사다리를 이용해서 저장실에 올라갈 수 있었다. 고고학자들은 얼마나 많은 사람들이 여기에서 생활했는지 추정하고 있다. 난로가 있는 방의 수에 기초해서 추산한 결과, 절벽 궁전에는 100에서 150명 정도의 아나사지 사람들이 거주했을 것으로 생각된다.

절벽 궁전에는 몇 층 높이의 사각형 및 원형 구조물인 탑들이 몇 개 있다. 이 유적에서 가장 훌륭한 석조물 중 일부가 이 탑 안에 있다. 이 단지의 남쪽 끝에 있는 4층짜리 탑 내부에는, 탑 안의 원래 회반죽위에 그려진, 추상적인 문양들이 포함되어 있다.

또한 절벽 궁전에는 의식에서 중요했던 동그랗고 움푹 패인 방들이 있는데, 이들은 키바라 불렸다. 한 개의 키바는 유적의 한가운데 위치해 있다. 이 지점에 있는 전체 구조물은 여러 개의 벽으로 구분되어 있다. 이곳에는 문도 없고 기타 출입할 수 있는 통로도 없다. 키바의 한쪽 벽면은 한 가지 색으로 칠해졌고 반대쪽은 그와 다른 색으로 칠해졌다. 고고학자들이 이 이상한 구조물을 연구했다. 그들은 두 공동체가 이곳에서 살았을 것이라고 결론지었다. 이 키바는 두 공동체를 통합하기 위해 사용되었을 것이다. [또 다른 가능성이 이 미스테리한 건축물을 잘 알고 있는 몇몇 고고학자들에 의해 제기되었는데, 이곳은 포로를 가두어 두는 공간으로 사용되었을 수도 있다.]

고고학자들은 나무의 나이테를 이용한 연대 측정법으로 절벽 궁전의 연대를 알아낼 수 있다. 이로써 절벽 궁전의 건축과 개조가 지속적으로 진행되었고, 이는 1190년부터 1260년까지 이루어졌다는 점이 밝혀졌다. 또한 건물의 대부분이 20년 동안에 지어졌다는 점도 밝혀졌다. 1300년경 절벽 궁전은 아직까지 밝혀지지 않은 이유로 버려졌다.

Vocabulary Check-Up
p.282

Ⓐ 1 ⓐ 2 ⓒ 3 ⓓ 4 ⓑ 5 ⓓ
6 ⓒ 7 ⓓ 8 ⓐ

Ⓑ 1 ⓖ 2 ① ⓘ 3 ⓐ 4 ⓙ 5 ⓗ
6 ⓔ 7 ⓕ 8 ⓑ 9 ⓒ 10 ⓓ

Actual Test

Actual Test 01
p.286

1 Ⓑ	2 Ⓓ	3 Ⓑ	4 Ⓒ	5 Ⓑ
6 Ⓐ	7 Ⓓ	8 Ⓒ	9 **4**	
10 ①, ②, ⑥				
11 Ⓓ	12 Ⓑ	13 Ⓐ	14 Ⓒ	15 Ⓐ
16 Ⓒ	17 Ⓐ	18 Ⓑ	19 **1**	

20 Place Value: ①, ③, ⑤ Zero: ④, ⑦

해석

[1-10]

주기율표

인간은 금이나 은과 같이 자연 속에 존재하지만 다른 물질로 분해되지 않는 특정 기본 물질들에 대해 늘 알고 있었다. 1669년부터는 기타 화학 원소들도 점차 발견되기 시작했다. 이때 독일의 상인인 헨닉 브란트가 흔한 금속들로부터 금을 만들어 내는 방법을 찾으려고 시도하던 중 우연히 인을 발견했다. 1809년경에는 알려진 원소의 수가 47개로 늘어났다. 원소를 연구하던 화학자들은 화학 물질이 반응하는 방식에서 패턴을 알아채기 시작했다. [하지만 이런 패턴들을 보여 주는 형태로 원소들을 분류하는데 성공한 사람은 없었다.] 현대적인 최초의 화학 교재는 1789년 앙뜨완 로랑 드 라부와지에에 의해 쓰여졌다. 그는 밝혀진 원소를 나열하고 이들을 금속과 비금속으로 구분했다. 하지만 그의 목록에는 기체가 빠져 있었다. 또한 빛이나 열량과 같이 물질이 아닌 것들도 일부 포함되어 있었다. 따라서 정확한 분류 체계로 인정받지 못했다.

원소의 중요한 특징 중 하나는 주기성으로, 이는 원소들을 핵 안의 양성자와 중성자를 합한 수인 원자량에 따라 배열했을 때 비슷하게 행동하는 원소들이 규칙적인 간격으로 나타나는 것이다. 프랑스의 지질학자인 알렉산드르 에밀 베가이에 드 샹쿠르투아가 이러한 주기성을 최초로 발견했다. 그는 주기율표의 전신을 고안했다. 이는 텔루륨의 나선이라고 불렸다. 그의 시스템은 원소들을 원자량의 순서에 따라 나선형 기둥 모양으로 배열했다. 비슷한 물리적 특징을 지닌 원소들은 원주에서 수직으로 나타났다. 하지만 샹쿠르투아의 1862년 논문은 지질학적 용어를 사용했고 그림이 포함되어 있지 않았기 때문에, 화학 분야에서는 그의 주기 시스템이 인정을 받지 못했다.

1800년대 전반기에 새로운 원소들이 발견되었다. 따라서 화학자들은 원소의 물리적 특성이 규칙적으로 반복된다는 사실을 확인할 수 있었다. 화학자들은 이러한 주기성을 나타낼 수 있는 새로운 원소 분류법에 대해 연구했다. 1863년 영국의 화학자인 존 뉴랜즈가 당시에 알려져 있던 56개의 원소를 동일한 특징을 공유하는 그룹으로 나누었다. 각 그룹에는 8개의 원소가 포함되는 것처럼 보였기 때문에 그는 자신의 체계를 옥타브의 법칙이라고 불렀다. 피아노에서 한 옥타브가 8개의 건반으로 이루어진다는 점에 착안하여 그러한 이름을 붙였다. 하지만 뉴랜즈의 아이디어는 조롱을 당했고 그의 이론은 받아들여지지 않았다. 1919년이 되어서야 원소가 8개씩 그룹이 지어진다는 점이 인정되었다.

원소 주기성의 기본 개념은 1869년 러시아의 화학자인 드미트리 멘델레예프에 의해 보다 효과적으로 수정되었다. 그의 획기적인 업적은 원소의 중요한 두 가지 특성, 즉 원자량과 핵의 양성자 수인 원자 번호가 하나의 표 안에 합쳐질 수 있음을 발견했다는 점이었다. 그의 표는 주기율표라고 불리게 되었다. 멘델레예프의 표는 솔리테르라는 카드 게임에서 영감을 받았는데, 이 게임에서는 카드가 가로로는 무늬에 의해, 세로로는 숫자에 의해 배열된다. 동일한 패턴을 차용함으로써 멘델레프는 원소를 7개의 그룹으로 나누었다. 그는 가로로는 원자 번호가 높아지는 방식으로, 세로로는 비슷한 성질을 지닌 일곱 개의 그룹이 나타나는 방식으로 배열을 했다. 따라서 금, 은, 그리고 동과 같이 유사한 금속들은 세로로 같은 칸에 나타난다. 마찬가지로 헬륨, 아르곤, 그리고 네온과 같은 반응성 기체들은 다른 칸에 나타난다. 가장 흔한 원소인 수소, 헬륨, 그리고 리튬은 원자 번호가 낮기 때문에 첫 번째 열의 시작 부분에 나타난다. 가장 희귀한 원소인 우라늄과 플루토늄은 핵에 있는 양성자 수가 가장 높다. 이들은 주기율표의 끝 부분에 들어가 있다.

멘델레프의 시대에는 63개의 원소만이 발견되어 있었다. 하지만 그의 표가 탁월해서 원래 표의 빈 자리에 들어갈 새로운 원소들이 발견될 것이라는 점이 예상되었다. 오늘날 이 표는 120개의 원소를 보여 주는데, 92개는 자연 상태에서 존재하는 것이고 28개의 원소는 실험실에서 탄생한 것이다. 과학자들은 보다 많은 원소들이 발견될 것으로 믿는다. 주기율표는 "이제까지 고안된 것 중 가장 멋진 조직표"라고 불린다. 멘델레프의 표는 오늘날에도 유용하다. 하지만 새로운 원소들이 지속적으로 발견되고 만들어짐에 따라 수정되어 왔다. 그리고 1914년에 헨리 모슬리가 원소의 X레이 파장과 원자 번호 간의 관계를 알아냈다. 그래서 그는 원소들을 전하량에 따라 재배열했다. 또 다른 중요한 발전은 1946년 글렌 T. 시보그에 의해 이루어졌다. 그는 악티늄족이라는 무거운 원소로 이루어진 수직 그룹을 추가할 것을 제안했다.

[11-20]

계산의 역사

가장 오래된 계산의 증거는 고대의 사냥 물품에서 찾을 수 있다. 기원전 30,000년 전의 동물 뼈에 새겨져 있는 홈이 일종의 셈법일 수 있다. 셈 표시는 물건을 기록하기 위해 사용되었다. 양치기는 양 한 마리가 풀을 뜯으러 나갈 때마다 자갈을 하나씩 쌓곤 했다. 밤에 양이 돌아오면 자갈을 하나씩 치웠다. 자갈이 남아 있으면 양이 없어졌다는 점을 의미했다. 하지만 그러한 셈이 진정한 계산은 아니었다. 두 무리의 대상을 비교했을 뿐이었다.

이집트는 진정한 숫자 체계를 도입한 최초의 문명 중 하나였다. 기원전 약 3,000년을 시작으로 이집트인들은 상형 문자 또는 수를 나타내는 기호로 숫자를 표현했다. 따라서 1부터 9까지의 수는 세로획의 조합으로 표현되었다. 10은 U자를 거꾸로 써서 나타냈고, 100은 고리 모양의 로프로 나타냈으며, 그리고 1,000은 연꽃으로 나타냈다. 문화에 따라 계산법에서 사용되는 기본 숫자들이 서로 다르다. 이집트인과 같은 많은 사람들은 양손의 손가락 수인 10을 반영한 십진법을 사용했다. 바빌로니아인들과 같이 60진법을 사용한 사람들도 있었다. 하지만 이 시스템에서는 60까지의 각 숫자 또는 10단위의 숫자를 위한 또 다른 기호가 필요했기 때문에 불편했다. 하지만 60진법은 오늘날 기하학에서, 각을 60분과 60초로 측정하고, 원의 각도를 360도, 직사각형의 각도를 180도로 측정하며, 그리고 시간 기록에서 1분은 60초로, 1시간은 60분으로 나타낸다는 점에서 사용되고 있다.

계산에서의 최초의 놀라운 발전은 자리값 개념이었다. 바빌로니아인들이 개발한 자리값은 기수법에서 각 자리의 값을 나타내는데 필요했다. 예를 들어 236이라는 숫자는 대부분의 시스템에서 쓰기가 복잡했는데, 그 이유는 여러 개의 기호와 획이 필요했기 때문이었다. 하지만 10진법의 각 자리에 위치한 값을 통해 우리는 숫자 6이 6을, 숫자 3이 30을, 그리고 숫자 2가 200을 나타낸다는 점을 알 수 있다. 자리값이 정확한 수를 나타내기 위해서는, 예컨대 숫자 236이 236을 나타내는 것인지, 2,360을 나타내는 것인지, 혹은 2,306을 나타내는 것인지와 같은 혼동을 같은 혼동을 피할 수 있도록, "0"이 필요했다. 처음에 0 또는 "비어 있는" 자리는, 2306을 의미하는 23_6의 경우처럼, 숫자 사이에 빈 공간을 둠으로써 표시했다. 마침내 제로를 나타내는 특별한 기호, 즉 현재 사용되는 0이라는 숫자가 만들어졌다. 이 기호는 아랍의 계산법을 위해 만들어졌으며, 650년경에 널리 사용되었다.

수학에서 0과 자리값이 유용하게 쓰이기 위해서는 기본적인 수에 각각의 기호를 만드는 일이 필요했다. 따라서 1부터 9까지의 수를 위한 각기 다른 기호들이 만들어졌고, 10 간격의 수, 즉 10, 20, 30, 40 등을 나타내기 위해 각 숫자 뒤에 0이 추가되었다. 그리고 100, 1000, 그리고 10,000과 같이 그보다 훨씬 더 큰 숫자를 나타내기 위해서는 여러 개의 0이 추가되었다.

아라비아 숫자는 17세기까지 서양 유럽 역사를 지배했던 로마 숫자를 대체했다. 이는 현재 대부분의 지역에서 사용되는 숫자이다. 초기 형태의 아라비아 숫자는 기원전 200년경 인도에서 등장했다. 인도의 수학자들은 0이라는 기호가 포함된 자리값 시스템으로 숫자를 적고 조작하면 수학 연산이 가능하다는 점을 알게 되었다. 주요한 계산 수단이었던 장치인 주판보다 빨랐다. [주판은 최소 기원전 2300년부터 사용되었고, 고대의 유럽, 이집트, 그리고 아시아 사람들에게 알려져 있었다.] 숫자를 적어서 계산하는 방식은 아랍인 수학자 알-콰리즈미가 수에 관한 논문을 발표한 9세기 이후에야 인도 이외의 지역에 알려지게 되었다. 하지만 그의 논문은 12세기까지 라틴어로 번역이 되지 않았기 때문에, 그때까지 유럽 사람들은 이에 대해 모르고 있었다. 레오나르도 피보나치라는 이탈리아 사람이 알고리즘이라고 불리는 아라비아 계산법에 대한 책을 씀으로써 이를 대중화시켰는데, 그의 책은 부기 계원들과 상인들에 의해 읽혀졌다. 그들은 상거래에서 이 계산법을 사용하기 시작했다.

피보나치 이후 몇 백 년 동안 학자들과 상인들은 십진법 대 주판의 장점에 대해 논쟁을 벌였다. 인쇄기의 발명으로 알고리즘에 관한 책이 널리 알려지자 약 1,500년부터는 이것이 계산법으로 인정받게 되었다. 1,600년경 대부분 계산에서는 로마 숫자가 아라비아 숫자로 대체되었다.

Actual Test 02
p.302

1 Ⓐ 2 Ⓒ 3 Ⓓ 4 Ⓐ 5 Ⓑ
6 Ⓐ 7 Ⓒ 8 Ⓓ 9 **3**
10 ②, ③, ⑤

11 Ⓒ 12 Ⓐ 13 Ⓑ 14 Ⓓ 15 Ⓒ
16 Ⓐ 17 Ⓓ 18 Ⓒ 19 **3**
20 ②, ④, ⑤

해석

[1-10]

광물

광물은 자연적으로 존재하는 단단한 물질로, 지구의 지질 운동에 의해 형성된다. 광물을 특징짓는 주요 특성은 이들이 무기물이고, 무생물로 이루어져 있으며, 결정 구조를 지니고, 그리고 화학 성분이 독특하다는 점이다. 광물의 유형은 결정 구조 및 화학 성분에 따라 결정된다. 결정 구조는 광물 내의 원자들이 광물 전체에 반복되는 기하학적 무늬로 배열되어 있을 때 나타난다. 모든 결정 구조는 원자의 배열 방식인 14개의 가능한 격자, 즉 규칙적인 패턴 중 하나에 들어 맞는다. 이러한 격자는 X레이로 확인할 수 있다.

광물의 물리적인 특징은 결정 형태의 영향을 받는다. 예를 들어 다이아몬드와 흑연은 모두 동일한 원소인 탄소로 이루어져 있지만, 전자는 가장 단단한 광물인 반면 후자는 무르다. 그 이유는 흑연의 결정 구조에서는 서로로부터 미끄러질 수 있는 판 모양으로 탄소 원자들이 배열되어 있는 반면에 다이아몬드의 탄소 원자는 단단하고 촘촘한 그물 형태로 배열되어 있기 때문이다. 동일한 결정 구조를 지닌 두 광물도 화학적 조성은 다를 수 있다. 따라서 암연과 방연광은 동일한 결정 구조를 가지고 있지만 서로 다른 화학 물질로 이루어져 있다. 반대로 두 광물이 동일한 화학 성분을 가지고 있지만 결정 구조가 다른 경우도 있다. 예를 들어 황철광과 백철광은 둘 다 황화철로 이루어져 있다. 하지만 이들의 원자 배열은 서로 다르다.

국제 광물 학회에 따르면 현재까지 확인된 광물은 4,000개이다. 이 가운데 150개 정도만 풍부하다. 약 50개는 "흔하지 않은" 광물로 분류된다. 나머지는 거의 발견되지 않는 것들이다. 이들 중 일부는 암석의 매우 적은 부분만을 구성한다. [따라서 이들을 찾아내기 위해서는 전문적인 장비가 필요하다.] 광물은 종종 암석의 성분에서 찾아볼 수 있는데, 암석에는 광물뿐만 아니라 유기 물질도 포함되어 있다. 일부 암석들은 방해석으로 이루어진 석회암처럼 하나의 광물로만 이루어져 있다. 반면에 다수의 광물들이 들어 있는 암석도 있을 수 있다. 오늘날 볼 수 있는 거의 모든 암석에는 약 15개의 광물 중 한 개 이상의 광물이 포함되어 있다. 석영, 운모, 장석 등이 여기에 포함된다.

암석에서 볼 수 있는 광물은 세 가지 요소에 의해 결정된다. 첫째, 암석의 화학 성분이 특정 광물에 적합해야 한다. 예를 들어 규소가 들어 있는 암석에는 석영이 포함되어 있을 가능성이 높다. 둘째, 암석이 형성된 상황이 암석에서 발견되는 광물의 종류에 영향을 미칠 것이다. 그렇기 때문에 고온 고압 상태의 화산 활동으로 생성된 암석에는 화강암이 포함되어 있을 수 있다. 셋째, 광물의 분포는 암석이 현 상태에 이르기 전에 거치는 지질학적 단계의 영향을 받는다. 예를 들어 수분 및 산성 물질에 노출되는 경우 일부 광물들이 부식되어 이들의 자리에 다른 광물이 들어설 수도 있다. 생태학적 시대가 전환되는 기간에는 암석이 모래나 흙으로 붕괴될 수도 있다.

광물학자들은 물리적인 특성이나 화학 성분 중 하나에 의해 광물을 분류한다. 광물은 여러 가지 측정 가능한 물리적인 특성을 지닌다. 경도는 모스 경도계로 측정된다. 이는 0부터 10까지의 경도를 나타낸다. 모든 광물은 모스 경도계 상보다 높은 경도를 지닌 광물에 의해 절단되거나 자국이 표시될 수 있다. 따라서 경도가 10인 다이아몬드로 경도가 7인 석영을 자를 수 있다. 광택은 광물의 표면에 따른 빛의 반사율이다. 금속은 표면에 구멍이 많은 석고보다 광택이 높다. 쪼개짐은 어떤 광물이 자연적인 결을 따라 갈라지는 방식을 가리킨다. 깨짐은 자연적인 벽개면으로 깨지지 않는 정도를 가리킨다. 조흔은 광물을 특수한 면에 문질렀을 때 광물에 생기는 잔류물의 색이다. 비중은 광물의 밀도이다. 광물의 질량과 같은 부피의 물 질량을 비교함으로써 계산된다.

광물은 또한 화학적 특성에 따라 분류될 수도 있다. 가장 흔히 볼 수 있는 광물은 규산염인데, 규산염에는 상당량의 규소와 산소가 포함되어 있다. 거의 모든 암석이 여기에 해당된다. 두 번째로 흔한 광물은 탄산염이다. 여기에는 탄소와 산소가 포함되어 있다. 탄산염은 부패한 플랑크톤이 축적되어 만들어진 것이기 때문에 해저에서 찾아볼 수 있다. 또 다른 부류인 할로겐 화합물은 물이 증발한 곳에서 찾아볼 수 있다. 말라버린 호수 바닥과 유타의 그레이트 솔트 레이크와 같은 육지로 둘러싸인 바다에서 찾아볼 수 있다. 기타 흔한 종류에는 황산염, 이산화물, 황화물, 그리고 인산염이 포함된다.

[11-20]

흰꼬리사슴과 검은꼬리사슴

북미에서 몸집이 큰 모든 동물 가운데 가장 수가 많은 것은 흰꼬리사슴이다. 이 사슴종은 꼬리를 등 위로 들어올려 파닥거리는 습관으로 유명하다. 이러한 행동으로 하얀색 배 부분과 엉덩이가 드러난다. 이러한 숨길 수 없는 표식은 이들이 달아날 때 종종 목격할 수 있다. 꼬리를 내리면 꼬리는 갈색을 띠며 그 주변은 하얗게 보인다. 계절에 따라 변하는 흰꼬리사슴의 색은 여름에는 붉은색, 그리고 겨울에는 회색이 된다. 수사슴으로도 알려져 있는 다 자란 수컷은 키가 1미터를 넘는다. 몸무게는 110킬로그램 정도이다. 수컷은 뿔을 가지고 있는데, 수컷들 사이에서 뿔이 엉키는 경우가 있다. 이렇게 되면 두 동물 모두 서서히 죽음을 맞게 된다.

버지니아사슴으로도 알려져 있는 흰꼬리사슴은 미국 본토의 대부분의 지역에서 서식한다. 또한 캐나다 남부, 멕시코, 중미, 그리고 남미 북부의 국가에서도 찾아볼 수 있다. 또한 북유럽에도 유입되었다. 흰꼬리사슴은 적응력이 매우 뛰어나다. 대부분 나무가 울창한 숲에서 살지만, 탁 트인 사바나에서도 적응해서 살 수 있다. 텍사스 평원 및 베네수엘라 야노스 대초원 지대가 여기에 포함된다. 짝짓기 철은 가을이다. 수컷들은 암사슴이라고 불리는 가능한 많은 암컷 사슴들과 짝짓기를 하려고 한다. 암사슴은 늦은 봄에 한두 마리의 새끼를 낳는다. 암사슴은 한 번에 몇 시간씩 새끼들을 혼자 내버려두기도 하는데, 새끼들은 자연적인 위장을 통해, 즉 점박이 무늬를 갖고 있고 냄새도 풍기지 않는다는 점 때문에 대부분의 포식자들의 눈에 잘 띄지 않는다. [이로써 어미가 먹이를 찾는 동안 새끼는 안전할 수 있다.] 암사슴은 새끼에게 먹이를 먹이기 위해 주기적으로 다시 돌아온다.

충분한 먹이와 보금자리가 있는 경우 흰꼬리사슴의 개체수는 빠르게 증가한다. 하지만 때때로 너무 빠르게 증가하는 경우도 있다. 이러한 경우, 사슴의 먹이가 되는 작물을 재배하는 농부들에게 종종 피해가 생기기도 한다. 또한 도로를 가로지르면서 자동차와 충돌하는 경우도 많다. 그러면 사슴이 죽고, 운전자들도 부상을 입거나 사망하게 된다. 제한적인 사냥으로 과도한 개체수를 조절하게 된다. 또한 사슴 사냥은 여러 지역에서 중요한 문화 의식이다. 일부 지역 경제에 활력을 불어넣는 중요한 기능도 담당한다. 상업적인 개발을 목적으로 한 산림 벌채로 인해 많은 사슴 무리들이 자연 서식지를 빼앗겼으며, 이로 인해 사슴들이 굶어 죽거나 고속도로에서 충돌 사고를 당할 위험성이 높아지고 있다.

검은꼬리사슴은 수백 만 년 전 사촌 관계인 흰꼬리사슴으로부터 진화했다. 과학자들은 흰꼬리사슴이 북미 대륙의 동부 해안가로 내려왔다고 생각한다. 이들은 멕시코를 건너 캘리포니아 해안가로 들어왔다. 이곳에서 마침내 검은꼬리사슴으로 진화했다. 이들의 조상이 같다는 점은 이 두 종이, 신체적인 외형 및 정신적인 특징에 있어서, 서로 유사한 이유를 설명해 준다. 사실 이들 두 종은 구별하기가 어렵다. 검은꼬리사슴의 꼬리가 검정색이기는 하지만, 이들은 꼬리를 들어올려 하얀색 배를 보이는 습성을 공유한다. 이로써 하얀색을 띠는 아랫부분이 드러난다. 그리고 두 종의 수컷들 뿔 모양도 비슷하다. 하지만 검은꼬리사슴은 미대륙의 서쪽 가장자리 부분에서만 찾아볼 수 있다. 캐나다의 브리티시 컬럼비아에서 캘리포니아 남부 지역까지 해당되는 지역이다. 뿐만 아니라 검은꼬리사슴은 흰꼬리사슴보다 몸집이 약간 더 작다.

최근까지도 과학자들은 검은꼬리사슴이 뮬사슴의 아종이라고 믿었다. 하지만 DNA 검사 결과 별개의 종임이 밝혀졌다. 뮬사슴은 진화를 통해 흰꼬리사슴 및 검은꼬리사슴과 구분되는 종이 되었다. 경험이 많은 사냥꾼들은 검은꼬리사슴이 사냥하기 가장 힘든 사슴종이라고 말한다. 한 가지 이유는 검은꼬리사슴이 훨씬 더 더운 곳에서 서식하기 때문이다. 캘리포니아의 사냥 시즌 중 여름의 낮 기온은 약 화씨 100도까지 올라간다. 이러한 더위에서 수컷들은 낮 동안에 조용히 있는다. 어둠이라는 보호막이 생길 때에만 몸을 움직인다. 우기가 되면 검은꼬리사슴은 낮에도 활동을 한다. 하지만 악천후 속에서 모험을 하려는 사냥꾼은 거의 없다. 서부의 주들의 사냥 기간이 짝짓기 철 전에 끝난다는 사실 때문에 검은꼬리사슴 사냥은 더 힘들어진다. 이때는 많은 수사슴들이 암컷들을 찾아다니느라 가장 활동이 활발한 시기이다. 따라서 사슴 사냥이 주에 의해 금지된 기간에 가장 잡기가 쉽다.

MEMO

MEMO

How to
Master Skills for the

TOEFL® iBT

Second Edition

READING Intermediate